TEACHER'S INTERNET COMPANION

ANN HEIDE & LINDA STILBORNE

Based on the Award-Winning
Teacher's Complete & Easy Guide to the Internet

Trifolium Books Inc.

A Fitzhenry & Whiteside Company

For Jack, Jessica, Alex and Christine, with love and thanks for your encouragement and support.

Trifolium Books Inc.
A Fitzhenry & Whiteside Company
195 Allstate Parkway
Markham, Ontario, Canada   L3R 4T8

In the United States:
Fitzhenry & Whiteside Limited
121 Harvard Avenue, Suite 2
Allston, Massachusetts 02134

National Library of Canada Cataloguing in Publication

Heide, Ann, 1948 –
    Teachers' Internet companion / Ann Heide, Linda Stilborne. – 3rd ed.

Previous eds. published under title: The teacher's complete & easy guide to the Internet.
Includes bibliographical references and index.
ISBN 1-55244-045-1

    1. Education–Computer network resources. 2. Teaching–Computer network resources.
3. Internet in education.
I. Stilborne, Linda II. Heide, Ann, 1948 – . Teacher's complete & easy guide to the Internet.
III. Title.

LB1044.87.H43 2003   025.06'37   C2003-905546-9

Printed and bound in Canada
10 9 8 7 6 5 4 3 2 1

Trifolium's books may be purchased in bulk for educational, business, or promotional use. For information, please write: Special Sales, Trifolium Books Inc. 195 Allstate Parkway, Markham, Ontario, Canada L3R 4T8
Email: info@trifoliumbooks.com

Fitzhenry & Whiteside acknowledges with thanks the Canada Council for the Arts, the Government of Canada through its Book Publishing Industry Development Program (BPIDP), and the Ontario Arts Council for their support in our publishing program.

Cover design: Kerry Plumley
Page layout: Darrell McCalla

Acknowledgements:

The authors would like to thank Liz Simms for contributing her research on ICT and learning theory, Trudy Rising (Trifolium Books, Inc.) for her support and encouragement with previous editions and Jim Chiponis for his delightful cartoons. We also especially thank the many teachers who so generously share their work in the vibrant learning community of the Internet.

About This Book

It is challenging and sometimes frustrating to keep up with the constantly changing environment of the Internet. For teachers, an even greater challenge is integrating this technology into their classrooms in a meaningful way. Teachers who have used *The Teacher's Complete & Easy Guide to the Internet* found it to be an invaluable resource for learning about this technology and locating relevant curriculum resources. In this new edition, *Teacher's Internet Companion*, we provide even more information to help teachers further explore classroom resources and online learning environments.

Teacher's Internet Companion offers an updated and expanded view of the Internet. We explain the range of ways that the Internet can be used to enhance learning, with many lesson ideas, practical tips and step-by step instructions for both new and experienced users. Here are some of the questions you will find answers to in this book:

What impact is the Internet having on learning?

See Chapter 1, which explains why the Internet is an increasingly important tool for educators and how telecommunications technologies have the potential to transform the ways in which teacher teach and students learn.

How can the Internet be integrated into the curriculum in a meaningful way?

Find out how to organize student Internet projects, from keypals to global classrooms — and how to ensure that the use of the Internet results in a meaningful learning experience for students. Learn about Webquests as a practical model for curriculum based projects that promote active learning.

How are teachers in the early, middle and higher grades using the Internet for student projects?

You'll find ideas throughout this book, but see especially the Project Ideas features. Project Ideas are provided for most grade levels. Some are cross-curricular, and many projects can be extended or adapted for use with younger or older students.

How are teachers dealing with controversial and unacceptable material on the Internet?

Student security issues (such as student safety and acceptable use) are a major issue with teachers and with parents. Chapter 3 discusses acceptable use policies (AUPs) and offers practical guidelines for safe and productive online learning.

What are some strategies for using the Internet with special needs students?

Chapter 3 identifies some of the ways in which the Internet can provide support for special needs students and identifies a range of useful resources for enabling exceptional students.

What are the newest tools and resources available on the Internet?

Chapter 4 and 5 will provide will provide you with the latest information about the World Wide Web. Find out about Webquests and how to share your bookmarks online. In chapter 8 you will learn about some newer Internet applications, including video and audio streaming, classroom conferencing, how to download Web sites for offline viewing and file formats such as MP3.

How can I use the Web more efficiently?

If you sometimes feel overwhelmed by too much information on the Internet, Chapter 4 will introduce you to strategies for finding what you are looking for quickly and easily. In Chapter 5 you will find guidelines for evaluating and citing Web resources.

How can I create effective Web pages for class activities and school communications?

Chapter 6 provides simple explanations for developing your own Web pages. In this chapter you will also find tips for developing school web pages, great sources for graphics and software options for editing Web pages.

How can I connect with other teachers on the Net?

See Chapter 7 for a discussion of e-mail, as well as suggestions for listservers (discussion forums) and newsgroups of particular interest to teachers. You can also find out where to obtain free e-mail accounts and learn about a great new Internet tool for easy Web posting: Weblogs or blogs.

Where can I find curriculum-related information on the Internet?

Many of the best Web sources for curriculum and student projects are cited in Chapters 2, 3, 4 and 5 as well as in the hints and Teaching Tips that appear throughout the book. You will also find an extensive list of sources in Appendix B.

Where can I get information on technological planning?

See Chapter 9 for resources that can help administrators and teachers meet the continuing challenge of implementing technological change.

How can I get my classroom involved if funding is limited?

Funding is another challenge for integrating the Internet into the classroom. Chapter 9 also offers practical suggestions for enlisting corporate, government and community support to make the Internet a reality in your school.

What additional opportunities exist for teachers outside of the classroom?

Find out about initiatives that support homeschoolers and provide distance education. In Chapter 10, you can learn about ways that teachers are using distance education for professional development and as a new teaching venue. Here you will also learn about new tools for online teaching, such as virtual classrooms and learning management systems.

About This Book's Features

We have designed the *Teacher's Internet Companion* in a way that we think will make good sense to teachers. We explain all the basics on how to use the Internet and provide practical tips and project ideas that will help teachers turn the Internet into a useful tool for the classroom.

Here are some of the exciting features of this book:

Project Ideas. We think this is one of the most exciting features of this book! These take you step by step through a range of Internet projects that you can use in the classroom. Projects are included for all grade levels and for varying levels of connectivity. You'll be able to implement some of these with just a basic Internet connection.

A Sampling of… Great Internet Sites. Our "site samplers" identify many of the very best educational sites currently on the Internet. We've also provided space for you to add your own personal favorites, as your list of exciting educational resources on the Internet continues to grow.

HINT

Hint. Scattered throughout the text, these highlight extra suggestions for learning about the Net and using it effectively.

Teaching Tips. These time-saving tips will help you and your students make the most of your time online as you integrate the Internet into your classroom.

Tech Talk. These are technical points that are not essential, yet are useful to know about. If a particular point seems obscure at first, you can highlight it, and return to it once you've gained more experience. It's not necessary to understand everything all at once. In fact, we hope this guide will continue to be useful to you over the long term.

Teacher Quotes. Our teacher quotes (most of them culled from the Internet!) offer practical hints and insights into the value of this technology for learning. We hope you'll find these as exciting, motivating, and helpful as we did.

Glossary. Check the back of the book for an up-to-date glossary of Internet terms, based on a glossary originally developed by the Unisys Corporation.

Curriculum Links: Online Resources. Appendix B lists links that will lead you to resources in your specific teaching area. We include everything from Art to the

Environment to Special Needs. The list is designed to help teachers link the Internet to practical learning outomes. Even teachers who are already familiar with the Internet will find this list of selected curriculum resources invaluable.

How to begin?

We suggest you read Chapter 1 first because it gives an overview of the ways that the Internet can be used in the classroom. Even if you are an experienced Internet user, Chapter 1 will help you learn more about the role of technology in schools and generate new ideas about how the Internet can be used to support learning.

Chapters 2 through 9 offer down-to-earth instructions on "how to" that you can explore in whichever order works best for you. Use the Table of Contents and the Chapter Goals to help determine which chapters will be most immediately useful to you. Some teachers may want to focus initially on using electronic mail, while others will prefer to start by sampling some of the curriculum resources on the World Wide Web. Be aware that Chapters 6 and 9 are somewhat more technical than the other chapters. You may want to explore these two chapters after you have mastered basic Web navigation. If you are an experienced user, these may be among the first chapters you'll want to delve into.

Our most important goal in designing the *Teacher's Internet Companion* has been to try to make it work for individual teachers. Thus, we have relied on the suggestions, ideas, and experiences of teachers like yourself. Their input has helped us to identify many issues that need to be addressed for the Internet to be successfully implemented in schools. We welcome your comments and suggestions about sections of this book that you have found particularly useful.

"I am proud to be able to use the Internet as a way of speaking to people all over the globe to help provide quality education to my future students! We've only just begun!"

Cheryl Janik, Elementary School Teacher, currently a graduate student in the Elementary Education Program at the University of New York at Buffalo.

Linda Stilborne (left), Ann Heide (right)

About the People Behind This Book

Ann Heide (B.A, B. Ed, M.Ed.)

Ann has been a classroom teacher, consultant in Educational Technology for the Ottawa Carleton Catholic District School Board, and content provider for educational CDs and Web sites. For several years she taught Educational Technology and Curriculum Design courses in the Teacher Education Program at the University of Ottawa and presently teaches online courses in Computers in the Classroom. She has 12 years' experience in developing materials and teacher training for integrating technology across the curriculum. Ann is the co-author of *The Technological Classroom* (Trifolium Books Inc.1994), *The Teachers Complete & Easy Guide to the Internet* (Trifolium Books Inc.1996, 1999) and *Active Learning in the Digital Age Classroom* (Trifolium Books Inc.2001).

Linda Stilborne

Linda is a learning technology consultant and distance learning specialist. She has taught at Deer Park High School in Cincinnati, Ohio, and St. Joseph's High School in St. Thomas, Ontario. Her classroom subject specialties are English and computers. As a member of the technical support team for Canada's SchoolNet, she conducted research into the educational applications for the Internet, with a particular focus on classroom integration issues. Linda has also served as an Eastern Region representative to the Ontario Colleges' Computer Based Learning Project and as a research project co-ordinator for the Education Network of Ontario.

Contents

Chapter 3: Planning Your Own Projects   67

Chapter 6: Developing Web Pages for Learning   191

Chapter 7: Communicating over the Internet   213

Chapter 8: Additional Internet Tools   253

Chapter 9: Bringing the Internet into Schools   275

Introduction

"Having been a teacher for 39 years, I've experienced many initiatives to engage the learner and make the educational experience more meaningful. Never in all those years have I seen students work harder and learn more than they do with international collaborations and worldwide communication…. It's a great time to be a teacher, an awesome time to be a learner, and a wise school system that encourages everyone in the school building to experience both roles."

— Janet Barnstable, Teacher, Percy Julian Junior High School, Oak Park, Illinois

Online at **http://4teachers.org/testimony/barnstable/index.shtml**, 14/04/03

In education today, we find ourselves in exciting and challenging times characterized by constant change. While the Internet brings us closer to being able to deliver on the promise of technology to re-shape our education systems, we know that educational media alone do not influence the achievement of students.

In this book, we examine the use of the Internet within the overall context of educational reform, in which the integration of technology is neither simply to speed up the process of learning nor to teach new technology skills. Rather the intent is to combine technology use with other reform efforts (e.g., new instructional strategies, new uses of time and staffing), in helping schools become environments that empower students to successfully attain new learning goals. This book is for any teacher who wants to learn more about how to use the Internet to enhance student learning. It is especially for teachers who approach the Internet with reluctance and perhaps with a touch of skepticism about its value in the classroom.

Your guide

Teacher's Internet Companion is intended to help you, the teacher, experience the excitement that the Internet can bring to your classroom. It explains key concepts and helps you learn to use basic Internet tools. Learning the mechanics of using new tools is just one element of technology in education reform; another is developing lesson plans and projects that incorporate the resources available over the Internet into curriculum. You do not have to do all this yourself; this book tells you where to find some of the best educational resources on the Net. Most importantly, it will help you to discover how the Internet can help your students learn.

The global village

We read and hear a great deal these days about how the world is shrinking. Traditional political, economic, and social boundaries are being redefined almost daily. As we search for common values and a common understanding, we develop an appreciation for the complexities of managing a world of profoundly different cultures and social structures.

Education will be the key to resolving economic and cross-cultural problems, and it is the younger generations that will need to find solutions. We are all aware that we have a responsibility to provide today's students with the skills they will need to succeed in a workplace that is increasingly information based. These skills certainly include knowing how to use computers; even more important are the personal and social skills that must be developed.

Veterans of the education technology movement say teachers learn best from each other. Fortunately, teachers who have ready access to the Internet are discovering, inventing, and sharing the kinds of practices and programs in their own classrooms that illustrate true education reform. And because the Internet is an incredibly effective communications tool, these teachers are finding one another, sharing with one another, and organizing collegially in new ways. In the past few years there have been substantial efforts aimed at making the Internet a more teacher- and student-friendly place. Resource lists and lesson plans have sprung from a variety of sources both public and private; we highlight some of the best in this book.

A central skill

We feel strongly that the Internet is a powerful force for helping students develop a sense of personal responsibility for their own learning. Students expand their horizons by learning how to communicate, how to collaborate, and indeed, how to learn. Most new teachers entering the profession today are already very comfortable with the role the Internet plays in their personal and professional lives. Teachers who understand that the world is changing also understand that classroom learning needs to change in response. Schools must play an integral role in bringing about the necessary social adjustments as we move from an industrial to an information-based economy. The Internet will be a vital tool for bringing about such change. It is increasingly clear that we as teachers must think about the impact telecommunications can have on education and respond in positive ways to it.

Educators who have begun using the Internet as a learning tool know the critical role it can play in linking students to the world of telecommunications and information technology. Others are excited by the vastness of the information resources on the Internet. More than anything, teachers who have begun to explore the Internet with their classes are thrilled by its potential as a communications tool.

The opportunity

A major challenge is that we often feel bombarded by the proliferation of new technologies. Even seasoned "Internauts" are still struggling to keep up with the technology and sort out the technical, political, and pedagogical issues. Major improvements need to be made to our telecommunications infrastructure to accommodate increasingly complex applications, such as multimedia and videoconferencing. Then there are the serious social questions, such as "Should there be complete freedom of information on the Internet?" Educators must play a part in helping to resolve some of these issues. We have a unique opportunity to ensure that knowledge and understanding, rather than power and greed, are the forces that will steer the growth of the information highway.

A team approach

As you and your class become familiar with the Internet's many resources, learning can become a team effort in which everyone is encouraged to share knowledge, skills, and new discoveries. A team approach to learning is one of the things that makes the Internet fun for students. Many innovative teachers have involved their classes in designing learning units for other classes — including establishing learning outcomes and evaluating learning. A team approach also allows students to become active in their own education and reinforces the value of personal responsibility.

The three keys to keeping this dynamic environment manageable are
- committing enough time to become reasonably familiar with Internet tools
- seeking out others who can help when you get stuck
- moving slowly enough to make sure that you understand each stage before moving on to the next

You are about to embark on an adventure that will change the way you teach and the way your students learn. It will also change the ways in which you — and they — see and respond to the world. It is our hope that *Teacher's Internet Companion* will help to make this adventure a mutually exciting and satisfying one.

Ann Heide
Linda Stilborne

Learning about the Internet will

- be exciting
- take time
- sometimes be frustrating
- change the way you solve problems
- change the way you teach
- give you new confidence
- broaden your horizons

Most importantly,

- using the Internet will ensure that you and your students have a place in a global world.

Ten tips for Internet success

Here are some approaches you and your students can use to get started quickly and avoid common pitfalls. Many of these suggestions are based on the idea of sharing expertise, which is the best way to master the Internet. Because integration of technology into the curriculum is a requirement of the educational reform that is occurring everywhere, you are not alone. Take advantage of what other teachers, students, administrators, and the broader community are offering to help you bring this technology into your classroom.

1. **Consult others before proceeding on your own;** if you know someone who uses the Internet effectively, ask him or her to help you get started. Check with your local school district resource people, teacher organizations and national as well as provincial/state online networks to find out what projects are already available for your students to join. If other teachers in your school have experience using the Internet, offer to help them manage an Internet project.

2. **Find a learning partner,** possibly another teacher in your school who also wants to use the Internet. You can compare notes on resources and encourage each other. (If you find yourselves complaining to each other, find a different partner!)

3. **Sign up for any local courses** that promise to help you learn more about the Internet and its tools. Your school district may offer such courses or may be willing to fund a course, particularly if you agree to share some of what you learn with your colleagues. (Hint: Taking a course with a partner is also a good way to ensure you don't miss key points.)

4. **If your school does not have Internet access,** get your own account. Shop around for a service provider until you find one who is willing to provide help with the installation. Seek out Windows- or Macintosh-based access, since these bring you the best of the Internet's multimedia features.

5. **If you know of any student technowizards at your school,** ask them to help with such tasks as installing plug-ins. As you may have discovered, many students (particularly those in the upper grades) are already knowledgeable about the Internet, and are eager to share what they know.

6. **Visit your school or local university** library to see what books and magazines about using the Internet in education are available. Many

educational journals such as *Electronic Learning, Learning and Leading with Technology, American Journal of Distance Education, Technology and Learning,* and *Journal of Computer Assisted Learning* focus on the role of technology in education reform and provide lesson plans, projects, and useful advice from teachers.

7. **Once you're online,** seek out online tutorials and education resources. This book suggests many helpful sources.

8. **Don't try to master everything at once;** take time to explore. In particular, give yourself ample time to learn before beginning a classroom project. If you spend even 30 minutes a day learning something new, you'll be amazed at what you've mastered in a month.

9. **Once you're comfortable with electronic mail,** join one of the educational listservs such as Kidsphere. (See Chapter 7 for more information about these.)

10. **Although Net browsers let you keep track of resources online,** keep a small notebook or card file of some of the interesting resources you find. A personalized, computer-based card file or database is great for quick searching.

Hope you find our hints helpful! We will provide more useful tips throughout this book.

If you live in a country where the grade levels K–12 are not used, please note the following approximate ages of students at each grade level. This chart will permit you to see readily which projects in the book are at the appropriate level for your own students.

kindergarten (K)	grade 1	grade 2	grade 3	grade 4	grade 5	grade 6
ages 5–6	ages 6–7	ages 7–8	ages 8–9	ages 9–10	ages 10–11	ages 11–12

grade 7	grade 8	grade 9	grade 10	grade 11	grade 12
ages 12–13	ages 13–14	ages 14–15	ages 15–16	ages 16–17	17–18

1
Chapter

The Role of the Internet in Today's Classroom

"Technology is not the only change in the American classroom in the last 28 years, but it is the most dramatic and arguably the one with the most far-reaching implications for how we teach and how children learn ... If anyone had told me even five years ago that I would have integrated technology into my daily teaching, and at the level I do now, I would not have believed it. But I am inspired and motivated by the changes it has wrought."

— Christine Arkwright Clemon, Teacher

Marshall McLuhan, the communications visionary of the sixties, said that new technologies are always used to do the old job — that is, until some driving force causes them to be used in new ways. It can be argued that, so far, this has been our experience with computers in education. Today there are computers in schools, but as yet they have not significantly changed the nature of teaching or of learning. Computers can deliver learning in novel ways, but they still fall far short of delivering the kinds of school experiences we want for our children. With the advent of the Internet, this situation is changing and very quickly. Again, it was McLuhan who captured the concept that is now the driving force behind the Internet — as well as behind an impending revolution in education. The concept is that of the global village. Since Marshall McLuhan coined the term in the 1960s, few of us have truly understood what the term *global village* means. Most of us have been impressed with CNN's instantaneous global video broadcasting, but the passive medium of television gives few of us the feeling of much involvement beyond our favorite reclining chair. Yet today, thousands of children in dozens of countries around the world are living the reality of the global village in personal, hands-on interactive ways. Through the medium of networking and telecommunication technologies, these students are for the first time learning to think of themselves as global citizens, seeing the world, and their place in the world, in ways much different than their parents.

This chapter looks at the Internet and its potential to bring about revolutionary social change in education and society. The availability of so much information and so many opportunities to share and communicate with people at a distance may not at first appear to be sufficient justification for schools to spend the amounts of money needed to link classrooms to the

Internet. This chapter discusses some of the reasons why the Internet is an increasingly important tool for educators and shows how telecommunications technologies have the potential to transform the ways in which teachers teach and students learn.

The Internet today

The Internet is an extensive network of interlinked yet independent computer networks. In less than two decades, the Internet has gone from being a highly specialized communications network used mostly for military and academic applications to a massive electronic bazaar. Today, the electronic network includes, but is not limited to

- e-learning
- e-commerce
- e-shopping
- e-banking
- e-mail
- online games
- digital music
- digital video

The Web, though still only a young child in human years, continues to grow exponentially, becoming daily more robust and sophisticated. If something you want is lacking, check again in a few months and it may have appeared. Like religion and politics, it seems as if the Internet is large enough to accommodate our interests, needs, and preferences. American statistics indicate that in just a year and a half, from December 1998 to August 2000, the share of households with Internet access doubled, rising from 26.2% to 41.5%. Rural households are catching up. The data show a 75% increase in rural household access over this 18 month period, so that today 38.9% of rural households have Internet access.[1] Families who find themselves stranded on a desert island are more likely to request a computer with online access than a telephone or television and more than one in three families admit to redesigning, reconfiguring, or renovating their home to accommodate their computers.[2] The increase in home use indicates that the Internet has something for everybody. Statistics Canada reports that the number of households in the top 15 Census Metropolitan Areas with at least one regular Internet user increased from 35.9% in 1998 to 61.6% in 2002.[3] People reported that they use the Internet to

- communicate by e-mail (95.2%);
- do electronic banking (51%);
- purchase goods and services (30.5%);
- find medical/health information (63.9%);
- pursue formal education and training (47.3%);
- search for employment (35%);
- play games (50%)
- obtain music (47%)
- make travel arrangements (59.1%).[4]

In terms of spending time on the Internet, a 2001 study revealed that the average Canadian family spends more than 32 hours per week surfing in cyberspace. And while parents tend to go online together with their young children and show them the ropes, parents with older children tend to let them do their own thing, and find themselves learning from the older children.[5]

The Internet and schools

Information and communications technologies are *the* driving force in our culture and our economy today. The technological revolution has produced a generation of students who have grown up with multidimensional, interactive media sources, a generation whose understandings and expectations of the world differ from those preceding them. The world is available as a curriculum resource and the implications for schools are profound. In 1994, the American federal government established a goal of linking every school to the Internet by the year 2000. From 1994 through 1998, the percentage of public schools with Internet connections jumped from 35% to 89%.[7] The percentage of instructional rooms with Internet access in public schools increased from 3% (elementary) and 4% (secondary) in 1994 to 76% (elementary) and 79% (secondary) in 2000.[8]

An examination of how schools are connected to the Internet tells us more about how it is being used. A dedicated line is much faster than a dial-up connection and allows higher-level use of the Internet. The percentage of public schools in the United States using a dedicated line for Internet access increased from 65% in 1998 to 77% in 2000, whereas schools using a dial-up connection decreased from 22% in 1998 to 11% in 2000.[9]

School connections are improving and bandwidth is increasing as decision makers realize the potential of the Internet for learning.

Another indicator of Internet use is that the ratio of students per instructional computer is fast approaching that recommended by the President's

Committee of Advisors on Science and Technology. The proportion of instructional rooms with Internet access in public schools in the United States increased from 50% in 1998 to 85% in 2001.[10]

While some troubling differences in computer access and Internet connectivity still exist between inner-city and rural schools and suburban and medium-sized city schools, the level of computer access for teachers and students is rapidly improving in the United States.[11]

How is the Internet being used in these schools? American educational statistics indicate some clear trends in Internet use. Teachers reported using computers and the Internet to a moderate or large degree for the following instructional purposes:

- classroom instruction (66%);
- practice drills (31%);
- research using the Internet (30%);
- solve problems and analyze data (27%);
- produce multimedia reports/projects (24%);
- graphical presentations of materials (19%);
- demonstrations/simulations (17%); and
- correspond with others (7%).[13]

Teacher preparation statistics also attest to the fact that new teachers to the profession are coming equipped with better online skills. In a 1999 American study, 45% of teachers with three or fewer years of teaching experience reported that they felt well/very well prepared to use computers and the Internet for instruction compared to 27% of teachers with 20 or more years of teaching experience.[14] These teachers with three or less years of experience reported that they use computers or the Internet a lot at school to

- communicate with colleagues (30%);
- gather information for planning lessons (21%);
- access model lesson plans (11%);
- access research and best practices for teaching (11%); and
- communicate with parents or students (6%).[15]

Conversely, there are a number of reasons why some schools and teachers have been less than enthusiastic about bringing the Internet into the classroom. These reasons include

- reduced funding for public education
- lack of release time for teachers to learn, practice or plan ways to use the Internet
- lack of support regarding ways to integrate telecommunications into the curriculum

- outdated, incompatible or unreliable computers
- lack of technical support
- concern about student access to inappropriate materials
- lack of administrative support.[16]

There is also the problem that — at least at first glance — the Internet may seem to be dominated by technowizards who appear to be more concerned by what the technology can do than about how it can improve the teaching and learning processes. Some teachers may be daunted by the fact that their students know so much more that they themselves do about the Internet. These are all real problems, problems that are addressed in the upcoming chapters of this book. But they are problems that are being overcome by educators who recognize and use the benefits of the Internet for learning.

The Internet and education

On the Internet, educators recognize long-time friends like reference materials, resources and lesson plans, but these are just the tip of the iceberg in terms of the Internet's potential. Teachers who want to truly exploit the power of the medium don't look for the online equivalent of their textbooks or handouts, but rather "the sparks that create insights, the contrasts that excite problem solving, the bells and whistles that motivate, the passion that inspires."[17] The power of the Internet can be demonstrated by its characteristics.

- The Internet is immediate. On September 11, 2001, people around the world witnessed the dawn of a new era live on the Internet. And when teachers wondered how to talk with their students about this disaster, help was immediately forthcoming online from psychologists, counsellors and colleagues. Also in connection with these events, the Bush administration launched the Friendship through Education Consortium (**http://www.friendshipthrougheducation.org**) to encourage communication and understanding between U.S. schools and those in Islamic countries. As the conflict between the United States-led coalition and Iraq unfolds, we can expect to find similar advice and support for parents and teachers.
- The Internet is primary-source resource-rich. Consider the online collections of paintings and artefacts from the National Gallery of Canada (**http://national.gallery.ca**) and the Smithsonian (**http://www.si.edu**). The Thinker (**http://www.thinker.org**), an American museum, offers more than 70 000 images online. With the increasing role of digital imagery in our world, teachers are exploring ways to use primary sources in classroom instruction. The University of Virginia's Digital

Media Center (**http://www.lib.virginia.edu/clemons/RMC/collections-home.html**) has assembled links to sites with image resources that can be used in K–12 schools at this time.

- The Internet is interactive, putting control under the fingertips of the user. Java-scripted simulations, Flash animations and virtual reality allow students to actively participate in their own learning. The virtual simulations online at the San Francisco Exploratorium (**http://www.exploratorium.edu/exhibits/f_exhibits.html**) can be easily integrated across the curriculum. Thousands of simulations are now readily available at the JARS.com directory of Java-based science resources (**http://www.jars.com/jars_categories_java_science.html**).

- The Internet is a community of experts. Webcasts, as the name suggests, are live broadcasts over the Web. They generally include a presentation from an expert in a certain field and an opportunity for students to ask questions. Support materials such as Teachers' Guides, biographies, background information and archives are often provided.

Figure 1-1
This NASA Webcast (**http://quest.arc.nasa.gov/aero/events/marsplane**) focused on planetary flight. The page also has links to the curriculum standards addressed by the activity.

- The Internet is authentic. In the international project, Connecting Math to Our Lives (**http://www.iearn.org/projects/math.html**) students explore how math is used in their communities, use math skills to investigate community social concerns and then take action to promote greater equity in the world around them. In the Australian project, Book Rap (**http://rite.ed.qut.edu.au/oz-teachernet**) students from across the country or around the world discuss scheduled books via e-mail. Teachers or teacher librarians can nominate a book for discussion by becoming a Book Rap Coordinator.
- The Internet is passionate. A huge variety of causes and ideologies are represented: environmental and human rights advocacy groups, animal rights organizations, and any number of individuals who really believe in something. The Space for Species project (**http://www.spacefor species.ca**) allows students to track endangered species in Canada using satellite telemetry and to communicate directly with the scientists who are conducting field research on species at risk. The project is the brainchild of Canadian Astronaut Robert Thirsk.
- The Internet is clever and funny. Visit the Museum of Bad Art (**http://glyphs.com/moba**) "dedicated to the collection, preservation, exhibition and celebration of bad art in all its forms and in all its glory." At The T.W.I.N.K.I.E.S. Project (**http://www.twinkiesproject.com**) you'll find a series of experiments to determine the properties of "that incredible food, the Twinkie."
- The Internet makes learning fun. The Yuckiest Site on the Internet (**http://yucky.kids.discovery.com**) uses multimedia to engage learners as they discover the inside story of roach anatomy or what happens to old dirty earwax.
- The Internet is a virtual world. We can go on field trips around the universe, to museums and galleries, through human body systems, within animal colonies, back in time — all by simply using an Internet connection. To get an idea of the variety of virtual field trips available for students, look at Vicki Blackwell's Internet Guide for Educators (**http://www.vickiblackwell.com/vft.html**).
- The Internet spawns invention. E-books are but one example. E-books are digitized versions of books that can be downloaded from a Web site and read on a desktop or laptop computer, a hand-held device or a dedicated e-book reader. Imagine integrated reference and testing tools, opportunities for teachers to add and customize content, embedded hyperlinks to Web sites, and information search capabilities. Until publishing companies receive enough demand from schools, lack of content in E-book formats may continue to be problematic, but this exciting technology holds a great deal of promise for the near future.

- The Internet makes data accessible. Businesses and government agencies place data in online data banks, thus providing real data for authentic student investigations. This data can be useful in social sciences, humanities and mathematics explorations. For example, the "Exploring Data" Web site developed by the Education Services Directorate in Queensland, Australia, (**http://exploringdata.cqu.edu.au**) provides a wide variety of data sets ranging from air pollution to pottery. Often this data can be transferred from the Web site to your school server and opened in a spreadsheet such as Microsoft Excel. Learners' accessibility to information using the Internet allows them to develop their own styles of information retrieval and organization.
- The Internet is all about communicating. Every day, events occur that provide "teachable moments" for teachers and students. The Media Awareness Network (**http://www.media-awareness.ca/eng/med/class/teamedia/tmintro.htm**) has created a "teachable moment" section to provide teachers with a forum with which to share these opportunities for learning with other educators.

With the depth and breadth of the Internet becoming ever more accessible to more learners, we are now seeing the marriage of technology with learning come to fruition.

The Internet and learning theory

In recent years the philosophies that have long governed educational practice have been challenged by a number of new theories, which place the learner at the center of the educational universe. "Buzz words" from these theories are all around us: "Active Learning," "Agency," "Anchored Instruction," "Collaborative Learning," "Multiple Intelligences," "Situated Cognition" and "Social Constructivism." These theories and others put technology into the hands of learners to assist in their developing higher order cognitive skills and speak of technology's power to access, store, manipulate, and analyze information, thus enabling learners to spend more time reflecting and understanding.

Active learning

Active learning isn't a new idea. It goes back at least as far as Socrates and was a major emphasis among progressive educators such as John Dewey. Active learning involves putting our students in situations that compel them to read, view, listen, think deeply, and communicate. Using the Internet as a tool, students can explore environments, generate questions and issues, collaborate with others, and produce knowledge rather than passively receiving it. For example, to meet Science learning outcomes, students at a school in

Virginia used the National Geographic Kids Network (**http://www.nation algeographic.com/kids/index.html**). In the Acid Rain Project they explored a variety of issues surrounding acid rain. They designed acid rain collectors, studied energy and powerplants and analyzed Civil War tombstones for rain damage. In addition to these real-world activities, they compiled and critiqued their data and shared it with students from distant schools through e-mail. Online collaborative learning allowed the students to consider different views and sources and debate them in real time.

An example of active learning in Language Arts is the Harry Potter "In Character" Novel Project (**http://schools.sd68.bc.ca/coal/potter/ mainpott.htm**) in which older students, who serve as impersonators of the Harry Potter characters, are paired with younger students who ask questions of them by e-mail.

In such an environment, acquiring content changes from a static process to one in which learners define their own goals. Students are active, rather than passive; they produce knowledge and present that knowledge in a variety of formats. The teacher's role is to guide and structure the learning environments and experiences such that learners are fully engaged in their learning, recognizing that when students are investigating, asking questions, writing about what they're learning, and doing those things in an authentic context, then they are learning to think and to learn.

Agency

Agency is a term introduced by American psychologist Jerome Bruner. Teachers who accept that learners control their own learning will understand the concept of agency. Bruner says we are the agents in our own meaning making. We control our own mental activity, using a cognitive structure, which allows us to be agents of our own learning. The international ThinkQuest program (**http://www.thinkquest.org**) accomplishes this by encouraging students to use the Internet to create Web-based educational tools and materials. Structured as a contest, ThinkQuest works with teams of students who build educational materials. These teams collaborate electronically to develop innovative, high-quality educational tools that take advantage of the strengths of the Internet. Teachers, parents and other interested adults support the participating young people as coaches, technology mentors, and subject-matter guides, but they leave the hard work of defining the project, organizing the work, conducting the research and mastering the Web technologies to the participating ThinkQuest team members.

Collaborative learning

It takes planning and intervention to build successful collaborative groups with or without computers, but computers and the Internet are effective teamwork tools that facilitate collaboration. Classroom activities can be structured so that the Internet encourages collaboration by building on the learners' desire to communicate and share their understandings. Beyond the classroom, communication tools like e-mail, bulletin boards, and chat groups allow students to communicate and collaborate with content experts as well as with peers around the world.

A Grade 4 Spiders Project at Yes Net is an example of a classroom-based collaboration (**http://www.yesnet.yk.ca/schools/jackhulland/classes/colberg/spiders**). In this project, each group of students collects information about a specific type of spider. Together with the teacher, they post their findings, cross-curricular outcomes statements, and a resources list. In this example, insightful student evaluations are included. An effective presentation format becomes a research tool for others.

"Comparing High School Timetables" is an example of a school-to-school collaboration (**http://www.gsn.org/pr**). Students use surveys, e-mails and discussions between responding classes to find timetable efficiencies and to compare percentages and ratios of time spent on different areas of curriculum.

Situated cognition

All learning is situated in a context that gives it meaning. Situated learning means that we use this context to make sense of what we learn. So whether you're learning by doing, listening, reading, or writing, it's always situated in the social context in which you make meaning of what you are learning. We transfer what we learn constantly from context to context, of course, as we move from community to community keeping our same identity. When we think about schools as part of the larger context of society as opposed to an exclusive centre of learning, we see learning as a constant process that doesn't end at the 3:30 bell. Learning how to learn is what we do at school. When teachers integrate the Internet with curriculum objectives, they are giving their students a good collection of tools and the time to practise new skills for learning. The complexity of the knowledge building process requires skills for a lifetime of learning. The builder is the learner and multimedia technologies provide an ideal environment in which to work.

The Learning Circles program, found at iEARN (**http://www.iearn.org/circles**), develops theme-based, scheduled, cross-classroom Internet projects, which connect a small number of schools internationally. Classes post their project requests and are assigned to a circle of between 7 and 9 classes, and they "telecommunicate." Each class posts and receives information as weekly updates. Students prepare class subprojects for a real audience of international friends. Learning is situated in a meaningful context in which everyone's ideas count.

"... there's a bit of a problem with this notion that learning can be viewed as taking place exclusively or even primarily in a self-contained context and the rest of life is application.... What I have trouble with is that idea that the best way for students to learn is to isolate them from real life, have them focus completely on the learning, package knowledge in such a way that it can be most efficiently transferred from head to head, and then send them off into real life and expect them to apply what they've learned."[18]

— Dr. Etienne Wenger, author of *Situated Learning: Legitimate Peripheral Participation* (1991), and *Communities of Practice: Learning, Meaning and Identity* (1998)

Communities of practice

Learning is fundamentally a social phenomenon, and people organize their learning around the social communities to which they belong. These communities, which share values, beliefs, languages, and ways of doing things, are called "communities of practice." Communities of practice form and share knowledge by creating mechanisms for practitioners to reach out to other practitioners. The "communities of practice" approach to learning suggests that educators create opportunities for students to solve real problems with adults, in real learning situations. The Electronic Emissary (**http://emissary.wm.edu**) is a "matching service" that helps K–12 teachers and students locate other Internet account-holders who are experts in different disciplines, for purposes of setting up curriculum-based, electronic exchanges among the teachers, their students, and the experts. In this way, the interaction that occurs among teachers and students face-to-face in the classroom is supplemented and extended by exchanges that occur among teachers, students, and experts online, via electronic mail, text-based chats, Web pages and desktop teleconferencing. To date, the Emissary has supported more than 400 electronic teams of students, teachers, facilitators, and subject matter experts. The Internet lends itself to exploration, and circumstances in which students engage in real actions that have consequences for both them and their community create powerful learning environments.[19]

Social constructivism

In the 1930s, Russian psychologist and philosopher Lev Vygotsky described learning as a knowledge-building process. According to Vygotsky, our social and physical world combined with our biological and cultural ancestry, all play a part in the "construction" of our own reality. Today, we know this as "Social Constructivism." This concept is easy to understand if you think of learning as a creative building project, controlled by the learner who, over time, uses both people and environments as sources of knowledge. Social Constructivism now forms the basis of new teaching methods—many of which are fundamentally supported by using the Internet as a learning tool. [20]

Constructivists believe that knowledge is constructed uniquely and individually in multiple ways and that learners each bring their own prior knowledge, experiences and beliefs to a learning situation. The Internet provides a mixture of text, pictures, sound, and motion to address the diverse learning styles of students. WebQuests are a vehicle through which constructivist teachers put these beliefs into action. A WebQuest is "an inquiry-oriented activity in which most or all of the information used by learners is drawn from the Web. WebQuests are designed to use learners' time well, to focus on using information rather than looking for it, and to support learners' thinking at the level of analysis, synthesis and evaluation."[21] A WebQuest uses online resources, selected in advance by the teacher, to challenge

"If I were to become a teacher, I would hope to use the computer to allow my students to get information or allow them to gain knowledge through research and exploration…. Using computers has enhanced my education by allowing me to explore a whole new world of things I could not have otherwise seen already. It also allows me to do much neater and more professional work. I think that everyone should have access to computers and the Internet for many reasons. Mostly though, because I know that computers are the future and I think everyone should be a part of the future, not just those who are lucky enough to have access to a new and important tool."

— Katie, a 7th grade student online at **http://4teachers.org/kidspeak/kat ie/index.shtml** 10/01/01

students in their critical examination of a given issue, event or topic drawn from the curriculum. Students involved in WebQuests can be self-directed and independent. They can choose what sources to examine and what links to follow. They can work through the WebQuest at their own pace. Teachers can provide individualized attention to those who begin to fall behind, while others can be encouraged to tackle more complex tasks. If you are new to the WebQuest concept, begin your orientation at **http://webquest.sdsu.edu/webquest.html**. You will find a more detailed examination of WebQuests in Chapter 5.

Constructivists believe that learning is internally controlled and mediated by the learner and that learning is both active and reflective. Using the Internet as a research tool or as a communication channel to share ideas with other learners, students build on their own understandings. An online conversation through e-mail is an active event, but such discussions usually prompt reflection. They help learners think about ideas and modify their understandings. Writers In Electronic Residence (**http://www.wier.ca**) connects students with professional writers, teachers and one another in an animated exchange of original writing and commentary. The writers, well-known Canadian authors, join classrooms electronically to read and consider the students' work, offer reactions and ideas, and guide discussions between the students. Students compose their works and responses to the works of others offline before posting their writing in the WIER online conference. WIER operates conferences at the elementary, middle and secondary school grade levels.

In the constructivist paradigm, knowledge is constructed through a variety of real world tools, authentic data, relevant resources, engaging experiences and meaningful contexts. The Internet provides opportunities for students to manipulate and analyze raw data, critically evaluate information, and operate hardware and software within the context of a variety of different situations. The Global Grocery List, is a project that generates real, peer collected data for student computation, analysis, and conclusion-building (**http://landmark-project.com/ggl**). Students find and share local grocery prices for items on a common list to build a growing table of data from around the world. This data can then be used for comparisons, finding patterns and discussion on the factors that control food prices.

The technological literacy required for these types of learning experiences also imparts a very important set of vocational skills that will serve students well in a world in which IT is now the fastest growing industry. [22] The U.S. Bureau of Labor Statistics predicts that 70% of the jobs available in the workforce will somehow be related to the acquisition and manipulation of digital knowledge. Ninety percent of those jobs will go unfilled if this need is not addressed today in our schools. [23]

Constructivist teachers create collaborative online projects that involve students in long-term problem-solving and product-generating tasks that utilize Internet resources and a variety of digital communications. Constructive learners are in control, they are "in the driver's seat" – an apt metaphor for the information highway.

Anchored instruction

"The Adventures of Jasper Woodbury" (**http://peabody.vanderbilt.edu/projects/funded/jasper/Jasperhome.html**) is a collaborative online project that uses a technique called "anchored instruction." In the Jasper series, real life situations depicted in video stories become the "anchor" or the basis for constructing a useable database of knowledge. In the process of buying a used boat, students identify the mathematical problems, which must be solved before Jasper can fulfill his dream. They find information about navigation, weather, gasoline costs and motor consumption rates so Jasper can travel to the marina to see the boat. They calculate repair costs when Jasper's old motor breaks down. Students learn by collaborating with each other, but stay anchored to the content by solving problems for Jasper's real life drama. Students determine what questions, if any, must be answered. This process of dialogic inquiry uses questioning and discussion or negotiation skills to know if there's a problem, to understand and agree on a statement of the problem, and to find possible solutions. Jasper's helpers identify the small steps in the progression of problem solving in the complex challenge of buying a used boat:

- Is there a problem?
- What's the problem?
- How can we solve it?
- Who's got any ideas?
- What do we need?
- Where will we go?
- How will we get there?
- Can anyone help us?
- When will we know if the problem is solved?
- What else might happen?
- How can we avoid this again?
- What have we learned?

Several key concepts of Social Constructive learning theory are also used in this project. The context is authentic because learning is situated in the familiar. Stories connect real life problems to other subject areas in the curriculum in a relevant way. Groups of students work together to identify the questions, break down the tasks, and test their assumptions in order to answer the challenge. All ideas are valued, every little bit of information helps. The social interaction involved when comparing perspectives or negotiating practical solutions is motivating and reflects real life.

Multiple Intelligences

Most of us are aware of Howard Gardner, who challenged the theories of I.Q. Gardner defined our brain capability in terms of eight intelligences:

1. *Verbal-Linguistic* — ability to use words and language
2. *Logical-Mathematical* — capacity for inductive and deductive thinking and reasoning, use of numbers and recognition of abstract patterns
3. *Visual-Spatial* — ability to visualize objects and spatial dimensions, and create internal images and pictures
4. *Body-Kinesthetic* — wisdom of the body and ability to control physical motion
5. *Musical-Rhythmic* — ability to recognize tonal patterns and sounds, sensitivity to rhythms and beats
6. *Interpersonal* — capacity for person-to-person communications and relationships
7. *Intrapersonal* — spiritual, inner states of being, self-reflection, and awareness
8. *Naturalist* — strong appreciation for and understanding of the natural world

At the New Dimensions of Learning site (**http://www.multi-intel.com**) you can get a closer look at these eight types of intelligence. The New Dimensions site will help you respond to students' learning preferences by providing exercises and lesson ideas in every subject area as well as a planning chart of activities and subject connections.

You can probably picture one of your own students who may be wonderfully gifted at music, but who has little interest in sports or one who writes great stories but struggles with math. These different types of intelligence indicate the range of ways in which students are most likely to become engaged in learning. Activities that are inquiry-based and encourage students to work to the best of their ability, using all their "smarts" are applications of Gardner's theories.

Pollution Solutions (**http://www.stemnet.nf.ca/pollution**) demonstrates how awareness and real activities improve the quality of learning. The purpose of the Pollution Solutions project is to develop awareness of pollution issues at home, in the community, and to propose and implement realistic solutions for pollution control. This is a structured, collaborative project for communities of participating classes. Students are grouped into teams in order to investigate recycling. Over a period of four weeks, they collect data, and then prepare a report, predicting what their community will look like 50 years from now if the pattern continues. Challenge activities include designing, implementing and reporting on a cleanup project for their community.

Pollution Solutions provides many opportunities for cross-curricular and Multiple Intelligences learning. Learning outcomes statements are listed for each subject area. Learning outcomes for Math (statistics, data collection, logical problem solving), for Science (recycling, environmental awareness, stewardship, ecosystems) and for Language and Creative Arts (designing, presenting, reporting) can be targeted in one project. When integrated with other theme related resources such as Earth Day's global action site (**http://www.earthday.net**), pollution reduction becomes the "anchor." Students are challenged to find global connections. They use their own knowledge, their capabilities as a collective of learners, their skills and their resources to build a useable proposal. Using real-life statistics, found at environmental statistics sites such as **http://www.atl.ec.gc.ca/pollution**, encourages logical and mathematical thinking skills.

Including artwork and creative recycling options from The Imagination Factory (**http://www.kid-at-art.com**) can provide alternatives for presentations. These examples show Multiple Intelligences and Social Constructive theories in action. The diversity and connectivity of the Internet provide powerful curriculum delivery tools. Students who are actively engaged in knowledge construction tap into their "unique smarts" and develop more and better skills at all levels of functioning. Learner labels are not needed.

Learning environments, like the ones in these projects, respect all questions and all contributions. Collaborative, digital and inquiry-based learning provide opportunities to let learning happen naturally for each student.

Education in the 21st century includes teaching about research, information management, interpretation, synthesis, guidance, facilitation, cultural connections, and the construction of a knowledge base through collaboration, inquiry, dialogue and reflection. Figure 1-2 outlines some of the shifts between the old and the new models of learning, together with their implications for students. The characteristics of the new model of learning can be more easily accomplished when Internet technologies are wrapped into your curriculum goals.[24]

Time for a change

The technological revolution has produced a generation of students who have grown up with multidimensional, interactive media sources, a generation whose understandings and expectations of the world differ from those preceding them. Only by revising educational practices in the light of how our culture has changed can we give these students an appropriate education. Technology consultant and award-winning teacher Alan November describes the necessary changes to our schools as changing "job descriptions":

> The job descriptions of everyone in school will fundamentally change because of the [information] highway. Students will move from working in the test-preparation business to building information products that can really be used by "clients" around the world. For teachers, perhaps the most difficult job change will be that we'll no longer be at the center of learning for our stu-

"If I had a teacher that incorporated the Internet with their lessons, I would definitely be more interested in school. Some examples of this would be having an economics teacher get on the Internet and give the kids a shopping list; and their job was to find the best deal. Or you could have an English teacher have kids get on the Internet and read movie reviews, then have the kids rent the movie and see if they agree with the experts. Maybe they could write their own review and send it to Siskel and Ebert!"

— David, a high school student online at **http://4teachers.org/kidspeak/thelan/index.shtml** 10/01/02

dents. We'll become brokers—connecting our students to others across the nets who will help them create and add to their knowledge in a way that one teacher alone could only dream of.

— Quoted by Thérèse Mageau (1994, May/June), "Will the superhighway really change schools?" Electronic Learning, 13 (8):24.

Some teachers might raise an eyebrow at November's unconventional views, but others would insist that the reality he envisions is not far off.

It is often the case that, at least initially, people approach new technologies with the thought that they are somehow replacing something more familiar. Sometimes this perception proves to be true. Television has in large part replaced radio, just as the car has replaced the horse and buggy. We may worry that the Internet has the potential to replace the textbook, the school library, and, ultimately, the classroom teacher. Undoubtedly the role of the classroom teacher will change, but teachers will not become redundant. In fact, the best guarantee that teachers, and not technology, will be at the heart of the classroom of the future is to ensure that we as the teachers of today master new tools for learning, such as the Internet. "For teachers, technology should be a means to new ends, to more dynamic learning, but technology should not be the issue. The real issues are about new forms of perception and awareness required by change, new definitions of what it means to produce knowledge, and a willingness to abandon old forms of authority for the more democratic assets found in a true learning community." (Rowe, 1994) With access to the Internet, the classroom becomes an even greater cooperative learning environment in which the teacher provides focus, guidance, and inspiration.

	Old model	New model	Implications for learners
Figure 1-2 New models for learning.	Teacher centered	Learner centered	Students are empowered as learners
	Passive absorption	Learner participation	Student motivation is enhanced
	Individual work	Team learning	Team building skills are developed; learning is enhanced through sharing
	Teacher as expert	Teacher as guide	Framework for learning is more adaptable to a fast-changing world
	Static	Dynamic	Resources for learning (textbooks, existing knowledge base) are replaced by an online link to the real world. Resources can be adapted to immediate learning needs
	Prescribed learning	Learning to learn	Development of skills for the information age

Today, more than ever, we need teachers who are able and willing to become side-by-side learners with their students. Teachers who are not afraid to acknowledge, "I don't know," and then can turn around and say, "Let's find out together." These teachers need to know how to use various technologies to shape and process and manage information, to look for relationships, trends, anomalies, and details, which can not only answer questions, but create questions as well. We need teachers who understand that learning in today's world is not just a matter of mastering a static body of knowledge, but also being able to discover the rapidly changing ideas about that knowledge itself.

— Al Rogers. The Failure and the Promise of Technology in Education, Global SchoolNet Foundation, **http://www.gsn.org**, *03/10/97.*

Keys to using the Net

As with any learning venture, success depends on mastering the basics and then gradually expanding knowledge through practice. Although the Internet is a huge and ever-expanding universe of information, the good news is that you don't have to know it all. For teachers, the key to using the Internet successfully is to learn to use a few basic tools—and then to focus on using a few key educational resources.

This chapter briefly describes some basic Internet tools. Subsequent chapters will discuss each of these in detail. The paragraphs that follow are intended to give a preview of some of the ways that you can access educational resources over the Internet. With the exception of the World Wide Web (described below), most of these applications are possible even on an outdated computer with a relatively slow connection.

World Wide Web

The World Wide Web, along with special software called Web browsers (such as Netscape, Opera, or Microsoft's Internet Explorer), provides point-and-click access to text, graphics, sound, and sometimes video files, often integrated around a specific topic. The World Wide Web provides easy access to a vast array of information. A Web page can be a "clickable" children's book, an online museum exhibit, an art gallery display, a government information resource, a lesson from a distance learning course, a weather map, or even an interactive frog dissection. The World Wide Web also provides a great opportunity for students to publish their own information.

You can use a Web browser as a communications tool to send e-mail or to participate in online discussions. Technologies such as Web conferencing, in which messages are posted to the Web for ongoing discussions, and Flash, a technology developed by Macromedia which is used to deliver interactive content over the Web, have greatly enhanced the relatively static presentation of text and graphics. Increasingly, Internet applications that have traditionally been separate and distinct are now all accessible through the

World Wide Web. Newsgroups, FTP (File Transfer Protocol) sites, and online chat groups are all available through the Web. For many teachers, the Web is the real focus of the Internet, to the point where some people have come to think (erroneously) that the Web and the Internet are synonymous.

E-mail

Electronic mail, or e-mail, rivals the Web as the most common Internet application, as well as one of the most powerful. Electronic mail allows you to send and receive messages over the Internet. Using electronic mail, you can communicate with anyone else who has an Internet address. You can also send messages through "gateway" services to other systems, such as bulletin boards or America Online. Many classroom projects may use electronic mail, which provides an opportunity for interactions with students and teachers around the globe.

In addition, through electronic mail you can join worldwide discussion groups. There are literally hundreds of discussion groups for educators on the Internet. Favorites among elementary and secondary school teachers include Kidsphere, an international discussion group for teachers; Edtech, which focuses on the use of technology in the classroom; and Kidlit-L, a discussion group that explores children's literature. There is a wide range of discussion groups with a specific curriculum focus. Such groups include **k12.lang.art**, for language arts education; **k12.ed.soc-studies**, for social science teachers; and **k12.ed.life-skills**, for school counselors.

You will be amazed at the number of projects you and your students can undertake using e-mail. Chapters 2, 3, and 7 provide a wealth of examples and ideas.

Audio and interactive video

With the proper computer setup (including speakers, a sound card, and Web phone software, which you can buy at your local computer store), you can use the Internet in place of the telephone. It is estimated that more than one million people currently do this.

You can also have instant access to radio and other audio broadcasts with technologies such as RealAudio. Desktop videoconferencing and video over the Internet are still limited on slower-speed networks (such as those that depend on ordinary telephone lines), but new techniques for compressing and transmitting data may make these high-end applications widely available in just a few years.

The proliferation of cable Internet services, WebTV (for Internet access via your television), and satellite communication technologies are helping to bring interactive audio, video, and broadcast services to average technology users.

One American study indicates that the percentage of households with broadband access increased from 8% in 2000 to 17% in 2002.[25]

Streaming audio and video can provide multimedia content for lessons, projects, primary source data collection and interactive experiences. Streaming audio and video refer to audio and/or video that play over the Internet without downloading to the end user's computer. Think television and radio for your computer. Streaming is different from downloading in that playback starts immediately with just a mouse click for the viewer, and the large file is not saved to the viewer's computer.

Streaming audio is like an audiotape or CD, except that you play the file over the Internet. The digitized audio file is kept on a server, and can be accessed, listened to and downloaded by a number of listeners, in different places, at the same time. All that's required are an Internet connection (the faster the better) and the freely downloadable RealPlayer plug-in. If you have a slow modem connection or are behind a firewall that prohibits real-time audio streaming, many of these presentations can be downloaded for local playback from your hard drive. If you have a sound card and a good set of speakers on your home computer, you can listen to streaming audio presentations through the speakers. In school, have students use earphones, which plug into a jack which itself is connected to the "speaker" jack of the computer's sound card.

An educational site that uses the technology of streaming audio and video is the Virtual Chautauqua Performing Arts Center (**http://128. 138.144.49/vchautauqua**). This center celebrates Colorado's performing arts and creates a means for artists and audiences to interact. Here students use RealAudio Player, a free plug-in available on the Web, to experience a variety of music, poetry, theatre, and dance. Netscape is in the process of building a library of on-demand streaming audio presentations available worldwide over the Internet 24 hours a day. You also have access to both live and archived radio broadcasts with technologies such as RealAudio.

Ask any high school student about .mp3 and you'll learn about the popularity of this file format used for the storage and transmission of music. The .mp3 format was designed to compress sound efficiently in a way similar to how .jpeg compresses pictures. Downloading songs from Web sites and saving them to writable CDs, DVDs or .mp3 players is very common today. It is, of course, illegal to distribute copyrighted songs without a license.

Streaming video, as you might expect, is like a videotape, except that you play the file over the Internet. In order to view streaming video clips, you need appropriate software loaded on your computer such as Microsoft's Windows Media Player or RealPlayer. Not only is streaming video a great tool for student learning, teachers can also take advantage of the many online opportunities for lifelong learning such as a video available at **http://www.edtechtv.org/index.php?topic=profer** that provides highlights from the 2001 California Student Technology Showcase.

"If you want to see a good example of streaming video, have a look at the TERENA (Trans European Research Network Association) conference given in Lund, Sweden in June 1999 (**http://www.cultivate-int. org/ issue4/scenes/#ref-02**). The whole conference was streamed out live across the Internet. When I watched it, I realised that streaming technology for distance learning had finally arrived. The quality of the video and audio was much better than anything I had ever seen or heard before. It was as good as actually being there at the conference. In fact it was better, because during parallel presentations I could pull down the separate streams and easily switch between sessions without having to shuffle between rooms. That's the real benefit of interactive Web media — doing things that can't be done in real life."[26]

Other Internet tools for communication and collaboration

For the past two years, six school boards across Canada have connected by CA*net3 for ongoing collaborative learning. CANARIE-supported LearnCanada (2000–2002) and the CRC/NRC Virtual Classroom (1997– 2002) program have facilitated dozens of multi-site broadband videoconference sessions providing innovative opportunities for teacher professional development and student collaborative learning. MusicGrid is an example of a current project that pioneers large-scale broadband E-learning. In this project, Canadian students and teachers, the National Arts Centre, industry, universities and international partners share knowledge, best practice, culture, and passion for music using broadband visual communication tools, including video-conference and videoservers. For more details on this exciting project, see **http:// www. musicgrid.ca/ index.php**.

Webcasts take advantage of both streaming audio and video to bring people and events live to your classroom. Webcams, video cameras that attach to a computer, can also bring real life in real time into your classroom. Students can watch pandas as they go about their lives and journal their activities the way research scientists do. They can see what's happening at any given moment on Paris's Champs Élysées or New York's Times Square. The people with whom students are collaborating become real people when they are revealed on camera. Videoconferencing involves the transmission of full images and sound. In other words, a group of learners in one site can see and speak with learners in another using cameras and TV or computer screens. Desktop videoconferencing brings this possibility out of the studio and into your classroom. You need a color video camera, a microphone, videoconferencing software (CU-SeeMe is a popular videoconferencing software application), and an Internet connection. The quality of the video and audio, however, will depend upon the speed of your Internet access. Despite the fact that most of the examples we have seen to date feature miniature, distorted images with halting, jerky audio, this technology may well be ready for the average classroom much sooner than you expect.

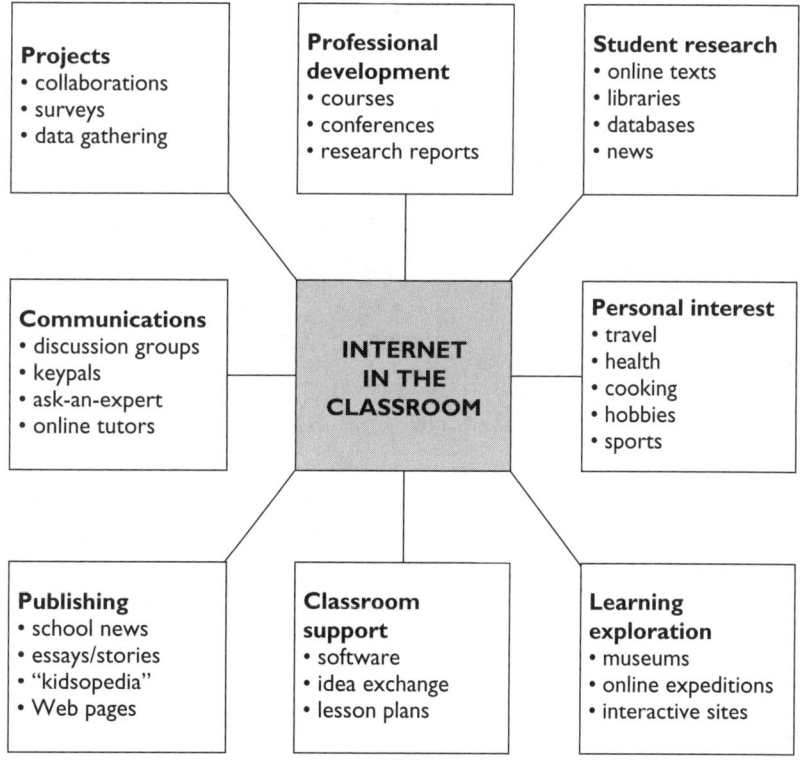

Figure 1-3
The Internet in the classroom.

These types of Internet resources, especially when combined with a laptop or hand-held computer, let students study whenever they want, wherever they want. You'll find out more about these technologies and their educational potential in Chapters 8 and 10.

Internet in the classroom

Each Internet tool has a specific function, and most teachers exploring the Net will want to become familiar with all of them. For teachers, these tools can be used to provide students with exciting opportunities to access and interpret the world around them. Teachers in a traditional classroom often have to create an artificial world, from whatever resources are available, to create learning opportunities that capture some dimension of the real world. But such resources have always been limited, and the classroom environment has never been quite "real." By becoming familiar with a few basic Internet navigation tools, teachers can bring the real world into the classroom. Following are some examples of typical Internet learning activities.

Learning through connectivity

Possibly the most powerful feature of the Internet is its potential as a communications tool. Students delight in being able to connect with people around the world. A fairly simple educational activity using electronic mail involves linking individual students with their counterparts in other places. This is an excellent way for them to learn about life in other countries, to develop and improve their language skills, and to share their thoughts on contemporary issues and problems.

> When the earthquake happened in San Francisco, we read about tidal waves in kids' swimming pools, earth movement in soccer fields, and kids being thrown down stairways—kids' perceptions of what it was like to be in an earthquake. When the Berlin Wall came down, we had classes in Berlin that were giving us day-by-day reports on what it was like to be there. When the Gulf War was going on, kids in Saudi Arabia's schools talked about the crocheted gas mask backpacks that their mothers made.
>
> — *Margaret Riel, Consultant, AT&T Learning Network*

Being able to see world events at the same level of detail at which ordinary people actually experience them is one way that students can discover the basic humanity they share with people around the globe.

Students can also use e-mail to involve other classes in a project. One seventh-grade class used e-mail to conduct a survey. They wanted to know how much time other students their age spent watching television, so they designed an electronic questionnaire and distributed it to other students over the Internet. This project provided students with an opportunity to learn about gathering and analyzing data. The project was also an interesting way to explore an important social issue.

A somewhat younger group of students used e-mail to find out about food resources around the world. Through a single e-mail account, they requested that students in other countries send them messages about what foods were native to their area. The responses they received provided the basis for developing a classroom map on which foods from various regions were displayed. Being able to interact with other students around the globe in this way brings a new and exciting dimension to learning.

Finally, electronic mail connectivity is a powerful tool for accessing experts and tutors. Purdue University in Indiana operates an online writing lab (OWL) that provides some excellent writing resources as well as human writing coaches. Along a similar line, the Canadian-based Writers In Electronic Residence has professional writers reviewing student writing samples. Other programs link students with scientists and researchers to help with class projects and units of study. Students themselves can even become mentors for their peers, using a rubric to evaluate writing samples or comparing solutions to a common math problem submitted by e-mail.

Connectivity is also a powerful tool for teachers. Global classrooms, in which several classes from around the world work on a common theme, allow teachers to collaborate on lesson planning, student activities, and assessment techniques. Many hours of preparation time can be saved by taking advantage of shared resources and strategies. Professional growth is a natural outcome as teachers learn together and benefit from one another's expertise. The Marsville project challenged students in many locations to research, design, and build a Martian colony. Organized into teams, students designed one of the eight support systems needed to establish a colony on Mars: air supply, communications, food production and delivery, recreation and leisure, temperature control, transportation, waste management, and water supply. A Marsville Web site allowed the students to post messages, read updates, and view designs from other participating schools. Communication via phone, fax, video e-mail, and videoconferencing enhanced the excitement and collaboration of the participating schools. **(http://marsville.enoreo.on.ca)**

Learning through online resources

As classrooms are able to connect to Internet resources, learning can become an endless adventure. Not only are there substantial text-based resources on topics ranging from planets to politics, but a wide range of resources is available for electronic field trips involving pictures, text, sound, and sometimes interactivity. Here is a sampling of some online exhibits sponsored by museums and other educational institutions.

- Honolulu Community College offers a fascinating dinosaur exhibit that features pictures, textual information, and an opportunity to take a narrated tour of the exhibit.

- The Institute of Physics in Naples offers an exhibit of some early instruments used to study physics. Specialized exhibits of this type abound on the Internet, and many of them are exhibits that few people would have a chance to visit otherwise.

- The Smithsonian Institution makes available an exhibit, Oceans of the Earth. Students electronically visiting the exhibit electronically can learn about fascinating sea creatures and about how the oceans affect climate. Teachers can download video clips from the Undersea Flyby or access educational resources such as the *Killer Whale Teacher's Guide*.

- At another exhibit sponsored by the French Ministry of Culture, students can learn all about the discovery of a Paleolithic painted cave. The University of California at Berkeley sponsors the online Museum of Paleontology with exhibits on geology, fossils, and pre-history. A computer server in Oxford, England, provides a gateway to these and many other museum sites.

- Classes can visit the Louvre and other art galleries as well as photography exhibits. Students can download graphics and incorporate them into their own printed or electronic reports. They must first ensure that their teacher allows the use of such graphics and that no copyright laws are being broken by reproducing them. Of course, students must correctly reference all materials taken from the Internet.

- At Questacon, Australia's hands-on science center, students can explore current exhibits, read about intriguing science discoveries and applications, practice problem-solving skills with something called Puzzlequest, and do experiments online. Like many resources on the Internet, these are available at no cost, apart from the cost of basic connectivity.

You'll find the addresses to these and other great sites in upcoming chapters, as well as on the Web site that accompanies this book. In addition to Web sites, which offer multimedia and interactivity, a great many less exciting but equally useful text-based resources are available on the Internet. These include online books, magazines, and references sources (such as an online dictionary and table of chemical elements). Selected news features, back issues of popular magazines, and full-text encyclopedias are increasingly available on the Net. Extensive archives of historical topics and online documentation of current events provide a depth and breadth of learning resources unmatched by anything previously available in even the best-equipped schools. The Internet is a very good resource for students researching current events, science, or social science topics. In addition, many discussion groups publish basic information about their area of interest. From these resources students can obtain information on topics ranging from pet care to astronomy to ballet. While the Internet may not have the very best information about "everything," it is a substantial information resource. In most communities, it is a welcome supplement to the generally limited resources available in a local library.

Students can also construct knowledge by collecting and sharing information with one another. In one cooperative project, students analyzed the quality of rivers in their area and compared the data they collected with data gathered by other students in their state. In another project, students reported on when various wildflowers started to bloom in their area, with data being collated centrally.

Perhaps one of the most rewarding ways to use the Internet in a classroom is to participate in a real-world adventure. An interesting example of how this can happen is through the On-Line Expeditions project. This Internet site is designed for teachers and students to explore live, field-based destinations around the world. Participants are connected to live expeditions to places like the Amazon, the Antarctic, and other destinations and have access to a wealth of curriculum activities and resources. The primary goal of On-Line Expeditions is to increase student engagement in learning and to increase overall student achievement.

Figure 1-4

The On-Line Expeditions project connects students via the Internet to live, field-based expeditions, and provides an arts and technology-integrated, inquiry-based curriculum framework which engages students in investigating real-world environmental, social, and cultural issues. Through the project, students become explorers of new and exciting destinations, people, wildlife, and issues, and bring their learning full circle by linking global learning to local action initiatives.

Learning by becoming involved

Electronic publishing can provide an authentic audience for student writing. Online magazines and newspapers, catering to all ages of students, abound on the Web. Some focus on current events, others on current issues relevant to students of particular ages, still others on book reviews or artistic creations. Some evidence has been gathered showing that students who write for a distant audience of their peers, as compared to those who write for their teachers

- are more fluent
- are better organized
- state and support their ideas more clearly
- include content that is more substantive and better supports their thesis
- consider the limits and needs of their audience
- enjoy writing more
- are more willing to write, proofread, revise, and edit their work
- are more careful about their spelling, punctuation, grammar, and vocabulary (Cohen and Riel, 1989)

School home pages are also used as a forum for publishing student work. Parents and families appreciate this easy access to examples of exemplary student products.

Many classes use the Internet to facilitate and organize collections of traditional music, games, folk tales, or customs from around the world. Because physical barriers such as race, gender, and disability do not exist in a virtual online world, these information exchanges promote multicultural acceptance and appreciation of diversity. The isolation experienced by some rural schools can also be addressed by having the students become involved in virtual events. A few years ago, 12,000 children from nine countries competed with one another in track-and-field events without having to leave their own schoolyards. This one-day event, which was billed as a "virtual" Olympics, was facilitated by the Internet.

Learning to learn

An important development in current thinking about education is that we now acknowledge the need for students to develop skills for lifelong learning. The Internet is an ideal mechanism for encouraging students to assume responsibility for their own learning. In accessing the diverse range of learning resources on the Internet, students become active participants in their quest for knowledge.

Incorporating the Internet into classroom learning gives students significantly more opportunities to structure their own learning than are available in traditional classrooms. Years ago, in the days of the one-room schoolhouse, it was assumed that there was more knowledge inside the schoolroom than outside. Today, there is much more knowledge outside the classroom. Moreover, given the diversity of learning styles, it is difficult if not impossible to "repackage" the world of knowledge to suit individual learner needs. More and more, the role of the teacher is to facilitate learning, not to prescribe it. Learning becomes an evolving process rather than a prescribed set of tasks, and the teacher's relationship to the students shifts from that of an all-knowing authority to that of a facilitator, a counselor, and a guide.

Students learn to define their learning needs, to find information, to assess its value, to build their own knowledge base, and to communicate their discoveries. Having them create their own lessons is one way of facilitating this process. All the higher-order skills come into play — defining the question, gathering resources, sifting and sorting them, and figuring out how to present them in a way that is meaningful to somebody else. And the result is something of genuine value: high-quality student work helps fill the need for well-vetted content in the online world. In the ThinkQuest Project, teams of students and coaches are encouraged to build educational tools through their own Web pages to help them and other students prepare for the future. Submissions are collected in ThinkQuest's online library of entries (**http://www.thinkquest.org/library/index.html**). A peek into this library revealed the following lessons:

- An in-depth analysis of *Macbeth*
- Anatomy of a murder: A Trip Through Our Justice System
- CHEMystery: An Interactive Guide to Understanding Chemistry
- Chernobyl: A Nuclear Disaster
- Collab-O'-Write
- Creative Nexus — the center for artistic expression
- Economics and Investment: A Stock Market Simulation
- Interactive Tour of the Cell
- Science and Beauty of Fractals
- Science Quest: An Exploration of Experiments
- Shadowball: The Story of the Negro Leagues
- Southern Native American Pow Wows
- The Spanish Missions of California
- Stamp on Black History
- Tangerine! Poetry Site Extraordinary
- WarEyes

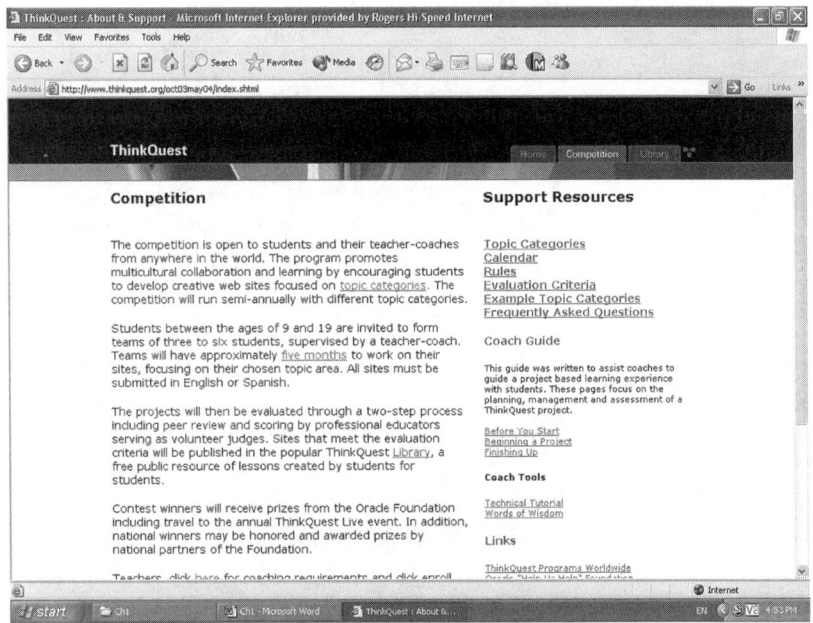

Opportunities for problem solving of all kinds — mathematics, games, quizzes, design and technology — are easy to find on the Internet. Students can get involved individually or in collaborative groups. Online tutorials provide "just-in-time" training for virtually any technology-related skill you and/or your students need to learn. Teachers equipped with a computer and an Internet connection can tap into hundreds of project ideas on the Internet. Online discussions expand a teacher's network of colleagues to include teachers from around the world. This is especially important for teachers in small schools or in rural communities who may not otherwise have the opportunity to interact with teachers in their area of specialty. The Internet is a source for electronic books and journals, for educational research, and for professional development opportunities in the form of conferences and courses.

Summing up

The Internet as a learning tool is an ongoing work in progress, one that is being produced by communities of learners, many of whom have come together through new ways of communicating made possible by the Internet itself. The educational value of the Internet ultimately will depend on what we put into it and what we do with the information we take out of it. The best way to ensure that the Internet is relevant and meaningful in your own classroom is to join with other learners in becoming familiar with the range of its resources. Technology literacy facilitates growth, change, empowerment, independence, knowledge building, collaboration, and communication. Once you know what is available and how it can benefit your students, you will be confident in developing original projects and ideas. This chapter has examined some interesting ways in which teachers are using the Internet. The chapters that follow will present many more exciting examples of classroom Internet use.

> To have students who are explorers, we need teachers who encourage exploration. To deal with the Information Age in and out of the classroom, we need teachers who can teach students how to manage information through available technologies and who can aid students in turning information into knowledge.

> — *Nancy Hechinger and Melissa Koch (1993), "Beyond the lightbulb."*
> Technos: Quarterly for Education and Technology, 2(1): 23.

Snapshots: Classroom experiences on the Internet

These are comments from classes that participated in the Weber-Malakov expedition, a project that had students use electronic mail to interact with a research team exploring the Arctic. The team was led by a Canadian and a Russian, and the project generated student interest in the respective cultures. Here are some of the learning experiences that stemmed from this event.

"We have discovered among our students technical experts who have all kinds of Internet knowledge, way more than their teachers! These students are now busy training their classmates on how to send e-mail and 'surf the Net.'"

"We have established a team of students who correspond with children in Russia. They are learning to communicate at an appropriate level as they share common interests. Do you know that seven-year-old Sergei in Russia knows who Van Halen is and enjoys this 'heavy metal' music as much as fifteen-year-old Kevin in Canada?"

"We have learned how students at a school in the Northwest Territories track a herd of caribou by monitoring the whereabouts of three cows that have transmitters attached to their ears. These students too are using satellite data. The topic of caribou and the use of technology in remote areas tied in nicely with our study of Farley Mowat's novel, *Never Cry Wolf.*"

"We have learned to question, to reflect on and wonder about matters beyond a superficial level. We wondered what time the sun got up when Richard and Misha first left for the pole, or did it get up at all? When did or when will twenty-four hours of daylight begin? How will sunlight affect the trip and the explorers themselves?"

Notes – Chapter 1

1. United States Department of Commerce, Economics and Statistics Administration and the National Telecommunications and Information Administration. *Falling Through the Net: Toward Digital Inclusion*. Washington, D.C. 2000. Online at **http://search.ntia.doc.gov/pdf/fttn00.pdf**

2. Capannelli, H. *Families Click with Online Lifestyle* The Globe and Mail Online, Jan 23, 2001 **http://www.globeandmail.com**

3. Online at **http://www.statcan.ca/english/Pgdb/arts51a.htm** 06/01/04

4. Online at **http://www.statcan.ca/english/Pgdb/arts52b.htm** 06/01/04

5. Capannelli, H. *Families Click with Online Lifestyle* The Globe and Mail Online, Jan 23, 2001 **http://www.globeandmail.com**

6. Capannelli, H. *Families Click with Online Lifestyle* The Globe and Mail Online, Jan 23, 2001 **http://www.globeandmail.com**

7. Online at **http://www.kidsource.com/education/teaching.ss.internet.html** 10/10/01

8. Online at **http://nces.ed.gov** 11/01/02

9. Online at **http://nces.ed.gov** 11/01/02

10. Online at **http://nces.ed.gov** 06/01/04

11. Online at **http://www.kidsource.com/education/teaching.ss.internet.html** 10/10/01

12. Schrum, L. Education World online at **http://www.educationworld.com/a_tech/tech004.shtml** 10/01/02.

13. Online at **http://nces.ed.gov** 11/01/02

14. Online at **http://nces.ed.gov** 11/01/02

15. Online at **http://nces.ed.gov** 11/01/02

16. Online at **http://nces.ed.gov** 11/01/02

17. March, T. *Working the Web for Education* online at **http://www.ozline.com/learning/theory.html** 10/01/02

18. Wenger, E. *Situated Learning: Legitimate Peripheral Participation* (1991), and *Communities of Practice: Learning, Meaning and Identity* (1998) online at **http://www.microsoft.com/education/default.asp?ID=SituatedLearning** 10/01/02

19. Online at **http://www.funderstanding.com/communities_of_practice.cfm** 11/01/02

20. Online at **http://www.sedl.org/pubs/tec26/cnc.html** 10/01/02

21. Online at **http://edweb.sdsu.edu/webquest/overview.html** 03/04/00

22. *Bridging the IT Skills Gap*, Canadian Software Human Resource Council, 2000

23. McKenzie, W. *Are You a Techno-Constructivist?* Education World, 2000 online at **http://www.education-world.com/a_tech/tech005.shtml** 10/01/02

24. Sims, Liz. adapted from original research and material created for Online Lecture Series, 2000

25. UCLA Internet Longitudinal Study. Online at **http://ccp.ucla.edu/pdf/ UCLA-Internet-Report-Year-Three.pdf**

26. Online at **http://www.cultivate-int.org/issue4/scenes/#ref-02** 17/02/02

2
Chapter

Tapping into Existing Projects

*"In a world often over enamored of change for change's sake ...
advocates of technology in our schools should have a compelling answer to
the question, 'Technology for what?' The answer, we suggest, is twofold: to
promote equal educational opportunity for all our children; and to raise the
academic achievement of all children. Technology can advance both equity
and excellence in education."*

— Diane Ravitch (1993, January), "The promise of technology: Eight ways to take full
advantage of technology." *Electric Learning*, 50.

Educational technology will continue to advance at an ever-increasing pace. As educators, it is our job to plan for and implement the use of technology in ways that are best for all our students. Technology must be understood in a context; in education, the context is learning. This means integrating Internet use into the curriculum in a meaningful way and incorporating it into current successful classroom practices such as outcomes-based education, collaborative projects, active learning, and student portfolios. Internet projects can provide an authentic context in which students develop knowledge, skills, and values. Knowing how to use the Internet is not an end in itself; rather, it is a gateway to lifelong learning.

> I am involved in a totally online school.... The students dial up from their homes via modem, download their specified lessons for the day, then upload them to a computer or to the teacher of the class. There are also group discussions in the specified disciplines. I am currently examining their learning with standardized tests, and our faculty is amazed at their progress. We even have parents now enrolled. I think it's the way of the future, and it's happening now.
>
> — *Kevin Gerrior, Teacher, California, U.S.A.*

Perhaps the easiest way to begin is to participate in an Internet project started by others that meets your educational goals. These goals should include developing social and cooperative learning skills in addition to knowledge and task-related skills. This chapter describes some different types of projects and provides concrete examples of how teachers are using the Internet to enhance student learning. Helping students learn to use some basic Internet tools will be critical to your success. The strategies included in this chapter come from teachers who have learned from experience.

■ **To describe some ongoing Internet projects that invite participation**
■ **To provide strategies for helping students learn how to use Internet tools**

Types of projects

As you investigate other teachers' projects in your reading and online explorations, you will discover a wealth of Internet activities to satisfy many styles of learning and student interests.

Learning through connectivity

Keypals

This is the electronic equivalent to penpals and is probably the most common of all school telecomputing activities, though not always the best as a beginning project. Individual students can be paired; the students communicate about themselves and share their interests and activities or a specific school project. Other keypal projects involve sending more general mail to a class rather than using one-to-one communication. Group-to-group exchanges are easier to manage than person-to-person messages with regard to quantities of e-mail. A suggested timeline for an introductory keypal activity could be this:

- Week 1 — write introductory letters stating name, age, grade, and one special interest

- Week 2 — respond with a second letter giving information about family, school, hobbies, other interests

- Week 3 — discuss a special topic, e.g., pets, jokes, creative writing, a curriculum theme

- Week 4 — decide if communication will be ongoing or regularly scheduled, or if you wish to get involved together in a collaborative project

HINT Listservers, commonly known as listservs, are special-interest groups available through the Internet. Members post messages to the list owner, and listserv software distributes these to all members of a given discussion group. To join a listserv, you need only know how to send an e-mail message and specific information about how to subscribe to any given list. Chapter 7 discusses listservs and how to subscribe.

Some of the most successful keypal exchanges derive from teacher-to-teacher acquaintances. Sustainability, the most difficult aspect of keypal exchanges, is enhanced if the two (or more) teachers involved have things in common, either personally or through similar curriculum and pedagogy. The topics around which students correspond vary greatly. Common topics include comparisons of aspects of life such as sports, school, weather, customs, hobbies, communities and food. Locating keypals' locations on a world map and graphing these comparisons are often logical curriculum connections.

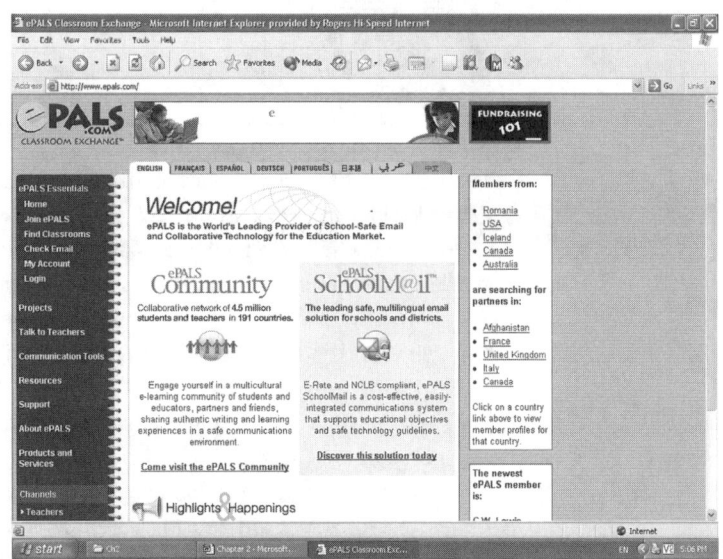

Figure 2-1

A scan through the letters archived at popular e-mail sites like ePALS (**http://www.epals.com/about/testimonials**) will turn up many other curriculum related examples such as these:
• Australia students providing specifications on the Great Barrier Reef,
• an Indian student's perception of Gandhi's contributions, and
• a French Muslim student's description of Ramadan.

You can find lots of ideas for topics for student exchanges by visiting Filamentality's Idea Pool at

> http://www.kn.pacbell.com/wired/filamentality/topics.html

There are different ways to find keypals for your class. One way is to visit a Web site that hosts keypal information, browse through the database and then contact any class that is listed. Here are some suggested sites:

Classroom-2-Classroom

This is a forum to help teachers and their students connect with other classrooms around the world. In addition to exchanges hosted by Teachnet, the forum allows Teachnet contributors to host their own activities, complete with updates and information.

> http://www.teachnet.com/lesson/class2class/index.html

Mighty Media

Mighty Media hosts the KeyPals Club, a place for teachers and students to locate and correspond with other youth and students around the world. The service provides a database to quickly locate and contact a student or a class from around the world.

> http://www.teaching.com/keypals

Intercultural E-mail Classroom Connections

IECC is a free service to help teachers link with partners in other cultures and countries for e-mail classroom pen-pal and other project exchanges. Since its creation in 1992, IECC has distributed over 28,000 requests for e-mail partnerships.

> http://www.iecc.org

Tips for Keypal Exchanges

- Be clear about the curriculum focus and desired outcomes.
- When looking for keypals, be sure to leave enough time for people to reply to your request. Some flexibility may be required but be clear about your expectations. Send out your request several times and repeat the message one or two weeks before the desired start date.
- You will want ten to fifteen classes to respond to your project to ensure that students get replies to their letters.
- Sample survey questions help younger students get started — e.g., sports, weather, seasonal activities, countries of origin, wishes, favorite books.
- Before exchanging information with another class, review online safety rules with your students. Students and parents should have signed an Acceptable Use Policy. Review the safety rules that they agreed to when they signed this AUP. Students that have not signed an AUP should not participate in this classroom information exchange. In Chapter 3 you can find out more about Acceptable Use Policies.

Electronic postcards and greeting cards have added a twist to traditional keypal activities by allowing you to send an image along with your message. Electronic postcards add variety and creativity to student exchanges, but there is a catch. Because the various graphics formats don't always travel well over the Net, the card doesn't just magically pop up on the recipient's computer screen. Instead, he or she must visit an electronic post office to view it.

To send an electronic postcard, you must first locate a World Wide Web site that offers the service. Here are just a few of the many free sites available:

The Electric Postcard

This is one of the best card collections, offered by the Massachusetts Institute of Technology. You can choose images from categories such as famous paintings, photographs, and science.

http://postcards.www.media. mit.edu/postcards

Marlo

This excellent site features award certificates in addition to postcards and greeting cards. There is a good selection of cards for special occasions such as Halloween, Christmas, Hanukkah and Martin Luther King Day. You can add a bit of music to your card also.

http://www.marlo.com

Warner Brothers

Warner Brothers provides several cards featuring their cartoon characters.

http://wbwebcards. warnerbros.com

Family Planet House of Cards

Disney's favorite characters are found here.

http://www.family.com

Multimedia Greeting Cards

Multimedia Greeting Cards allow you to add music and video to your custom cards.

http://www.multimedia greetings.com

To find other sites, type "postcards" into a search engine and browse through the results.

Simply follow the instructions at the site for selecting, addressing, and sending a card. It's free. Soon after you send the card, the recipient will be notified by e-mail that a card is waiting. Using the address and password provided, he or she can then log onto the appropriate site and view the postcard. The cards are stored for about two weeks from the date they are sent.

A listserv is another good way to locate keypals. Before submitting your request for keypals however, be sure that this is appropriate for the particular listserv, as each listserv targets pre-determined topics and discussions. If you are looking for a particular location, you may be able to find a school online that has teachers' e-mail addresses posted and send your request directly to a teacher. You can find a list of schools around the world that are online at **Web66: WWW School Registry**. Once you have established your topic and located partners, develop a timeline with the partner teacher(s) but keep it flexible. Changing schedules and special events in schools sometimes make it difficult to adhere to timelines that are very strict.

Figure 2-2
Kidlink (**http:www. kidlink.org**) is a global, non-commercial service that operates 86 conferences on the Internet in 19 languages. Kidlink's focus is to help kids and youth create interpersonal networks and collaborate with peers around the world. Since its start in 1990, over 175,000 kids from 144 countries on all continents have participated. Their primary means of communication is e-mail, but chats, various types of Web-based dialogs, regular mail, fax, videoconferencing, and ham radio are also used.

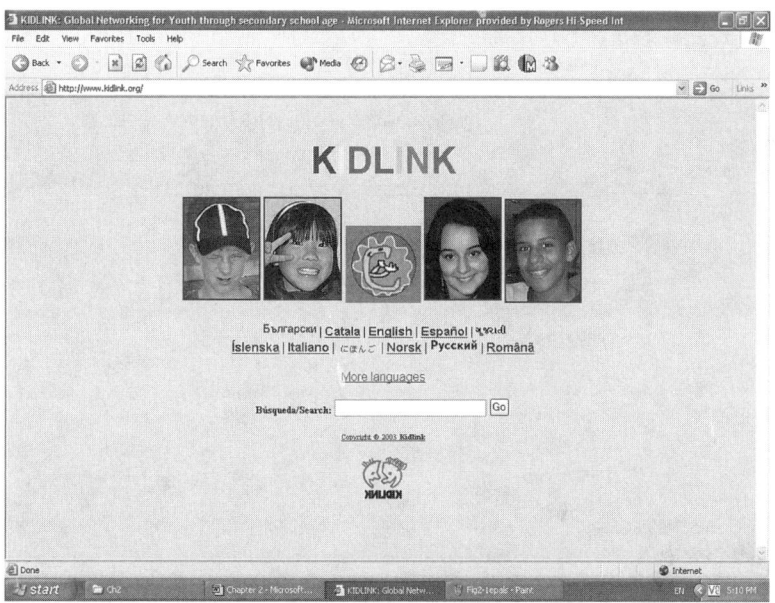

Online safety rules

1. Use only your first name.
2. Do not give out personal information such as your address, telephone number, parents' work address/telephone number, or the name and location of your school without your parents' and teachers' permission.
3. Tell your parents or teacher right away if you come across any information that makes you feel uncomfortable.
4. Never share a password for an Internet game or chat room with an online keypal.
5. Never agree to meet with someone online.
6. Do not send your photo to your keypal. It's all right to send class pictures as long as individuals are not named.
7. Never attach pictures or other files to an e-mail message unless the people receiving the message have given you permission.

Adapted from
http://www.4j.lane.edu/safety/rules.html 26/01/03
You can find Yahooligans' rules for online safety at
http://www.yahooligans.com/docs/safety/index.html.

Global classrooms

E-mail and other collaborative communication tools are components of virtually all Web-based projects. An example of a simple project that relies on e-mail is **http://www.bullying.org**. This is a project created to help youth cope with issues related to bullying and teasing. Students from around the world contribute their personal reflections, poems, music, drawings, voices (audio files) and even animations and films. An example of a more complex project that uses a variety of collaborative communication tools is Space Day^{SM} sponsored by ePALS.

Participants use two sites: the Space Day^{SM} Web site offers space-based information, tools, and activities, while ePALS provides a wide range of collaborative tools and an online classroom community. The ePALS collaborative tools include

- monitored e-mail, which offers teachers the safeguard of profanity filters that flag any messages sent or received by a student containing inappropriate content or attachments;
- moderated discussion boards, which offer students and teachers the opportunity to post questions and answers about their Design Challenges for other participants around the world;
- private chat rooms, which provide students with a password-protected area where real-time discussions can take place between collaborating classes;
- instant translation, which breaks down the language barrier for any global participants or second language learners.

Figure 2-3

Students around the globe have worked on the Space Day^{SM} Design Challenges (**http://www.spaceday.com/index.html**). These challenges focus on real-life situations that scientists, engineers, and researchers deal with in their work. The focus of Space Day 2003 was "Celebrating the Future of Flight." The 2003 Design Challenges, for 4th–5th and 6th–8th grade students, use an interdisciplinary, inquiry-based approach and incorporate national education standards.

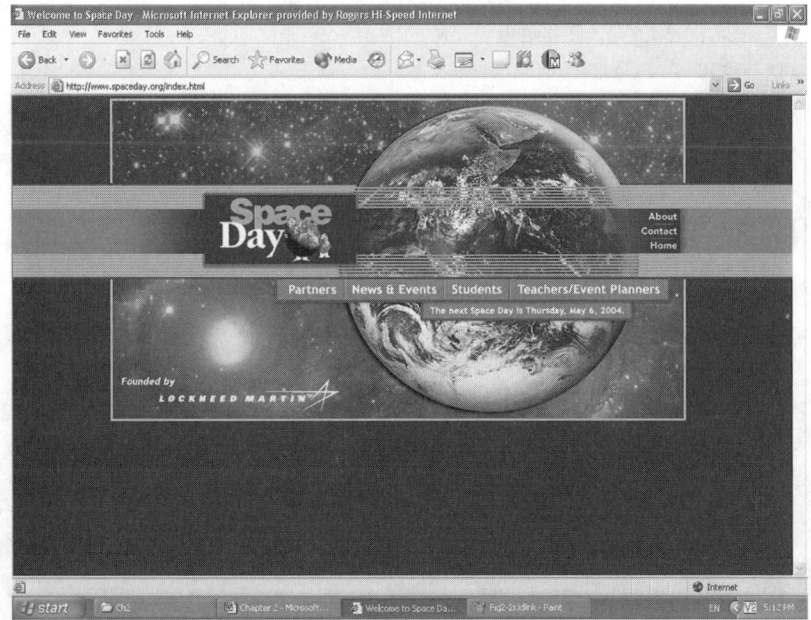

The goals of the Space Day^{SM} Design Challenges are to:

- Increase student interest in science, mathematics, and technology.
- Give abstract concepts concrete meaning.
- Help students develop realistic processes of cooperation, communication, critical thinking, and problem solving.
- Increase student autonomy and responsibility for their own learning.
- Encourage students to develop positive perspectives about learning.
- Increase student commitment to learning.
- Help students pose questions and find pathways to answers.

In 2003, students were invited to develop a solution for one of the following Design Challenges:

1. Design and build a model aircraft of the future. Your design must be based on, and incorporate, factual research. Write and illustrate a story that involves your aircraft. Create a timeline of important past and future events in flight.
2. Design and build a working model spacecraft that can fly on Earth. It must be designed with characteristics that would allow it to also fly on another planet or moon in our solar system. Write and illustrate a story that involves your spacecraft. Create a timeline of important past and future events in flight.
3. Design and build a working model of an aircraft that is self-propelled, uses a renewable energy source, and can remain airborne for a short distance. Write and illustrate a story that involves your aircraft. Create a timeline of important past and future events in flight.

Each eligible *Design Solution* received by the deadline date was reviewed for national recognition in one of the following categories:
- Most Creative
- Best Overall
- Best Design

Teachers choose the Design Challenge(s) in which their students participate. The whole class can work on the same Design Challenge or teachers can divide the class into groups that work on different Design Challenges. Teams are limited to 12 students or less. Each team member also has at least one role on the team. The roles are as follows:

- Lead Scientist(s): Collects and maintains all team members' research information.
- Design Engineer(s): Coordinates the designing of the solution.
- Team Ambassador(s): Main liaison between teams. Keeps records of all collaboration.
- Mission Specialist(s): Oversees team. Keeps team on task, using the schedule as a reference.
- Writer(s): Develops the plot line and characters for the story. Incorporates team members' ideas into the story.
- Artist(s): Draws the illustrations to accompany the story. Assists with technical drawings for the Design Solution.

Rubrics are provided to guide students' work. An extensive teachers' guide contains teacher and student resources such as background information, recording sheets, lists of relevant Web sites for research, teamwork reports, activity logs and templates.

Special activities are provided at regular activities, for example:

- live Webcasts featuring international experts in the fields of aviation, aeronautics, and propulsion.
- an opportunity to ask an expert questions about your proposed Design Solution.
- electronic lessons online.
- Webchat with Orville and Wilbur Wright in which students can find out how they achieved manned and powered flight.
- experts from the Johnson Space Center who address students and answer questions about flight, aircraft development, and space exploration.
- winning solutions announced during the Space Day[SM] Opening Ceremony from the Smithsonian's National Air and Space Museum in Washington, DC.
- several teams featured in the Cyber Space Day[SM] Webcast.

Mentors

Specialists in a variety of fields make themselves available to students via the Internet. Some examples are Ask Dr. Math, Ask Dr. Science, Ask a Geologist, and Electronic Innovators in the Schools.

A good place for your students to look for an expert is at Pitsco's Ask an Expert site at **http://www.askanexpert.com**. This directory of links includes over 300 Web sites and e-mail addresses where they can find experts who have volunteered their time to answer questions. Students can select from twelve categories (such as religion, science/technology, career/industry, international/culture, and arts) or they can conduct a search for their specific topics.

Sometimes, experts respond to listserv postings from students; however, it is unwise to count on this.

> One team spent hours in libraries looking for documents on sundials. They found nothing. After posting a request for information on the Internet, they received recommendations from distinguished professors from several renowned universities. Even when expert-student collaboration is brief, it really boosts student morale.
>
> — *Mathieu Dubreuil, Teacher, École Secondaire Dorval, Quebec, Canada*

True mentorship involves more than simply answering one-time student questions. Students and teachers need to engage in ongoing dialogue with knowledgeable professionals as they analyze information and solve problems. Many curriculum issues are multidisciplinary, technically sophisticated, or dependent upon current and highly specialized research and theory. Curriculum content takes on real meaning when students have authentic opportunities to interact with someone for whom it is part of everyday life. The following online mentorship programs are designed to accomplish this.

International Telementor Program

The International Telementor Program provides project-based mentoring opportunities for students from around the world. Students are matched with career professionals who can assist them with a wide range of projects, including these:

- studying whales in the North Atlantic;
- developing Web sites; and
- assembling a statistical analysis for the performance of a professional baseball team.

Since 1995, when this program started, more than 16,000 students, mentors and teachers from around the world have participated.

http://www.telementor.org

The Electronic Emissary Project

The Electronic Emissary, in operation since 1993, is a global service coordinated from the University of Texas. Its goal is to help K–12 teachers and students with access to the World Wide Web locate other Internet account-holders who are experts in different disciplines, for purposes of setting up curriculum-based, electronic exchanges among the teachers, their students, and the experts. The Electronic Emissary is also a research project, which focuses upon the nature of telementoring interactions in which K–12 students are active inquirers. You can look at sample telementoring experiences at the Web site.

http://emissary.wm.edu

The Four Directions Project

The Four Directions Project, funded by the U.S. Department of Education, is designed to help address the educational needs of Native American students. Many of the schools which serve Native American children are located in remote, rural areas and do not have access to the information resources and assistance available to students in urban settings. This project is a "matching service" that helps teachers locate volunteers for purposes of arranging curriculum-based, electronic exchanges between their students and on-line mentors.

http://www.tapr.org/4d

Learning through online resources

Information collection

Data can be collected from multiple sites and analyzed in the classroom. The simplest type of activity might involve students electronically issuing a survey, collecting responses, analyzing the results, and then reporting their findings to all participants. Students can gather information by conducting their own online surveys and polls or by collecting statistics, comparative prices, or athletic records. Examples include these:

HINT www.statcan.ca is your direct route to statistical information profiling Canada's business, economy, and society. It should be your first stop for the latest numbers.

- water acidity measurements at various sites and comparing with others
- global grocery lists to compare prices of common items around the world
- wildlife studies that track migration paths of butterflies, whales, and birds
- election projects in which students vote electronically and compare their choices with national returns
- Olympics projects in which schools conduct Olympic-like events and submit their statistics for a competive comparison

What starts as an information collection project will often lead naturally to additional online experiences, as shown in Dalia Naujokaitis's project, "Buy Nothing Day: Be a Consumer Hero." Created and illustrated entirely by students (9-11 year olds) the site challenges students especially in

Figure 2-4

"Be a Consumer Hero!" is a student-created project on consumerism built around the celebration of the International Buy Nothing Day. (**http://www3. sympatico.ca/dalia/buy0**).

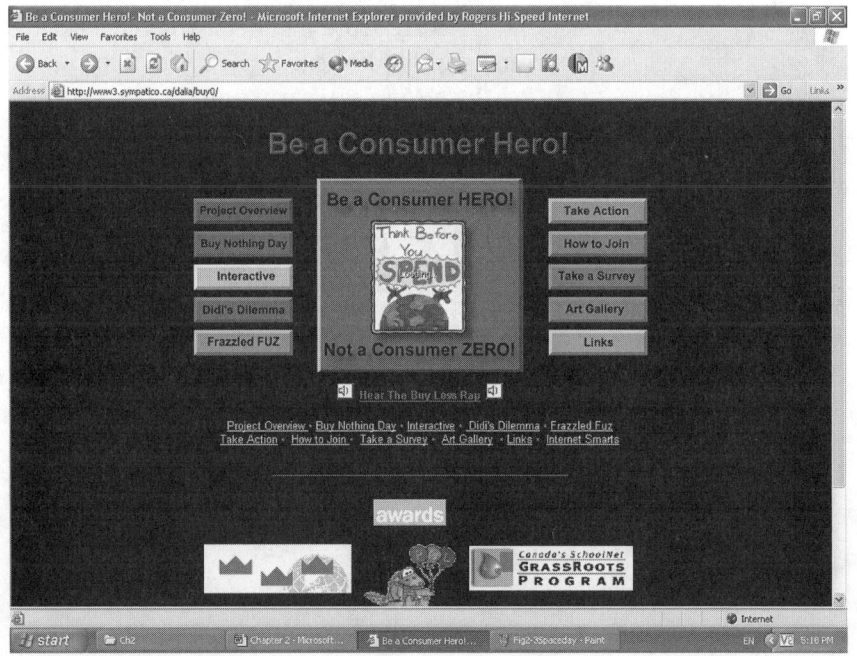

well-developed countries to reflect on the difference between wants and needs and to understand and begin to practice the 6 R's of environmental and global citizenship locally. This is done through student research, student-created "choose-your-own-adventure" stories ("Didi's Dilemma" and "FUZ Gets Frazzled"), an art gallery, action plans, a survey, an acrostic, a rap song and multimedia presentations.

Online field trips and expeditions

A virtual field trip is a Web-based teaching tool that presents multimedia content appropriate for whole group viewing or collaborative/individual learning. These can be as simple as sharing information about the community or as complex as monitoring an expedition to reach the North Pole by dogsled. Students can share observations and experiences made during local field trips with teachers and students from other cities and countries by posting trips for others to see and asking relevant questions. You can find Yahoo's virtual field trips site at **http://www.yahoo.com/Recreation/ Travel/ Virtual_Field_Trips**. It provides links to online tours such as Amazon Adventure, Odyssey in Egypt, and Live from Antarctica.

An online trip could be to a museum or gallery anywhere in the wor[l] Each group or pair of students could visit a different institution and s[u] rize their findings. This compilation of visits and ratings makes a g[o] ence source for future individual student research. Museums, gall[e]

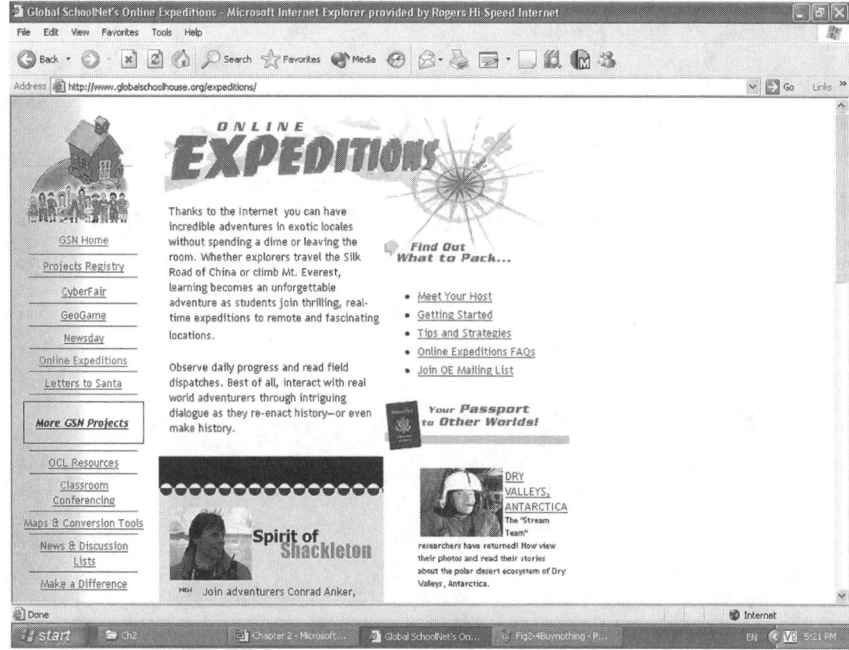

other educational institutions offer text, pictures, sound and sometimes even interactivity.

> My favorite project focused on virtual museum visits. These allow learners to experience the multimedia strength of the World Wide Web. The esthetic and other curriculum goals that can be enhanced by multimedia museum visits have great learning potential. My favorite museum listing can be found at **http://vlmp.museophile.com**.
>
> — *Robert Christina, Associate Professor, Oakland University, Rochester, Michigan, U.S.A.*

There is a variety of starting points for locating electronic field trips, from commercially sponsored sites to school-hosted databases. As you might expect, many have a cost associated with them and are supported by learning materials of all sorts. Here are some other good places to look.

The Virtual Field Trips Site

The Virtual Field Trips Web site is devoted to providing online guided field trips. It includes specific focus trips such as salt marshes or volcanoes, ...bject matter experts, stops en route that describe each site and prepared ...ocuments that you can print out for each student on the trip. **http://www.field-guides.com**

teaching tip

Tour Canada Without Leaving Your Desk is at **http://www.2.cs. ...du/Unofficial/ ...ravelogue. ...int-**

Vicki Blackwell's Internet Guide for Educators

Links to all kinds of virtual field trips
   http://www.vickiblackwell.com/vft.html
Visit the publisher's Web site for links to lots more virtual field trips.

Ancient Olympic Games Virtual Museum

   http://minbar.cs.dartmouth.edu/greecom/olympics

Car factory

Take a tour of an automobile factory to learn how cars are built.
   http://ipl.sils.umich.edu/autou

Classroom Connect

Enter as a visitor and take a look around. You may decide to join.
   http://www.classroom.com

Mountainzone.com

This is the best source for online Everest coverage including cybercasts from climbs, interviews and profiles of climbers, books, scientific information, IMAX Everest interviews, news and features.
   http://www.mountainzone.com

National Geographic Xpeditions: Interactive Learning Museum

Here you can climb a mountain, hover over the earth or visit an archeological dig. Activities and lesson plans are provided!
   http://www.nationalgeographic.com/xpeditions

oz-TeacherNet

At oz-TeacherNet, a virtual field trip is considered to be a partnership between two or more classes. One class acts as the local host for the field trip and the other class is the remote partner for the field trip. The host class gathers data, answers questions and reports their findings to the remote class using e-mail. The host class may use a local point of interest near the school or a site being visited during a school excursion. Digital photographs, video clips or captured sound can either be attached to e-mail or published on Web pages to add to the exchanges between the students. Students may also use live events during a virtual field trip by using Internet Relay Chat, Microsoft netMeeting or ICQ chat.
   http://rite.ed.qut.edu.au/oz-teachernet/index.html

Phil Gordon's Ongoing Journey Around the World

Phil has been on a backpacking trip around the world since July 1997.
He carries a digital camera and laptop along.
   http://www.pgordon.com

U.S. White House

Visit the White House and look around.
   http://www.whitehouse.gov/history/whtour

Volcano World Virtual Field Trips

Pick a volcano and go for a look.
   http://volcano.und.nodak.edu/vwdocs/kids/vrtrips.html

Wonders of the Ancient World

Visit each of these amazing wonders and follow links to find out more.
   http://ce.eng.usf.edu/pharos/wonders

World Travel Destinations

   http://www.learn-travel.com

Learning by becoming involved

Electronic publishing

Teachers are always looking for authentic ways to publish student work.
Donating student products to the school library, publishing books for
younger students or peers, reading original work to seniors and displaying
work in shopping malls, banks and other public places are popular methods.
Now teachers can add to this list the opportunity to publish on the Internet,
an idea that is often very motivating to students. Student products published
on the Web include artworks, stories and poems, digital images, Web pages
and multimedia productions of various sorts. Hyperstudio, Kid Pix and
PowerPoint presentations are easily adapted for the Web. You will find wonderful writing by students published on many of their school Web sites.
Students can also publish their original works in an online newspaper, anthology, or magazine. One of the most popular is Midlink, an electronic magazine
for middle school students at **http://longwood.cs.ucf.edu/~MidLink**.
One issue featured a virtual tour of battlefields by students at an English
school; original poems and parodies using Hyperstudio from a school in
Canada; a study of various qualities of athletic shoes from American students; and much more.

Electronic process writing is facilitated by programs such as the Writers In Electronic Residence program sponsored by York University in Canada. Writers In Electronic Residence (WIER) connects students across Canada with writers, teachers, and one another in an animated exchange of original writing and commentary. The writers, who are all well-known Canadian authors, join classrooms electronically to read and consider the students' work, offer reactions and ideas, and guide discussions between the students. (**http://www.wier.yorku.ca/wierhome**) Another variation is having students from several schools work on collaborative writing of the same piece. More publishing sites for students include these:

Children's Express   Children's Express publishes "news and comment by young people for everyone." It is a site to encourage learning through journalism for young people aged 8–18. The members regularly see their work in local and national newspapers, and hear one another on radio and television. In five years they've published more than 350 stories.
   http://www.childrens-express.org

E-LINK Magazine   This electronic elementary magazine, published four times each year, welcomes submissions of stories, art work, riddles, and more from students aged 5 to 11.
   http://www.inform.umd.edu/UMS+State/MDK12_Stuff/ homepers/emag

LDOnline   Every week LD OnLine chooses an artist of the week and a writer of the week whose work will be displayed on the home page of LD OnLine. Any student between the ages of 5 and 18 who has a learning disability can enter, with parent permission.
   http://www.ldonline.com

Stone Soup   This site features writing and artwork from students up to age thirteen. Since Stone Soup accepts only about one percent of all work submitted, this would be of most interest to especially talented student writers.
   http://www.stonesoup.com

Writer's Window Writer's Window is a friendly site for student publishing.
   http://english.unitecnology.ac.nz/writers/home.html

We shared students' writing among various schools in our province. Students had the opportunity to analyze and critique each other's writing. This was a great experience for them, since we are a small school and students don't often get the opportunity to see much writing by students their own age.

— *Jill Colbourne-Warren, Teacher, H.L. Strong Academy, Springdale, Newfoundland, Canada*

Information exchanges

Many classes organize or contribute to compilations of games, folk tales, music, holidays, or recycling practices from around the world. This sharing of information is intrinsically interesting for children and provides an excellent way to foster international acceptance and an appreciation of cultural diversity. This type of activity can also involve many classes without becoming too overwhelming. The Classroom Pet Exchange Project (**http://208.183.128.8/cpe**) exemplifies a creative approach to student information exchange, especially for the beginner internaut. This project enables students in Grades K–5 to connect with another class and share their experiences via e-mail, the Web, and journaling. Classes exchange a stuffed animal and its journal by snail mail. When the class pet arrives, students in turn take it home with them. Upon their return to school, students write or dictate a story about their adventures with the class pet. These adventures are kept in the pet's journal. Students can also communicate weekly with their partner class via e-mail. Travel tales of the pet's adventures may be shared at the Classroom Pet Exchange Web site by sending these in an e-mail. A list of learning outcomes, a schedule of the exchange, a sample parent letter and suggested activities are available through the project Web site. After its visit, the pet is returned by snail mail to the original school along with its journal.

Virtual events

Students who participate at their local school in athletic events, read-a-thons, or collections can submit their results to a larger arena. This is a good way to overcome the isolation of some rural schools.

> "A host school runs the virtual track meet. The students create and send out entry forms to the schools interested in being involved. A certain number of participants are allowed per event, with age and gender categories. A deadline is set as to when results are sent back to the host school (e.g., results for the high jump or 100-m sprint). The students of the host school then figure out the placings and send back their results sheet."
>
> — *Margot Alwich, Teacher, Lindsay Place High School, Pointe Claire, Quebec, Canada*

Learning to learn

Games and quizzes

Students enjoy learning through interactive games that revolve around a curriculum topic. Such projects are extremely motivating to most students of all ages. Students can learn a game and share it with others from a site such as Clever Games for Clever People at **http://www.cs.uidaho.edu/~casey931/conway/games.html**, which features games from John Conway's book, *On Numbers and Games* (New York: Academic Press Inc.).

Here are some other quiz sites:

Insect Wacky Facts Insect Wacky Facts is a fun way to get students to look up information about insects. Students are given a wacky question and they try to answer it. There are seven questions in all. When they send in their answer they receive a response from Bob, the online science teacher, and interesting information to go with it as well as a new question. Students are encouraged to find the answers using reference materials available to them (books, CD-ROMS and the Internet) and to write their source with their answer. Good Internet site addresses which participants share are made available on the Insects Wacky Fact Web pages for all to use. Students will often find that there can be more than one answer. It is a great opener to a science class.

http://www.qesnrecit.qc.ca/cc/ff97-98/INSECTD.HTM

GetSmarter This is an animated, interactive testing and learning site. Students can assess their own academic achievement in math and science, and compare themselves to other students around the world. The site also provides opportunities for practice, hints and links to tutorials.

http://www.getsmarter.org

Quizbrain Quizbrain features quizzes on all sorts of topics such as sports, movies, school and wildlife. Students can also contribute their own quizzes here.

http://www.quizbrain.com

12teach.com Here you can make online quizzes with multiple choice or fill-in-the-blank questions. Quizzes are scored and the results are stored. The free license is limited to a total of only 100 questions in all your tests. For more, you must purchase a license.

http://12teach.com

Environmental News Network ENN features a variety of quizzes related to environmental issues such as energy and water, native plants, recycling, healthy eating, ecology, sun safety and more.

http://enn.com/features/quiz.asp

Problem-solving activities

Similar problems can be presented to students in various locations, or two or more classes can take turns presenting problems for peers in other locations. A Day in the Life of an Ice Cube (**http://www.windsorct.org/icecube**) is a project organized to test the hypothesis that global location and climate affect the amount of time it takes ice to melt. Students in participating classes make predictions of meltdown times, conduct the experiment, analyze the results, and then interpret and submit the data electronically along with their explanations. Teams of students can use telecommunications to plan strategies, discuss projects, share results, and solve projects collaboratively. They might even produce a joint final report. Odyssey of the Mind at **http://www.odysseyofthemind.com** involves students at all levels in solving problems in a variety of areas, from building mechanical devices such as spring-driven vehicles to giving their own interpretations of literary classics. Science Olympics (**http://www.psd70.ab.ca/sgchs/Science_Olympics/internet.htm**) posts challenges such as building a boat that can hold the most pennies afloat for one minute, building an Alka-Seltzer powered rocket, and building a bridge that can hold as much weight as possible. Entrants submit results and digital photos of their projects. In the Landmark Game, sponsored by Kidlink (**http://www.kidlink.org/KIDPROJ/landmark01**), students from around the world choose a local landmark and work on creating nine clues about it, which they then submit to the project. The goal is for others to determine what and where the landmark is. Each week the game moderator posts three clues to the Kidproject board and during that week a question requiring a yes or no answer can be asked of each participating school.

"This project brought excitement and enthusiasm to our classroom, our school and to the learning process. It allowed me to be the guide on the side instead of the sage on the stage as my students organized the game, used both public and private e-mail to send the announcement and all the correspondence. They wrote and worked in small groups as they not only researched the clues for our landmark but researched the clues submitted by the participating schools. As the clues came in weekly my students posted them to boards in our classroom and to a general board in the students' cafeteria and teacher's lounge so that many students and teachers throughout the school participated. They submitted questions each week to the participating schools, helped participating schools with questions of organization or rules which needed to be clarified, submitted our guesses to participating schools and kept a tally of all landmarks guessed correctly by setting up a data base. This project has many wonderful aspects. It not only crosses the curriculum areas allowing students to call on their writing, problem solving, critical thinking, map reading and organizational skills but it also crosses grade levels and cultures."

http://www.kidlink.org/KIDPROJ/landmark01/announce.html, 01/10/01

Here are some math-oriented problem-solving sites for students.

MathSoft Puzzler Puzzles and their solutions for high school students.
http://www.mathsoft.com/puzzle.html

Mega Math The goal of the MegaMath project is to bring unusual and important mathematical ideas to elementary school classrooms so that students and teachers can think about them together. The site includes graphs, stories and games with lots of helpful teacher resources.

http://www.cs.uidaho.edu/~casey931/mega-math/menu.html

Word Problems for Kids Elementary school students can tackle these problems in pairs and check their answers when they've completed them.

http://juliet.stfx.ca/people/fac/pwang/mathpage/math1.html

Problem of the Week The goal of this site is to challenge elementary students with non-routine problems and to encourage them to verbalize their solutions. Student submissions are answered by "Visiting Math Mentors" and students also have an opportunity to act as mentors themselves. All those who correctly answer the challenge appear on the Web site, and the most creative solutions are highlighted.

http://forum.swarthmore.edu/sum95/ruth/elem.pow.html

A group presents a complex task as a challenge or contest. Participants attempting to complete the task e-mail requests for specific help as needed. For example, a math problem may be posed and the solution is required to be described in words; or a physics experiment may be explained and the distant students are asked to repeat the experiment within a defined error tolerance.

— *Shelley Martin, Student, Department of Graduate Studies, Carleton University, Ottawa, Ontario, Canada*

Social action projects

When students focus on a real-life problem, the Internet truly becomes a tool for learning. Students electronically research solutions to local or global issues and often get involved in awareness projects or fund raising as a result.

Several of my students have been using Internet Relay Chat to speak with people around the world. Social studies students listen to the nightly news for foreign events, such as the recent earthquake in Russia, and then try to contact individuals from the countries mentioned in the hope of hearing from people who are involved.

— *Rick Pyles, Teacher, Tyler Consolidated High School, Sisterville, West Virginia, U.S.A.*

These projects also illustrate ways in which the Internet can help students get involved in authentic issues at the local level:

Save the Beaches Save the Beaches is an international project in which students do a sweep of a local beach and analyze and categorize the litter. They then share the data with the participating schools. Through graphs and online discussions they reach conclusions based on what was found and develop practical ways to eliminate the litter. This helps students see a direct relationship between the solution to the problem and their own actions.

http://www.swindsor.k12.ct.us/Schools/tems/beaches/index.html

Figure 2-6

A good place to begin your search for a social action project is iEARN's project list (**http://www.iearn.org/projects/project_list.html**) because, in addition to meeting a specific curriculum need, every project proposed by teachers and students in iEARN has to answer the question, "How will this project affect the quality of life on the planet?"

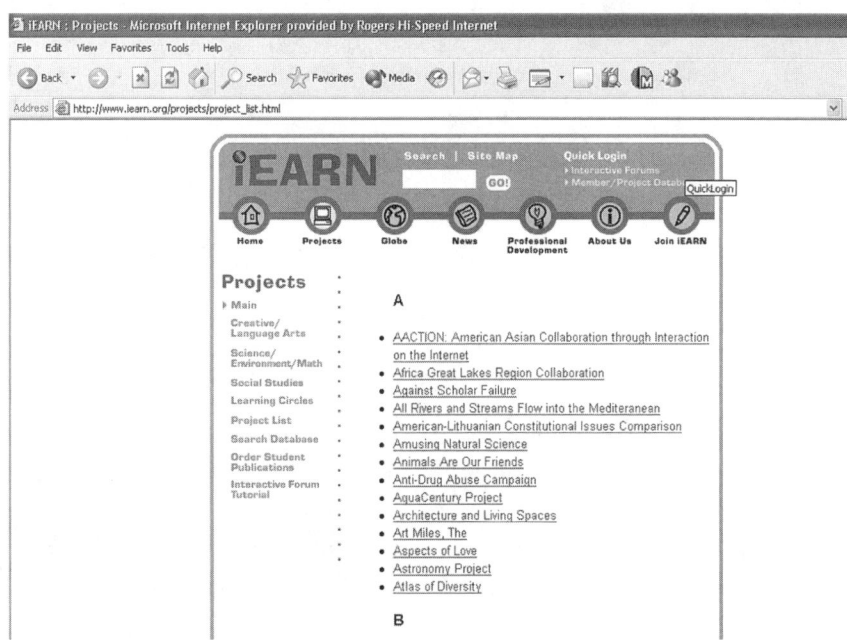

The Earth Day Groceries Project The Earth Day Groceries Project is one of the oldest and largest educational efforts coordinated on the Internet. Students borrow bags from a local grocery store, decorate them with environmental messages and return them to the store to be given out to customers on Earth Day. School reports are posted on the Web site.

http://www.earthdaybags.org

The following activity, Environmentally Friendly Community, is another example of how students can get involved in authentic issues.

ENVIRONMENTALLY FRIENDLY COMMUNITY

Description
Students will discover what it takes to make their community more environmentally friendly. They will research what is presently being done with respect to reducing and recycling waste and then determine what further action is needed.

Grade levels: 6–12

Learning outcomes
Students will
- research the roles required to run a community
- find out how their municipal government deals with environmental issues
- access Web resources related to environmental issues
- take photos using a digital camera
- use e-mail to communicate with community members
- create an environmental checklist for their community
- examine forms of energy available in their community
- investigate energy or water use in the home or school and record results in a spreadsheet
- produce a graph from a spreadsheet
- explore methods of reducing energy or water consumption
- assess the effectiveness of local energy or water conservation programs
- prepare a report on the environmental health of the community

Class management ideas

- Students work in small groups, with each group responsible for researching and reporting on one aspect of the community.
- Each team prepares a report to share with the whole class.
- Consider using a *jigsaw model* in which students become experts in their chosen field and share their knowledge with other teams.
- Students could take on roles such as environmental engineer, environmental officer, environmental health specialist, environmental scientist, environmental lawyer, biologist, naturalist.

Scenario

Friends of your family are planning to move to an area near your community. They are members of an environmental awareness organization and are most concerned that the community is environmentally friendly. They have asked you and your family to help them make the decision as to where they should purchase a house. They have given you some very specific topics to investigate.

Problem

Create a plan for determining how your community addresses environmental issues. You will need to find out how the municipal government deals with these issues:

- waste management
- water protection
- transportation
- sewage treatment
- green space
- recreation
- alternative forms of energy

Prepare a report suitable for your friends. Outline how your community stacks up.

Internet resources

Locate Web resources concerning your local community as well as surrounding communities of a similar size and composition. Visit ecology and environment sites to prepare tips for your local government.

Ask a Naturalist at **http://www.ontarionature.org/home/ask-the-naturalist.html**
Federation of Ontario Naturalists will answer questions on a variety of issues.

Ask the Eco Wiz at **http://www.gbr.org**
Ask questions about ecological and environmental issues.

Canadian Department of the Environment at **http://www.ec.gc.ca/envhome.html**
Canadian information on the environment.

Destination Conservation at **http://www.dcplanet.org/index.php**
Links to many sites worldwide.

Energy Probe at **http://www.energyprobe.org/energyprobe/index.cfm**
Information about the wise use of energy, alternative sources of energy, energy in the home.

Envirolink at **http://envirolink.org**
Wide variety of issues and links to other sites.

Environmental Organization Web Directory at **http://www.webdirectory.com**
Large list of Web sites on environmental issues.

Evergreen Foundation at **http://www.evergreen.ca**
Links, activities for green environments, school projects.

Environmental Solutions http://strategis.ic.gc.ca/Ces-Web/-index-.cfm?target=english
Industry Canada's Web site on environmental solutions.

Greenpeace at **http://www.greenpeace.org**
Information about the organization and links.

Urban Agricultural Notes at **http://www.cityfarmer.org**
Links to many sites related to environmental city living.

Urban Forest Centre at **http://www.utoronto.ca/forest/ufchome.htm**
Information on planting trees in urban settings, landscaping benefits.

Suggested student activities

- Brainstorm in your group the elements needed for a community and the issues related to making it environmentally friendly. Record your ideas in an electronic journal.
- Research the roles required to run a community. Use a class database to record your findings.
- Carry out Internet research into one of the major topics. Prepare a report for your team members. Add it to the electronic journal for sharing and use it in the final report.
- Create an environmental checklist for the community. Go on a walking tour and record your findings. Take pictures using a digital camera (or scan photos) for your database and presentation.

- Examine the forms of energy available in the community and determine the advantages and disadvantages of each. Using e-mail, contact representatives to ask for information about current practices and future plans.

- Investigate how energy consumption (or water usage) is measured in your home or school and calculate how much energy (or water) is used in a week, month and year. Record your results in a spreadsheet and turn it into a graph.
- Explore methods for reducing the amount of energy or water consumed. Consider asking an expert for information; use e-mail.
- Look at energy conservation programs in your community and determine how effective they have been. Create a chart or graph to demonstrate your findings.
- Examine water management programs in your community and others. Explain the reasons for the different methods and e-mail your findings to the local politicians and water facilities.

- Determine the importance of green space in maintaining environmental quality, and identify public interest groups that work to preserve urban green space. E-mail them to find out their opinions about the health of your community.

Final activity

Create a final report on the environmental health of your community for your friends, considering creative methods of demonstrating your findings. Prepare a report to be submitted to various environmental agencies and your local municipality.

— Sheila Rhodes (1998), *Connecting the Web: Successful Student Internet Activities*, Trifolium Books Inc.

Joining an existing project

Once you start looking around, you'll be delighted by the number and variety of projects that students can join. Some are specific to a particular age or grade level, while others are more general. All you need to get involved in an interactive Internet project is access to Internet e-mail. As we will discuss in Chapter 9, you can get this easily through a commercial service such as America Online, through a local Internet service provider, or through your school network. Once you are online, look for forums, conferences, or special interest groups related to education. You can also subscribe to one of many listserv groups, which are discussion groups interested in a specific topic. When you subscribe to one of these mailing lists, you receive all messages posted to the list by other subscribers around the world.

When reviewing the many available projects, look for one that is consistent with the learning outcomes you have in mind for your students. You might begin by selecting a curriculum-specific project that focuses on process writing, geography skills, or science. Consider simple projects before trying more complex ones: you might begin by participating in a survey, exchanging writing samples, or responding to keypal requests.

> Getting students online can be frustrating at first because everything is new— the hardware, the software, and all the tools of the Net. But don't get discouraged. Make sure you know some good resources that will help the kids get started.
>
> — *Sholom Eisenstat, Teacher, Earl Haig Secondary School,*
> *Toronto, Ontario, Canada*

1. **Before going online**
   - Locate a collaborative project you want to join.
   - Introduce the topic to the class by presenting background information, holding a class discussion, visiting the local library, and/or inviting local guest speakers.
   - Send home a note describing the collaborative research project students will be conducting and inviting parents to participate or contribute in any way they can.
   - Divide the class into groups of four or five students.
   - List and describe each of the tasks needed to conduct the project.
   - Assign each student within the group a job title and task to accomplish.
   - Review proper online behavior and Net etiquette.
   - Have students sign an AUP (Acceptable Use Policy) stating they have read the rules and will follow them.
   - Have parents also sign an AUP form indicating that they have reviewed the online rules with their children and will assist the teacher in enforcing those rules.

2. **During the collaborative project**
   - Begin your activity with a "hello" greeting message. Rather than have each student write a separate hello message, it is more effective if groups of two or three students create different sections of the message. For example, one group might write about their school; another can describe their city; another can tell nearby places to visit, and so on. The result is a single collaborative document that reflects the input of all the individual students.
   - Have all students keep a written or typed log of their activities describing their research, their explorations, and their findings (this helps ensure that students are staying on task).

   - Schedule students to meet periodically and report the highlights of their activities to their group and the entire class.
   - Exchange lesson plans with other teachers and discuss ways to refine and improve the project.

3. **After the collaborative activity**
   - Write thank you notes to project partners.
   - Prepare a list of questions about the collaborative project and practice answering them by interviewing one another (students could videotape each other).
   - Make presentations about the project to other classes and to the community.
   - Organize the findings in a shareable format (including images, audio, and video clips) and post the information on the Internet.
   — Yvonne Marie Andres, *Electronic Learning*, March 1995

As your students become more comfortable with the technology and see what is possible, they will be eager to get involved in more sophisticated projects, such as tracking an expedition or working cooperatively with others to address an environmental problem. Once you are involved in a project, learning outcomes that you had not anticipated are likely to emerge. Be sure to document and assess the skills and values your students develop as they proceed.

You'll find many examples of projects you can join throughout this book.

You can find a comprehensive list of projects to join at **http://www.siec.k12.in.us/~west/online/join.htm**.

Teaching students how to use Internet tools

Many students today know what the Internet is all about, but younger students may know the language without truly understanding how the Internet works. Consider inviting a guest speaker from your community to provide an overview, or do a quick introduction yourself.

I tell my kids that the Internet is an international network of computers, connected to each other by modems and telephone/fiber optic cables. I explain the different machines that are connected over the Internet, such as the servers, which "serve" people the information they need in many different ways: mail servers, file servers, Gopher servers, FTP sites, and HTML file servers, or Web sites. This is easiest to do with a diagram. I then explain the various tools available across the Internet, and how students should use these tools depending on what they are looking for and where they wish to go. My lab has TurboGopher, Fetch, InterNews, Eudora, and Netscape on each computer. Although each program works differently, all navigate the international network of computers to help people trade information. I explain that the WWW is just a small subset of the Internet, specifically the patch of Internet traffic conducted and controlled by HTML. My third to sixth graders seem to "get it" just fine.

> — *Sally Grant, Teacher, Sewickley Academy,*
> *Sewickley, Pennsylvania, U.S.A.*

Your students may need a combination of free exploration, direct instruction and skill-building activities to learn how to use the Internet and its tools effectively. Explain, demonstrate, and illustrate each skill you expect them to use in their project. Then provide exercises and allow time for them to practice before expecting them to use the skill independently.

> The first time you introduce students to The Weather Underground, you might lead them step-by-step to the site, show them how to locate the current temperature of a given city, then how to successfully leave the site. Next, you might have them attempt to return to the site on their own and locate weather conditions in a city of their choice. You might allow teams of students to compete in scavenger hunts to locate information. All of these activities help students practice the needed retrieval skills. Once they know how to retrieve the information, they will be ready to put the available information to real instructional use.

> — *Patricia Ross (1995, February), "Relevant telecomputing activities."*
> *The Computing Teacher, 28–30.*

Direct instruction

If your school does not have a data projector, LCD tablet, smart board or a means of connecting a computer to a large screen TV, students can gather around a single monitor as you demonstrate a Web site or a skill such as effective searching. Keep demonstrations brief and focused. Concentrate on the specific features that students will need to perform the task at hand, rather than trying to show all the things the software can do in one session. Take 3 to 5 minutes each day during an extended project for a mini-lesson in which you, or a student, share a tip or new feature. Rather than try to show 30 students at once, you could divide the class into groups of four or five and have a student expert, helping teacher, or parent volunteer assist with the instruction.

Many schools require students to complete a yearly Internet training session. Students must demonstrate their mastery before being awarded a license to use the Internet at school. Take a look at the following site for an example. **http://www.pekin.net/pekin108/tech/tutor/index.html**

The grandfather of one of my students was wonderful! For six weeks during our whales unit, he came every morning. He worked with pairs of students, helping them to find information about whales and to contact scientists. By the time the unit was complete, everyone had used the Internet and we had many great resources to share!

— Joanne Dillon, Teacher, Elmridge School,
Gloucester, Ontario, Canada

The technical skills necessary to navigate the Internet cannot be taught in a vacuum. Introduce and practice each skill only as it is needed to accomplish a curriculum task. For example, an isolated lesson on how to do a Web search is soon forgotten if students are not involved in a related activity. However, teaching that same lesson while students are engaged in researching earthquakes provides them with a valuable tool to use immediately for a specific purpose.

Along with directly teaching students how to use Internet tools through lessons and discussion come the other important issues that students must learn: netiquette, copyright rules, and citing of Internet resources. These are addressed in Chapter 5.

Free exploration

Most experienced computer users will tell you that the way they learn new hardware and software is by trial and error. You may be uncomfortable with this method if you have not had many opportunities to learn this way yourself, but it is very effective with technology. Set aside time periods for students to freely explore topic-related sites that you have gathered. Again, pairing students for this activity often leads to better problem solving.

Guided exploration

You can provide step-by-step instructions for using a particular Web site or learning an Internet related skill. By rotating students according to a schedule, you can then give everyone practice time.

Peer tutoring

It can be a challenge to keep students on track in a lab setting, but you do not have time in your busy day to introduce a new computer skill to every student individually. Therefore, teachers who are familiar with using computers in their classrooms are finding a variety of alternative methods. Recognizing the different learning styles of students and providing alternatives is one of the keys to training students how to use technology. Here are a few ideas you can try:

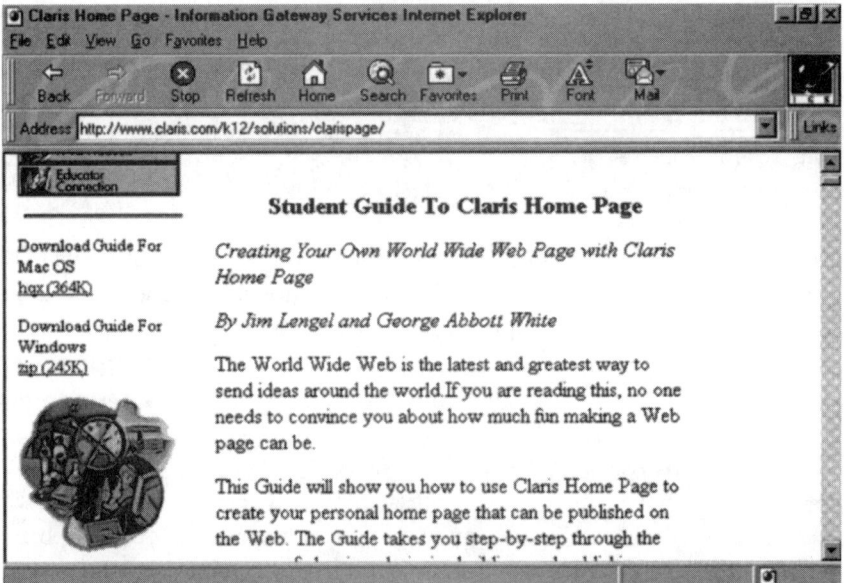

1. Train one student and have that student instruct others, one at a time, how to accomplish a specific task such as saving a graphic from a Web site or changing the background color on a Web page. Choose a different student for each new item and soon you will have a network of experts in your class. Post the names of these experts together with their areas of expertise. This is time consuming if you have only one computer and one expert, but it is effective.

2. Train one student who in turn trains another: "each one teach one." Continue until every student has been both a student and a teacher. Again, this is time consuming, but every student will try to learn it well knowing that they have to teach another. The risk is that the training will get "watered down" or start to include errors as it is passed from one student to another.

3. Team up younger students with older as computer pals or mentors. In a high school setting, course credits can be given to students who work as mentors for a specified number of hours. Provide specific skills that must be taught and tasks to be accomplished. Both parties benefit from this approach.

Tutorials

You can find tutorials within software, in books and online. If these are not at an appropriate difficulty level for your students, you can make your own,

A recent visit to the school found students helping each other with software or the Internet in almost every class at almost every moment. Unlike in many schools where children immediately call for the teacher when they get stuck, students here often look first to their peers in their small groups.

"I teach them to do that," says 2nd grade teacher Rhonda Willome. She says she tells the children, "Don't interrupt me while I'm teaching."

"You learn which kids can help the other kids," adds Jane Farris, a 4th grade teacher. "The teacher just can't be everywhere at one time."

http://www.edweek.org/sr eports/tc98/cs/cs3.htm 22/08/00

If you teach young children, you can find great lesson plans from Loogootee Elementary School in Indiana. Go to **http:// www.siec.k12.in.us/ ~west/surf/lessons.htm**.

though it is a tedious and time-consuming process. As more teachers in the school develop learning guides for Web sites and Internet skills, however, you will develop a bank of shared resources. The following are just some of the many Web sites that offer useful online tutorials you and your students might use:

Internet 101

Internet 101 was created for those who want to know just the basics. This guide will provide you with enough knowledge to be successful on the Internet without too many details. It includes searching, browsers, e-mail, viruses, safety, file sharing, newsgroups, chat and more.
> **http://www.internet101.org/internet101.html**

Learn the Net.com

This is a very comprehensive site suitable for older students and adults. It includes basics, surfing, e-mail, newsgroups, multimedia, searching and basic Web site design.
> **http://www.learnthenet.com/english/index.html**

Learning Space

In this Macintosh based tutorial, students explore the features of Netscape and practice searching and bookmarking.
> **http://www.learningspace.org/tech/tech_skills/ manage_bookmarks/netrain.html**

Monroe City Schools

This is a comprehensive collection of links that will lead you to tutorials on all sorts of software and Internet related skills.
> **http://www.monroe.k12.la.us/mcs/training**

The Kids' Computer Room

Young students can learn about emoticons and bookmarking here.
> **http://www.chirpingbird.com/netpets/html/computer/computer.html**

The Virtual Lounge

The Virtual Lounge has lots of information for any new user to the Internet as well as technical information on topics such as electronic mail, publishing on the Internet, digital movie and sound formats.
> **http://www.sofweb.vic.edu.au/lounge**

Welcome to the Web

This is a great place for beginners to learn interactively about guestbooks, safety, browsers, favorites, bookmarks, searching, copying and printing.

Students get a secret code by visiting each section and take a final quiz to get a certificate.

http://www.teachingideas.co.uk/welcome

WOW Online

At Internet 101, students can learn how to use the Web, including Web language, browsers, e-mail and other Internet tools.

http://www.wowusa.com/Internet101

Volunteer helpers

Particularly with younger students, an adult at the computer center or as a lab helper can be a real blessing. Many parents, co-op students and student teachers are happy to share their Internet skills.

Student experts

You don't have to teach the whole group yourself. Identify student experts in each class, train them, and let them teach others. Everyone benefits from this experience. Explain and discuss the learning outcomes you expect in these roles. Look for students who have leadership skills and will attend the school for a few years to come. Get a long-term commitment from them. Some schools award bonus marks or course credits for such services. Having one student teach another is also an authentic evaluation tool, since the ability to teach a particular skill is a demonstration of how completely it has been mastered. Use cooperative learning strategies to take advantage of the strengths of the technowizards in your class by distributing them among the groups to act as leaders during the technology-related parts of the project.

Learning together

Some school systems have initiated training sessions or courses that include teachers, students, and parents. The groups could be mixed or handled separately, but all learners gain expertise at approximately the same rate. Working as a community reinforces the goal of lifelong learning and breaks down some of the traditional barriers between home and school.

> I created a system that targets entire school families for Internet training to "jump-start" as many educators, students, and parents as possible. I bundle teacher training, student training, and parent training into a five-part, ten-hour series I call the Internaut Academy. I cover Net basics, classroom management, and other practical issues, and rotate the teacher, student, and parent

Generation Yes: Kids at the Head of the Class

The "Generation Y" model teaches students the skills necessary to introduce technology into the curriculum, pairing one student with one teacher to create partnerships. Teacher and student cooperatively develop a technology-integrated lesson and use it in the classroom. (**http://genyes.org**).

sessions in order to maintain equity among the groups. Ten hours is enough to launch people in individual directions.

— Mike Abbiatti, Teacher, Woodlawn High School/Louisiana State University, Shreveport, Louisiana, U.S.A.

Summing up

Once you have participated in a project or two, you'll be eager to continue incorporating the Internet as an exciting component of many subjects and units of study. As you and your students become more familiar with Internet tools, you can design your own project and invite participants from around your community or around the world. In the next chapter, you'll find some strategies for planning successful projects.

The change process

Integrating the Internet into regular classroom use will be a continuing challenge, and every experience won't be a success. Change is a journey, a non-linear trip loaded with uncertainty and excitement. Educational experts in implementation and the change process state that

- change takes place over time,
- change involves anxiety,
- change involves learning new skills through practice,

- successful change involves pressure,
- the people who must implement the change need to see why the new way works better,
- problems are our friends,
- connection with the wider environment is critical for success,
- both top-down and bottom-up strategies are necessary,
- every person is an agent for change.

3
Chapter

Planning Your Own Projects

"As the Internet provides connectivity among nations, it generates opportunities for connectivity within K–12 educational realms. As we come to realize the full potential of using the global reaches of the Internet within our school classrooms, we come to realize that we are able to build local to global, multicultural understandings of human experiences across and integrated among all content areas including literacy, social studies, science, math, languages, economics, history, politics, agriculture, vocational."

— Online at U.S. Dept. of Education
   http://www.ed.gov/teachers/how/tech/international/guide_pg12.html#tips3,
   06/01/04

After participating in at least one project organized by others, you may be eager and ready to try initiating your own project. This is an exciting venture for both students and teachers, and there's plenty of help available from others who are eager to share their ideas and tips.

The main benefits of designing your own project is that it truly fits your curriculum, it occurs at the right time of year for you, and it can be reasonably predicted to engage your students. Careful planning will be essential to the success of your project. In this chapter, we've synthesized information from experienced teachers to put together a series of logical steps that will help you to be assured of providing a valuable, meaningful learning experience for your students. If you have not already done so, you will also want to make decisions about student accounts and establish some classroom routines for acceptable Internet use before you begin. These issues are addressed in the pages ahead.

Chapter goals
- ■ **To outline strategies for developing original projects**
- ■ **To establish student procedures for accounts and use of Internet tools**
- ■ **To examine issues of acceptable use**

Planning your project

Step 1: Select a topic.

A teacher's choice of topics is usually controlled by curriculum set in place by the school or school district. Working within these guidelines, involve your students as much as possible in selecting a topic, giving them scope to pursue their own related interests. If you are planning to invite participation

The International Society for Technology in Education has developed standards, performance indicators describing technology-literate students at key developmental points in their pre-college education, and examples from classroom practice. These standards are very useful for planning and for developing assessment and evaluation tools. Technology standards are also available for teachers and administrators at all levels. Take a look at **http://cnets.iste.org**.

from others, give your project a snappy title that reflects its process or its content goals: "Fast Food Flash," "Great Gourmet Gastronomy," "Taming the Tube." Your students will enjoy creating novel project names.

Step 2: Establish learning outcomes.

Effective use of the Internet in education requires standards and outcomes for student learning. Without specific learning expectations for Internet-based activities, students will lack direction and focus and will be overwhelmed by the sheer quantity of information available to them. Learning outcomes define the criteria by which to measure both student progress and teacher effectiveness in using the Internet as a tool. Learning outcomes related to Internet use in the classroom fall into two broad categories:

- those associated with the knowledge, skills, and values of the curriculum unit (e.g., "Students will describe regional, national, and global environmental problems related to the use of technology and investigate ways of sustaining life in the future.")
- those related to effective use of the technology itself (e.g., "Students will send e-mail letters to peers in other parts of the country.")

Whether learning outcomes are teacher-selected or designated by the core curriculum, keep them foremost in mind as you plan your Internet project. Ask yourself the following questions:

- What learning outcomes do I want the students to achieve?
- Are these outcomes clear, specific, and measurable?
- Am I trying to fit the outcomes to the technology, or am I using the technology as a tool to meet the outcomes?
- To what extent will Internet use assist students in achieving the desired learning outcomes?
- Could these learning outcomes be achieved just as effectively or more effectively using other methods?

Step 3: Investigate other projects.

Examine other teachers' successful projects and identify the common elements that contributed to their success. Consider the timelines and number of classes involved. Look for situations that parallel your own with regard to anticipated learning outcomes, student ability, access to computers, time available, and teacher experience. Find a good project that has already been tried, and then improve it by customizing it to suit your own needs. You can find many good sites to look for projects throughout this book.

Step 4: Decide the type of activity and plan a timetable.

Choose the type of activity — keypal, information exchange, etc. — and decide how much time you plan to devote to it, keeping in mind the amount

of Internet access time available to your students. Peak use on an educational network is geared to traditional cycles of the school calendar. October through December, February through May, and July (with summer school) are very busy times on the network. However, most of the successful networking activities were planned, and announcements posted, six to eight weeks before the actual project was to begin. Carefully consider the types of teaching/learning strategies that are appropriate for your students and the type and amount of Internet access available in your school and classroom.

- **Whole-class activities.** If you're a beginner, start with a teacher-directed whole-class activity, especially if you have a limited number of computers with Internet access. Corresponding with another class either locally, nationally, or internationally is a good way to introduce students to the Internet. E-mail can be integrated into just about every subject and grade: reading, writing, social studies, science, business, second language learning. You can use e-mail as a vehicle for teaching both curriculum-related skills (such as letter-writing, devising questions, or improving punctuation) and Internet-related skills (such as addressing, formatting, and sending e-mail, and online etiquette). Once students have mastered electronic messaging in the group setting, they will be able to use it individually as a tool for other assignments.

    You don't have to limit yourself to e-mail. Information gathering related to a particular theme or project can be done by a pair of students who then report back to the whole class.

    Not only is whole-class instruction an effective means to learn the basic skills of Internet use: it is also an appropriate forum for exploring such topics as

- sources of information found on the Internet
- accuracy of information found on the Internet
- evaluation of Web sites
- copyright issues
- citing of Internet sources
- security issues
- acceptable use

    The issues of evaluation, copyright, and citing are discussed in detail in Chapter 5.

- **Cooperative learning activities.** In a well-structured, active learning environment, the Internet can become one of a number of tools that a group of students (or one or two members of each group) can use for a specific purpose, as in the Environmentally Friendly Community project described on pages 56 and 57 in Chapter 2. In such a setting, student experts emerge and peer tutoring happens naturally. Most Internet projects involve a great deal of learning offline. This might involve manipulating graphics or information files that have been gleaned from the Internet, or developing e-mail messages in a word-processing package for uploading later. It can also include posting new findings on a bulletin board, or tracking responses to a questionnaire on a graph or map. Each student in the group can play an important role, yet all need not have access to the Internet. Computer networks allow us to look at cooperative learning in a new way. Students can learn to work in teams whose members are separated by distance. This reflects the reality of our changing world of work. Before getting involved in a cooperative Internet activity, you can simulate this situation using your school's local area network. For example, while one team member gathers observational data about reptiles in the science lab, another might research the topic in the library, and another might scan drawings and diagrams in the multimedia room. Team members communicate strictly via computer. Following this experience, students will be eager to try collaborating with others in more distant places.

When student teams work in collaboration with other schools (virtual grouping), they know that the other group is counting on them and that they have to trust them.

— *Mathieu Dubreuil, Teacher, École Secondaire Dorval, Dorval, Quebec, Canada*

- **Individual activities.** You'll need a lot of student access if you expect all students to engage individually in an Internet activity as a mandatory course requirement. However, many schools are fortunate enough to have all their computers online. To be fair, ensure that all students have mastered the basic skills of Internet use, have attained a certain level of expertise through practice, and can get help when they need it. One of the great strengths of individualization, of course, is that no two students learn in exactly the same way. While one may approach an information search in a step-by-step manner, another may prefer to "surf" through a variety of sites. There is no right or wrong way, as long as the final goal is achieved within the specified timeframe.

Students need large blocks of time for Internet use. If you have explored the Internet at all yourself, you know how fast time goes while you're using it. It is very frustrating to get to the site you've been searching for only to find that there is not enough time left to download the information you want. It is also difficult to predict how long it will take to get to a particular site, or even if you can get there when you want to. Thus, it is inadvisable to create rigid timeframes. Involve your students as much as possible in establishing realistic time limits for the completion of projects, and try to keep your timetable flexible. By observing carefully, you can identify students who are off task and those who are using their time wisely. Have students keep a list of any sites they have used, with a brief description of their contents. If all are working on the same topic, share findings at the end of each computer ses-

teaching tip

If you have a computer with Internet access in your classroom, use it as a learning center that students access as one component of a unit. For example, in a study of whales, allow each student an opportunity to find the answers to specific questions about whales using the World Wide Web whale watching site (**http://www.physics.helsinki.fi/whale**). Visit the site yourself first to compose your questions.

sion. This fosters collaboration and saves time for everyone. By the end of the term, you will have developed an excellent resource package. Don't forget to build in time for sharing the finished products, whatever form they take.

> Be patient. Don't be discouraged. Things may not go as planned: they may go a lot slower, or they may not go at all. It's all part of the learning experience.
>
> — *Sharon Lewis, Teacher, Red Deer, Alberta, Canada*

If you teach in a setting where subjects are strictly segregated, team with another teacher. Your two subject areas can complement each other (e.g., language and history; math and science), and students can devote time from both classes to the project.

Step 5: Define roles of participants.

It's important to decide which staff will take a leadership role in initiating, managing, and monitoring a project. The most common method is for the adventurous and innovative teachers to be pioneers and then to encourage others. If you are eager to get involved in a project, brainstorm with interested colleagues and assign tasks according to the individual strengths of the team members. For example, classroom teachers might look after overall organization and student groupings; the computer resource teacher might schedule computer use and manage technical problems; selected students might act as Internet researchers and resource people; parent volunteers might supervise and assist individual students as they work; and the librarian might print a variety of the best projects and display them in the library. Discover your classroom and school student experts and tap into their knowledge by facilitating peer mentorship either in a formal or an informal way. If possible, try your project out with a close colleague first, on a small scale. This run-through can help you overcome technical problems as well as problems with the basic project design. You will find that having a sympathetic colleague available to discuss and solve problems will be a big help.

Step 6: Incorporate evaluation.

How will you evaluate the student learning outcomes you established for your project? How will you evaluate the usefulness of the Internet as a tool, perhaps even the primary medium, for your project? Teacher, peer, and self evaluation are all appropriate tools in an active, student-centered, technology-enhanced classroom. Develop checklists (see Figure 3-1) and rubrics (see Figure 3-2) of observable performance indicators to use as assessment criteria. Involve students in this process as much as possible. Use observational data, teacher-student conferencing, and a portfolio of work samples for formative evaluation. End your project with a tangible product such as an oral presentation, written report, video, or student/class portfolio that can be used for summative evaluation purposes.

Figure 3-1
A simple checklist can help teachers and students keep track of their growing telecommunications research skills.

Students will:	Jenna	Abdul	Guy	Sarah
1. access a Web browser on the network				
2. navigate the Web using a Web browser				
3. use Yahooligans search engine to locate information				
4. create bookmarks				
5. retrieve information from a Web site				
6. copy and paste an image from a Web site				
7. correctly cite Internet sources				

Electronic portfolios can be effective assessment tools for curriculum-based Internet projects. The real advantage of the electronic portfolio is that, in addition to printed text and graphics, it can include photographic, video and audio samples of student performance. Scanners and digital cameras are useful for recording work samples and computer-based projects can be stored directly. CDs and DVDs provide an excellent and compact storage medium. Guidelines for electronic portfolios should include exactly what students are to collect and how they are to structure the portfolio. When developing these guidelines, involve your students in designing an appropriate rubric for the portfolio itself.

Several software packages have been developed to help students and teachers create multimedia portfolios. They include

- *Electronic Portfolio* (Scholastic)
- *HyperStudio* (Roger Wagner)
- *The Digital Chisel* (Pierian Springs)
- *Kid Pix Studio* (Broderdund)
- *Learner Profile* (Sunburst)

As an alternative to purchasing software, you might choose to use multi-purpose software such as

- *ClarisWorks* (Apple)
- *Microsoft Office* (Microsoft)
- *KidWorks 2* (Broderdund)
- *Microsoft Works* (Microsoft)

Students' work on the Web is most appropriate for inclusion in an electronic portfolio. For example, high school students using the Internet to learn how to invest in the stock market created a PowerPoint slide show describing the project and what they learned. This summary was then included as an element of their electronic portfolios.

Figure 3-2
The rubric on page 73 is an example of what you might use to evaluate Web sites developed by students as a culminating project of a curriculum-related Internet project. Ideally, rubrics should be created in collaboration with students prior to beginning the project.

Web Site Evaluation Rubric

	Level 1	Level 2	Level 3	Level 4
Planning Process (plans must be submitted at end of week 1)	Planning is incomplete; it lacks necessary URLs, formats, and resources to complete project.	Planning is somewhat complete; it includes some elements, formats, necessary URLs and resources.	Planning is mostly complete; it includes many assigned elements in addition to most formats necessary URLs, and resources.	Planning is complete; it includes all assigned elements, in addition to formats, necessary URLs, and resources.
Subject Knowledge	Subject knowledge is not evident; information is confusing, incomplete or incorrect.	Some subject knowledge is evident; some information is confusing, incomplete or incorrect.	Subject knowledge is evident in most of the product; information is mostly clear, complete, and correct.	Subject knowledge is evident throughout; all information is clear, complete, appropriate, and correct.
Network Skills	Student has problems bringing up Web page within a Web browser.	Text or images do not appear or appear incorrectly images not saved in **gif** or **jpeg** format; one or more files in wrong location or have wrong file name.	All .html files properly organized in Web creation program; all images gif or **jpeg** format; all file names and group numbers correct.	Same as Level 3 plus student runs Web-creation program and Web browser simultaneously and shows efficient use of Internet access programs.
Writing Process	Difficult to understand; many spelling, grammar and/or syntax errors.	Somewhat consistent line of thought; some spelling, grammar and/or syntax errors.	Easy to understand; perfect spelling; one or two grammar and/or syntax errors.	Clear, concise, well written; perfect spelling; no syntax, or semantic problems.
Layout	Layout has little or no structure or organization; screens are either confusing or stark; graphics are used randomly.	Text broken into sections with labeled headings with some consistency; screens show some attention to visual design criteria.	Hierarchy closely follows meaning; headings and styles are consistent; text, images, and links flow together and reinforce one another.	Consistent format extends page-to-page; design is original and intentional; combination of multimedia elements with words and ideas delivers a high impact message.
Navigation	One page submission; buttons and/or navigational tools are absent or confusing.	2 page submission or one page with links to other resources; screens are difficult to navigate, but some buttons and/or navigational tools work.	3 pages with clear order, labeling and navigation between pages; screens contain working navigational tools and buttons.	Title page with other pages branching off, and at least 4 pages total; navigation path is clear and logical; screens contain all necessary navigational tools and buttons.
Images	Images are unrelated to text; most images were taken from other pages on the Internet; images too big/small in size or resolution; images poorly cropped or have color problems; no video, audio, or 3-D enhancements are present.	Images have strong relation to text; some images are student produced; images have proper size, resolution, colors, and cropping; limited video, audio, or 3-D enhancements are present.	Same as Level 2 plus images are from 3 or more sources such as scans, CD-ROM, digital camera photos, Internet, graphics design software; some video, audio, or 3-D enhancements are used appropriately.	Same as Level 3 plus more advanced student created graphics; appropriate amounts of video, audio, or 3-D enhancements are used effectively.

Keeping the electronic portfolios from year to year allows student, parents and teachers to visualize and value the student's educational growth and potential. The following portfolio sites provide additional information and first-hand experience with the use of portfolios:

American Association for Higher Education

This is AAHE's new Electronic Portfolios resource site, which includes links to related Web sites as well as a discussion site for individuals interested in further information on electronic portfolios, a database of institutions working with portfolios, and other resources.

> http://webcenter1.aahe.org/electronicportfolios/index.html

Dr. Helen Barrett's Electronic Portfolio Site

Dr. Barrett is an internationally known expert on electronic portfolio development for learners of all ages. This site links to her online publications, workshops and favorite sites.

> http://electronicportfolios.com

Electronic Portfolios: A New Idea in Assessment

Electronic portfolios are discussed. Questions such as what they are, why they should be used, use of technology in the creation of portfolios and various solutions and examples are examined.

> http://ericit.org/digests/EDO-IR-1995-09.shtml

Feasible Electronic Portfolios: Global Networking for the Self-Directed Learner in the Digital Age

Todd Bergman discusses Internet-based portfolios for students and teachers.

> http://www.mehs.educ.state.ak.us/portfolios/why_digital_portfolios.html

Mt Edgecumbe High School Digital Learner Portfolios

Portfolio guidelines and examples of digital portfolios created by students at an American high school.

> http://www.mehs.educ.state.ak.us/portfolios/portfolio.html

Using Technology to Support Alternative Assessment and Electronic Portfolios

This set of Web pages, developed and maintained by Dr. Helen Barrett from the University of Alaska, describes and discusses the use of technology to support alternative assessment.

> http://electronicportfolios.org/portfolios.html

Step 7: Outline the details of the project.

The following information will be required by other educators who wish to participate in your project:

- contact person's information (name, school, e-mail address, school address, and phone number)
- project title
- grade levels involved
- curriculum links (list as many as are relevant)
- anticipated student learning outcomes
- number of schools/classes to be involved
- summary of project including specific timelines
- registration details
- sharing of information at conclusion of project.

If you are applying for funding for your project, these details will be the basis of your proposal.

> For a successful cooperative project, be clear about your objectives, be sure the students understand the purpose, plan how you are going to manage the project, and be sure to follow through on your commitments to others.
>
> — *Connie Mark, Teacher, Pearl City, Hawaii, U.S.A.*

Are you looking for rubrics? Kathy Schrock's Guide for Educators has links to all sorts. **http:// school.discovery.com/ schrockguide/assess. html** Do you need help creating guidelines for projects? Try this site: **http://www.4teachers. org/projectbased/check list.shtml**.

Step 8: Invite others to participate.

Create your "Call for Participation" and post it to the curriculum conferences, Web sites, and/or listservs you have selected. Set definite starting and ending dates, and announce these when you call for participation. You may find that you need to advertise for participants several times, so the earlier you start, the better. Also, one teacher may see your project idea and think that it's great, but may need to pass it on to another. This takes time. It also takes time to gather and compile student input and prepare students to begin. If you expect submissions such as data or student writing, set realistic deadlines and stick to them, but set timelines that are broad enough to allow flexibility. You might provide examples of the kinds of writing or data collection that students will submit. Phased deadlines establish a sense of accountability to the other participants in the project and make it easier to ensure that they follow through. Even if the teacher is inclined to drop out, students who know the deadlines will often hold their own teachers accountable to complete the project.

> In cooperative projects, be clear on your expectations from other schools. If they lack the time to meet all project requirements, perhaps they can participate to a lesser degree.
>
> — *Sharon Lewis, Teacher, Red Deer, Alberta, Canada*

As soon as people respond to your call, send them a reply acknowledging their request for participation and a more detailed outline of the project that includes specific timelines and registration procedures. Keep track of the replies and registration details in a special file or folder; if you have enough classes before the registration date closes, be sure to respond to all requests stating that the project is full.

Step 9: Share your plans with parents.

Let parents know what you're planning and indicate that you would welcome their suggestions and assistance. This is a good way to identify contacts in your community who are knowledgeable about this new technology. You'll probably find that they will offer to help in a variety of ways, such as donating equipment, advising you of useful Internet sites, or spending time helping students.

> When our school's old modem finally bit the dust, I made a point of mentioning to my students that we could really use a modem, especially if their parents had upgraded their modems at work. Within a week we received three working modems. We were back online in no time!
>
> — *Chris McQuire, Teacher, Pope John XXIII School, Nepean, Ontario, Canada*

Step 10: Evaluate and bring closure to your project.

At the conclusion of the project, share the results with all participants. If you publish any student writing, send a copy to all who participated. Involve your students in writing a summary that describes the project, what they did, what they learned, and what changes they would make. Post the summary on the network for others to see, not just the project participants. Have your students send a thank-you message to all participants. You might also want to send a copy of your summary and a thank you to the principal of each school that participated in order to reinforce the value of using the Internet to achieve educational goals.

Students with special needs

The Internet is highly motivating for most students, and it can be used to implement and complement proven strategies in working with students with special needs. It can free the special student from a history of negative experiences with more traditional education and provide control and autonomy that may previously have been missing.[1] The Internet can open up the world to the student who is confined by socioeconomic or physical limitations. The multimedia technologies of the World Wide Web are powerful tools for meeting the needs of learning-disabled students and those with specific auditory or visual needs.

Teachers can individualize Internet activities to suit students with special needs by giving them a specific task to do online, such as searching an encyclopedia to make a list of the ten biggest cities in the world. Providing a "buddy" often makes it possible for students with special needs to participate in the regular activities of the classroom. A buddy can help a physically disadvantaged student manipulate equipment, read for a non-reader, check organization and completeness for a classmate with learning disabilities, help a distractible partner to stay on task or communicate in the first language of a non-English speaking friend. When faced with a particular student whose needs are very specific, the role of a buddy is easy to define. Cooperative and collaborative learning groups are another way to provide the support that the exceptional student often needs. The teacher's skill in facilitating collaborative learning and teamwork skills are just as important when using the Internet as in any other learning experience. Guidelines for group work, developed with the students, will help learning experiences to run smoothly. When roles are carefully assigned to group members, each student gets a chance to contribute in a meaningful way to the final product. Selfesteem is enhanced and confidence will grow. Curriculum-based Internet projects provide a further avenue for collaboration — across classrooms, linking students throughout the community and the world. One of the advantages of electronic communication is that gender, race, age, and physical characteristics are invisible. In online communication, we focus on what people say in their writing, not how they appear.

> I became aware that my students of low socioeconomic status had a harder time dealing with computers than those who had computers and video machines at home. We need to expose kids to technology at an early age in school. When pairing kids for computer use, I try to place them with kids at their own level, rather than with a more capable student who might unknowingly "take over."
>
> — *Heddi Thompson, Teacher, Chase County Elementary School, Cottonwood Falls, Kansas, U.S.A.*

The following additional strategies help in setting attainable standards for students with special needs, whether they are engaged with an Internet project or not:

- Encourage parents to use the Internet at home with the student if possible.
- Reduce the number of tasks and/or questions given within each task.
- Provide more structure by giving the student a prepared answer sheet or template (e.g., fill in the blanks).
- Ask for pictures or diagrams instead of language.
- Conference with the student to allow for oral responding instead of written.

Curriculum-related Internet Project Planning Template

Establish Learning Outcomes

Select the learning outcomes that best suit the curriculum focus. Look for opportunities for cross-curricular learning and integrate learning outcomes for each subject area. Review online curriculum guidelines from several sites to get ideas.

_____

_____

_____

_____

_____

Set the Context

Use questioning to determine the aspects of the subject area your students need to know. What do we need to know? What information do we already have? Where will we find more information? Who are the experts? Why are we doing this? How will we put it all together? Decide on the best learning experiences for your students in this context.

_____

_____

_____

_____

_____

Assessment and Evaluation

Determine the kinds of evaluation best suited to the project. Collaborative learning online will include critiques from outside sources. Teach critiquing skills so your students can teach others. Reflection, observation, journal writing, and portfolio management are tools for self-assessment. Teach students about criteria. Have them participate in rubric making.

_____

_____

_____

_____

_____

Outline the Process

Investigate online projects to determine the best kind of integration for your class. Look at simple information exchange and online collaboration. Publish a project goals statement so all partners will understand the focus. Break down the project into small steps. Develop timelines; schedule meetings, student conferences, speakers or trips. Have students help with the practical aspects.

_____

_____

_____

_____

_____

Identify Resources

Keep a list of all resources. Bookmark Web sites for fast access, encourage students to make a cumulative list of useable and authentic sites. Teach Web awareness, collaboration and information sorting skills. Teach electronic filing skills for storing information until ready for printing. Keep non-electronic resources accessible. Audio, video, software and paper resources can all be integrated. Artwork, posters, memorabilia, and theme-related objects all add to the motivation and encourage students to contribute and share knowledge.

_____

_____

_____

_____

_____

Conclusions and Next Steps

Reflection and student evaluation statements are critical. Summarize and conclude to assure all points of process have produced the established goals. Next steps can be identified and lead to new projects.

_____

_____

_____

_____

_____

- Give the student a small amount to do at one time, set a suitable time frame within which you expect it to be done and provide frequent feedback.
- Provide the student with an exemplar of the assignment as reference during task completion.
- Provide opportunities for individual electronic mentoring such as online projects in which students submit original writing to professional writers, teachers and other students and receive personal feedback.

You might want to check out some Internet resources associated with special needs, such as the following.

Closing the Gap

The organization focuses on computer technology for people with special needs through its bi-monthly newspaper, annual international conference and extensive Web site. You'll find suggestions, strategies, information and opportunities to chat.

http://www.closingthegap.com

Council for Exceptional Children

The CEC keeps you informed of ideas that work, recommends publications and products and outlines professional development events.

http://www.cec.sped.org

Education and Special Education Links

Here you'll find a comprehensive list of sites on everything from integration/inclusive education, IEP resources and also to links that relate to specific exceptionalities. It is an excellent resource.

http://www.isn.net/~jypsy/educatio.htm

KidsConnect

KidsConnect is a component of ICONnect, a technology initiative of the American Association of School Librarians. This Web site has answers to all the FAQs by K–12 students. The students can point and click their way through the questions that they most often receive at KidsConnect. It is categorized by subject headings and topics.

http://www.ala.org/ICONN/kcfaq.html

LD OnLine

LD OnLine is an interactive guide to learning disabilities for parents, teachers and children. A very comprehensive Web site that features highlights of new information, ABCs of LD and ADD, bulletin board, talk back, ask the expert, Kidzone, finding help, and first person essays on first-hand experiences with the challenges of learning disabilities.

http://www.ldonline.com

Windows XP includes Accessibility Options for users with special needs. These options include Filter Keys that ignore brief or repeated keystrokes or slow the response rate, High Contrast that uses colors and fonts designed for easy reading, and Show Sounds that display captions for accompanying sounds. Go to Control Panel to browse through the other options for keyboard, display, sound and mouse control.

Special Needs Network

This is a site that provides resources for parents, teachers, schools and other professionals in terms of discussions, events, e-zine, and resources.

http://www.schoolnet.ca/sne

Special Needs Opportunity Window

This Web site has an excellent bank of practical resources and curriculum materials. It is a place for educators to meet, share ideas, and develop their professional skills. Be sure to check out SNOWkids, a site with activities for young people with special needs.

http://snow.utoronto.ca

National Center for Learning Disabilities

This center's mission is to promote understanding and public awareness of children and adults with learning disabilities. It includes such things as fact sheets, behavioral signs, legal rights, and lists of resources.

http://ncld.org

KidSource OnLine

Here you will find articles about a variety of learning disabilities, links to student and parent sites such as homework helpers, and online forums.

http://www.kidsource.com/kidsource/pages/dis.learning.html

Learning Disabilities Association of Canada

The Canadian national organization is a focal point for articles of general information, research, legal issues, and links to other sites.

http://www.ldac-taac.ca

Learning Disabilities Association of America

LDA is a national organization of parents, professionals, and individuals with learning disabilities created to help parents and individuals of potentially normal intelligence who manifest handicaps of a perceptual, conceptual, or coordinative nature. They provide fact sheets, resources, and publications as well as links to other sites.

http://www.ldanatl.org

Deaf World Web

Deaf World Web is the central point of information on deafness on the Internet, with deafness-related information on all subjects from resources to references around the world.

http://www.icdri.org/dhhi/dww.htm

International Dyslexic Association

Of special interest here is the technology section, which includes assistive technologies, technology resources, and commercially available products and services.

http://www.interdys.org

National Centre to Improve Practice in Special Education through Technology, Media and Materials

From this interesting site, you can visit two exemplary early childhood classrooms, explore the use of voice recognition technology to address writing difficulties, look at an online workshop about assistive technology for students, or view a video of students using assistive technologies.

http://www2.edc.org/NCIP

Bobby

This is a free Web-based service that will help you to make Web pages accessible to people with learning disabilities.

http://www.ldresources.com

The Arc of the United States

The Arc of the United States is the nation's largest voluntary organization committed to the welfare of mentally challenged children and adults and their families. This home page provides links to support groups, reading lists, other disability-related sites such as dyslexia and autism, parenting information, assistive technology and software, and funding sources.

http://www.thearc.org

Children and Adults with Attention Deficit Disorders

This is an extremely well-organized site that provides resources and links related to children and adults with Attention Deficit Disorder.

http://www.chadd.org

listserv@ukcc.uky.edu

E-mail to this address. Type SUBSCRIBE DEAFBLIND <your name> to join this deaf-and-blind discussion list.

listserv@sjuvm.stjohns.edu

E-mail to this address. Type SUBSCRIBE CEC-TAM <your name> to join a discussion list for technology issues relating to exceptional children. Type SUBSCRIBE AUTISM <your name> to join the discussion list for issues relating specifically to autism.

> The primary value of using the Internet in my Learning Disabilities classroom is the willingness of my students to do their own research because the Net is (a) up to date, (b) does most of the labor for them (compared with looking through books and magazines), (c) is interactive through the e-mail contacts they make, and (d) is still a novelty with them.
>
> — *Gayle Fields, Learning Strategist, Queen Elizabeth Junior/Senior High School, Calgary, Alberta, Canada*

HINT Take a look at Tammy's Tech Tips: Nuts About the Net at **http://www.essdack. org/tips** for advice about physical setup, integration, policy and procedures, and training. Tammy is an experienced technology teacher with lots of good tips and ideas.

Adults often worry about socioeconomic, gender, and other issues regarding computer use, but the kids I see in my open-access lab don't show any of these problems. The experienced kids help the new ones, the gamesters defer to the workers, the girls and boys work in absolute equality, the age range in the lab is representative of the school, the Black-White ratio is also representative, and those students who have computers at home help the rest who don't have them. These concerns may stem from adult perceptions or preconceptions of young people rather than from observation of real kids at work. But maybe I'm just fortunate to have worked with an unusually great bunch of kids all these years.

— Elizabeth S. Dunbar, Teacher, Baltimore City College,
Baltimore, Maryland, U.S.A.

Student Internet accounts

HINT There are many kinds of free e-mail services, each with strengths and weaknesses. Large selections of e-mail providers also offer their services in languages other than English. You can find a guide that will help you choose a free e-mail service at **http://www. emailaddresses.com**.

All staff members and students need their own accounts. Students must understand that accounts and passwords are for their own protection, to ensure that someone else will not log on as them and steal their work or misbehave using their identity. When students use generic logins and passwords it's difficult to trace incidents and track student usage. One approach is to provide teacher accounts that give them full access to all Internet resources, while student accounts allow access to only certain sites and/or navigation tools.

Some schools provide individual student e-mail accounts hosted on their own servers while others allow students to use their personal accounts established through free e-mail services such as Hotmail or Yahoo. In some cases, schools require that the e-mail account used belong to the minor's parents, thus they have the right to examine all materials. When students do not have e-mail accounts or are not permitted to use personal accounts at school, teachers may decide to use their own e-mail accounts for curriculum projects, after establishing guidelines for acceptable use. If the computer is in your classroom, it's easy to monitor, and if you work with younger students a volunteer can assist. Naturally, those who abuse the privilege lose the privilege. One of the advantages of getting involved in a project through an established program such as ePALS (**http://www.epals.com**) is that monitored e-mail accounts for student use are provided.

"Across North America we are seeing huge networks installed which might support global e-mail exchanges and projects. The potential is enormous. But … In all too many districts the network professionals will fight against student e-mail accounts, using every excuse from workload to Internet abductions as a reason to prohibit student accounts. Imagine buying a Rolls Royce and keeping it in the garage!"[2]

Security and viruses

There always seems to be a new computer virus around these days. Some have only small effects but others can bring down entire computers and computer networks. It's a good idea for teachers to be aware of sources of computer viruses and how they are transmitted in order to act defensively. Traditionally, computer viruses were spread through infected diskettes or by downloading and running an infected program. If you use the Internet to

One example of an outside service provider is Power School Student Information System, a Web-based application that allows users access to important data while minimizing support and training costs (**http://www. apple. com/education/power school**). Instead of incurring an upfront charge for software, hardware, and installation, schools pay a subscription fee for each student per year. PowerSchool features include

- student demographics,
- a master schedule builder,
- attendance records,
- automated reports and form letters, and
- student/parent access.

exchange data (such as text or pictures) with known correspondents, virus infection is generally not a problem. The concern occurs when you download software programs and run them on your own computer.

E-mail messages can also carry viruses. Teachers should warn students against opening e-mail from any unknown source and particularly against opening e-mail attachments if they do not know exactly what they are. In particular, e-mail attachments with an .exe extension may contain a virus that will immediately affect the receiving computer. Suspicious e-mails should be reported to the school's network administrator and deleted immediately.

Whether you connect directly to the Internet or rely on your service provider to safeguard your security interests, be aware that you are exposing your network activities, online files, and electronic communications to some degree of risk from the "outlaws" of the Internet. A "hacker" is someone who is highly proficient at understanding and manipulating computer systems. A "cracker" is someone who maliciously and/or illegally enters or attempts to enter someone else's computer system. Computer security is unquestionably important, both in maintaining the security of the information residing on the school's network and in ensuring the proper behavior of all who use the network. In this area, not only school policy, but also provincial/state and national laws may apply. The good news is that Internet sites geared to school use have been spared the kind of attacks you read about in the press. While your school site is unlikely to be of great interest to computer intruders, they remain a possible threat, if only as a nuisance. A successful intrusion can result in theft of files, malfunctions in your system, installation of new and bogus user accounts, the generation of e-mail messages in your name, or the storage of alien files on your system.

Many schools have created Intranets, which are private networks that use Internet Protocol, common Web browsers and other software, but restrict information to those who are allowed access. Most Intranets contain confidential information such as student names, grades and personal records and possibly internal e-mail. A firewall, which is a set of programs that filters network information and requests, is used to secure the Intranet from the broader Internet. This means that when teachers wish to access student grades from home, for example, they require a password to gain access. Currently, many school districts put school data and applications together on their in-school network or Intranet. These days, however, increasing complexity is constantly adding to the cost of building and maintaining such a system, causing some schools to seek outside solutions for their data management.

Student safety

Parents and teachers are understandably concerned about the appropriateness of some of the material available online. The media have made us well

All teachers, students and administrators can become part of their school computer system's defense service by keeping the following security principles in mind:

• Choose your password carefully. The best passwords contain at least six characters combining letters, numbers and symbols. Ideally, they should be random and meaningless, yet simple to remember.

• Don't share your password with others. If you must write it down, don't identify it as such, and don't leave it near your computer.

• Be aware of oddities in your system that you notice but cannot explain, such as your e-mail account filling up with many messages from the same source or an unknown source. Report these to the network administrator.

• If you have a problem while online, sever your connection. (When in doubt, pull the plug!)

aware of online pornography, violence, and racism. Schools that are now online have taken precautions to keep inappropriate material out of the school setting. Those with broad Internet access usually require more procedures than those that have a single modem access in the school library. Some use special hardware and software to limit student access, some allow students to visit only approved sites, while others rely on strict acceptable use policies and close adult supervision. In order to implement procedures that meet the needs of a wide diversity of students, some schools distinguish between supervised, curriculum-related use of the Internet (available to all students) and independent use of the Internet (available only to those with parent permission). Students who have parent permission are allowed to conduct independent research with more latitude outside of structured class inquiries. Teams with guided access work independently from teams with unlimited access. Course options are provided at higher levels that involve research on the Internet with full access and parental permission, allowing groups of students with complete access to explore topics using a broader range of resources.[3] It's important to keep in mind that students who are fully engaged in creative learning activities will have neither the time nor the interest to seek out forbidden areas of the Internet, whereas students who are turned loose with inadequate forethought, preparation, and supervision are likely to find other ways to amuse themselves online.

Software that limits access to inappropriate sites

NetNanny, SurfWatch, and CyberSitter are examples of software designed to protect children on the Internet; such programs are often referred to as filtering software or Internet content screening tools. At the discretion of parents and schools, they monitor and block inappropriate sites and subject

In 2001, the American National Center for Education Statistics reported that 74% of schools using an acceptable use policy to define rules for Internet use were also using some form of software to filter Web pages. The Children's Internet Protection Act requires American schools to use filtering software in order to be eligible for E-rate and Title III technology funding. [4]

matter. In addition to preventing access to pornography, hate literature, and bomb- and drug-making formulas, you can prevent addresses, phone numbers, and credit card numbers from being sent out on the Internet. There are two types of screening tools available today. Client-based systems are designed for end-users, thus the software must be installed individually on each machine. Server solutions reside on a single machine to which all client machines are attached. Students cannot circumvent the screening mechanism as the server is under sole control of the system administrator.

These software babysitters screen and block both incoming and outgoing commands and content in two different ways. Keyword blocking involves blocking Internet sites that contain certain words. For example, if you enter the word "bomb" in your filtering software dictionary and someone sends the latest pipe-bomb recipe via e-mail, the terminal will shut down when the file is accessed. While this allows for good coverage, it also assumes that because one word at the site is objectionable, the entire site contains undesirable content. If a student tries to access **http://www.playboy.com**, a colorful "Blocked by ..." dialog box appears. However, while keeping students out of the Playboy site with the keyword "breast," you also deny them access to breast cancer research. Even though filtering software uses *knowbots* and *spiders* (Internet robots, in effect) to dig up and then filter any site that includes the use of various words, spelling can be changed and other words substituted.

A better way to block undesirable content is by reference to a database of undesirable material. Typically, a database is created, updated on a regular basis, and maintained by the software publisher, listing sites that fall into several categories that you can selectively turn on and off. A good system will offer daily automatic updates, a large database, and the ability to customize the database yourself.

Filtering Internet sites using software designed for this purpose is censorship. While school libraries and curriculum committees have always weeded out offensive materials before they are purchased, they have done this title-by-title, mindful that schools serve a range of family belief systems. The ALA (American Library Association) guidelines for libraries state that blocking of information violates freedom of access to information, which should be a family decision. You can read about the suit filed by the ALA to stop implementation of some of the aspects of the Children's Internet Protection Act at **http://www.ala.org/cipa**. For more information about filtering software, visit these Web sites:

CyberSitter

CyberSitter filters and blocks adult-oriented material, graphics and language from Internet newsgroups, chat areas, World Wide Web pages and e-mail. For stand-alone PCs and networks.

http://www.solidoak.com

Global Chalkboard

The designers describe this software as an Internet tool rather than filtering software. Educators can choose from Web resources reviewed by other teachers and add their own content for class lessons, generate reports on sites, create lessons online, and manage or turnoff other Internet services like AOL, newsgroups, and FTP.

http://www.bascom.com

Cyber Sentinel

Cyber Sentinel captures the offending screen and reports immediately to the network administrator. It also allows schools to control the hours in which students have access to specific features such as the Web, newsgroups, e-mail, or chat rooms.

http://www.securitysoft.com

NetNanny

NetNanny filters words, phrases or sites based on site lists and keywords. You can also have Net Nanny block instant messaging, online games, pop-up advertising and file sharing.

http://www.netnanny.com/index.html

SafeSurf

SafeSurf, a watchdog organization, has suggested a rating standard in which child-friendly sites identify themselves with HTML tags hidden inside the contents of their Web pages. Provided the child is using a SafeSurf browser, all tagless sites are invisible.

http://www.safesurf.com

SchoolMarshal

SchoolMarshal checks Web pages, e-mail, attachments and downloads. It blocks items based on the filtering rules set by each individual school. Schools can customize access for different groups of users and generate reports.

http://www.marshalsoftware.com

SurfControl

SurfControl offers both Web and e-mail blocking products in English, French, German, Spanish and Dutch. The Web content database contains millions of URLs and billions of Web pages. Daily updates are sent automatically. The software is customizable and can block files that are virus-infected or take up huge amounts of bandwidth.

http://www.surfcontrol.com

Websense

Websense monitors Internet activity in addition to allowing you to block undesirable sites. It uses a growing database of more than 800 million URLs, newsgroups and chat room addresses that fall into 81 categories. A person checks each site before adding it to the database and updates are daily.

http://www.websense.com

The ongoing costs of filtering software are high, usually requiring an initial investment plus a monthly update, money that might be better spent on learning related software. Filtering software may also create a false sense of security, and schools that claim they can keep students completely safe from controversial material may find themselves more at risk legally than others who make no such claims. Diverse family values and community values must also be considered, along with students' civil liberties. Some parents may question the school's right to restrict student access to information.

"Kid Safe" sites and search engines

Some schools post a list of sites known to be safe for the appropriate age of the students, and these are the only sites that students are allowed to visit at school. This strategy is used with young students; older students can surf and search within the guidelines of a good acceptable use policy, as described in the next section. Obviously, close supervision is always required. Here is one such list of sites for very young children.

Berit's Best Sites for Children

http://www.beritsbest.com

Carlos Coloring Book

http://www.coloring.com

Enchanted Learning

http://www.enchantedlearning.com/Home.html

Hands On Children's Museum

http://www.hocm.org

Jan Dembsky's Kids Excellent Web Links

Links to museums, sports, science, literature, homework and more.
http://www.cybercomm.net/~teach

Jellybean Kingdom

http://www.geocities.com/Enchanted Forest/3737

KEWL Kids Excellent Web Links

http://www.cybercomm.net/~teach

Kids Domain UK

This site contains downloadable files of games, educational software and pictures as well as reviews of the latest children's software on the market. Kids Domain UK also hosts an extensive range of craft activities, recipes, clip art and icons, holiday pages and original children's stories.

http://www.kidsdomain.co.uk

Kids' Wave

http://www.safesurf.com/kidswave.htm

Kids' Web

http://www.npac.syr.edu/textbook/kidsweb

Story Hour

Stories for children from the Internet Public Library

http://ipl.sils.umich.edu/youth/StoryHour

The Canadian Kids Homepage

http://www.canadiankids.net/default.jsp

Tukids

At this safe Web site where children and parents can download virus-free educational software. The files have been downloaded and tested by a review board to ensure that they are free from nudity, violence and explicit language. They also have some non-violent online games and coloring fun.

http://tukids.tucows.com

World Kids Network

Learn how to make a home page, join a club, find out more about animals, or play games at this site just for kids.

http://worldkids.net

Teachers report that it is often through a search that students run across questionable material on the Web. Several search engines have been developed specifically for the use of children; the sites in their databases have been screened and judged to be acceptable. By limiting younger students to these search engines, you may avoid an incident.

Alfy (portal site for young children) at **http://www.alfy.com**

Ask Jeeves for Schools at **http://www.ajschools.com**

Education World at **http://www.education-world.com**

Use your browser software to set up your selected Bookmarks as the Home Page where students begin their explorations. For example, Grade 6 students exploring whales as a class activity open the Home Page to see a list of approved sites.

Levels of protection

Many American schools that have acceptable use policies use various combinations of additional procedures and/or technologies to prevent student access to inappropriate material on the Internet. In a year 2000 study, 15% of American public schools reported using four additional procedures (filtering software, Intranet, teacher/staff monitoring and honor codes), 40% using three, 36% using two and 9% reported using one additional procedure only.[5]

Internet Public Library Youth Division at **http://www.ipl.org/youth**

Ithaki (metasearch for kids) at **http://www.ithaki.net/kids**

KidsClick! at **http://sunsite.berkeley.edu/KidsClick!**

Yahooligans at **http://www.yahooligans.com**

A number of major search engines can be set to filter out objectionable content. For example, AltaVista includes a "Family Filter" option. Check your search engine's preferences or customized features to set filters.

Another approach is to identify curricular and developmentally appropriate sites in advance for each grade level or theme and make these available as "pages" on the World Wide Web server. Students are told they must stay at those sites: no searching, no surfing. Violators suffer loss of Internet privileges or another appropriate consequence. While some teachers may be uncomfortable with this approach, time constraints make it appealing since pointing students toward worthwhile sites saves them time and effort.

School Intranets, private networks that restrict information to those who are allowed access, can include teacher-selected Web sites downloaded in advance. Users appear to be on the Internet until they try to access a link that is external to the downloaded sites on the Intranet. This is a restrictive but secure solution to student safety. It requires that the downloaded sites be regularly updated, as one of the strengths of the Internet is ready access to up-to-the-minute information.

Accceptable use policies

A balanced approach to using the Internet in schools emphasizes guidance rather than censorship. The strategies we use to teach children about risks in daily life work equally well with the risks associated with the Internet. By establishing clear rules and setting boundaries, we teach young children not to run in the school halls, not to talk to strangers, and not to use violence. We make judgments about how much supervision children require at various ages, and when the risk is extremely high, we keep them in sight or we employ some kind of structure such as a fence or a lock. As children mature, we teach them to respect boundaries and values without being physically blocked from entry. We expect our students to begin exercising judgment and restraint as they begin moving toward adult life.

It is important that schools develop clear policies to guide students' use of the Internet and establish rules and consequences for breaking them. Additionally, schools should consider integrating issues around technology and ethics into the curriculum. To protect the school and to reassure parents, most schools have developed and implemented an acceptable use policy. Such policies are frequently referred to as AUPs. An AUP is an agreement signed by students, their parents, and the teacher. It outlines the terms and conditions of Internet use. Some AUPs are instituted by school boards or districts. Others are school- or even classroom-specific. Find out if your school has an Internet AUP. If not, get together with interested colleagues and parents to develop one before allowing your students to access the Internet.

A thorough AUP contains the following:

- a description of what the Internet is,
- an explanation of how students will access the Internet at school,
- examples of how the Internet will be used to enhance student learning,
- a list of student responsibilities while online, which might address such issues as
  — privacy
  — morals and ethics
  — freedom of expression
  — legal constraints
  — safety
  — harassment
  — plagiarism
  — resource utilization
  — expected behaviors/etiquette
  — security issues
- the consequences of violating the AUP,
- a place for student, parent, and teacher signatures.

Rather than simply sending an AUP home for signatures, consider beginning the school year with a "cyberspace evening" to introduce the community to the Internet. Have students demonstrate some exciting Internet resources and projects. Talk to parents about how you plan to use the Internet in your classroom or school, and explain your AUP in detail. Stress that, with the privilege to use the Internet, students must accept the responsibility for proper use. Some schools adopt a "zero tolerance" attitude while others issue a warning letter after the first violation.

> Education is the key. We give a unit of Net Etiquette to each student and staff on the responsible use of the Internet account. You can find this agreement on our home page at **http://www.mvhs.fuhsd.org** under resources.
>
> — *Peg Szady, Teacher, Monta Vista High School, California, U.S.A.*

Sample AUPs abound on the Internet. At the following sites you can find examples and guidelines for AUPs.

Armadillo

Here you will find links to lots of sites for the guidance of students, teachers, administrators, parents, and board members in developing and understanding policy.

http://www.rice.edu/armadillo/acceptable.html

From Now On

This article, entitled "Creating Board Policies for Student Use of the Internet," contains lots of food for thought.

http://www.fno.org/fnomay95.html

The Electronic Frontier Foundation

This is a collection of the computer policies of many schools and critiques of some.

http://www.eff.org/pub/CAF/policies

HINT

Books of Internet acceptable use policies for schools

- *An Anthology of Internet Acceptable Use Policies* includes copies of twenty-seven university and K–12 school district policies. It's published by the National Association of Regional Media Centers and is available from Don Whitmarsh, NARMC Publications Chair, Area Education Agency 4, 1382 4th Ave. NE, Sioux Center, IA 51250, 712/722-4378.

- *Plans & Policies for Technology in Education: A Compendium* also includes sample plans and policies on other technology-related topics from a total of thirty-eight U.S. school districts. (March, 1995) It's available from the National School Boards Association Distribution Center in Maryland, (800) 706-6722.

My Rules for Online Safety

Name: _____

		YES	NO
1	I do not give out personal information (my address, telephone number, parents' work address/telephone number, or the name and location of my school) without my parents' or teachers' permission.	☐	☐
2	I never send a person my picture or agree to get together with someone I "meet" online without first checking with my parents.	☐	☐
3.	I tell an adult right away if I come across any information on the Web that makes me feel uncomfortable.	☐	☐
4.	I do not respond to any e-mail that makes me feel uncomfortable in any way. If I get a message like that, I tell my parents or teachers right away.	☐	☐
5.	I obey the Internet rules established by my home and school.	☐	☐
6.	I do not give out my Internet password to anyone other than my parents.	☐	☐
7.	I am a good online citizen and will not do anything that hurts other people or is against the law.	☐	☐

Responding to inappropriate material

The fact that your school has developed and enforced an AUP doesn't protect you or your students from possible violation from other less considerate Internet users. Though it's a relatively rare event, think about how you would respond if you or a student were to receive an e-mail message, containing language or content that you deem unacceptable. It is then up to the offending student's school to take appropriate action, which might include the submission of a formal apology and suspension of Internet privileges.

- I would treat [abuse of Internet privileges] much as I would treat a child who has been insulted on the playground or while going to or from school: I would counsel the child and try to deal with the offender.

- I would counsel *all* children about the possibility of this kind of message, so that they are not caught off guard. They should know to report this kind of message immediately to the teacher, who should print the message right away and then forward it to a safe location for future reference.

- I would ensure that all parents understood that this is a risk, but that the school doesn't sanction this behavior and that teachers try to prepare students to deal effectively with this.

- I would write a message to the offending e-mail address, with copies to the system administrator and postmaster complaining about this behavior, with full details of how the student was affected.
  — *Al Rogers, Executive Director, Global SchoolNet Foundation*

Talking about the issue of online safety in your school is the first step to dealing with it. Discuss one or more of these possible scenarios with a colleague or group, keeping in mind your school district's policies and procedures surrounding Internet safety.

Example 1

A Grade 9 student calls her classmates over to see a sexually explicit photograph she has found on the Web. She has parent permission to do independent work on the Internet in the library, but some of the other students do not. You are the teacher who observes this while on library supervision. What do you do?

Example 2

A student in your Grade 4 class accidentally stumbles across a Web site with photos of naked people. She follows your class's "No-Go-Tell" rule. After school that day, you receive a phone call from the child's mother demanding an explanation. What will you say to this parent?

Example 3

A Grade 7 teacher allows students to "surf" the Internet during "free time." He warns them to stay within the selected sites posted beside the computers. One day a group of his students' parents complain to the principal that their children have been looking at pornography at the back of the classroom while the teacher sat at his desk marking papers. You are the principal. What do you do?

Example 4

A system operator receives a threat from a high school student. It contains obscene words. He contacts the school and the student and parents are brought in for a conference. The student denies any knowledge or ownership of the e-mail in question. You are the principal. What do you do?

Resources for student safety

America Links Up: A Kids Online Teach-In

This is a public awareness and education campaign sponsored by a coalition of non-profit organizations, education groups, and corporations concerned with providing children with a safe and rewarding online experience. This site contains a number of valuable resources for parents, teachers and students.

http://www.getnetwise.org/americalinksup

Issues

Here is a list of issues that might be addressed by AUPs, developed by educational author Dave Kinnaman.

http://www.io.com/%7Ekinnaman/concerns.html

Media Awareness Network

These excellent resources have been created to help teachers provide students with the skills they need to evaluate online information and to protect their privacy and their personal safety as they surf the Net.

http://www.media-awareness.ca/eng/webaware/teachers/thome.htm

National Centre for Missing and Exploited Children

At this site you'll find the online game called Missing, designed for Canadian students in Grades 6 to 9. The game allows youth to play detective by searching for Zack, a fictional 14-year-old who has been lured away by an Internet predator. A parent/teacher guidebook is provided.

http://www.livewwwires.com

Netparents

This site contains guidelines to make it easier for parents to navigate online safely with their children.

http://www.getnetwise.org

SafeKids.com

Tips, advice, suggestions, the safe kids online song and a quiz are among the many offerings at this site.

http://www.safekids.com/index.html

The CyberTipLine

The CyberTipline handles leads from individuals reporting the sexual exploitation of children. Information is forwarded to law enforcement for investigation and review.

http://www.missingkids.com/cybertip/index.html

What's a (Teacher, Parent, Administrator) to Do?

This brief article is about how educators react when confronted in the classroom with unacceptable content or language.

http://www.ibiblio.org/cmc/mag/1995/jun/stratford.html

Netscape Navigator's built-in protection feature is called NetWatch. Once NetWatch is turned on, Netscape will read the rating on a Web page and compare it with the rating levels you have pre-selected as acceptable. To activate this service you must go to the Netscape Web site.

Microsoft's Internet Explorer uses a system called Content Advisor to control access. To find out more about this system and how to activate it, go to "Help," using the toolbar on your browser, and click on "Content and Index," and then search for Content Advisor in the Index.

The Internet Content Rating Association (**http://www.icra.org**) is an international, independent organization that empowers the public to make informed decisions about electronic media by means of labeling content. ICRA's aims are to protect children from potentially harmful material and to protect free speech on the Internet. Web authors fill in an online questionnaire describing the content of their site in terms of what is and isn't present. ICRA then generates a Content Label (a short piece of computer code) which the author adds to his/her site. Users can then set their Web browser to allow or disallow access to Web sites based on the objective information declared in the label and the subjective preferences of the user. The ICRA system can be used with Microsoft's Internet Explorer immediately. Wider applications are under development at the time of this writing.

Summing up

For those who have been teaching for a long time, but equally for beginners, the excitement of getting involved in an online project with other teachers and students around the world is inspirational. The Internet becomes one more tool students use to help them with critical learning; it's an information-tion giver, communication facilitator, and thought provoker. Using the Internet in your classroom projects increases the versatility and value of project-based learning as a curriculum tool by providing a rich environment for individuals and teams to carry out in-depth projects that draw on multimedia and information resources from around the world.

So much can go so wrong — a password typed incorrectly, server crashes, pornographic or illegal material. Yet so much can go so right. I can think of a hundred reasons not to get kids involved with the Internet, and I can think of a thousand reasons to get them actively participating. I am willing to put up with the small problems in order to achieve the results that I know will make my students self-motivated, critically thinking, lifelong learners.

— *Robert Steenwinkel, Teacher, Mary Butterworh School, Edmonton, Alberta, Canada*

Notes – Chapter 3

1.　Heide, A. & Henderson, D. (1994) *The Technological Classroom: A Blueprint for Success.* Toronto: Trifolium Books, Inc.

2.　McKenzie, J. (2001) online at **http://fno.org/apr98/quandaries.html** 10/10/01.

3.　McKenzie, J. (2001) online at **http://fno.org/fnojun95.html** 10/10/01.

4.　Gonsalves, A. (2003) Web Watchers. *Technology and Learning, 23* (6): 7–10.

5.　Online at **http://nces.ed.gov** 11/01/02.

4
Chapter

Exploring the World Wide Web

"The modern age has a false sense of security because of the great mass of data at its disposal. But the valid issue is the extent to which [people] know how to form and master the material at [their] disposal."

— Johann Wolfgang von Goethe, 1832

The World Wide Web inspires learning. Students and teachers are quickly excited by the vastness of this resource and the discovery of how easy it is to navigate. On the World Wide Web, students can learn about current news events and contemporary science. They can delve into the past and read correspondence from the American Civil War or visit a museum that provides a glimpse of an earlier time.

This chapter is an introduction to the World Wide Web. It describes some of the different kinds of applications that you can access over the Web. In addition, this chapter helps you learn how to search for information and introduces you to some good Web resources to help you get started using the Web in your classroom.

Chapter goals

- To provide an overview of the World Wide Web and its role in the classroom
- To provide an overview of Web browsers — options and common features
- To introduce the concept of client/server computing
- To introduce key concepts related to Web technology
- To describe how to search for information on the World Wide Web
- To suggest a selection of Web resources for teachers and students

The Web as a tool for learning

The World Wide Web is an important complement to traditional learning materials, both print and audiovisual. School librarians are constantly challenged to meet broad curriculum needs on limited budgets. Having access to the Web is an excellent way to supplement the school media collection. Ideally, students need to know beforehand how to use both print and Internet resources for their research, and how to assess the value of each for any given project.

In the classroom, the World Wide Web can also be used as a publishing tool, and as such it can be relevant to a broad spectrum of classroom learning activities. An exciting venture for students is to develop their own Web pages. We will talk more about student publishing on the Web in the next chapters.

Understanding the basics of the World Wide Web is the first step to using it effectively in the classroom. Chapter 1 briefly introduced the World Wide Web. In this chapter you will learn more about how it works. You will find that taking time to learn about the mechanics of using the Web will help you to become more confident about using the Web with students.

World Wide Web: Overview

The World Wide Web project was developed to provide easy access over the Internet to a variety of media. Web pages can display text, pictures, sound, video, and animated graphics. Web pages display paragraphs about a topic, and also provide links to further information, using a computer technology called *hypertext*.

Hypertext links lead you to more information whenever you choose to follow them. (See Figure 4-1, page 101.) A simple example of a hypertext link would be a situation in which you are reading a document on screen and are given an opportunity to click on a word to find its definition. Or you might be viewing a document about health and nutrition and discover a link to another document that provides in-depth information about vitamins. Hyperlinks can point to other references in the same document or to completely separate files on the Internet. Many educational Web pages include links to similar sites. School Web pages often provide links to individual classroom pages and student work.

Hypermedia is another term you will encounter on the Web. Hypermedia is similar to hypertext in that both denote the ability to access further information from a document. But hypermedia makes it possible to access other kinds of information, such as pictures or sound files, in addition to text. As you might guess, hypermedia is the basis for many multimedia applications. Web pages are becoming more complex in design, incorporating more sound and video files, so the World Wide Web can increasingly be described as a way of delivering multimedia over the Internet.

Client/server technology

A number of Internet applications, including the World Wide Web, are built on *client/server technology*. Client/server is a key concept in the world of the Internet. Simply put, in a client/server environment, two pieces of software work together as a team.

The *client* is responsible for
- the user interface (what the software looks like to you on your desktop),
- initiating the communications process, and
- displaying information sent from the server.

Figure 4-1

Clicking on highlighted hyper-links will bring up a new page.

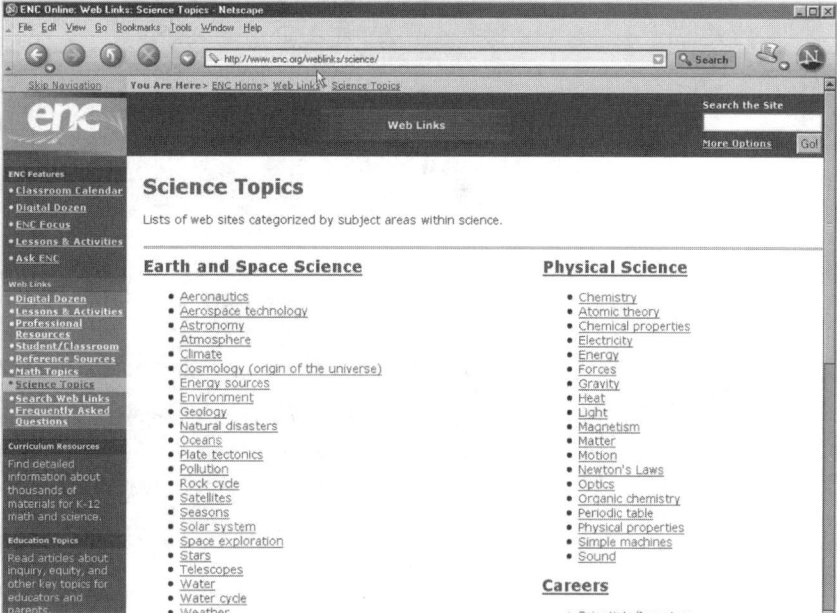

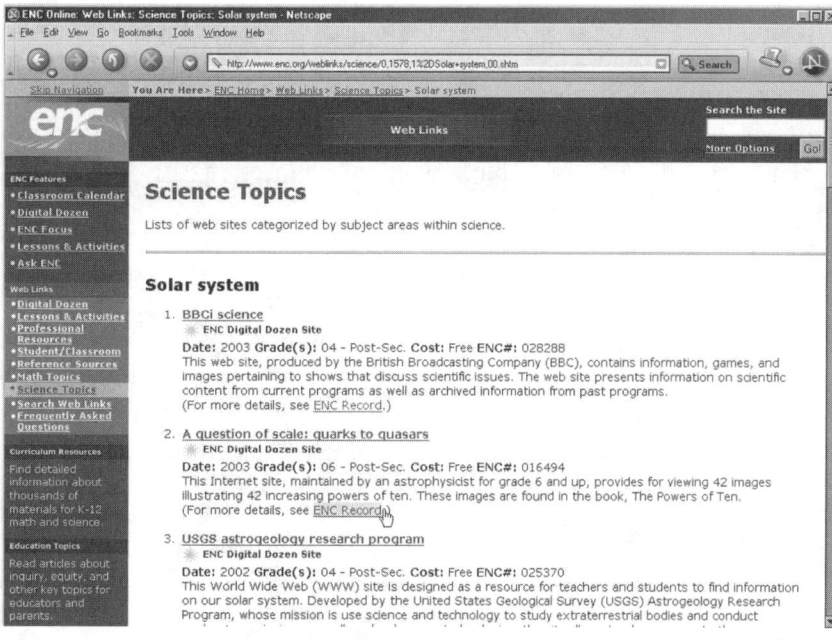

Figure 4-2
Client/server computing.

The *server*
- retains information (menus and file locations),
- analyzes requests coming from the client, and
- responds to requests by sending information back to the client.

In a nutshell, the client is the program that you use locally, and the remote server does what the client says.

A key advantage to client/server computing is that it allows you to use your desktop computing power (the client) while taking full advantage of more powerful remote computers (the server) to store the massive resources available through the Internet. Another advantage is that it allows information to be passed back and forth over the Internet without the connections between computers having to remain open. The connection on a remote server stays open only long enough to respond to your immediate request for a Web page. You, in turn, read the item only after it has been passed to your client computer.

Web browsers: Netscape vs. Explorer

The client software used to access the World Wide Web is called a *browser*. New and improved Web browsers are always on the horizon. The two most popular browsers are **Netscape** (available from **http://www.netscape.com**) and **Internet Explorer** (available from **http://www.microsoft.com/ie**), and versions of these browsers are constantly updated. Your access provider may have supplied you with a browser or told you where to obtain the latest versions of these popular Web browsers.

Both Netscape and Explorer offer many of the same features, and versions are available for both Macintosh and Windows operating systems. Both provide a toolbar for easy navigation and accept something called *plug-ins* for accessing many different types of files (such as sound files). With

Tech Talk

The latest versions of most Web browsers attempt to keep in step with current Internet applications, but not all will support the newest features on the Web. Find out about browser options, and keep up with the newest versions of your favorite browser at Tucows: **http:// www. tucows.com**.

HINT ChiBrow (**http://www.chibrow. com**) and KidSafe Explorer are Web browsers designed specifically for younger children. You can find a list of products for kid-safe surfing at **http:// www.tucows.com/ parent95_default.html**
.

either browser you will be able to track sites you've visited in the current session, save and print documents, and save references to sites you want to visit again. If you have configured your browser with information on how to locate news and mail on your Internet service provider's computer, you can also read and post to Internet discussion groups (called newsgroups), and receive and send electronic mail.

The very newest versions of these browsers include features such as the ability to chat and exchange files in real time, and the ability to create Web pages.

Because Netscape and Explorer offer very similar features, the choice between them is mostly a matter of personal preference. When you first start out, it's easiest to stick with the browser that is supplied or recommended by your Internet service provider (ISP), but don't be afraid to download and try another browser.

Other browser options

Although Netscape and Internet Explorer are the browsers of choice for an overwhelming number of users, they may not be ideal for your needs. In a non-graphical environment, you may be using something called **Lynx**, which is a text-only browser, and some Macintosh users prefer to use a browser called **iCAb** (**http://www.icab.de**). Even if you are using one of the two most popular browsers, you may or may not want to download the latest version. While Netscape 6 or 7 and Internet Explorer 6 offer many exciting features such as the file exchange and instant messaging features, some of these may not be suitable for schools if a teacher wants to limit the scope of student opportunities for communications over the Net. In addition, the latest browsers require a lot of disk space and computer memory, which may not be available on a school computer.

For many teachers, a browser called **Opera** (**http://www.opera.com**) is a practical alternative to Netscape and Internet Explorer. Opera is not well known, but it is becoming better known because it is a tidy, efficient browser that offers the basics and does so well. Here are several of the features that are available with Opera:

One nice feature of the Opera browser is that it will let you easily view Web pages that you have downloaded from the Web without the need to have Web connectivity software running in the background. Opera offers an Offline Browsing Mode. When this option is selected, the browser will automatically retrieve sites from your disk cache, rather than going online. The cache is a storage space on your hard drive where pages you have recently visited are saved. You can also capture pages for viewing offline by using an offline browser, such as Offline Commander. We discuss offline browsers in detail in Chapter 8.

- *Quick loading pages.* (Most people find that Opera will load pages noticeably faster than the mainstream browsers.)
- *Ability to access and view up to four Web pages at once in individual windows.* (This can be a real time saver. You can access several sites at the start of a class period and have other sites you'll be using waiting in the background. This feature will also let you easily compare two or more sites.)
- *Ability to save pages from one session to the next.* (This can be an advantage if your students' computers are located in your own classroom and a project will span several class periods.)

Figure 4-3

The Opera browser loads pages quickly and it requires less disk space than other browsers.

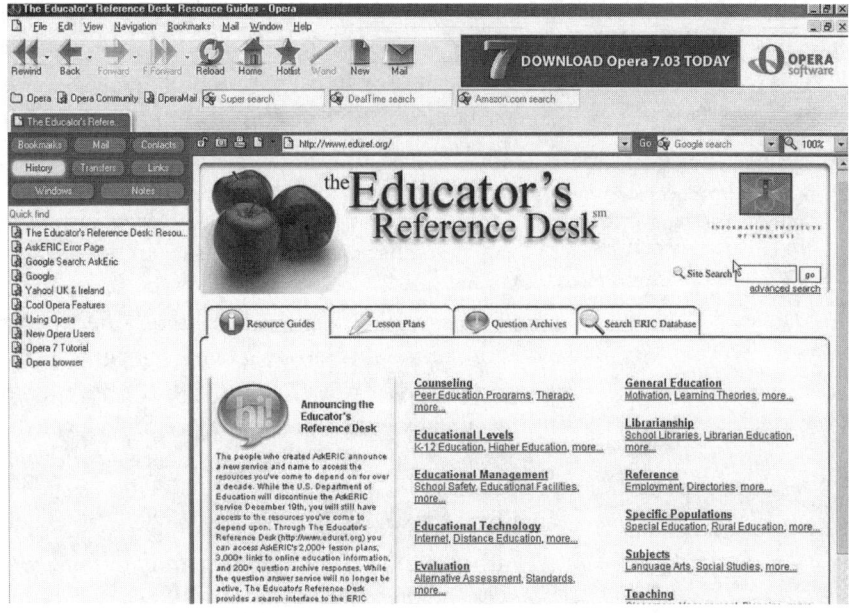

Figure 4-4

Right click on the toolbar to access the customize toolbar screen in Internet Explorer.

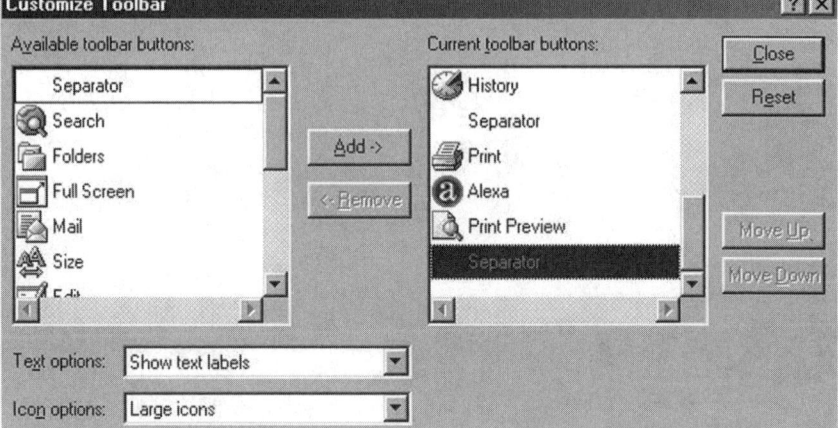

- *Quick access to look-up features.* (Double-click a word or right-click on a highlighted phrase to access a pop-up menu providing access to Web search engines, an online dictionary, encyclopedia, and translation.)
- *Limited requirement for computer disk space.* (This is a very significant feature for schools with older computers.)
- A number of design features (such as a zoom function for graphics and text) have been incorporated into the product, making it well suited for use with students with disabilities.

- *Print options.* Opera will let you increase or reduce the size of a print out, set margins and include or eliminate headers and footers.

It's almost impossible to talk about the Opera browser without making some reference to the story of David and Goliath. Opera's entry into the browser marketplace does remind us of the little guy challenging two big giants. It's not likely that Opera will seriously threaten either of the major browsers, both of which are very well established. Opera does, however, offer a number of features that could be particularly valuable for schools. You may want to investigate this browser for yourself or ask your school computer support person to check it out.

Basic navigation

When you first start your Web browser, it will connect to a Web server and display an initial home page (often the home page for the browser company or your Internet provider). From here, you can link to other documents by clicking on the words that are highlighted in some way. They may be a brighter color than other text, and they may be underlined. These links are usually blue. Once you have followed a particular link and you return to your original page, the links that you have followed will change color. Most new browsers will let you establish your own colors for links, but it's probably most convenient to go with the default settings.

Links are sometimes in the form of clickable images. If you use your mouse to slowly slide the cursor over a Web page, you can detect the hyperlinks by noting when the cursor changes to a grabber hand. Click and wait for a new page to appear. Be cautious about clicking more than once. Pages frequently take a minute or two to download through a modem connection. If a page does not download quickly enough, click on your browser's *Stop* button and try again. If the loading still seems very slow, try again later. When you want to navigate back and forth between pages, you can click on the back and forward arrows displayed at the top of your browser. You can also click and hold the back arrow to access a list of previously navigated links.

URLs

Although at first you'll probably navigate the Web simply by highlighting and clicking on the links that are incorporated into your Web browser or presented on a Web page, you can navigate more efficiently by using URLs (*Uniform Resource Locators*). In effect, URLs are "addresses" that specify the Internet location of computers having different types of information. The first part of the URL (before the colon) indicates the access method or the type of resource you want to retrieve. The part of the URL that follows the double slash (//) specifies a machine name or site. Here are some examples.

http://www.storybookonline.net/Default.aspx This is a Web site (http stands for *h*ypertext *t*ransfer *p*rotocol).

ftp://www.xerox.com/pub/file.txt With the FTP type of URL, you can access and transfer files. Software files that are not posted on the Web are sometimes available from "ftp sites."

telnet://dra.com The telnet URL will access a login screen for a remote computer.

news:alt.hypertext If your browser has been configured to point to your newserver, an address like this gives you access to newsgroups using your Web browser.

Most of the URLs you will encounter will be for Web pages. (We will explain more about the other types of files and applications in Chapter 8.) You have probably already encountered many references to Web sites. Many agencies, such as businesses, newspapers, and even television programs, now advertise, using an address starting with http:// or www.

The quickest way to access a Web site for which you have a specific address is to clear the window displaying the current URL and put in the URL for the site you want to go to. Most browsers will let you drop the http:// part of the address, but some people prefer to use the complete address. Most browsers locate the URL window at the top of the screen. You can also use a pull-down menu option or your browser tool bar to open a new location.

HINT Remember that Web sites are constantly changing. In particular, directory names and filenames may quickly go out of date. If a URL does not seem to work, check each character to be sure that you have entered it accurately. Then, try deleting the final filename and/or directories. Once you've accessed a specific location, you can often find the exact information you're searching for just by following the links. If you still are not successful, try finding the item using a search engine such as AltaVista.

HINT ZDNet from the publishers of *PC Magazine* and *MacUser* is a popular source for finding out about new hardware and software options. **http://www5.zdnet.com**. This site offers advice and how-tos from beginners to advanced. A number of other good sites are linked to print publications. You will find lots of helpful information at Mecklermedia's Internet.com at **http://www.internet.com** and at Byte Magazine's site: **http://www.byte.com**.

Making friends with your browser

Learning about the features available on your own browser is a good investment of time. While it's fairly easy to access links on the Net, many browser features are available to navigate quickly and to help you make the best use of a site once you get there. You can also customize various features on many browsers, such as the size of the print, how many links will be remembered as "followed links," and what program on your computer system you may want to use to display long text files.

To learn about the features on your particular browser, start by exploring the menu options at the top of the screen, and use the Help File for the program. Here are some basic features that are available on most browsers.

- Viewing many other types of files (such as multimedia files) with the addition of *helper files*, or *plug-ins*.
- Viewing newsgroup discussions and reading electronic mail if you have set up these options. (Some people use separate software for these functions, such as Eudora for reading mail.)
- Printing Web pages.
- Sending Web pages by e-mail.
- Cuting and copying text from a Web page for pasting into another document.

Speeding things up. Here are some things you can do:

- When typing in a URL, you can omit the http://. *Do not do this in electronic mail messages, however, or you will lose the automatic link feature.*
- Turn off image loading.
- Stop the transmission and click on the button to re-load.
- Check to see if another browser window has been opened. This can happen when you go directly to a link from your mail software, or if frames (a technique for splitting a Web display into several parts) are used, a second browser window may have been opened without your realizing it. This

is the case when suddenly you find that the Back button doesn't work. You can use the Windows Alt-Tab keys to determine if this has happened. If it has, close the window that is slowing things down.
- It is not always necessary to wait for a page to completely load before clicking on a new link. Be cautious however. Sometimes the link you intend to access is farther down on the page that is loading.
- If you are using Opera, you can split the browser screen and access one site while you are viewing another, or keep a search engine ready in a second window.
- If things are really slow — take a break and try again later!

The *right* mouse button offers a number of handy features in a pop-up menu. Try using this feature for moving forward or backward, saving graphics, and setting bookmarks. The options that can be accessed using your right mouse button vary from browser to browser, and the menu displayed when you click on your right mouse button will change depending on exactly where your cursor is positioned on a page. Some right button options:

- Setting up bookmarks or favorites that will let you easily return to a site whenever you want to come back to it.
- Select, cut and paste text.
- Viewing the source code for a document. This feature will give you a view of all the cryptic-looking codes that go into HTML tagging. You will find that this is a useful feature once you start developing Web pages.
- Print or e-mail a web page.
- Open a link in a new browser window

A common browser default is to display security messages of various sorts, such as asking you if you want to accept a cookie. A *cookie* is a server device for keeping track of who you are so the computer can send back the appropriate information to you. If, for example, you were taking an online quiz, the server might use a cookie to pass the test results back to your computer. Unless your system administrator advises against it, feel free to turn off these warning messages.

Explore the options for setting preferences on your browser. With most browsers you can change font size and colors. There will also be a range of security preferences, such as the option to display or not to display various warning messages and whether to accept "cookies." Don't be afraid to change things. You can always change them back. If you are unsure about some of the options, ask your school technician or a knowledgeable friend to explain.

HINT What to do when the back button doesn't work? This happens when your browser opens a page in a new browser window. Some sites are set up to automatically open a new window when you click on a link, so that before you know it you have several different windows open. Close the new window or use the *Alt|Tab* key combination to return to the original page.

- Saving Web pages. Newer browsers will let you save the complete contents of a Web page, including images and sound files if these are included. You can also save an HTML page as a text file and import the unformatted text contents of a site into your word processor. (Note: You can also download *Web sites* using an offline browser. Offline browsers are discussed in Chapter 8.)
- Retracing your steps. A *History* list saves links for places you've recently visited.
- Using *Bookmarks* or *Favorites*.
- Searching for text on the current page. Quickly find a word you are looking for on an unfamiliar Web page using *Edit/Find*.
- Performing a range of functions using the right mouse button. Depending on your browser, you can right-click when your mouse is positioned at targeted places on a Web page to save individual images; save a linked page without having to view it first; add bookmarks and cut and copy links. A right mouse click in the Opera browser provides quick access to a dictionary and encyclopedia.

Browser options

Many of the options settings for your browser are preset and for the most part you will want to stick with them. There are a few, however, that you may wish to change. Here are the most important options to be aware of:

- *Starting page* — Generally, browsers have been preset to load a specific Web page when they are first turned on (commonly that of your access provider). An option is available to change this URL setting to one that you might prefer, such as the URL for your favorite search engine, a good starting point page for a particular unit of study, or a Web page developed by your school or class.
- *Image loading* — Your browser will have a setting for easily turning off the *image loading* and then turning it on again when you want to access the images on a page. If you don't mind viewing pages without all the pretty pictures, this feature can save you time. Find the options menu on your browser and click to toggle the option on or off. With the Opera browser, you can access this feature by clicking on the camera icon just to the left of the URL window.
- *Title bars and button bars* — You can increase the size of the Web page window, by turning off the screen display for these features. Usually this is done by using a toggle selection that allows you to turn a feature on or off with a single click. If you turn off the screen display for the navigation bars, you can use your right mouse button to navigate.
- *Visual display* — If you want to increase the size of the print that displays for Web pages, it is possible to do so on most browsers. It is also possible to change the default color setting for the browser background and links.

HINT In Netscape, if either of the toolbar bars is not visible, pull down the **Options** menu and ensure that the **Toolbar** selection is checked.

The button bar provides one-click access to some additional features. The **Directory** (under Options) selection must be checked to view these.

These display features can be toggled on and off by clicking on the name of the item in the **Options** menu list.

Figure 4-5 The Netscape toolbar.

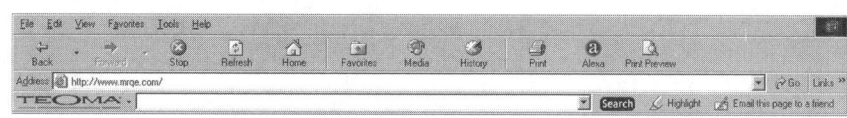

Figure 4-6 The Internet Explorer toolbar.

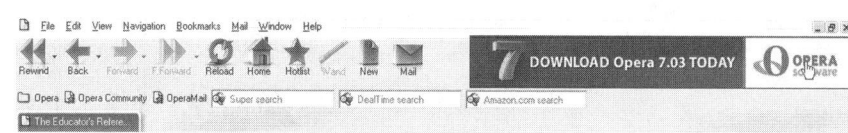

Figure 4-7 The Opera navigation bar.

BROWSER NAVIGATION

In this example, we describe the most common features available for navigation in Internet Explorer. The following functions will be available on all browsers, though the location of the features will not be identical to those on Internet Explorer.

Back.

Brings you back to the pages that you've previously viewed. As it accesses location, your browser retains information on where you've been (via a history list) and will quickly redisplay pages according to the most recently viewed page when you click on the Back button. Click on the small black arrow just to the right of the back button to display a list of recently visited sites or access the *History* panel.

Another way to access previously visited sites is to click on the tiny down arrow to the right of the location window.

Forward

Redisplay a page you have visited prior to using the Back button to retrace your steps.

Stop

Interrupts the data being transmitted from the network. Use this option when a page seems to be taking too long to load. Then, try to access the page again.

Refresh

Re-accesses the document you have just viewed and redisplays it on your screen. Use this option when a page appears incomplete or seems to have loaded incorrectly.

Home

Brings up whatever home or start page you have set as your preference. This is the page that automatically loads when you start your browser.

Search

One-click access to Internet search. Caution: IE's search is pre-configured with Microsoft's search engine choice. Also, without a secure firewall, the search option can unexpectedly access inappropriate content. You can easily remove Search as a toolbar choice using the Toolbar customization option.

Favorites

Provides quick access to your list of favorite sites.

History

Provides a list of recently visited sites.

Toolbar customization

To customize what is displayed on your toolbar, use the *View|Toolbar|Customize* menu option.

You can add and delete toolbar buttons, such as Media or Mail that may not be suitable for use in your school environment. Some special Internet navigation tools (such as the Copernic search program) provide an icon for toolbar access. These too can be displayed or hidden using the customization option.

Explorer bar

Internet Explorer's Explorer bar displays as a panel on the left side of the screen. Clicking on *View|Explorer* will list display options for the left browser panel.

Hotlists — Create Your Own **http://www. essdack.org/hotlists**. Use this site to create hotlists for online lessons or search for lesson hotlists created by other teachers. There are also services that will let you store your bookmarks online. This is useful when you want to access your bookmarks at home and at school. You can also use these services to share your bookmarks with colleagues. You can store your bookmarks online at any of these sites:

Backflip
http://www.backflip.com
Baboo
http://www.baboo.com
Bookmarktracker
http://www.bookmark tracker.com
Bestbookmarks
http://www.bestbook marks.com.
KeepBookmarks
http://www.ikeepbook marks.com (This site includes an example of a school that has used the online bookmarks site for sharing Internet resources.)

Using a hotlist

Once you start navigating you will quickly identify sites that you'll want to return to again and again. Luckily, it is not necessary to type in a complete URL each time you want to return to a location. Once you access a site that interests you, you can add it to your list of bookmarks or favorites. Use your right mouse button to add bookmarks. You can also left click and hold your mouse button as it is positioned over a URL to drag and drop a bookmark or favorite into the file where you want to store it.

Hotlists can be a great help for organizing classroom projects. Once you master the basics, you can save a great deal of time by using your browser's features for organizing and managing bookmarks or favorites.

Here are some tips to help you use browser hotlists effectively:

- Set up separate bookmark folders for curriculum areas or class projects.
- Use your right mouse button to quickly add new bookmarks.
- In Netscape Manage Bookmarks, the *Tools* menu option will let you import and export bookmarks. The import function will let you add bookmark files from other browsers or from colleagues to your bookmarks. Imported bookmarks will attach themselves at the end of your current bookmark file. The export feature lets you save your current bookmark file as an HTML file. You can edit this file like a normal Web page. When you save your bookmark file in this fashion, you can open it as a normal Web page using the *File | Open File* menu option. Some people like to use their Web page of bookmarks as the home page or browser starting page. Netscape's bookmark files are usually stored in C:\Program Files\Netscape\users\(username)\bookmark.htm. If you want to have a number of different bookmark files, you can use Windows file re-naming process to switch the bookmark file that Netscape is currently accessing.
- You can rename bookmarks. This is especially useful if the original name is not meaningful. Netscape lets you add a description under Edit | Bookmark properties. Use this feature to provide site summaries

HINT A number of teachers have posted their own bookmarks using "Backflip." Check out these Backflip pages to find out about sites that other teachers have found useful:

http://**www.backflip.com/members/ tonkteacher/9721407** (Teacher Resource page)

http://www.backflip.com/members/ donnamh (Technology)
http://www.backflip.com/members/ bjberquist (Arts resources)
http://www.backflip.com/ members/Dragonheart/8379061 (Science)

You can also search the Backflip public folders for additional sites of interest.

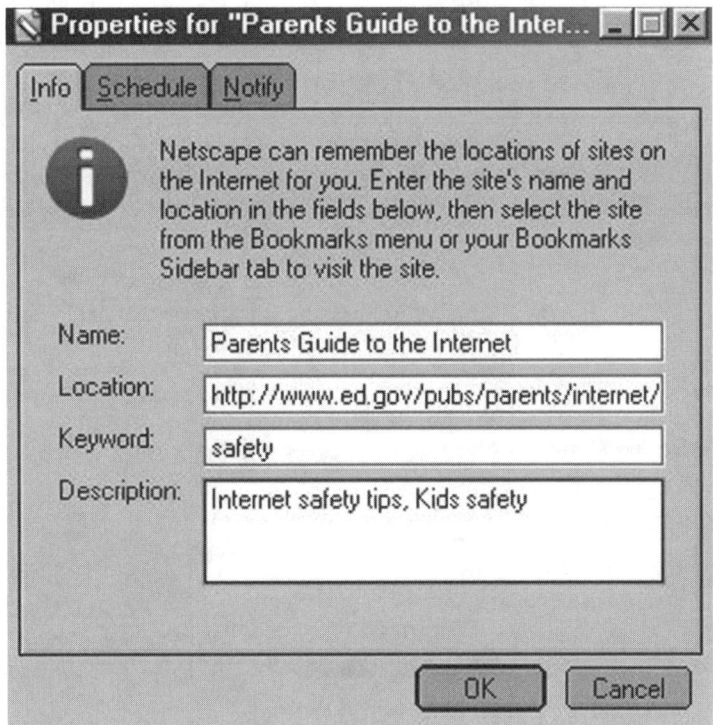

Figure 4 - 8
Netscape Bookmark Properties can to help keep bookmarks organized.

An online tutorial for teachers on using the Internet Explorer browser is available at **http://www.actden.com/IE5**. The tutorials can be printed and used offline for teacher workshops.

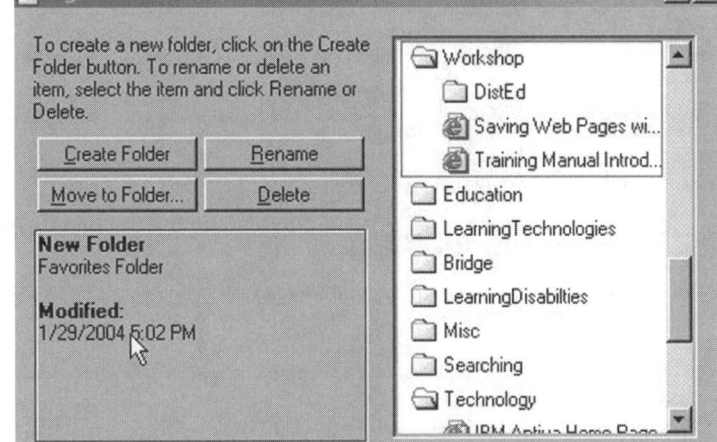

Figure 4-9
Internet Explorer lets you organize favorites in folders.

for students. Try adding a few descriptions to your existing bookmarks. Then open the bookmark file in your Web browser to see how the description is displayed.

- In Internet Explorer, use the Export Wizard under File | Import and Export to export individual bookmark folders as an HTML file that can then be opened in any Web browser. You can also use the export feature to export your bookmarks to Netscape. Use the Export feature to create a page of Web lists for class projects.
- Use Internet Explorer Quicklinks to set up quick access to dictionaries, encyclopedias and your favorite search engines. You can drag and drop links from the Address bar, use drag and drop to re-order links and use

Figure 4-10
The Opera Browser includes a drop-down search box.

HINT A number of bookmark utilities can help you manage your bookmarks. QuickLink Explorer for Windows will let you organize your bookmarks into folders and subfolders much like Windows Explorer. There is a freeware version available at **http://www. quiklinks. com**. Compass (**http://www.softgauge. com/compass**) is a similar shareware program that will let you organize bookmarks and add personal notes, outlines, and memos.

Your browser keeps track of the sites you have recently visited. Locate the "history" feature in your browser. Clicking on one of the items listed will let you quickly return to that location. While browsing, don't forget that you can bookmark your favorite locations so that you can easily revisit them at a later date.

the right mouse button to delete links. If the Links bar is not visible on your browser, click on *View|Toolbars|Links*.

- In Netscape, drag and drop the icon just to the left of the Location window to set-up a quicklink on your Personal toolbar or to set up a bookmark.
- If you use both Netscape and Internet Explorer, you can create a hot button link to your Netscape bookmarks from within IE simply by opening the file in the browser and then dragging the Web page's icon from the Address bar directly onto the Links bar.
- If you find yourself performing the same search for information again and again, try bookmarking the search results screen. Most search engines will update the search with the latest results. You can also incorporate the "URL" for a search into a student assignment.

Bookmarklets

Bookmarklets are small programs created in Javascript intended to be stored as bookmarks or quicklinks on your Personal or Links toolbar. (Javascript is a programming language used on the Web, but you can also just cut and paste available scripts so that you don't really need any programming skills to use Javascript.)

With a bookmarklet you can gain instant access to routine Internet functions such as changing a hard-to-read font or quickly accessing search options. You can even use bookmarklets to get rid of banner ads or a background that makes a Web page hard to read or set up quick access to a calculator. More than 150 bookmarklets are available for free. You can find a selection of them at **http://www.bookmarklets.com**.

Bookmarklet links are most convenient when they are stored as quicklinks. You can set up personal quicklinks in Netscape by filing the link as a bookmark in the "Personal Toolbar" folder listed in your bookmarks. In IE, just drag and drop the link onto the Links toolbar.

Find out more about how to create and use bookmarklets using the links provided at **http://www.bookmarklets.com/about/links.html**.

Tech Talk

As you explore subject trees in areas that interest you, you will undoubtedly find sites you want to return to. You can bookmark these sites, but be warned that bookmark lists can quickly become so long that you can no longer find things easily. A good strategy is to set up bookmark categories that make sense for you — e.g., Lesson Plans, Distance Education, Personal Interest. For quick filing, you can drag and drop the icon at or near the URL window directly into the folder where you want to file the bookmark. Alternatively, you can set up a "temporary" folder to collect new bookmarks for any given session. Then, at the close of the session, edit your bookmarks by moving new items into an appropriate category, establishing new headings for categories as you need them. Also take advantage of the opportunity to include a brief description of a site if your browser allows space for this on the bookmark edit screen. This will pay off later.

Searching the Web

If you have spent any time surfing the Net, you have undoubtedly already discovered that the Internet is chock-a-block full of information and useful resources for teaching. You will also have discovered that finding exactly what you are looking for can sometimes be a daunting task. One long-standing Internet joke compares the Internet to a library with 17 different card catalogs and "books" that get shuffled around every night. The Internet may be a great addition to the school library for students' research, but its lack of organization is often a source of frustration. Nevertheless, knowing how to use the Internet effectively as a tool for research is an increasingly important skill, and many teachers are now teaching their students how to find and evaluate information from this resource. Teachers also want to be able to locate useful lessons and learning materials without having to spend hours searching.

Effective Internet searching means knowing about the range of different tools available for searching and mastering techniques for developing and refining your searches.

Portal sites – getting an overview

An important part of finding what you are looking for on the Internet involves taking time to explore some of the resources that are available. There may be 40 different repositories for lesson plans on the Internet, but once you become familiar with one or two of them, you may find that that's all you need. Similarly, knowing about a handful of good resources on a subject is a significant advantage when it comes to quickly gathering material for a lesson. A good way to discover useful sites on the Internet is to browse, using a portal site as a starting point.

Portal sites (sometimes called Web directories or subject trees) allow you to explore the Internet using an organized list of categories and sub-categories. Portal sites also sometimes incorporate news services, online discussions and features that let you personalize your Internet experience. Yahoo (**www.yahoo.com**) is one of the best known Internet portal sites. Yahoo is intended to be a gateway to everything Internet. The best way to access Yahoo is using their search address: **http://search.yahoo.com**. This access point drops the flashing ads and makes it easier to find things. From the Yahoo search page you can search the entire Web or search just those sites listed in the Yahoo directory. If you search the directory only, you will get sites that have been preselected by Yahoo editors. A disadvantage to using Yahoo is that the "sponsored" results are always listed first. Sponsors have paid to have their listings go to the top of a search results screen.

Figure 4-11
Pandia Search Central
provides search helps.

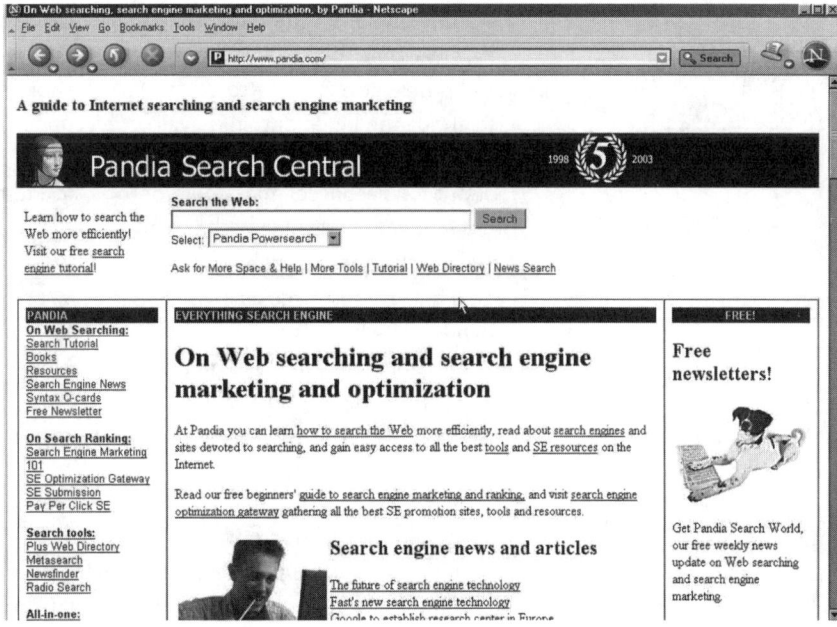

teaching tip

For an extra-quick access
to information in Yahoo's
directory, type in your keyword in the search box,
followed by an exclamation
point. For example, typing
in *lesson plans!* on Yahoo's
directory search will quickly list relevant sites on this
topic. Use Yahoo's preferences page to customize
Yahoo's results.

Yahoo has traditionally been one of the most popular Web directories.
Looksmart (**www.looksmart.com**) and Lycos (**www.lycos.com**) are two
other popular Web portals. A few less well-known directories are also very
good entry points to information on the Web. Here are some of our favorite
directories:

Pandia Plus

http://www.pandia.com/plus/index.html

Pandia is a site dedicated to fast and efficient Web searching. In addition
to providing access to a range of search tools and helpful search tutorials,
Pandia includes a Web directory based on the **Open Directory** database. The
directory is developed and managed by a large group of volunteer editors who
are experts in their areas of interest. You can browse the directory by category
or use the directory search to find some of the best sites on the Web.

Librarians' Index to the Internet

www.lii.org

Librarians at the University of Berkeley monitor the Internet and select
the best Web sites for research. The site does not provide an extensive list of
sites, but it does offer a reliable and efficient guide to good research sources.

Always "surf" with a purpose. If you are a newcomer to the Internet, it can be valuable for you to spend some time just exploring to get an idea about the kinds of things available on the Net. Always be on the lookout for resources that could be of value in your teaching. When you find something interesting, print a page from the resource as a visual reminder of what's there. File the sheet in a binder, and make an annotation on the page about how you might use the resource in your teaching. When you print from your browser, the URL for the page should automatically appear in the upper right corner of the page, so you won't lose track of where you found the resource.

At some point you might also want to create a printed binder of Web pages as a "where to look" file for students doing research on the Net.

HINT If you are interested in resources for a particular country, try one of the World Yahoos, such as **http://www.yahoo. ca**, which is a Yahoo page listing Canadian resources. There are Yahoo sites for Canada, Australia, France, Germany, Korea, Japan, and the United Kingdom and Ireland. Some of these can be a great source for foreign-language reading material. You will find links to each of these by scrolling to the bottom of the Yahoo starting page.

HINT Yahooligans is a Web guide for kids. It is a good place to browse or search for kid-safe sites. **http://www. yahooligans.com/tg/ index.html**.

Another good list of Web sites and online activities for kids can be found at the BBC Schools site at **http://www.bbc.co.uk/ schools**.

About.com

http://www.about.com

About.com is the ultimate "people-friendly" Web portal. It uses humans to organize resources and present information on a broad range of topics including arts, computers, education, homework help and travel. About.com doesn't just provide links to sites, it also offers background articles, online discussions and other special features. This is a good site, but watch for advertising pop-up windows in the background. These will slow down your computer. (Tip: The Opera browser preferences include a setting to filter out pop-up windows.)

Argus Clearinghouse

http://www.clearinghouse.net

This is another good place to start browsing. What's different about this source is that it is really a collection of subject guides to the Internet. When you want to get a good overview of what's available in a given subject area, the Clearinghouse is the place to start. Individual guides are put together by subject experts who identify, evaluate, and describe Internet information on a given topic. You will not find a guide on every topic, but there are hundreds of guides available and the guides themselves include extensive links to information.

Beaucoup

http://www.beaucoup.com/1geneng.html

Beaucoup is a directory of Internet search engines and directories. It includes links and brief descriptions of 1200+ indexing sites and is a good place to find out about many specialized search engines, including international search engines.

HINT For links to a number of search engine guides and tutorials, check out Internet searching at the Librarians' Index to the Internet, **http://lii.org**.

Education Portal Sites

While broad portal sites such as Yahoo are useful for general exploration of the Internet, using a site focused on education is a quicker way to explore useful education resources. A directory site that focuses on a specific topic such as education or health is sometimes called a vertical portal. Some boards or districts have established education portals and some are set up by commercial or government agencies. Here are some examples:

Education World

http://www.education-world.com

Education World offers a huge selection of resources. Resources include reviews of education sites, subject resources for curriculum planning, lesson plans, information on grants and funding sources, and articles on many special themes such as technology and classroom managment. The Education World search engine will help you locate resources of interest.

Awesome Library

http://www.awesomelibrary.org

Carefully reviewed education resources, including their pick of the top 5%. You can enter the site as a teacher, kid, teen, parent, librarian or member of the community. This is a well-organized site which includes standards, lesson plans, and resources for a range of special topics, including World Peace, the Environment, Terrorism and Current Events.

HINT Looking for new ideas or a solution to a problem? Search in Google Groups. Google's archive of newsgroup discussions includes a wealth of practical information. Great for finding travel tips and answers to technical questions.

Blue Web'N

http://www.kn.pacbell.com/wired/bluewebn/index.cfm

"Blue Ribbon sites for learning." The site offers a searchable database of about 1000 of the most useful sites for Internet learning. Sites are categorized by subject area, audience, and type (lessons, activities, projects, resources, references, and tools). This is a very good place to browse without getting overwhelmed. You can also subscribe to the Blue Web'N Weekly Update.

Canada's SchoolNet

http://www.schoolnet.ca/home/e/resources

This site offers links to 5000+ curriculum resources. The resources listed have been selected and reviewed by educators. At this site you can also find out about current SchoolNet sponsored activities and programs and links to Canadian schools online.

Figure 4-12
Education World is an
example of an education
portal site.

Figure 4-13
BBC has developed a
Web Guide for schools.

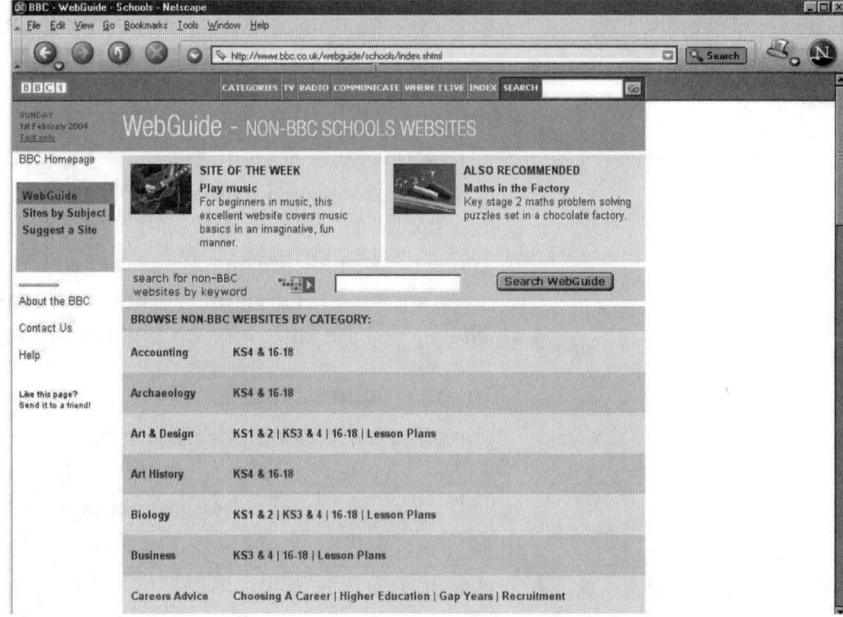

Eisenhower National Clearinghouse

http:// www.enc.org

This is a major portal site for math and science. It provides access to a huge collection of teaching materials, including lesson plans and activities, Web links, print materials and software. Search or browse for classroom resources. All of the resources are described. Covers Kindergarten through high school. The site also covers general education topics, educational technology and integrated approaches.

Kathy Schrock's Guide for Educators

http://school.discovery.com/teachers/index.html

This award-winning site for teachers includes curriculum links, teacher helps as well as links to news sources, magazines and reference materials for teachers and librarians. Teacher helps include access to slide shows for teaching, rubrics and professional development links.

SCORE

http://score.rims.k12.ca.us/index.html

This is an example of a portal site that has been set for California schools. The site lists resources and lessons by grade level for language arts, mathematics, science, and history and social science. Resources are Web links and example activities provided for many areas of the curriculum. There are discussion groups, examples of virtual projects and a newsletter that teachers can subscribe to.

Search engines

Subject trees and guides are good for browsing and for finding general reference information, but the best way to find something specific is to use a search engine. Search engines are tools that let you search for information using keywords that describe your topic. If you were looking for information on a specific topic, such as El Niño, it would probably take you a long time to find something on this by browsing through various weather sites, but you could quickly locate information using a search engine such as Google or Alta Vista." A number of search engines also let you search for images, newspaper articles, and audio files. Northern Light lets you search a special collection of magazine articles as well as Web sites.

Knowing how to search for information on the Internet is an essential skill for teachers and students. Teachers need to learn about different Internet search engines and how to use them effectively in order to teach their students how to use these tools. Both teachers and students can make

The Southern Regional Education Board has published a set of guidelines for selecting commercial Web portals — some of which charge for access to their activities and resources. You can obtain a copy of the guide in PDF format at **http://www. sreb.org/programs/ EdTech/pubs/PDF/ WebPortals.asp**.

Tech Talk

Search engines use a "crawler" or "spider" to scan the Web and build a database of Web documents and addresses. Crawlers use Web links to navigate from one document to the next. When you enter a keyword into a search engine, the search engine retrieves information from its database. Some search engines will index every word in a document, while others index the document title only or introductory text. Search engines use different techniques, called algorithms, for ranking documents and some search engines will be more up-to-date than others. Always consult a second search engine or metasearch engine if you are not successful at finding what you're looking for when using your favorite search engine.

HINT The BBC (British Broadcasting Corporation) has developed a WebGuide for Schools. The Guide lists top Web sites in a range of curriculum areas and includes links to lesson plan. Access the guide at **http://www.bbc.co.uk/webguide/education/schools/index.html**.

the best use of their time on the Internet once they have mastered a few basic search techniques.

The first step is to become familiar with a number of different search engines. Search engines differ from one another in terms of how comprehensive their coverage of the Internet is and how they rank results. The best search engines offer broad coverage and are successful at placing the most relevant results near the top of the list. Sample some of the following search engines. Which is your favorite?

Google

http://www.google.com

This is currently one of the most popular search engines. Google is a favorite because it provides fast and highly accurate results. Google uses a "link analysis" technique to rank results. Google places particular emphasis to authoritative sites, such as sites from educational or research agencies. If you have selected your search terms carefully, you will often find just what you are looking for at the top of Google's results screen. Google is also a good choice because it is one of the largest search engines and it incorporates the ability to search for news, images and documents available in Adobe Acrobat's PDF format. (We discuss PDF files in Chapter 8.) If you retrieve a Web page that is no longer posted on the Web, you can use Google's cache feature to view an archived copy of the page. Google offers a link to the **Open Directory** when you want to browse.

AlltheWeb

http://www.alltheweb.com

AlltheWeb has one of the largest indexes on the Web (2 billion+ documents), and is also one of the freshest. Its entire database is updated every 9–12 days. AlltheWeb also "spiders" 3000 news sites 12 times a day, which means that it is possible to retrieve news stories that are less than one hour old. In addition to searching Web pages and news sources, AlltheWeb also searches for pictures, videos, MP3 files (audio), and software. Advanced features include the ability to search for results in any one of 46 languages and to limit your search results to pages that have been recently updated.

AltaVista

http://www.altavista.com

This search engine has been around for a long time. While it currently is not quite as large as some of the other search engines, it can still be useful for precision searching. For example, in the Advanced Search Mode you can use Boolean (AND, OR, AND NOT and NEAR) searching and specify which word to place emphasis on for sorting results. AltaVista offers quick

Figure 4-14
Ask Jeeves for kids lets students type in questions to find what they are looking for.

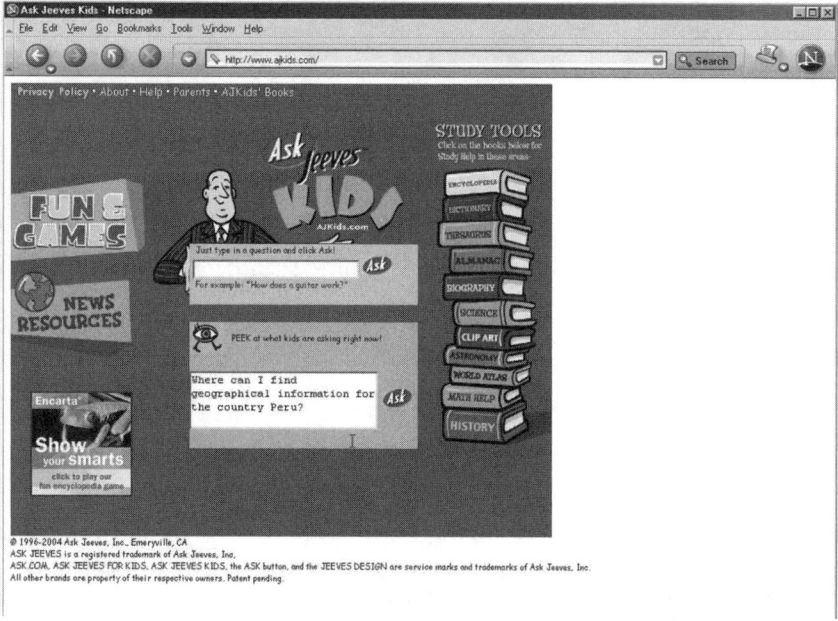

Figure 4-15
Ixquick is an example of a meta-search engine.

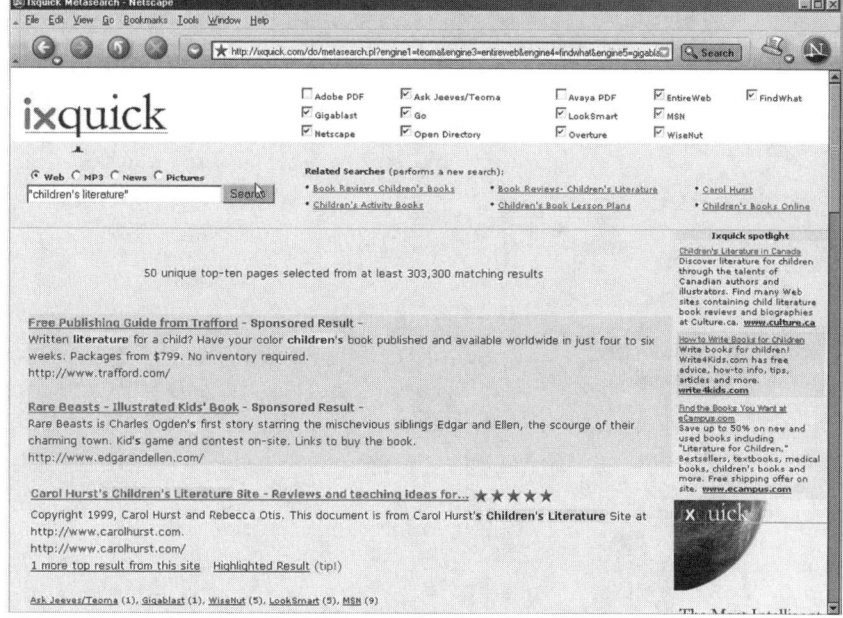

access to the Babblefish translation tool (**http://babelfish.altavista.com**) where you can copy text or type in a URL for access to a translation into your choice of languages.

WiseNut

http://www.wisenut.com

WiseNut is a newer entry into the search engine arena. It aims to rival established search engines in terms of size and accuracy and it's off to a good start. WiseNut offers "Wiseguides" which are categories semantically related to the keywords in your search. Wiseguide categories can help students refine their queries, particularly when broad search terms or words with multiple meanings are used.

Ask Jeeves

http://www.ask.com

Ask Jeeves combines technology and human intelligence to select top sites for locating information. Ask Jeeves attempts to answer questions rather than simply list Web sites. If you type in a question such as "Where can I learn about endangered species?", Jeeves will bring you directly to a Web page or site deemed to be the best place to find the information. Jeeves will also help you refine your search using variations on your questions and prompts. The question regarding endangered species will provide question prompts for information about specific endangered animals. Using Ask Jeeves, students can often efficiently find what they are searching for without having to sort through an extensive list of search results. Ask Jeeves for Kids (**http://www.ajkids.com**) is a "kid-safe" search engine for younger students.

Metasearch tools

Metasearch engines let you submit a query to several search engines at the same time and they consolidate the results. This can be useful when you don't get successful results using a single search engine. Some people like to use a metasearch engine all the time, but frequently this is not as satisfactory as selecting a top search engine and learning to use its advanced features. A disadvantage to using metasearch tools is that you are seldom able to refine a search to the same extent as you can with an individual search engine. Special features such as language filters and lists of related keywords may not be available. In addition, metasearch engines may first display the results that are retrieved most quickly and these may not be the most relevant results. Try the metasearch tools on page 126 to discover how they compare to your favorite search engine.

HINT A good source for learning all about search engines and search techniques is Pandia's Search Resources page at **http://www.pandia.com/resources/index.html**. Check out Pandia's Q-cards which provide quick summaries of search syntax for several popular search engines.

HINT To find out how search engines compare in terms of size, check out the Search Engine Watch report on Search Engine Sizes (**http://www.searchenginewatch.com/reports/sizes.html**.) A large search engine, such as Google or Fast, is particularly good for finding information on unusual or hard-to-find topics, but a small search engine may be more selective and provide equally good results for more common topics.

HINT Choose the best search for your information need at **http://www.noodletools.com/debbie/literacies/information/5locate/adviceengine.html**.

Vivisimo

http://vivisimo.com

This metasearch tool automatically organizes documents into meaningful groups. This can help you narrow a search and get more relevant hits.

Ixquick

www.ixquick.com

Ixquick awards each site in a results list a star for every search engine that placed the site in its top ten results. This is a quick way to determine which sites will likely be most relevant. Ixquick includes search options for news, MP3 files and pictures.

EZ2Find

http://ez2www.com

This metasearch engine combines results from a number of top ranked search engines and directories with easy-to-read search results. EZ2Find uses clustering to help narrow your search results.

SurfWax

http://www.surfwax.com

SurfWax displays a long list of search results on the left side of the screen and provides a quick preview of results (SiteSnaps) on the right. This split-screen approach can be confusing, but some people find it to be an easy way to scan results. You can also save and share your search results using SurfWax.

Magazine search

A normal search engine will not find magazine articles. Here are two sources you can use to search for articles that have been published in magazines and can be accessed over the Web.

FindArticles

http://www.findarticles.com

FindArticles.com is an extensive archive of magazine articles from more than 300 magazines and journals. Although URL changes at the site, user only has to type in **www.findarticles.com**.

MagPortal.com

http://magportal.com

Helps you to find individual magazine articles from all over the Web. You can also use MagPortal to keep abreast of current articles in education or another area of interest.

Search for lesson plans at the University of Illinois Collaborative Lesson Archive (**http://faldo.atmos.uiuc.edu/CLA/index.html**). This archive is used by thousands of teachers who share their classroom lessons. The archive contains lessons for all grade levels and subjects.

Desktop Search Tools
A number of useful desktop tools can help you streamline Internet searching.

Copernic is a downloadable desktop search program which can be accessed from within your browser. The program allows you to query a range of search engines at once (including many specialty search engines), customize results and save searches. You can download a basic version of Copernic for free at **www.copernic.com**.

Lexibot is a similar product. It includes a feature that lets you publish results lists as Web pages. Lexibot is available from **www. lexibot.com**.

Alexa is a popular "surfing companion." When Alexa is activated it will accompany you as you surf the Web and identify sites that are similar to the Web page that is currently displayed in your browser. If you are on a page containing environmental information, Alexa will give you a list of additional sites you can visit to learn about the environment. Alexa also provides one-click access to a range of search engines. Download Alexa from **http://info.alexa.com**.

ELibrary

http://ask.elibrary.com

This site provides access to magazine articles, newswires, maps and other useful sources, but you need a subscription to access these resources. A seven-day free trial is available.

You may also want to check with your local library to find out if they allow magazine searches over the Internet as a service. Many libraries have purchased subscriptions to indexing services with full text articles. In some cases, these resources can be searched over the Web if you are a registered user of the library.

Hints for searching the Internet

Finding exactly the information you are looking for on the Internet requires knowledge and persistence, but knowing how to search will help you use this resource as a learning tool. Here are some points to be aware of:

- **There are a number of different search engines**. Some provide full-text searches of Web pages, while others may index only the first 20 words on a page. That's why search engines sometimes yield wildly different results. Pick two or three search engines and learn to use them well. Be sure to explore the advanced searching techniques and make use of special features, such as the ability to search for news or to save searches. If you don't find what you are looking for using one search engine, try another, or try one of the metasearch tools.
- **Choose keywords carefully.** Rather than searching for general concepts, use concrete words that are likely to appear on a site and try to be as specific as possible. Search for "Labrador Retriever" rather than dogs. If you are having trouble identifying keywords try writing your question down and underlining main concepts. You can also list possible synonyms. Most search engines let you string synonyms together either just by listing terms one after the other or by using OR between the terms. Avoid using upper-case letters — unless you are searching for a proper name.
- **Learn to use search engine syntax.** Using a phrase (in quotes) and/or entering additional keywords using a + sign before individual terms is an excellent way to narrow your search. For example, if you were looking for travel information on Montreal and used only the keyword *Montreal*, you would find many Web pages that had nothing to do with travel. If, however, you included the phrase "tourist information" in your search, you would have a better chance of finding exactly what you were looking for. Use quotes to enter a phrase. Here's what your search should look

Figure 4-16
GEM is an example of a database on the Web. It lists thousands of high quality lesson plans and Web sites. To search GEM you must go to the site at **http://the gateway.org/welcome.html**.

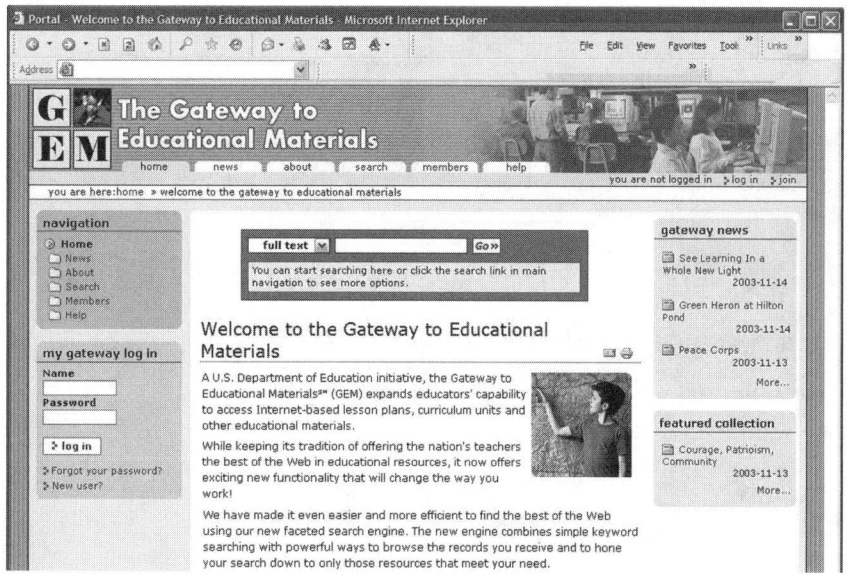

like: *Montreal* +*"tourist information"* (Note that there is no space between the plus sign and word or phrase that follows.)

You can also use "wedge words" to narrow a search. Wedge words are terms that designate the type of resource you are looking for. Here's an example: "Lord of the Flies" + "lesson plan." In this example, "lesson plan" is used as a "wedge word." Tutorial, rubric, and template are other applicable wedge words.

- **Invisible Web.** Information that is stored in databases rather than as Web pages is known as the "invisible web." This is because search engine crawlers are not able to locate this type of information. Generally, you have to go to a site to get information from a database that is available there. For example, you may need to go to a "white pages" directory such as Infospace to search for someone's e-mail address or connect to Amazon.com to search for a book in its database. A few gateway services pass searches through to targeted sites containing database information. The Invisible Web (**http://www.invisible-web.net**) provides a browsable (Yahoo-like) directory of searchable databases that can help you find hidden content on the Web. Some of the databases are fairly specialized (like the Tasmanian Index of Community Organizations); however, from this site you can also access a number of general interest sources, such as news and magazine archives, discussion databases and mailing list archives, legal databases, product reviews, medical databases and government information sources. The Invisible Web covers over 10,000 databases. ProFusion

HINT Looking for a particular reference on a very long page of information? Most browsers offer a tool that will search for a word on the page that is currently displayed. On Netscape, for example, the Find button on the toolbar performs this function.

(**www.profusion.com**) is a metasearch tool from the same company that has developed the Invisible Web. It permits direct searching of about 500 database sources. To learn more about search tools for the Invisible Web, check out the Weblens search portal at **http://www. weblens.org/invisible.html**.

CHOOSING THE RIGHT SEARCHING TOOL

Search Engines		
AlltheWeb	www.alltheweb.com	Extremely fast with relevant results. Try fast for multimedia and news searching.
AltaVista	www.altavista.com	Fast and comprehensive. Investigate the advanced search for precision results.
Ask Jeeves	www.ask.com	A user-friendly search engine that lets you use natural language queries.
Google	www.google.com	Comprehensive with highly accurate results. Currently a favorite among academic researchers.
WiseNut	http://www.wisenut.com	Includes links to resource collection from experts.

MetaSearch Tools		
Ixquick	www.ixquick.com	Use a star system to designate the top ranking results from engines searched.
Moonmist	www.moonmist.co.uk	Use this metasearch engine to access data from U.K. and international search sources.
Proteus	www.thrall.org/proteus.html	This search page lets you easily move between search engines without having to re-enter your keywords.
SurfWax	http://www.surfwax.com	"Site snaps" let you preview site contents in advance of loading a complete page.
Vivísimo	vivisimo.com	A popular metasearch engine that uses "results clustering" to group related documents.

Subject Directories		
Librarians' Index to the Internet	**www.lii.org**	Small but selective directory of resources selected by librarians.
Looksmart	**www.looksmart.com**	Good source for popular interest topics — travel, entertainment, etc.
OpenDirectory	**www.dmoz.com**	A directory created by subject experts. Also accessible from Google and Pandia.
Yahoo	**www.yahoo.com**	Best known directory. There are versions available for specific countries (e.g., yahoo.ca for Canada).
Yahooligans	**www.yahooligans.com**	A Web portal for children and young adults.

Education Portals		
Ask Eric	**http://ericir.syr.edu**	Access to ERIC Clearinghouse information and links to related Internet sites.
Community Learning Network	**www.cln.org**	An excellent annotated list of education resources.
Education Virtual Library	**http://www.csu.edu.au/education/library.html**	An education portal. Includes a list of education resources from many different countries.
Education World	**www.educaton-world.com**	An education portal. Safe search for teachers and schools.
Eisenhower National Clearinghouse	**http:// www.enc.org**	A major gateway to mathematics and science resources.
Kathy Schrock's Guide for Educators	**http://school.discovery.com/teachers/index.html**	Gateway to many useful education resources.

Searching for People		
Canada 411	**www.canada411.ca**	Canadian source for phone numbers, e-mail, etc.
Infospace	**www.infospace.com**	Find phone numbers and e-mail addresses and city information.
Switchboard	**www.switchboard.com**	Find people and businesses, maps and city guides.
The Ultimates	**www.theultimates.com**	Phone directories, travel and metasearching for e-mail addresses.

Beaucoup	**www.beaucoup.com**	Beaucoup will help you locate many specialty search engines.
MapQuest	**www.mapquest.com**	Search for street maps and driving directions.
My Virtual Reference Desk	**www.refdesk.com**	Search for dictionaries, quotations and factual information.
News Index	**www.newsindex.com**	Search for current news stories using this news-only search engine.
U.S. Department of Education	**http://www.ed.gov** This URL gets users to a search screen	Search for legislation, statistics, research, grants and links to other education databases.
The Gateway	**http://www.thegateway.org**	Search for educational materials.
Lesson Plan Search	**http://www.lessonplansearch.com**	Search for lesson plans.

- **Although there is abundant information on the Internet, not everything is readily or freely available.** It helps to have a sense of Internet resources — universities, government and research institutions, schools, museums, community groups and many commercial organizations provide information over the Internet. However, when information has been painstakingly gathered, or when it falls under the realm of traditional publishing, only sample files will likely be available, or the material will be available for a cost. *The Encyclopedia Britannica* is on the Internet, for example, but you must pay to access it. Spending time cruising the Internet and exploring resources such as Yahoo will help you become familiar with available resources.

- **Remember that one of the very best resources on the Internet is other people.** If you're searching for a specific piece of information, sometimes participants on a listserv or in a newsgroup can be a great help. The FAQs (Frequently Asked Questions) from some of the discussion groups can be useful as well. You can find pointers to these at Yahoo.

A sampling of educational Web sites

The number of Web sites on the Internet is growing at an astonishing rate. In addition to the great number of sites that are of professional interest to educators, more and more schools are developing their own sites on the World Wide Web. The Web has metamorphosed teachers and students alike into successful cyberjournalists. Appendix B contains many curriculum resources on the Internet, and listed below are some particularly noteworthy Web sites that you can sample as a way of familiarizing yourself with the wealth of educational resources on the Internet.

Armadillo This directory of WWW educational resources has been developed for elementary and secondary school teachers and students. It lists resource materials that teachers can quickly access for lesson plans or as supplementary educational resources for students.

> **http://www.rice.edu/armadillo/Rice/Resources/reshome.html**

Artsedge An outstanding resource for arts information, with many links to learning resources.

> **http://artsedge.kennedy-center.org**

AskERIC Virtual Library Here you'll find lesson plans, satellite images, and links to many other educational resources.

> **http://ericir.syr.edu**

A to Z Teacher Stuff Lots of original lesson plans, and more than 50 teaching themes, as well as resources for building thematic lessons, including seasonal activities. This resource also offers teacher tips, discussion boards, articles, links to educational sites, and printable worksheets.

> **http://atozteacherstuff.com**

Awesome Library for Teachers, Students, and Parents With 10,000 sources, it would be easy to become lost at this site, but there is a helpful alphabetical index and a search engine to help you find things. Many of the resources include brief descriptions. Comprehensiveness and good organization combine to make this a valuable resource for teachers.

> **http://www.neat-schoolhouse.org/awesome.html**

Bell South Education Gateway Offers a quick search for Lesson plans, homework helpers and curriculum aids. ThinkQuest, the popular student Web site development project, is a Bell South sponsored project. Find out about other interactive learning and e-trips at this site.

> **http://K12.bellsouth.com**

Berit's Best Sites for Children This site points to some excellent resources for elementary and secondary school students aged 5 to 14. The site is organized by general topics that are easy to relate to curriculum areas, including Animals, Astronomy, Dinosaurs, Environment, as well as pointers to elementary schools on the Web.

> **http://www.beritsbest.com**

Figure 4-17
Blue Web'N Homepage.

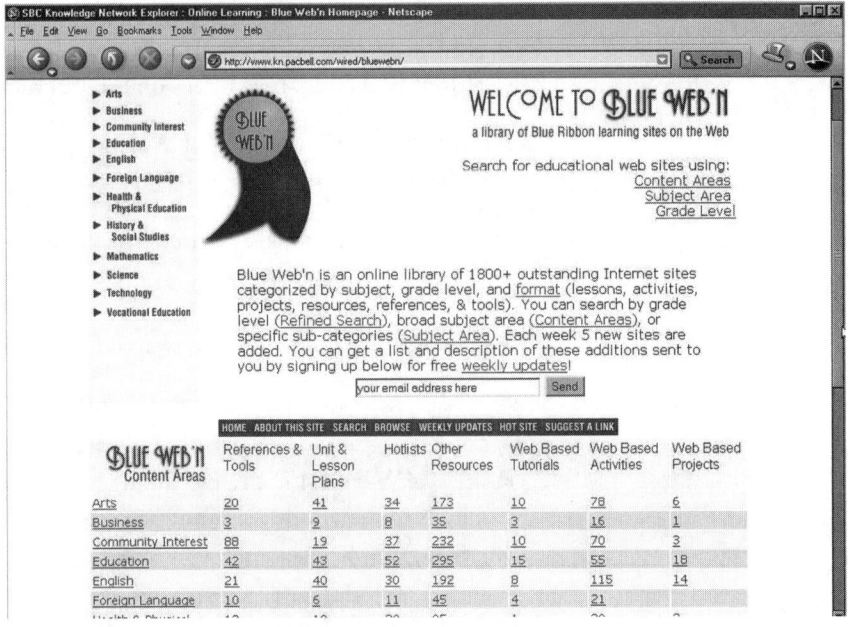

Blue Web'N Learning Applications Sponsored by Pacific Bell, this site offers an excellent collection of curriculum-related lessons, activities, projects, and resources. You can browse the content table or search for a topic. You can enter your e-mail address to receive updates.

http://www.kn.pacbell.com/wired/bluewebn

Busy Teachers' WebSite This site was developed with two goals in mind: to offer teachers direct-source materials, lesson plans, and classroom activities; and to provide an enjoyable and rewarding experience for the teacher who is learning to use the Internet.

http://www.ceismc.gatech.edu/busyt

Cisco Educational Archive Links to the NASA SpaceLink, Frog Dissection, and more. This site has a *Virtual Schoolhouse* with a meta-library of elementary and secondary school Internet links. The Classroom area at this site offers educational links by subject. The *What's New* feature at the archive is a useful way to track current resources, and *Schoolhouse NOC* provides information on school networking.

http://sunsite.unc.edu/cisco/edu-arch.html

Classroom Connect This is an exceptionally good resource for teachers looking for helpful information on the Web. There is a searchable index of educational links as well as a resource station of online materials for educators, and a teacher contact database. Classroom Connect's Connected University offers online courses and learning activities for teachers. Some areas of Classroom Connect require a subscription to access.

http://www.classroom.net

Community Learning Network Contains a well-developed set of links to many K–12 resources from the British Columbia Ministry of Education. Highly recommended.

http://www.cln.org

Connections+ Internet resources, lesson plans and learning activities for K–12. Includes arts, social studies, language arts and maths and sciences — linked with corresponding subject-area content standards.

http://www.mcrel.org/lesson-plans/index.asp

Cool Sites for Kids These sites have been selected and evaluated by the American Library Association. Categories include *Reading and Writing*, *Facts and Learning* and *Just for Fun*.

http://www.ala.org/alsc/children.links.html

CyberDewey If you long for the Internet to be as carefully organized as your local public library, try a visit to this site. The traditional Dewey Decimal library classification system has been used to structure the links.

http://www.anthus.com/CyberDewey/CyberDewey.html

Children's Literature Web Guide An excellent resource for elementary school teachers. The focus here is on children's literature. One teacher states, "This may be the single most useful site for elementary teachers that I have found to date."

http://www.ucalgary.ca/~dkbrown/index.html

Education World Another comprehensive set of links. Here you can search a database of over 50,000 sites. Features include K–12 Schools Online, Regional Resources, Employment Listings, and Events Calendar.

http://www.education-world.com

Educational Hotlists at the Franklin Institute You'll find many valuable resources at the Franklin Institute Science Museum. The hotlists identify Web sites of value to educators. Items are added to the hotlists every day, so you may want to consult this source often.

http://sln.fi.edu/tfi/hotlists/hotlists.html

Eisenhower Clearinghouse for Math and Science A repository for elementary and secondary mathematics and science instructional materials funded by the U.S. Department of Education.

> http://www.enc.org

Exploratorium From the Palace of Fine Arts in San Francisco, this site includes hundreds of interactive exhibits on broad subject areas such as color, sound, music and emotion. Elementary and secondary students will find this a fascinating site to explore. Includes a monthly selection of the best science and art sites.

> http://www.exploratorium.edu

Frank Potter's Science Gems Popular resource for science activities and resources by category, subcategory and grade level. Approximately 2,000 resources are available.

> http://www.sciencegems.com

Gateway to Educational Materials (GEM) U.S. Department of Education sponsored site where you can search for curriculum-based Web resources by subject and by grade level.

> http://www.thegateway.org

History/Social Studies Web Site for K–12 Teachers The focus for this site is to encourage the use of the Web for learning with a particular emphasis on history and social sciences. Resources are included for American, European and non-Western history and there are sections for diverse populations, including Asian-American, African-American, Native American, and Hispanic.

> http://www.execpc.com/~dboals/boals.html

Internet Public Library You will find a wealth of material here. There are special sections devoted to children, teens and online reference sources. This is also the place to access online magazines, newspapers and books. The "Reading Zone" includes a "story hour" and links to online picture books.

> http://www.ipl.org

Addison School District This is an example of a school district Web gateway. It includes links to Internet resources linked to curriculum areas and grade levels, links to sources for lesson plans, and links to student search engines and other resources. School and district sponsored Web sites are among the best sites to visit because resources are carefully reviewed before being listed and there is no commercial "agenda" determining what's included. Visit school district Web sites in your own state or province.

> http://www.asd4.org

Figure 4-18
Middle School.net.

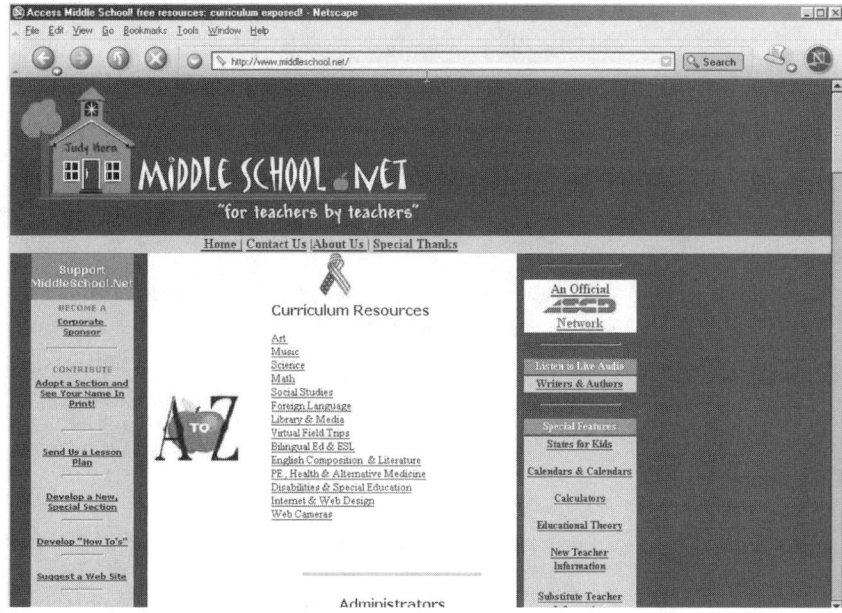

Middle School.net Developed and managed by Judy Horn, an instructional technology specialist with the Governor's Best Practice Center of the Virginia Department of Education, and sponsored in part by ASCD (Association for Supervision and Curriculum Development). Links at this site are carefully selected and the site is very easy to browse.

> **http://www.middleschool.net**

Middle Web Focus on middle school reform with links to many resources for teaching strategies, assessment, professional development, and more.

> **http://www.middleweb.com**

NASA Spacelink Very good resource for science information and projects.

> **http://spacelink.msfc.nasa.gov**

NCRTEC (North Central Regional Technology in Education Consortium). Includes a lesson planner template, a selection of customizable rubrics and a search for pictures that can be used in the classroom. Visit other regional educational technology centers at

> **http://rtec.org**

New England College Ed Links This is an ideal place to locate curriculum resources on the Web. It also includes Teaching and Pre-Service Teaching Resources. Sites listed include helpful annotations and ratings. A

Frameworks and Standards area contains links to organizations specializing in standards or to the frameworks of various states.

http://www.necedlinks.org

Physics Lecture Demonstrations A must if you are interested in physics. From astronomy to magnetism to waves, this site covers it all.

http://www.mip.berkeley.edu/physics/physics.html

Pitsco's Launch to Educational Resources The Resources for Educators Link at this site provides a comprehensive set of links to a wide range of sources that will interest educators, including funding, projects, technology plans, and special-education links.

http://www.pitsco.com

Quest: NASA K–12 Internet Initiative One of a number of NASA educational resources on the Web, this site is intended to help elementary and secondary teachers fully utilize the Internet as a basic tool for learning. A good resource for information about classroom projects, grants, and international projects such as MayaQuest. Access *Bring the Internet into Your Classroom* to find out more about what's available.

http://quest.arc.nasa.gov

Ron MacKinnon's Educational Bookmarks This is a great place to browse.

http://juliet.stfx.ca/people/stu/x94emj/educt1.htm

SchoolNet Canadian-based educational resource with a wealth of useful content, including links to Canadian provincial education networks.

http://www.schoolnet.ca

Science Learning Network Science activities and more. An online resource for teachers, students, schools and museums focusing on inquiry science education. Use this resource to visit Exporatorium sites, and browse the archives for Inquiry Almanac, an older, but excellent online resource from the Franklin Institute. The site also provides links to education hotlists for science topics, as well as literature, careers, schools on the Web, and technology helps.

http://www.sln.org

Teachers Connect Includes a gateway to educational materials, "Tried and True" Web resources, best practices and professional resources. This is one of many state-sponsored teacher sites. Visit your own state, provincial or regional Internet education gateway. You can access many state education agencies at **http://www.ed.gov/Programs/bastmp/SEA.htm**.

http://www.teachers-connect.net/

Teacher's Edition Online This site features lesson plans, a teacher's forum as well as instructions for subscribing to the online newsletter.

http://www.teachnet.com

Teachers.net Teacher portal site and a place for teachers to meet online. Teachers.net sponsors teacher message boards and weekly live text-chat meetings. Lesson plans are regularly submitted by teachers.

http://www.teachers.net

Teacher Tap Professional development resource for teachers with helps for technology integration. Starting points, thematic topics, lesson plans and teacher tools.

http://eduscapes.com/tap

The Teachers Guide Free software, clip art and print outs. There are also sections for students with special needs, new teachers and job links. A free e-mail service is available.

http://www.theteachersguide.com

UCI Science Education Programs Office An excellent collection of science and math resources on the Web.

http://www-sci.lib.uci.edu

WebSites and Resources for Teachers A collection of sites and resources for classroom use developed by professors of elementary education.

http://www.csun.edu/~vceed009

You Can This is a "must-visit" for Grades 3 to 6 (ages 8 to 12).

http://www.beakman.com

Personal favorites

Use this form to make notes on your own favorite Web sites.

Site: _____

http:// _____

Notes: _____

_____

Site: _____

http:// _____

Notes: _____

_____

Site: _____

http:// _____

Notes: _____

_____

Site: _____

http:// _____

Notes: _____

_____

Site: _____

http:// _____

Notes: _____

_____

Site: _____

http:// _____

Notes: _____

_____

Site: _____

http:// _____

Notes: _____

_____

Summing up

In this chapter we have presented topics to help you become familiar with the Web environment and introduced a number of sources that are particularly useful for teachers. While knowing how to find information on the Net is an important stepping stone to learning, the real goal is to use the Net in a meaningful way in the classroom. In the next chapter, we will discuss practical techniques and resources that you can use to integrate the use of the Web with your goals as a teacher.

5
Chapter

Bringing the World Wide Web into the Classroom

"Technology is useful as students construct meaning. While [some] contend that the student-teacher relationship is at education's core, I would contend that it is the student-meaning relationship that is at education's core, and that both technology and faculty are tools to build that relationship."

— Diane Walton, Ph.D. Candidate University of Oregon Chronicle of Higher Education Colloquy (posted 1/19/98, 3:10 p.m., E.S.T.)
http://chronicle.com/colloquy/98/skeptics/21.htm

Once you have become confident about using the Web yourself, you will undoubtedly begin to think about some of the ways in which the Web could be used for student learning. In the first three chapters, we provided an overview of the kinds of student projects that use the Web as a learning resource and noted some of the things to think about as you are planning your own projects. In this chapter we will look at several different models for projects that you can adapt for your classroom and we will provide ideas for introducing your students to using the Web as a research tool.

Chapter goals

- ■ **To provide sample exercises to introduce students to the Web**
- ■ **To provide guidelines for evaluating and citing online resources**
- ■ **To offer some examples of Web-based student research projects**
- ■ **To provide a range of ideas for curriculum-based projects**
- ■ **To introduce WebQuests as a model for curriculum-based projects**

The Project Ideas for student activities outlined in this chapter are of three general types.

The *first* are activities to introduce your students to a Web browser and to show them how to find things on the Internet. It is essential that students know how to go about finding the information they need for reports and assignments. This is similar to learning how to use a card catalog to find information in a library. Students will need to know how to search the Net using LookSmart or some other search engine. The Project Ideas that follow contain specific lessons to help students master these skills.

HINT
**Teaching and Learning
on the WWW**
http://www.mcli.dist.
maricopa.edu/tl

Maricopa Center for
Learning & Instruction
(MCLI) has collected over
500 examples of Web
resources for learning. At
this site you can search
for examples of learning
activities ranging from
sources to supplement a
specific lesson to complete
courses available on the
Web.

Learning how to navigate the Web can be spread over several lessons. Use your judgment about how much time to spend on navigating activities and which features of the browser will be the most useful to your students. For example, a basic skill would be knowing how to use browser buttons to navigate, but saving a file or viewing source information are skills that can be learned later.

A *second* category of Project Ideas shows students how to use the Internet to complement print-based information for classroom projects. For the most part, the World Wide Web can help teachers greatly extend the research that students do for projects and reports. A study of earthquakes, for example, can extend beyond the culling of print materials in the library to accessing online weather research stations, news reports, and even special sites set up for reporting on earthquakes.

The wealth of resources on the Internet helps students gain skill in evaluating and organizing information. These extensive resources also provide an ideal context for group work. One goal in such a project might be to learn something about earthquakes, but more importantly, the objective is to learn how to locate, sift through, and organize a body of information. We will introduce some valuable Internet research sources such as museums and news media. Being able to evaluate information from the Internet is an important research skill.

Figure 5-1
High School Hub is a good starting point for student research.

Many museums, government agencies, and news organizations have compiled re-sources that you can simply download and use in the classroom. Lots of educational Web sites will point to these resources. Also, check out these sources for lessons plans:

AskEric at
http://www.askeric.org/Virtual/ Lessons

The lesson collection at the Awesome Library for Teachers, Students and

Parents at
http://www.awesomelibrary.org

Discovery School of K–12 lesson plans at
http://discoveryschool.com

WebSites and Resources for Teachers
http://www.sitesforteachers.com

Collaborative Lesson Plan Archive
http://zubov.atmos.uiuc.edu/CLA

Guidelines for using the World Wide Web in the classroom

- A good rule of thumb is to avoid pursuing Web project activities that would work just as well without the Web. For example, don't search for poetry re-sources online if your school library already has several excellent poetry anthologies. Do, however, think about using the Web if you are in search of in-depth, up-to-the-minute weather information or an interactive learning resource.
- One of the best ways to organize classroom use of the Web is to set up a series of bookmarks related to your research project that students can use as a starting point. Ask the school librarian for help with this. If your librarian knows how to use the Net, he or she may be able to identify quickly some of the best resources for your project. If necessary, a preconfigured bookmark file can be copied to individual student machines.
- A valuable technique for enhancing learning is to create opportunities for students to share what they have learned. One way to share would be to have students

create a Web page with pointers accompanied by short personal accounts. These can be stored on a local hard drive. Alternatively, you could have students cut and paste information from a Web site, print it, and collect it in a binder that other students can then leaf through.
- Although it is generally preferable to have students use the Web only for specific projects, a number of sites can be used as a resource for gifted students or as an enrichment activity for students who finish classroom work early. You could set up your own page with pointers to safe sites (see Chapter 3), selected kids' sites (such as Berit's Best Sites for Children, Interesting Places for Kids, or B.J. Pinchbeck's Homework Helper), favorite museum sites, or a "site of the week."
- When assigning students Web page projects, warn them that URLs can change. If you are having them investigate particular sites (such as museums on the Net), be sure to have addresses for some back-up sites that

students can explore if the original sites don't work out. Assign an older student to check site addresses shortly before introducing an assignment to your class.
- Remember that your aim is not to explore everything that's on the Web, but to work with students in uncovering resources that are particularly relevant to your classroom. If Net access is available in the classroom or school library, try featuring a different subject area each month—geography, wildlife, astronomy, government.
- Probably the most important point to keep in mind is that you don't have to know everything about the Internet or the World Wide Web to introduce a Web project to your students. In fact, an ideal way of using this resource is to involve your students in researching sites and then have them share their discoveries with one another. The teacher's role is not to have all the answers, but to delight in and also learn from students' discoveries.

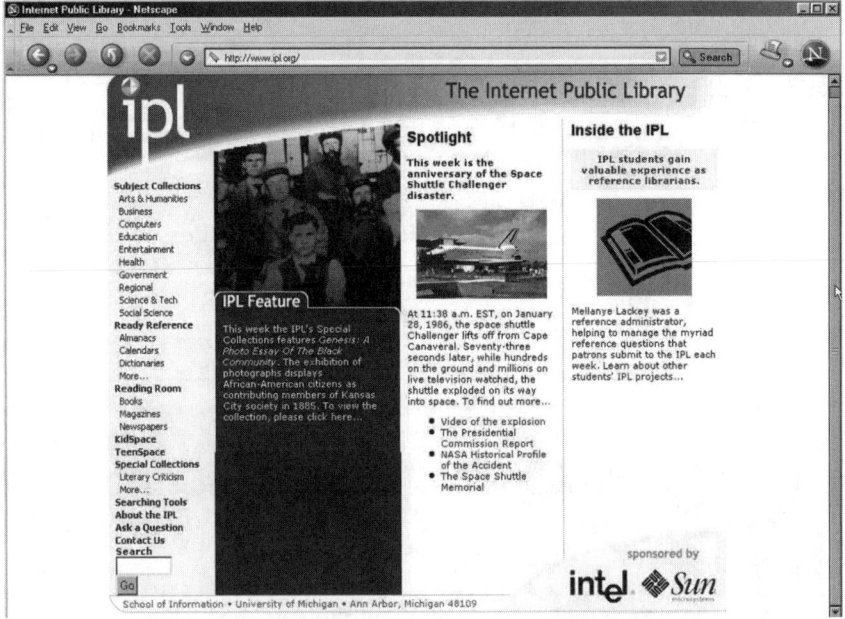

The *third* type of Project Ideas will give you a sense of the range of curriculum possibilities. One of the best ways to organize student work on the Web is to organize student activities and learning goals using a WebQuest. We will describe how WebQuests work and provide a collection of practical ideas that you can use to get students using the Web as a learning tool.

ABCTeach offers a collection of student worksheets that can be printed directly from your browser. Teachers have permission to reproduce these pages for classroom use. **http://abcteach.com/sitemap.htm**

Project Ideas

Learning to Navigate the World Wide Web

Learning outcomes
- Students will learn to use a Web browser and become familiar with the kinds of information they can find on the World Wide Web.

Grade levels: 4–8

Getting started
- Identify the default home page that should appear when your students first log on to the World Wide Web. It is simplest to use the default home page that comes with your browser, but if you have been using the Net for a while yourself, you may want to have them go to a different home page or even a customized home page on the local system that you've set up yourself, such as a bookmark page that you have set up in advance.
- Take time to allow students to become familiar with their Web client software. Explain and have them explore the various menu options and buttons for navigation. Show them how to turn the image loading off, and how to load images again as they are needed. Explain the concept of links, and have them sample various links. Point out how the information in the URL window changes as they access different sites.

Developing
- Explain the concept of a URL to your students. You may want to explain how the Internet can be used to access different kinds of resources (e.g., Web pages, software, and audio files). List some examples of URLs on the board. Be sure to include URLs for local files (e.g., *file:///C\ /inter-net/randy.htm* in which the file *randy.htm* is located in the Internet subdirectory on the local C drive).
- Review some of the reasons a URL might not work, reminding students that a server might be down or excessively busy, or that a file might be removed. Be sure to suggest that they try the technique of omitting the filename at the end of the URL if they have trouble accessing a site the first time.

Extending

- Now your students are ready to apply what they have learned. Following is a sample scavenger hunt. In this exercise, students are given a series of specific URLs and will be asked to provide one or more pieces of information from each site. In some cases, they may have to explore to find the required information. Be sure to give them ample time to complete the assignment. Accessing each site and having a chance to explore will likely require more than one class session. Tell them that if they have difficulty accessing one site, they should move on to another and try again later.

You can get many good ideas for integrating Web technology from published articles by teachers and experienced technology users. Techlearning.com offers articles from *Teaching & Learning Magazine* and from *Educators Outlook*, a resource for learning about technology in the class-room. Access these publications and archives from **http://www. techlearning.com**.

Students will need time to explore the Web browser on their own before using it in a class project.

INTERNET LEARNING HUNT

Directions: Complete as many of the items below as you can. In each case, begin by typing the designated URL. Once you access a site, hunt for the information you are asked to provide. If a site you are trying to reach seems to be taking too much time, cancel the connection and return to it later.

1. **http://volcano.und.nodak.edu**
   Name a place where a volcano has recently erupted. _____

   _____

   When did this eruption take place? _____

2. **http://sln.fi.edu/tfi/virtual/vir-summ.html**
   Benjamin Franklin was an expert in many different fields. You can find out about Benjamin Franklin at the Benjamin Franklin Museum. Name two fields in which Benjamin Franklin excelled.

   _____

3. **http://animaldiversity.ummz.umich.edu**
   The Animal Diversity Web offers an Animal Information Database. This is one place to find out about animals. Use this resource to find out the Latin name for a Big Brown Bat. _____

4. **http://www.seaworld.org**
   Next visit Sea World. Check out the Animal Bytes database. What today is the typical length of a blue whale? What is the current population of blue whales? How many blue whales once roamed the seas?

   _____

5. **http://sse.jpl.nasa.gov/index.cfm**
   Find out about our solar system at the Solar System Exploration site. This resources tells us that Jupiter has numerous moons and also rings, so that Jupiter itself is a "mini-solar system." How many rings does Jupiter have and what are these named? _____

   _____

6. **http://www.sas.upenn.edu/African_Studies**
   This URL is for the African Studies Center. Select the link for Country-Specific Pages. Next, select a country from those listed. Now look for World Fact Book information.

   What country did you select? _____

What is the population for your country? _____

What is the population growth rate? _____

What is the life expectancy? _____

7. http://www.ipl.org

On the Internet, you can get whole books to download and read. The Internet Public Library Reading Room is one place to obtain electronic books. Access this site. Can you find the author of the text titled *Mudfog and Other Sketches*?

_____

Name one other title that you can download from this site.

_____

8. http://www.unesco.org/whc/heritage.htm

Here you will find the UNESCO World Heritage list. What heritage site is shared by the United States and Canada? _____

_____

Name another heritage site in either the United States or Canada.

_____

9. http://www.profusion.com

There are a number of places on the Web where you can search for current news stories. Profusion is one of them. Access this site and click on "Headlines." Select several news sources and locate a recent story on weather or the environment.

What news source did you search? _____

Write the headline for your story here: _____

Would you find this news source helpful if you were writing a class report on this topic? _____

10. http://www.yahooligans.com

You can also find magazines on the Internet. Many magazines for kids and teens are listed at Yahooligans. Use Yahooligans to locate a magazine that interests you.

Write the title of the magazine here: _____

Click through to the magazine site and write below the name of an article in the current issue. _____

11. Use the **Back** button on your browser to return to Yahooligans. Navigate to a site that interests you. Write down the URL and a brief description of the site you've found.

URL: _____

What is this site is about?: _____

Bonus question

Try this question if you have extra time.

12. http://www.google.com
Google is one of a number of search engines that will let you search for information on a topic of your choosing. Access the site. Put in the name of your state or province. Click on Google Search. The system will return a list of Web sites. Review the list and name two resources you found that could be helpful if you were doing a school report on your state or province.

Project Ideas

HINT The Internet Public Library posts a step-by-step guide for writing and research, an information search tutorial and a set of links to help students with their writing and online research. Check out the Aplus Research & Writing for High School and College Students at **http://www.ipl.org/div/aplus/toc.htm**.

Searching for Information Online

Learning outcomes

- Students will develop thinking skills related to searching for information electronically.

Grade levels: 6–10

Getting started

- Discuss with students some of the ways in which the Internet is the same as, or different from, a library. Here are some points to consider.

LIBRARY	INTERNET
Clear organization by subjects	No clear organization
Subject headings assigned to information	Finding things requires a keyword search
Librarian available to help	No Internet experts—people have to find things for themselves
Librarian selects materials to suit users	Organizations post their own materials; some subjects might be neglected
Resources limited by physical space	Resources almost unlimited (just add new servers)
Information can be out of date	Can include very latest information
Printed format not easily captured	Electronic format easily captured
Sometimes closed when you need it	Sometimes too busy; information may have moved to another site

You can find a selection of Internet scavenger hunts for specific areas (such as math, science and social studies) at Cyberbee: **http://www.cyberbee.com/hunts.html**.

Developing

- Ask students to think about some of the things they might need to consider when searching for material online. Have them work out the following questions with paper and pencil and share their answers:

  1. List the following topics (or alternatives) across the top of your page:

     animals   weather   politics

2. Under each word, give examples of some more specific terms you could use to search for information on the topic (e.g., *Animals: dogs, livestock,* or *wildlife*).

3. Pick one of the more specific terms and think of some alternative terms you might use to search for information on these (e.g., *dogs: canines; livestock: farm animals*).

4. Take one of your more specific terms and try to think of a term you could combine it with to make it more specific (e.g., *dogs and training; wildlife and habitat*).

- Pose this question to your class: *How might you go about finding a resource that would tell you the name of the configuration of stars that looks like a bear?* Ask students to think of some other examples where the computer might be confused about what you're looking for if you enter only one term. Here are some samples to get them thinking: Indian (for information on North American Aboriginal peoples), football (for information about soccer), courts (for information on the legal system).

Extending

- Draw a diagram on the board to illustrate the concept of Boolean searching — that is, using *and, or,* and *not* in a search. Explain that most search engines on the Internet assume that when you include two words in your search you want those words to occur together (e.g., *dog training*).

- Have students list all the reasons they can think of to explain why they might not be able to find the information they are seeking on the Internet. (Reasons could include a faulty search strategy, spelling mistakes, lack of information, information available only in a specialized database that needs to be searched separately, such as a database that stores full-text magazine articles.)

Figure 5-3
Boolean logic.

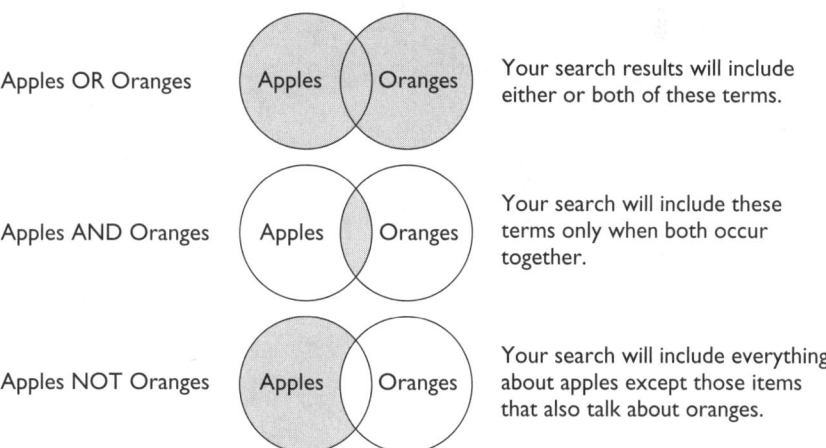

Apples OR Oranges — Your search results will include either or both of these terms.

Apples AND Oranges — Your search will include these terms only when both occur together.

Apples NOT Oranges — Your search will include everything about apples except those items that also talk about oranges.

Analyzing their search strategies helps students to sharpen their reasoning and organizational skills.

Some teachers who are well versed in HTML (the computer language of the Web) write Web assignments, including information scavenger hunts and Web searches for their classes, and include them on their school's Web pages. I found out, however, that searching for an answer and then having to refer back to a home page for the questions is more time consuming than having the questions printed out and being able to look over the entire assignment. That way, also, you don't have to know HTML, and you'll have a paper that the students can hand in when they are finished.

Jean Johnson in "So You're Finally Online. Now What?"
http://www.gsh.org/wce/jjohnson.htm

Project Ideas

Searching for Information on the World Wide Web

Learning outcomes
*   Students will develop skill in locating information on the World Wide Web using Yahoo, Google and AlltheWeb.

Grade levels: 5–9

Getting started
*   Ideally, this exercise should be done in conjunction with an actual research project. Alternatively, each student could select a suitable topic for online searching. Be sure to approve student topics in advance to ensure that searching is appropriate and well focused. Sample topics include tundra, rain forests, deserts, lakes, oceans, stars, forests, taiga, grassland, earthquakes, volcanoes, nutrition, wasps, place names, animal species, current events.

You can create an online learning resource or activity sheet for your students to use with the Web Worksheet Wizard at **http://wizard.hprtec.org**. This is an interactive site that steps you through the creating of a Web page that can include images and links. When your resource is complete, you can direct your students to the site to work on the lesson. If want to include an online quiz, you can use QuizStar at **http://quiz.4teachers.org** or Quia at **http://www.quia.com**.

Print and use Pandia's Search IQ cards (**http://www.pandia.com/q-cards/index.html**) to review with students how they can combine terms and search for phrases at specific search engines. A printable worksheet focusing on Web search concepts is available from **http://www.teachingideas.co.uk/welcome** Students can use this to document their understanding of key concepts.

WORLD WIDE WEB SEARCH

1. Access Yahoo at **http://www.yahoo.com**.
    Input your search term(s) in the search window and then click on
    Search.
    (If no matches are found, the Yahoo search will pass the search to
    Google.)

    How many items did your search return? _____

    List two items that could be helpful for researching your topic.

    _____

    _____

HINT Proteus gives you quick access to several different search engines. If you have not found at least four good references by searching the above sites, try your search using AskJeeves, Hotbot or one of the other search engines listed at Proteus **http://www. thrall.org/proteus.html.** You can also try Ithaki, which is a metasearch engine for kids: **http://www.ithaki.net/ kids.**

    Be sure to set up a bookmark or write down the URL for any resources
    that you want to return to later.

2. Now try the search again using Google. Access Google at
    www.google.com. Input your search terms and click on Google Search.

    How many items did your search return? _____

    List an item from here that could be helpful for researching your topic.

    _____

    _____

3. This time search AlltheWeb, which is at **www.alltheweb.com**. At this
    site, check out the Advanced Search to see the ways that you can cus-
    tomize your search. Use the Advanced Search to search for your topic.

    How many items did this search engine return? _____

    List two items that could be helpful for researching your topic:

HINT Use Pandia's index to find out about many spe- cialized search tools, includ- ing audio and video files, encyclopedias and and statistical search sources: **http://www.pandia.com/ powersearch/index.html.**

    _____

    _____

Variations

- (Grades 5–12): Have teams of three or four students each select a different search engine to search for information on the same topic. Ask one student in each group to browse for resources by using a subject tree such as Yahoo or the Google Directory (access Google at **www.google.com** and click on the Directory tab) or by visiting the Librarians' Index to the Internet at **http://lii.org**.

  Have all students prepare a list of any useful resources they have found, and discuss together which search technique was most useful. Then have them report back to the class.

- (Grades 5–10): You will find a number of places on the Net that offer a range of searching tools from a single site. Examples are Proteus at **http://www. thrall.org/proteus.html** and Pandia's Power Search Page at **http://www. pandia.com/powersearch/index.html**. These searches offer a selection of tools for locating information on the Internet. Pandia also offers access to many specialized search sources, such as reference books and science search engines. Searchers can use a drop-down menu or click on links to perform a search. Have students access Pandia's Power Search Page. Choose a topic that might interest your class, such as nutrition or beluga whales. Assign one Web search engine to each student or pair of students. Have them report their findings to the class. What useful references did they find? Was the search tool easy to use? Was there anything they didn't like about this particular searching tool? Students will want to make note of this page for future projects.

- (Grades 1–4): Develop a list of animals and assign an animal to each student for research. Have students access KidsClick at **http://sunsite.berkeley.edu/ kidsclick!**. This search engine has a user-friendly interface that younger students will be able to use easily. For younger students, you can enlarge the print size using the browser options settings. Explain how they can type in the name of their animal to retrieve information about it. Have them sample one or two items and write down something they have discovered about their animal. Have students access any of the following sites to obtain more information.

NetVet: **http://netvet.wustl.edu**
Electronic Zoo: **http://netvet.wustl.edu/e-zoo.htm**
SeaWorld Animal Database: **http://www.seaworld.org/animal-info/ index.htm**
Yahooligans Animals: **http://www.yahooligans.com/Science _and_ Nature/Living_Things/Animals/**

There are also a number of online learning tutorials about animals. Have students try these pages.

All About Bats (from Bat Conservation International): **http://www.batcon.org**
Backyard Nature **http://www.backyardnature.net**

HINT There are a number of sources for obtaining full-text magazine articles over the Internet. These include Northern Light **http://www.northernlight.com** Electric Library **http://ask.elibrary.com** CARL Ingentia **http://www.ingenta.com** In each case there is some cost involved in obtaining articles, but you can also use these sources to get references to articles that might be obtainable through your local library's interlibrary loan service. School librarians in particular will want to be aware of what's available from these sources.

Evaluating online resources

While the Internet is an increasingly important tool for student research, as many teachers are aware, not all of the information is valid. Newspapers and magazines are scrutinized by proofreaders and editors, but the Internet looks a lot like an information free-for-all. Although in some respects this is to be lamented, it also presents an excellent teaching opportunity. Students need to learn to evaluate the quality and accuracy of everything they read — including traditional news sources, the validity of which is sometimes taken for granted.

Students need to learn to evaluate Web sources for such things as currency and objectivity. They also need to be able to determine which sources are likely to be of most value for their projects. Take time to discuss with your students some of the reasons why information on the Web might not be totally accurate. As a group, consider such things as what interest the agency sponsoring the site might have in presenting the information with a particular bias. Ask students their views on whether a site developed by an individual is likely to provide inaccurate information — or may in fact contain more accuracy and detail than information available in the press. When was the material last updated? Can the information presented be verified? Is this information complete or are you left with many questions about the subject? What do spelling mistakes, incorrect grammar, and typographical errors indicate about the validity of the information on that site? Have students use the checklist on the next page to evaluate Web resources for their research projects.

There are many online resources for helping you to teach students how to evaluate Web resources.

Kathy Schrock provides a very good list of evaluation resources at **http://school.discovery.com/schrockguide/eval.html**.

The Wolfgram Memorial Library offers a list of sites that can be used to discuss specific concepts, such as accuracy and objectivity. It is available at **http://www2.widener.edu/Wolfgram-Memorial-Library/web evaluation/webeval.htm**.

The Media Awareness Network provides a number of excellent resources for evaluating Web pages and other resources that will let you extend the learning to other media. Access this site at **http://www.media-awareness.ca**.

teaching tip

Understanding how bias works is best taught using examples. Create a folder of materials from both newspapers and the Web that illustrate this concept. Have students review the examples and identify statements that they think might not be totally accurate. Have them explain why they feel the information may not be entirely believable.
You can use a search engine "filter" to include or filter out sites from commercial agencies. You can also access some examples of sites to compare at The Good, the Bad, and the Ugly (**http://lib.nmsu.edu/instruction/evalexpl.html**) and at the Gordon Library Evaluating Web Resources page at **http://www.wpi.edu/Academics/Library/Training/webeval.html**.

WEB SITE EVALUATION CHECKLIST

1. What topic are you researching?

   _____

2. What is the URL of the Web source you are evaluating?

   _____

3. What is the name of the site?

   _____

4. What is the main purpose for this site?

   _____

5. What group or individual is responsible for this site?

   _____

6. Do you feel that the group/individual responsible for
   this site is a good authority on the subject you are
   researching?   YES/NO

7. Are pages at this site easy to load and navigate?   YES/NO

8. Is the information presented in an interesting way?   YES/NO

9. Does the site seem to provide enough information
   about your topic?   YES/NO

10. Is the information easy to understand?   YES/NO

11. Is the information on this page up-to-date?   YES/NO

12. Does this page lead you to other useful resources
    for your topic?   YES/NO

13. Is there anything you particularly like about this site? YES/NO

    Describe:

    _____

14. Is there anything you dislike about this site?   YES/NO

    Describe:

    _____

15. Would you recommend this site to another student
    wanting to learn about your topic?   YES/NO

Project Ideas

Museum Reports

This is similar to a book report but with a Web twist. The exercise is designed to help students explore the World Wide Web in a meaningful fashion. The information they collect can become a helpful resource for other students.

Learning outcomes

- Students will explore Internet sites that have a learning focus.
- Students will evaluate Web resources and communicate information to others.

Grade levels: 4–8

Getting started

- Museums and science centers offer a wealth of interesting opportunities for learning on the World Wide Web. Any of these might prove to be relevant for a particular unit of study. To find out what is available, have your students prepare museum reports. One site that you can use to visit a number of science centers around the world is **http://www-2.cs.cmu.edu/~mwm/sci.html**. Access the site or use the Yahooligans list of Museums and Exhibits.
- Have students each select a science center they would like to visit. Then have them fill in the information sheet that follows and report back to the class.
- Instruct them to design an eye-catching header for their museum report in which they include the name of the museum and a small picture reprinting its theme. If you have a graphics program and a color printer, students might want to download sample graphics from the site to use for their headers.
- File student reports in a binder and make this available as a reference for other students to use in exploring the Web.
- Consider this "class report" strategy for collecting references to other types of sites on the Web, such as a selection of sites with environmental information or some favorite kids' sites. Develop a bookmark or Web page (museums.htm) to help other students easily access sites that have been reviewed favorably.

Link to the Virtual Library Museums Page:
http://vlmp.museophile.com

HINT Investigate these resources to learn more about teaching information literacy skills: Media Literacy Online Project (**http://interact.uoregon.edu/MediaLit/HomePage**), an online publication that includes feature articles, Web links and lesson plan ideas; Directory of Media Literacy Sites **http://www.chebucto.ns.ca/CommunitySupport/AMLNS/internet.html**.

Figure 5-4
Museums on the Internet.

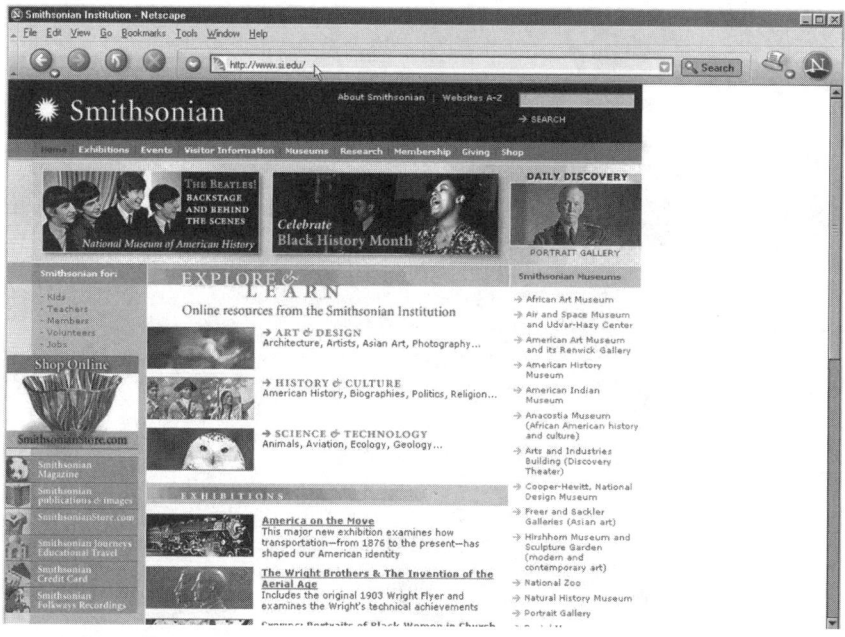

MUSEUM REPORT

What is the name of the museum that you visited? _____

_____

_____

What is the URL? _____

_____

What is the focus of this museum? (e.g., art, sea animals, history of computers, insects) _____

_____

Describe a special exhibit or feature at this museum that your class-mates might find interesting to explore. _____

_____

_____

_____

_____

Did you find any other resources at this museum that might be help-ful if you or one of your classmates were researching a project?

_____

_____

_____

_____

What did you like best about this site? _____

_____

_____

_____

_____

Overall, how would you rate this site? (Circle one)

| Great | Pretty good | OK | Could be better | Could be a lot better |

Variations

- (Grades 1–4): In this activity, students will create a classroom "scrapbook" of a visit to a museum exhibit. Have each student draw a picture of something in the exhibit and write one or two sentences about what they discovered.
- (Grades 9–10): Have students visit an online museum as a way to further explore a period of history. Invite them to develop a virtual time capsule. They are to visit a museum and select artifacts and works of art or documents that illustrate some aspect of life in that era. They should briefly describe the resource, designate its location on the Net, and explain its historical significance. Examples of sites that could be used for this exercise include The Vatican Exhibit **http://www.ibiblio.org/expo/ vatican.exhibit/Vatican.exhibit.html**, The Soviet Archives Exhibit **http://www.ibiblio.org/expo/soviet.exhibit/soviet.archive.html**, Canada's Digital Collections **http://collections.ic.gc.ca** and American Treasures Library of Congress Exhibitions **http://www.loc.gov/exhibits**.

HINT An interactive gallery and other space exploration resources are available from NASA at **http://www. nasa.gov** and from Hands On Universe at **www. handsonuniverse.org**. The Space Telescope Science Institute offers space-related downloadable activities and software. You can download electronic picture books, an electronic tutorial and a number of electronic reports from the Exploration in Education page at **http://www.stsci. edu/exined/exined.home.html#C2**.

Copyright

With so much material easily downloadable from the Net, teachers need to be sure that they and their students are knowledgeable about copyright. As a general rule, teachers are permitted to make "fair use" of material for instructional purposes. With print materials, "fair use" (or "fair dealing") often means *limited* use *for classroom purposes only*. This guideline also pertains to text and images available on the Internet. While it may be permissible for a student to use a downloaded photograph of dinosaur remains in a report, a teacher may not, in turn, be able to post the report on a school Web site. Some Web sites intended for educational use post a notice authorizing use for educational purposes. When in doubt about whether material can be downloaded for school use, send a message to the Webmaster or the author of the document informing them of your intended use. It is particularly important to seek permission to copy when material may have some commercial value. One enthusiastic Winnie-the-Pooh fan found himself threatened with legal action when he attempted to establish a Winnie-the-Pooh Web site.

Jamie McKenzie offers a very good discussion of the copyright issue in an article entitled "Keeping It Legal: Questions Arising out of Web Site Management," available from **http://www.fno.org/jun96/legal.html**. In the United States the Copyright Office of the Library of Congress is an important source of information about copyright legislation and trends. If you want up-to-date authoritative information, this is the place to go. For a slightly less intimidating introduction to copyright, try The Educators Guide to Copyright and Fair Use, available from Education World: **http://www.education-world.com/a_curr/curr280.shtml**. The article deals with "Copyrights and Copywrongs," Fair Use and copyright issues related to new technologies.

In Canada, the Council of Ministers of Education have published a booklet entitled "Copyright Matters: Some Key Questions and Answers for Teachers." You will find a copy of this publication along with other useful copyright information at the Education Network of Ontario Web site: **http://www.enoreo.on.ca/resources/copyright.htm**.

Other useful documents include these:
The Fair Use Guidelines for Educational Multi-media
http://www.ohiou.edu/imts/copylink.html

Copyright and K–12: Who Pays in the Network Era by David Rothman
http://www.ed.gov/Technology/Futures/rothman. html

Copyright Resources: K–12
http://www.groton.k12.ct.us/mts/pt2a9.htm

Copyright Sites
http://sisnet.ssku.k12.ca.us/~imcftp/copyright.html

Copyright Management
http://www.msu.edu/user/stewa158/Copyright.htm

Copyright Tips and Issues
http://www.siec.k12.in.us/~west/online/copy.htm

You can access more copyright information from the Stanford University Copyright and Fair Use Site at **http://fairuse.stanford.edu** and from ALA Copyright Education Program at **http://copyright.ala.org** Information on Canadian copyright legislation is available from the Canadian Intellectual Property Office at **http://strategis.gc.ca/sc_mrksv/cipo/cp/cp_main-e.html**.

HINT At Peter Milbury's Network of School Librarian Web Pages you can access Web pages developed by school librarians around the world. Many of these include good lists of curriculum sites that school librarians have found useful for their teachers and students. Consider using some of these sites in a workshop for teachers. The site is located at **http://www.school-libraries.net/#K-12 web**.

Having a good understanding of copyright is important for all teachers, since students will look to their teachers for guidance. Unfortunately, copyright legislation is very complex, particularly as the law attempts to grapple with such things as digitized images, networked computers, and distance education. Ask your board to sponsor a copyright workshop for teachers, or work with your school librarian to initiate one in your own school. As a group, teachers can review some of the references above and share ideas on how to deal with specific issues. You may even be able to find a knowledgeable expert who is willing to talk to the group about this issue.

Citing Internet sources

As students make use of the Internet, they should be expected to provide the same level of care with respect to citing sources as they would use when referencing print resources in a bibliography. The difficulty with Internet resources, however, is that material can disappear or change location from one time to the next, so in addition to providing information about the authorship, title, and location of a Web resource, a citation should include the date the material was available at that site.

Although the exact format for citing online sources can vary depending on the reference you consult and the publication characteristics of the item you wish to cite, a basic format you can use for citing Web sites in a bibliography is this:

Author Last Name, First Name (if available). "Title of item." Date on the document or date of last revision (if available). [Online] Available: URL, Day Month Year.

Example:
Kronk, Gary. "Comets & Meteor Showers." 1999. [Online] Available: **http://comets.amsmeteors.org**, 31 January 2003.

Here is a basic format for citing an e-mail message:
Sender Last Name, First Name. "Subject Line from Posting." [Online posting] Available E-mail: to@address from @address, Day Month Year. (In this case, the date is the date the message was sent.)

A succinct guide to formats for citing electronic sources, including useful links to Web sites about citations, is maintained by the William Paterson University of New Jersey:

Guide for Citing Electronic Information
http://ww2.wpunj.edu/~library/citing.htm

For a more detailed list of rules and examples, you can consult Columbia Online Style: MLA-Style Citations of Electronic Sources at **http://www. columbia.edu/cu/cup/cgos/idx_basic.html** or you can compare citation styles using Online! Citation Styles: **http://www.bedfordstmartins.com/ online/citex.html**.

Using online newspapers and magazines

A major resource for student research projects is available through online newspapers and magazines. With the Internet, students can have access to up-to-the-minute news sources, such as news discussion groups or Web pages set up to follow current events. This provides an excellent opportunity for students to compare different versions of news stories and to examine such issues as how news can be slanted or what kinds of stories are considered newsworthy.

News resources on the Internet can easily be used to track coverage of a story over a period of weeks. For example, students might look at how an election is reported in two different newspapers. Such an activity might be enhanced by accessing discussions within newsgroups dedicated to political issues. Some newspapers and magazines provide archived stories. These can be used to study the events that led up to a story in light of its outcome.

At NewsDirectory.com (**http://www.newsdirectory.com**), you will find links to sites for hundreds of newspapers and magazines. Many of the magazines offer archives of past articles. This resource includes English-language magazines from different parts of the world. By browsing sources such as NewsDirectory.com, you'll discover ways to use online news and magazine stories in the classroom. One magazine recently featured an article on climate change, while another offered a full-text article on animal poaching in the Amazon rain forest. Such topics could easily be tied to the curriculum.

Because the magazines at this site are intended for adults, this is not a good location for students to roam freely, but it is a valuable resource for teachers. Visit NewsDirectory.com to identify a selection of publications that would be suitable for student research, then have students directly access the magazines that you have selected.

You can find specific news articles by searching for current news topics using Google's News search (**http://news.google.com**) or Alltheweb News search at **http://www.alltheweb.com**. Many full-text magazine articles are also available online, and many offer at least some free content. Online magazines provide students with the ability to locate up-to-date information for their research projects. You can search for full-text magazine articles at FindArticles.com (**www.findarticles.com**) and at MagPortal (**www. magportal.com**). More comprehensive access to newspapers and magazines is available through services such as the Electronic Library (**http:// ask.elibrary.com**).

A sampling of good Internet news sources

Canada.com

Canadian newspaper site. Search the Calgary Herald, Ottawa Citizen, National Post and others.

http://www.canada.com

Canoe (Canadian Online Explorer)

A Canadian online news source that issues a daily news update and provides links to top stories from a range of Canadian news media sources.

http://www.canoe.ca

CBC (Canadian Broadcasting Corporation)

Traditional broadcast sources are another source for online news. Some, such as the CBC, offer programs in an audio format. CBC for Schools is a current affairs audio subscription series.

http://www.cbc.ca

Christian Science Monitor

Full-text version available. Excellent resource for comparison with popular press to illustrate different journalistic styles in news coverage.

http://www.csmonitor.com

CNN

Source for current news, including complete transcripts of broadcast news.

http://www.cnn.com

Environmental News Network

This is a news service for environmental education and awareness. The Environmental News Daily provides informative articles on a wide range of issues at a good reading level for students. Note that access to some of the information requires a subscription.

http://www.enn.com

Globe and Mail (Toronto)

Canadian newspaper with national coverage.

http://www.globeandmail.ca

Guardian Unlimited United Kingdom and World News

Includes an archive search with coverage back to 1998.

http://www.guardian.co.uk

JournalismNet

Terrific journalism resources page developed by Julian Sher for professional journalists, but with many useful links for schools. Includes links to news archives.

> http://www.journalismnet.com

Media Channel

This is a nonprofit, public interest Web site concerned with the political, cultural and social impacts of the media. It offers news, reports and commentary media-issues organizations and publications worldwide. A thought provoking news site for students which includes a teachers toolkit.

> http://www.mediachannel.org

New York Times

Registration is required, but access to articles appearing within the last seven days is free. Older articles from the archives must be purchased.

> http://www.nytimes.com

News Directory

Source for newspapers and magazines from many different countries. At this site you can search for newspapers and magazines by title or browse by regions.

> http://www.newsdirectory.com

News Index

This is a news-only search engine. News Index currently indexes over 200 news sources from around the world.

> http://www.newsindex.com

NewsCentral

This site links to a whopping 3,200 newspapers around the world, including some student newspapers. Because this site includes newspapers from many different countries, it is a good resource for foreign language studies.

> http://www.all-links.com/newscentral

NewsLink

This source claims to be the most comprehensive news resource on the World Wide Web, and it probably is. It includes pointers to newspapers, broadcast sources and magazines, and an excellent selection of special links. From this source you can also access a news-only search engine.

> http://www.newslink.org

Newspapers – USA and Worldwide

This site offers up-to-date links to newspapers around the world.

> http://www.refdesk.com/paper.html

If your curriculum includes a study of censorship around the world you can access many fascinating examples from an online database called The FileRoom (**http://www. thefileroom.org**) which is a cultural archive that has been featured as an exhibit in many places around the world. It is now available online and can serve as a research source for senior students in media, history and political science classes.

Use Newspapers in Education (**http://nieon line.com**) for some sample lesson ideas on using newspapers in the classroom. The activities will work equally well with online or printed newspapers.

Figure 5-5
Media on the Internet.

PBS

Online News Hour and a number of exciting learning projects, including electronic field trips.

http://www.pbs.org

The Learning Network

This is a news resource specifically for students in Grades 3–12. It includes news summaries, a daily news quiz, vocabulary features, a science feature and an opportunity to talk with a reporter.

http://www.nytimes.com/learning

Time-Warner's Pathfinder

This gateway links to full-text information from *Time* and other magazines from Time-Warner.

http://www.pathfinder.com

Time Classroom

Time magazine offers a weekly teachers' guide to facilitate bringing the news into the classroom. Lessons include links to complementary Web learning sites. *Time* magazine also makes available the Time Archives Student Centre, a collection of cover stories and feature articles suitable for student research.

http://www.time.com/time/classroom

You can search for up-to-the-minute news at Google (**http://news.google.com**) and at Alltheweb (**http://www.alltheweb.com**). Have students use these sources to access news stories on a controversial issue from a range of different news sources. Ask them to compare the stories to determine which is most informative and how details are used to support different perspectives.

Times Newspapers Ltd.

British news source that includes the *Sunday Times* and many excellent news features. Registration required.

http://www.sunday-times.co.uk

USA Today

Regularly updated news and a number of useful archives for student research, such as archives of stories on health issues.

http://www.usatoday.com

Washington Post

This is a very well-respected online newspaper. It includes a supplements feature that provides links to background articles related to current news stories.

http://www.washingtonpost.com

The next Project Ideas is intended to help students discover biases in news reporting and to develop analytical thinking skills as they consider what news reports suggest about Russian society and how it differs from their own.

Figure 5-5a
Google News Search.

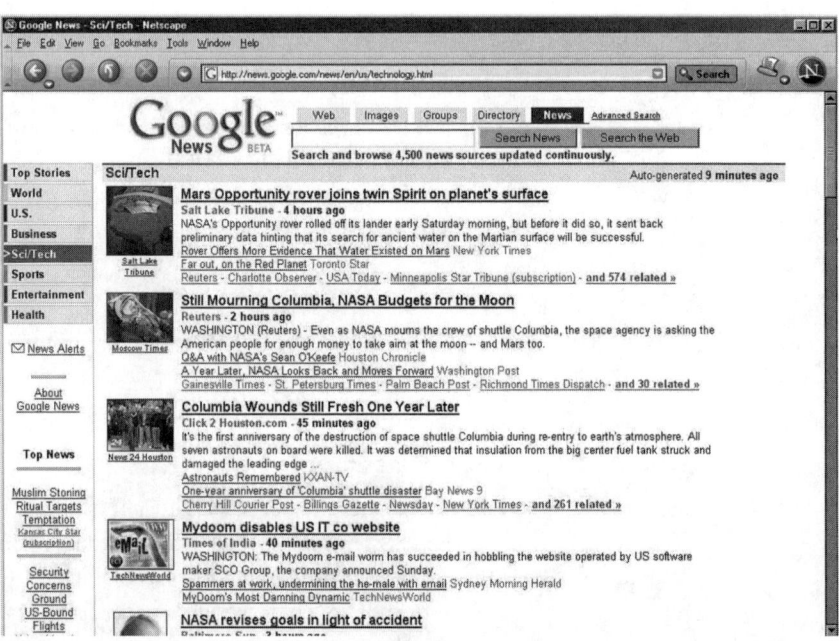

Project Ideas

News from Russia

Grade levels: 7–8

Learning outcomes

- Students will use news reports to learn about a foreign culture.
- Students will consider how well news reporting reflects a community.
- Students will develop writing skills as they translate their findings into a letter to a friend.

Getting started

- Have students locate St. Petersburg, Russia, on a map.
- Give students some background on Russia's political history, and take time to discuss what students might already know about life in Russia.

Developing

- Have students access the *St. Petersburg Times* (**http://www.sptimesrussia .com**), a weekly English-language newspaper from St. Petersburg. While its intended audience is English-speaking people living in Russia, it is nevertheless a good way to give students a glimpse of day-to-day news events in Russia.
- Have all students look at one or two current issues of the newspaper, and have a class discussion in which students are asked to consider how life in Russia is reflected in the news stories. Have them compare the news stories with stories appearing in their own local paper. Discuss in particular how well newspaper reports reflect their communities. This is a particularly interesting exercise, because a look at a foreign newspaper calls into high relief the tendency of all newspapers to focus on "bad news" rather than "good news."
- Next, have students delve into the newspaper's archives. Assign a different issue of the paper to each student. Issues should include feature stories, breaking news, business, commentary, classifieds, and culture. Allow sufficient time for students to examine their assigned issues carefully. If time allows, some students may want to look at more than one issue.

teaching tip

TeachNology makes a number of Web Tools available, including a tools that will allow you to make graphic organizers by filling out a simple form. You can choose to create a concept map, timeline, SQ3R chart, or KWL organizer (What I Know, What I Want to Know, What I Have Learned.) The organizers can be printed and distributed to students. When the organizers are saved in HTML format, they can also be modified and posted to the Web. Access TeachNology Graphic Organizers at **http:// www. teach-nology. com/web_tools/ graphic_org**. Check out the other Web tools available at TeachNology to create learning contracts, certificates, schedules and more.

Extending

- As a last step, have students write about their discoveries. Ask them to imagine they are student visitors in Russia. They are writing a letter home and will be using the incidents they read about to communicate to someone who has never been to Russia just what Russia is really like. Emphasize that in their letters students should communicate both the things that are different about Russian issues and those that are similar to news at home.

For a great collection of lessons and activities for teaching about media, visit the Media Awareness Network at **http://www. media-awareness.ca**. If you want to challenge your students with a different perspective on the news, you will find links to some interesting alternative news sources at Cafe Progressive **http://www.cafe progressive.com**.

Online traveling

Part of the value of the Internet is the fact that through it we can reach more than 160 different countries. Tapping into online information from and about countries around the globe will captivate students and stimulate learning. Ideally, students will use online resources to supplement printed material that is available in their classroom or library. The advantage of online resources is that they are wide-ranging and can be kept totally up-to-date. Learning about another country and compiling a report on it can be relevant to geography, history, and other social studies areas, as well as language studies (e.g., using travel information about France as project resources for French-language studies). You can link to resources for countries around the globe using the Yahoo Regional Index at **http://www.yahoo.com/ Regional/Countries**. You can also use the many travel and geographical information resources available on the Net.

A sampling of Internet travel guides

CIA World Factbook

Published annually in July by the Central Intelligence Agency for the use of U.S. government officials, this is a great resource for factual information about countries around the world. The Factbook can be found at many places on the Internet, such as

> http://www.cia.gov/cia/publications/factbook

Columbus World City Guide

Good guide to cities around the world.

> http://www.cityguide.travel-guides.com

Clearinghouse Net

This is a repository for many different subjects. There is a good selection of country specific guides. Look for resources under Places and Peoples.

> http://www.clearinghouse.net

Use travel sources to explore a country along with a class project involving students who exchange e-mail with keypals from other countries.

CountryReports

This site pulls together information from a range of sources on the Net to provide a substantial repository of country information.

http://www.countryreports.org

Google Directory

Use the Google Directory to access comprehensive information about individual countries. Most countries feature at least one portal site that may include information related to history, economics, geography, ethnic groups, arts and culture, and photographs of the country are commonly featured. The Google Directory will also point you in the direction of maps, guides and government country information sources. You can access Google links to country information at

http://directory.google.com/Top/Regional/Countries

Greatest Cities of the World

Detailed profiles of major cities around the world. City profiles are taken from the Encarta Encyclopedia.

http://www.greatestcities.com

Some good travel writing in the form of travelogues can be found at the Yahooligans site. Use this resource to generate ideas for student writing projects or to enhance a geography lesson. Travelogues are available at **http://www. yahoo ligans.com/Around_ the_World/Travel/ Travelogues**.

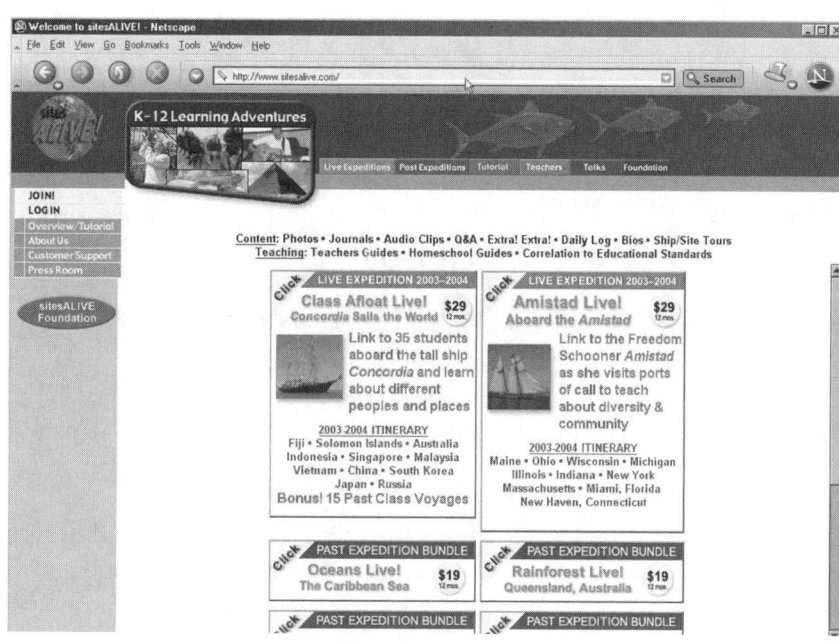

Figure 5-6
At sitesALIVE! students can connect to adventures around the world.

Library of Congress Country Studies

This resource offers over 85 detailed studies of countries around   the world. The reports include information on geography, history, society, culture, and the economy. If hyperlinks for a particular country do not work, use the search engine to retrieve sections of the reports.

http://lcweb2.loc.gov/frd/cs/cshome.html

Lonely Planet

The Lonely Planet's World Guide lets you click your way to a region of the world that is of interest to you. When you arrive at a destination, you can learn about the area's history, culture, environment and, of course, travel information: weather, currency, and attractions. The interactive presentation will engage students and there are many fascinating things to learn about here.

http://www.lonelyplanet.com

Map Machine

Country maps, including political maps and physical maps, flags, and other country information from *National Geographic*.

http://www.nationalgeographic.com/resources/ngo/maps

National Atlas of Canada Online

Canadian resource with an interactive mapping tool, a community atlas, a geographical factbook, a place name search, a geography quiz, and more.

http://atlas.gc.ca

National Atlas of the United States

This interactive map lets you select areas of interest (such as crops, ethnic population or metropolitan areas) and then click on an area of the map to get a visualization of the data for the selected area.

http://nationalatlas.gov

Tiger Mapping Service

Census and geographic information for the United States. Students will enjoy looking up place names and being able to zoom in on them on a map.

http://www.census.gov/geo/www/maps/CP_OnLineMapping.htm

World Flag Database

Pictures of flags from countries around the world, as well as state and provincial flags. Brief factual information about each country is provided, including main cities, population, languages and religion. This site is a good supplement to student exploration of other countries.

http://www.flags.net

WorldSkip

This resource puts a wealth of country information at your fingertips. Select a country using the drop-down menus to access newspapers, maps, business and government information, and information about the people, culture, education and tourism. The inclusion of current news sources, including regional news sources and magazines, makes this site particularly complete for research projects.

http://www.worldskip.com

Yahoo Countries

Have students take an imaginary trip and report on sights from around the world. Yahoo points to travel information for specific countries.

http://dir.yahoo.com/Recreation/Travel/By_Region/Countries

The following Project Ideas are designed to have students explore the Internet as a way of refining and developing their understanding of Africa and its peoples.

Project Ideas

Exploring Africa Online

Grade levels: 5–8

Learning outcomes

- Students will use the World Wide Web to learn about Africa.
- Students will question their assumptions, synthesize their ideas, and express their ideas in writing.
- Students will find information on the Internet and work as part of a team.

Getting started

- Post a map of Africa in your classroom. Have a brainstorming session in which students discuss what they already know about Africa. When information relates to a specific country, pinpoint that country on the map.
- Have students access an Internet news resource, print news source, or print encyclopedia to obtain basic information about Africa.

Developing

- Before attempting further research, have students respond to the true/false questions listed on the next page. Compare answers and discuss. (The online version of this questionnaire is available from **http://www.sas.upenn.edu/African_Studies/K-12/ Perceptions_16165.html**.)

Curriculum resources about Africa on the Internet are particularly rich. Pointers to educational resources about Africa are available from **http://www.sas.upenn.edu/ African_Studies/K-12/menu_ EduBBS.html**.

This site offers lesson plans, hand-outs, and full-text articles for studies in African history, geography, politics, languages, religions, social studies, and culture.

QUESTIONNAIRE: PERCEPTIONS OF AFRICA

True or False?

1. Much of Africa consists of rain forest.

2. Most African economies are based on agriculture.

3. Few modern/technological cities exist in Africa.

4. All Africans are Black.

5. Most African nations are governed by White regimes.

6. Africa has an abundance of mineral wealth.

7. Traditional African religions are prominent in Africa.

8. Africa is a country with Nelson Mandela as president.

9. Africa changed little until its contact with the West.

10. Most African nations received their independence in the 1960s.

11. Africa is the same size as the continental United States.

12. One can see snow in Africa.

13. Most African men tend to marry more than one wife.

14. Africa is a place of great physical danger from wild animals, which roam freely through the countryside.

15. Most African art forms, such as carved masks, would never be used for decoration in an African's home.

16. Divination is a popular form of traditional religion.

17. Drums are the primary form of communication used in Africa.

18. Swahili is a major language spoken in Africa.

19. Most Africans speak several languages.

20. African political and economic affairs have little interest for the rest of the world.

- Use the questionnaire as a springboard for Internet research about Africa. Have the class identify the broad areas of knowledge reflected in the various questions (e.g., geography, people, history, politics, religion, languages, culture).
- Divide the class into pairs or groups of three, and assign a different African country to each group. Each student should take responsibility for researching on the Internet two or more topics identified in the previous step. Their task will be to prepare one or two paragraphs on their area of research. Students may want to begin their research by accessing the Country-Specific Pages available at the University of Pennsylvania African Studies Web page at **http://www.sas.upenn.edu/African_Studies/Home_Page/ AFR_GIDE.html**.

  They should also conduct Web searches using Yahooligans or Google or consult one of the resources listed under "Internet Travel Guides." Invite them to share with their teammates any particularly good resources they locate.

Extending

- As a follow-up, have the class exchange African discoveries. Ask each student to tell the group what he or she has learned about Africa that he or she didn't know before or found particularly surprising.
- Have the class return to the Perceptions of Africa questionnaire and see if any assumptions have changed.

Variations

- (Grades 5–8): Assign student groups to investigate the broad topics identified above for other countries and develop similar reports. For more in-depth reports, select a single country and assign different topic areas for students to investigate.
- (Grades 3–5): Assign each student an African country. Locate the countries on a classroom map. Have students access the African Country-Specific pages and identify just a few key pieces of information for their country: climate, population, capital city, language spoken, etc. Have students record their findings on a chart. When they have finished assembling their data, have them discuss similarities and differences they have discovered among the countries.

Project Ideas

A Potpourri of Web Projects

The goal for many teachers is to get enough of an idea about what's available on the Web to be able to pick up on relevant resources that complement existing curriculum and classroom activities. These project ideas provide some examples of what is available and how to make use of it in the classroom. You will discover more ideas for projects as you explore the sites listed in Appendix B.

- **Book Reports (Grades 4–8).** Have students sample the book reports posted at the KidsBookshelf. The site provides some good ideas for books to read and review. Students can select one of the books reviewed at the site or another of their choosing, then write and submit a review to KidsBookshelf at **http://www.kidsbookshelf.com/**.

- **Studying Bees (Grades 4–8).** Divide the class into teams. Each team should research and be able to identify three different kinds of bees, three foods that depend on bees for pollination, and three different reasons why the bee population is threatened. In addition, each team should develop one "why" question and one "how" question about bees. Have students share their questions (and answers) verbally with the rest of the class, or you can redistribute student questions for further research. Students can use these sources for their research:

  Of Bees, Beekeepers and Food **http://www.queen.pollinator.com**

  Bee Research Center **http://gears.tucson.ars.ag.gov**

  P.O.'s Homepage **http://www.algonet.se/~beeman/index-f.html**

  Africanized Honey Bees on the Move **http://ag.arizona.edu/pubs/insects/ahb** (At this site, you will find a list of downloadable activities to extend this lesson.)

- **Youth in Action (Grades 8–12).** Youth in Action Network provides an opportunity for youth from all over the world to share ideas and come up with solutions to environmental and human rights problems. First, visit the site to get an overview of the kinds of opportunities for social

action that are available. You will need to register for the site, and you can register your class as a group. Select a specific area for your class to focus on. For example, in the area of human rights, your class could choose to learn about the rights of indigenous peoples. At the Youth in Action site, you can get background information and Internet resources and organizations relevant to this topic. Read and discuss with your students the ideas presented in the document "An Introduction to Social Action," which is available at the site. Discuss how students can make a difference locally, nationally, or internationally. Review the range of options for taking action — such as developing a petition or writing a letter to the media. As a group, agree on a strategy for taking action. You may prefer to use Youth in Action as an idea generator rather than as a tool for contacting agencies. If so, ask your school librarian to help track down addresses for sending letters to newspapers, local politicians, Congressional representatives, or members of Parliament. **http://www.teaching.com/act**

- **Windows to the Universe (Grades 4–8).** This is a terrific starting point for students studying the solar system. The site includes teacher resources and an Ask a Scientist link. Have younger students search for the names of the planets and their relative sizes, and record this information on their own handmade charts. Older students can prepare in-depth reports, following relevant links and searching for other information on the Web. **http://www.windows.ucar.edu**

- **Learning about World War II (Grades 7–10).** The SchoolNet Digital Collections offers resource material that can be used to learn about Canada's social, cultural, or natural history. Included in the collections are photographs from Kryn Taconis, an underground photo-journalist during the Dutch Resistance of World War II. In conjunction with a unit of study on World War II, have students visit the site and study the photographs. Discuss what the pictures reveal about the experience of war. Have students assume the role of war-time journalists. Use the photographs as a starting point for writing "news stories" that describe conditions that existed during the war. You will find the Taconis collection at **http://collections.ic.gc.ca/taconis**. You will find related material for learning about World War II at these sites:

  What Did You Do in the War, Grandma **http://www. stg.brown. edu/projects/WWII_Women/tocCS.html**

  World War II Time Line **http://history.acusd.edu/gen/WW2Timeline/start.html**

Edhelper.com makes available reproducible lessons and student worksheets for Grades 1 through highschool for math and language studies. This site also provides access to many online WebQuests. Edhelper is at **http://www.edhelper.com**.

Grolier Online World War II Commemoration Page **http://gi.grolier.com/wwii/wwii_mainpage.html**

Rutgers Oral History Archives
http://fas-history.rutgers.edu/oralhistory/orlhom.htm
This site provides text transcripts of interviews with veterans and links to other WW II archival sites.

- **Flags of the World (Grades 4–8).** Have students download images of flags from around the world and incorporate them into geography reports. This site provides images of flags from a great many countries with links to additional information about the country. **http://www.infoplease.com/countries.html**

- **Solving Math Puzzles (Grades K–12).** MathMagic is a stimulating Web site for kids who like solving mathematical puzzles. Current and past puzzles are posted for different grade levels. Visit the site yourself, or select a student to visit this site and come back with a puzzler to present to the class for solution. **http://mathforum.org/mathmagic**

  Another resource for developing math and reasoning skills is 21st Century Problem Solving, a database of problems and solutions for grade school through graduate school. **http://www2. hawaii.edu/suremath/journal.html**

- **Online Scrapbooks (Grades 4–10).** Have students make an electronic scrapbook. First, check out Amy's Amazing Adventure. This site is a creative account of Amy's experience at summer camp. Amy has also identified resources on the Net where a visitor to her Web page can learn more about a topic. The site will generate other ideas for similar classroom projects. The exercise will help develop student skills in writing and Web-based research. Use the online scrapbook project to develop skills for more complex online portfolios. **http://sln.fi.edu/camp/camp.html**

- **Learning about Energy (Grades 5–8).** Have students identify and discuss the pros and cons of various forms of energy that they are aware of. Assign one form of energy to individual students or teams. As a group, create a large chart (or Web page) that lists the various forms of energy described at the site, along with the advantages and disadvantages related to each energy form. List or include as links information sources for each energy form being researched. Have students select one form of energy to learn more about and report on. Students can use their knowledge

of Web searching and these sources of information to find out more:
Energy Information Administration Kids Page **http://www.eia.**
doe.gov/kids
Energy Quest **http://www.energyquest.ca**

- **Kapili.com Science Research (Grades 5–10).** Kapili is a resource for exploring scientific topics in astronomy, biology, chemistry, geography and physics. The easy-to-read online tutorials are a good way to introduce students to topics or to complement classroom learning. The tutorials, including an introduction to the scientific method, matter, the biosphere and climate, can also be used as "reach ahead" activities for students with a particular interest in science.
  http://www.kapili.com/topiclist.html

- **Creating a Personalized Newspaper (Grades 4–12).** Crayon is an online resource that allows students to create their own version of an online newspaper. The site draws its news items from current Web sites, then mixes and matches them according to your specifications. Allow students to access the site and develop their own customized versions of a newspaper. The newspaper templates that the students create can be saved as HTML files. These then can be accessed and read periodically or daily as a way for students to learn about current events. Take a few minutes each day to have students share with the class items from their online newspapers.
  http://crayon.net

- **Women's History (Grades 7–12).** Students can learn about the contributions women have made by visiting The Women's International Center Biography Index, The National Women's Hall of Fame (U.S.) or Herstory (Canada). These resources provide brief biographies of women who have made a contribution in some area. Have students sample these resources and select a woman to research. Identify key questions to get them started: When did this woman live? What contributions did this woman make? What challenges did she face? Have students use the above resources to start their research, and then have them use a search engine to see what additional information they can find for their biographical reports. After your students have developed their reports, have them share what they've learned with the class. This project can form the basis for a class project Web page.
  http://www.wic.org/bio/idex_bio.htm
  http://www.greatwomen.org/index.php
  http://library.usask.ca/herstory/index.html

- **Learning about Tornadoes (Grades 4–8).** Have students research tornadoes and prepare oral reports for the class. They can find out such things as how tornadoes are formed, where they form, how they are rated, how they die, and what to do if a tornado hits. For comprehensive information on this topic, they can visit the Tornado Project Online: **http://www.tornadoproject.com.** Other weather-related resources are available from The University of Michigan Weather Site, **http://cirrus.sprl.umich.edu/wxnet** and Weather Mania **http://www.weathermania.net.**

- **Learning about Hurricanes (Grades 4–6).** The five-part series Storm Science is a resource developed with the elementary student and teacher in mind. You can supplement this resource with recent online news reports on hurricanes or other storms. **http://www.miamisci.org/hurricane**

- **Earthweek (Grades 4–8).** Each week, this resource provides a look at the weather on the planet. Have each student select a continent and document the weather phenomenon on that continent for a week. They can then research and report on a weather event they would like to know more about. Use the Earthweek Classroom Companion for more classroom ideas.
  http://www.earthweek.com

- **Learning about Other Cultures.** The Cultural Profiles Project provides an overview of life and customs for many different countries around the world. For many countries, the site includes information about family life, work, health care, holidays, arts and literature. Have students select a country and use this site to report on how life in another country compares to their own.
  http://www.settlement.org/cp

- **Learning about Maps (Grades 5–10).** Use this resource as an introduction to a map-study unit. Have students access the site to learn about different types of maps and to view examples of each. **http://www.epa.gov/ceisweb1/ceishome/atlas/learngeog/learnmaps.html**
  Also check out the wonderful set of map resources available from the Perry-Castañeda Map Collection at **http://www.lib.utexas.edu/maps/index.html**.

- **Midlink Magazine (Grades 4–8).** This is an electronic magazine for students in the middle grades. Issued bi-monthly, Midlink offers an exciting range of learning activities. It includes written contributions

from kids, reports on student Internet projects, and pointers to resources that students will enjoy. Each month features a special theme. Some issues contain examples of student portfolios that have been prepared using largely electronic resources. The magazine is an appealing way for middle grade students to get involved in online activities, and you can use this resource to generate your own ideas.
http://www.ncsu.edu/midlink

Kidsworld Online (**www.kidsworld-online.com**) and Cyberkids (**www.cyberkids.com**) are similar resources with stories and artwork by kids. Older students can submit work to Cyberteens at **http://cyberteens.com/fg/fb/an/aa.**

- **Planning a Trip (Grades 6–10).** Students respond positively to the way that this activity is anchored in the real world. Have students select a country to travel to. They are allowed $4000 for travel, including hotel and transportation. In addition to planning travel to and from their destination, they must convert their dollars to the currency of their country of destination. A trip planning worksheet is available from **http://www.scetv.org/ntti/lessons/2000lessons/activities/currencyA1.html** Planning transportation can be done at **http://www.expedia.com**. Currency conversion can be done at **http://www.xe.com/ucc**. Use The Lonely Planet (**http://www.lonelyplanet.com**) or other travel site to find information about travel to different countries.

- **Viewing the Earth (Grades 5–9).** This resource gives students a different perspective on the earth. They can specify longitude and latitude and view locations from the perspective of the sun or moon, and they can see the division between night and day in different time zones. This site also points to some public domain software for downloading.
http://www.fourmilab.ch/earthview/vplanet.html

- **Parts of Speech (Grades 4–6).** Wacky Web Tales is a fun resource that tests students' skill at identifying parts of speech. Students select a story, then fill in parts of speech in the designated fields. They submit their completed forms, and a "wacky" story is returned. (Some teachers may remember this activity as "Madlibs" in pre-computer days.) There are Madlibs elsewhere on the Internet, but this source has an exceptionally clear focus.
http://www.eduplace.com/tales

- **Math Puzzlers (Grades 3–10).** A new set of puzzles is offered every week at this resource. Select a puzzle for your class to solve. Then check for the answers each Wednesday when new puzzles and answers to the previous week's puzzles are posted. Puzzles are available for Grades 3/4,

5/6, and 7+. Strong math students may enjoy exploring the math puzzle archives, where previous puzzles are posted along with their solutions.
http://www.eduplace.com/math/brain

- **Learning about Earthquakes (Grades 1–12).** The Internet provides many outstanding resources for learning about climate and geological phenomena. The U.S. Geological Survey's Earthquakes for Kids site provides links for finding out about earthquakes. From this site, students can access earthquake data, take a virtual tour of several fault zones and find out about current research. The site also has activities and lesson ideas for younger students.
http://earthquake.usgs.gov/4kids

- **Writing (Grades 5–8).** Have your students contribute something to KidNews. This publication publishes student writing in a number of different categories, including news, sports, feature stories, creative writing, reviews, and personal profiles. Preview the publication and select sections that you would like to have students focus on. Writing can be submitted using conventional e-mail or an online form posted at the site.
http://www.kidnews.com

[By contributing to online projects], students can easily become part of a much larger project, while appreciating the uniqueness of their own area. When my class began work on our school Web page, we used it as an extension to the social studies program.

— Nancy Barkhouse, Teacher, Atlantic View Elementary School,
Lawrencetown, Nova Scotia, Canada

- **Resume Writing (Grades 9–12).** About.com features many good articles about resume writing, along with templates and advice for submitting resumes electronically. Select from among the articles those that you would like to have your students read. Include articles offering tips for resume writing and cover letters. Students may discuss and compare their findings before developing their own resumes, either for imaginary careers or for part-time or summer work.

About.com Links:
http://careerplanning.about.com/cs/resumewriting
http://jobsearchtech.about.com/cs/resumes

Students can use CareerWeb (**http://www.careerweb.com**) or other online career service to explore career choices and find out about entry level job opportunities in a field that interests them.

HINT You will find site reviews for online learning sites and teaching ideas at Education World's "Best of Series." Here you can locate top resources for arts, math, science, as well as special topics, such as the Holocaust and 9-11. Annual reviews can be accessed at **http://www.education-world.com/best_of/2002/reviews.shtml**. Also check out the links to lesson plans and curriculum topics at Blue Web'N at **http://www.kn.pacbell.com/wired/bluewebn**.

Figure 5-7
Search for online activities for kids at Yahooligans.

WebQuests

Using the Web effectively depends in part on having a good sense of the kinds of learning resources you can find on the Internet. If you have taken time to explore some of the resources we have talked about so far, you have likely found a number of activities that you could use in your classroom. The next step is to develop an effective method for introducing students to useful resources in a way that ensures the learning will tie closely to curriculum. WebQuests provide a model for linking Web-based research and learning outcomes in a practical and engaging fashion. WebQuests as a way of learning on the Internet were first developed by Bernie Dodge, an educational technology professor at San Diego State University. His definition of a WebQuest includes the following description: "an inquiry-oriented activity in which some or all of the information that learners interact with comes from resources on the Internet...." In addition, WebQuests can be short term (from one to three class periods), or long term, requiring a week, a month, or even more. The appeal of WebQuests has to do with the fact that they can be adapted for a range of technology environments and many different curriculum areas. In addition, WebQuest projects can easily be used in cross-curricular learning situations.

Here are the basic elements of a WebQuest:

• An introduction, which provides background information to interest students in the assignment.
• An interesting task.
• Process or steps involved in completing the task.
• Resources to be used. Typically, these are primarily Internet resources, but other sources, such as library resources, can be included.
• Guidance in organizing information and completing tasks.
• Conclusion (what's been learned with suggestions for learning more).

Optional elements can include

• Group activities/discussion
• Online conferencing (audio or video)
• Motivational context (controversial theme, role playing, real-world environment)
• Creating of a learning "product" online or offline.

WebQuests foster active learning in which the instructional goal is knowledge acquisition and integration. Ideally, the learner will deal with a significant amount of new information, interpreting it through synthesis and analysis and ultimately transforming information into knowledge.

Another appealing feature of WebQuests is that they can readily be shared among teachers, and with some attention paid to keeping them up-to-date, they can be used from one year to the next, so that the value from the time a teacher spends developing an assignment is maximized. Some teachers have posted their WebQuests on the Web. A good selection of WebQuest examples for various grade levels is available from Edweb: **http://edweb.sdsu.edu/webquest/matrix.html**.

The best way to get a sense of how WebQuests work is to look at an example. The following WebQuest about the dangers of tobacco was created by Ginger Nehls of Magnolia Elementary School.

Tips for developing WebQuests

- Think about real-world issues (e.g., political, interest groups, scientific controversies).
- Use real-world roles to motivate (e.g., you are a judge, you are part of a visible minority).
- Think of a new perspective on an old topic.
- Use imaginative or historical settings.

- Think about topics that interest kids.
- Think about new areas of learning to explore.
- Think about investigative research projects your students have done "offline." How might these be extended to the Internet in the form of WebQuests?

- Consider a multi-discipline approach.
- Don't forget about opportunities to communicate online.
- Provide imaginative texture as a motivator (e.g., Does the Tiger Eat Her Own Cubs?).

Webquest
Instructional Technology Development Consortium

The Real Scoop on Tobacco

You have been hired by the parents of Icabod, a sixth grade student. They suspect their child of smoking or about to start. He's gone through D.A.R.E. and listened to the lectures of his parents and teachers. However, he thinks they are all just handing him a line. After all, he sees lots of adults smoking and figures it isn't really so bad. In fact, he thinks it's pretty cool. But he might listen to you. After all, you're his peer. That's what his parents are counting on. They've hired you to convince him to quit smoking. To do so, you must show your commitment to the fight against youth using tobacco and create a memorable message for him. Do a good job - it could be a matter of life and death.

The Task

Your client's son doesn't particularly like to read, so you must approach him in a more creative way. He is, after all, much like you, a member of the MTV generation. He'll listen to a rap song; he'll hang a poster in his room. But to earn his respect, you must first demonstrate your knowledge of tobacco and your commitment to fight its use by young people. So here's what you're being paid to do:

- Become an expert about tobacco use and issues surrounding its use.
- Create an ad or poster that visually conveys the message you want to get across.
- Demonstrate your commitment to fight tobacco use by writing a letter to a tobacco company and an editorial for the local paper.
- Get Icabod's attention and give him a memorable message using a music video, skit, or TV commercial.

The Process

1. Determine how you will organize information in your journal. You will use this to record all information and activities throughout the project, including a log of your daily activities, brainstorming questions, notes from research, comments from other students, drafts of project tasks, etc.
2. Conduct research on tobacco and respond to the following questions:
   - What diseases are caused by smoking cigarettes? smoking cigars? chewing tobacco?
   - What influences people to smoke?
   - What keeps them smoking?
   - What are the facts about nicotine?
   - What can you find out about the tobacco industry?
   - Identify and explain the significance of recent court cases involving the tobacco industry.
   - Collect any other interesting or important facts.
3. In your journal, brainstorm the position and supporting facts you will use to convince Icabod to stop smoking.
4. Collect tobacco ads, posters, etc. and analyze them using the following questions:
   1. What graphic design techniques did they use to appeal to you?
   2. What does the ad say directly?
   3. What does it say indirectly (hinting, suggesting)?
   4. Who do you think this advertisement is designed to interest? How does it do this?
5. Based on your research, design an advertisement or poster to convey your message about tobacco use. Consider analyzing any ads aimed at your age level for techniques graphic designers use to attract you. Use these techniques in your ad to promote your position on tobacco use.
6. Spread the word by writing an editorial to your local newspaper making a persuasive statement about one of the issues related to youth using tobacco. To get a feel for style and format of this type of writing, read a variety of editorials published in newspapers or magazines. Does the editorial convince you to agree with the author's position? If so, how was it convincing? If not, why wasn't it convincing? How can you relate this to your task of writing an editorial?
7. Go directly to the source! Write a letter to tobacco companies stating your concerns for their impact on youth. Support with facts from your research and ad analysis.

Page: 1

8. Give a message that'll stick! Determine how you will convince Icabod to quit smoking. Select from the following presentation ideas or propose your own idea. Regardless of your approach, you need to be convincing, relate important facts, and connect with your audience. You can create a:
   - song and a music video for it
   - skit using a scenario related to youth using tobacco
   - TV commercial
9. Prepare a presentation to Icabod and his parents in which you can offer your letters and ad/poster as testimony to your knowledge and commitment. Then deliver your message to Icabod in a way he won't forget!
10. Present your final product to Icabod and his parents on a designated "Youth Against Tobacco" day in your class.

Resources

Below are some sites that will help you accomplish your tasks. Many have links to additional sites. Stay focused on your tasks, however, and know what you are looking for, or you can waste a lot of valuable time.

Master Anti-Smoking Page is a great resource for links to organizations working to combat the smoking habit. It also provides a way to ask an expert specific questions. You'll need to scroll down quite a bit to find the Anti-Smoking page listed under "Specialty Pages -General Interest".

American Cancer Society is the site specifically targeting tobacco control. It provides facts about smoking cigars and includes a position statement and cigar fact sheet.

Quit-Net is a site by the Massachusetts Tobacco Control Program with information on how to quit, resources, news items, and great links.

The Learning Trip has easy-to-understand information on the physical reasons people continue to smoke and on nicotine's effects on various parts of the body.

If Tobacco Ads Really Told the Truth is a fun site showing kids' versions (parodies) of tobacco ads.

Campaign for Tobacco Free Kids includes information about recent legislation (laws) and policies. Be sure to check out the "Kid's Corner". It's written just for you!

Adverse Effects of Smoking has some interesting information — including a picture of a smoker's lung.

Learning Advice

Feedback: Get feedback from at least two other people while each part of your project is still in rough draft form. Have them record their feedback (what's good, suggestions for improvement) in your journal. Record your reaction to their feedback and any changes you made based on their suggestions.

Writing a song: If you're having trouble designing both the music and lyrics, pick out a catchy tune or a popular song to which you can rewrite the lyrics.

Performing: Determine whether you would prefer to act out your presentation live or videotape it. If you choose to videotape it, become familiar with the functions of your camcorder, storyboard the presentation, and determine effective shooting techniques.

Evaluation

Use the following questions to evaluate the quality of your work:

- Were you able to put together accurate and current information about the effects of using tobacco?
- Is your journal complete, including notes, feedback from others, log of activities, etc.
- Is your poster creative, appealing, and professional looking?
- Does your skit get your point across? Is it thought-provoking and interesting to watch?
- Is your letter to the tobacco company written in proper form and expressing a clear opinion substantiated by facts?
- Is your editorial to the newspaper written in proper form? Is it persuasive and supported with facts?

Page: 2

Reflection

1. Do you feel this was an effective learning experience? Explain.
2. How did you determine which information was helpful and accurate?
3. If you were doing this activity again, what would you do differently?
4. What suggestions or hints would you offer to future students doing this WebQuest?

Conclusion

What have you learned about the effects of tobacco that you didn't really know before? In what ways has this project affected you and your opinion about smoking and other forms of tobacco use?

Extension

Find out about smoking laws in your state and city. If there are laws restricting smoking, what are the restrictions? Why do you think these laws were enacted? What impact do they have on you and your community? Write to your council members supporting or urging action.

Notes to the Teacher

Lesson Title: The Real Scoop on Tobacco

Curricular Area: Health

Grade Level: 5–9

Goal/Purpose: To give students the opportunity to apply and make sense of the myriad of information available regarding tobacco and to
be able to personalize it so that the information can aid them to make better decisions regarding their health.

- learn to identify the effects of tobacco on different parts of the body.
- understand the influences that promote drug use including peer pressure, advertising, etc.
- develop and use interpersonal and other communication skills such as assertiveness, refusal, etc.
- become aware of the legal issues concerning tobacco use.
- identify ways of obtaining help to resist pressure to use (or to quit using) tobacco.

(quoted from the *California Health Framework,* 1994)

Interdisciplinary Connections: Language Arts, Visual and Performing Arts

Length of Lesson: 2–3 weeks

Materials:

- notebooks/journal for note-taking and organization
- magazines full of ads
- newspapers that have a kid editorial section
- names and addresses of tobacco companies
- camcorder (optional)
- tape player/recorder
- poster paper
- markers, glue, etc.

Teacher Resources:

- A List of Tobacco Industry Addresses
- Tobacco BBS (Bulletin Board System) is a free resource center focusing on tobacco and smoking issues. It features tobacco news, information, assistance for smokers trying to quit, alerts for tobacco control advocates, and open debate on the wide spectrum of issues concerning tobacco, nicotine, cigarettes and cigars.

Page: 3

- *Here's Looking at You, 2,000* 6th grade drug prevention program published by Comprehensive Health Education Foundation. Lesson 3 deals with smoking; lesson 4 deals with chewing tobacco; lesson 6 deals with advertising.
- *Microsoft Encarta '95* CD — look under "Smoking."

Prerequisite Learning: Students need to be comfortable with the following skills or supported throughout the process:

- cooperative learning skills
- willingness to solicit and consider constructive criticism
- note-taking and organizational strategies
- letter writing skills (format and style)
- ability to identify and target different audiences
- ability to use Internet resources

Suggestions:

1. Organize the students into small groups. Discuss the advantages of dividing up responsibilities. Be clear in what your expectations are for individuals and groups.
2. When presenting this project, provide students with a copy of the project to include in their journal. Conduct a brainstorming session to determine organizational strategies for notebooks, materials, computer use, etc.
3. Conduct small group or whole class sessions throughout the project to provide support on various activities and peer feedback opportunities.
4. Arrange a "Youth Against Tobacco" day in your class/school. Ask administrators or parents to participate as Icabod and his parents and have students present their products. Provide opportunities for students to share their projects beyond the classroom with their school, parents, and community.

Written by <u>Ginger Nehls</u>, teacher at Magnolia Elementary School, Upland Unified School District.

Page: 4

Ideas for WebQuest learning tasks

WebQuest activities can range from a simple set of questions that students are to answer using the Internet, to a more involved group assignment culminating in an online debate or publication. At the bottom of the page is a chart of some examples of the kinds of activities that could be the focus of student learning using the WebQuest model.

Where possible, students should share their knowledge over the Net.

WebQuest resources

Find out more about WebQuests using these sources:

The WebQuest Page
http://webquest.sdsu.edu

The SESD Teacher Resource Site List of Web Quests
(1200+ WebQuest examples submitted by teachers).
http://sesd.sk.ca/teachersresource/webquest.htm

WebQuest: Searching for China
http://www.kn.pacbell.com/wired/China/ChinaQuest.html

WebQuest: Does the Tiger Eat Her Cubs?
http://www.kn.pacbell.com/wired/China/childquest.html

WebQuest: What are They?
http://yesnet.yk.ca/schools/wes/webquests.html

QUESTIONS	SUMMARY	PROBLEM SOLVING	CREATIVE WORK	DEFENDING POSITION
open ended	outline	flow-chart	logbook	debate
targeted	concept map	report	journal	essay: compare and contrast
scavenger hunt	text summary	action	student news report	table: pros/cons
data collection	timeline	diagram	poem	
table completion			play	
			letter	

Whitehorse WebQuest Collection
http://www.yesnet.yk.ca/schools/wes/webquest_collection.html

WebQuests in Our Future: The Teacher's Role in Cyberspace developed by Kathy Schrock.
http://school.discovery.com/schrockguide/webquest/webquest.html

Templates for Developing WebQuests. There are a number of sources you can use to acquire a WebQuest template. Here are two examples.

• A WebQuest template with directions for modifying the template using Netscape composer is available from **http://www.internet4classrooms.com/composer_wqtemplate.html**

• Another WebQuest template with directions for its use is available from **http://www.spa3.k12.sc.us/WebQuestTemplate/webquesttemp.htm**. This template can be modified using Microsoft Word, Notepad or HTML editing software.

Summing up

In this chapter we have suggested some of the ways that the Internet can be used for student research. While the most dynamic Internet projects include collaboration with students in other classrooms, learning how to use the Internet as a research tool is an essential first step.

In the next chapter we will explain how to develop Web pages. Knowing how to develop Web pages will increase the ability of students to share what they have learned. Although such projects require a higher level of skill than just using the Web to find information, they are particularly exciting activities for students because they give them a way to present their own creative work and research findings to others. It is in designing and publishing their own Web pages that students and teachers will fully appreciate the power of the Internet.

6
Chapter

Developing Web Pages for Learning

"A Language Arts teacher asked me to teach her ninth- and eleventh-grade students how to make a Web page. Several of my student assistants volunteered to teach these kids enough to put a writing project or two online. These projects are not perfect nor very sophisticated, but they do function. It is also our first experiment in electronic portfolios as a means of alternative assessment."

— Currie Morrison, Technology Coordinator, Nathan Hale High School, Seattle, Washington, U.S.A.

Perhaps the most powerful application of Web technology for classrooms is as a publishing tool. With the ability to publish home pages, students can share their work with one another and even make the work they do available to the world. Knowing how to program in HTML (*Hypertext Markup Language*) and to create online learning resources such as WebQuests is a practical skill for teachers and the most exciting part of the Web for many students. *Be aware, however, that HTML programming is not for everyone.* Learning to develop Web pages is not hard, but it can be time consuming and frustrating for those who do not possess a good eye for detail. Many teachers have neither the time nor inclination to master this skill. Don't worry if you fall into this category. Read through this chapter to get a sense of what's involved, then find an eager student to develop pages for you. Using an HTML editor, which we describe later in this chapter, will also greatly simplify the task of creating Web pages.

Chapter goals

■ **To provide an overview of HTML tagging**
■ **To provide instructions on how to develop a Web page**
■ **To provide guidelines and resources for Web graphics**
■ **To offer some examples of how Web pages can be used in schools**
■ **To provide guidelines and ideas for developing effective school Web pages**

What the Web offers that books, magazines, or videos don't is the opportunity to publish their work for a worldwide audience, which motivates them to write. I wish you could have seen my students last spring creating a Web page for their school. They were so proud!

— *Karla Frizler, ESL Instructor and Founder, Frizzy University Network (FUN), San Francisco, California, U.S.A.*

Figure 6-1
A secondary school
Web page.

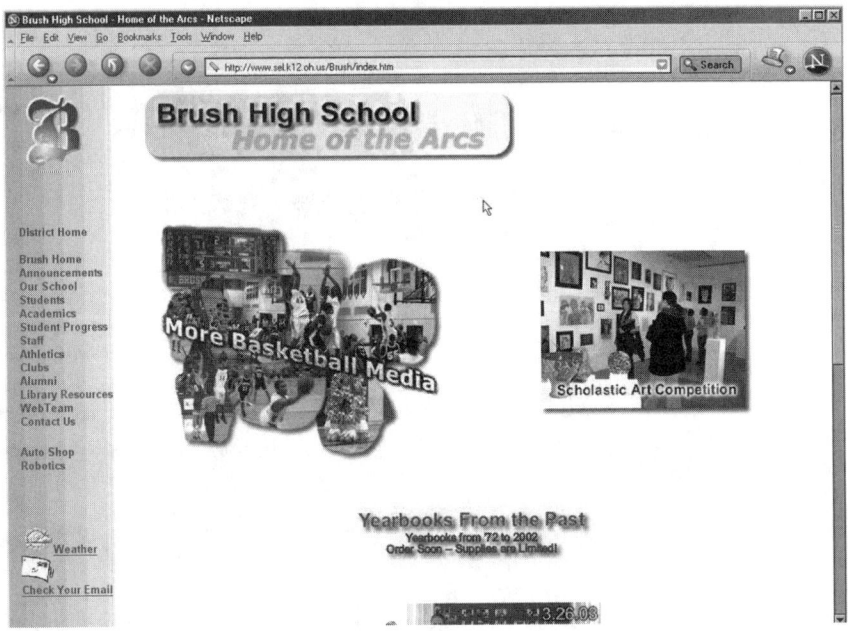

If the very thought of HTML causes your eyes to go out of focus, you'll be happy to know that there are a number of ways to create HTML pages that don't require any programming. Most newer word-processing programs offer an option to save in HTML format. Word 2000 does all of the grunt work, converting a word-processing document to HTML, handling graphics and packaging up everything into a folder that can be easily uploaded to a Web server. The HTML editors discussed in this chapter will also make things easy. A number of other programs such as Hyperstudio and Inspiration also include Web publishing features. Learning a bit about HTML will help you to know what's happening in the background and it is sometimes handy for troubleshooting.

Introduction to HTML

HTML stands for Hypertext Markup Language. Basically, HTML offers a set of tags that tell your browser how to format and display text on a Web page.

You can see how a Web page is constructed by using your Web browser to view what is called the *source document*. In Netscape, after accessing a Web page, click on **View** and **Source**. The cryptic-looking page that is revealed is in fact the Web page you have accessed. It displays the codes that are interpreted by your Web browser. Although a first look at a Web source page can be intimidating, if you take a closer look you'll see that it's not much more than a text document with a series of codes enclosed in brackets. Here's a sample:

```
<HTML><HEAD><TITLE>Online Educator
Samples</TITLE></HEAD>
<BODY bgcolor="#fffff0">
<A HREF="SAFETY.html">[Safety]</A>
<A HREF="OWL.html">[Writing]</A>
<A HREF="NASA.html">[Space]</A>
<A HREF="CUREVEN.html">[Events]</A>
```

```
<A HREF="CYBERJ.html">[Cyberjournalists]</A>
<A HREF="QUAKE.html">[Quake]</A>
<A HREF="GEOG.html">[Geography]</A>
<A HREF="EMAIL.html">[E-Mail]</A>
<A HREF="MUSEUM.html">[Museums]</A><br>
<A HREF="../OEWELCOME.html"><IMG WIDTH=220 BOR-
DER=0 VSPACE=4
SRC="../OEFOLIO.GIF"></A><br> <ADDRESS>A sample
article from our monthly publication
</ADDRESS> <hr NOSHADE SIZE=3> <STRONG>January
1995</STRONG>

<hr NOSHADE>

<H1>Caution and good sense keep Net safe</H1>

<P>Taking your students online will open up a
whole world of educational possibilities. It also
will present them and you with the opportunity to
come in contact with questionable material and
subjects.

<P>The Internet can deliver pictures from Jupiter
and Mars into your classroom, and it can also
bring nudes and other inappropriate photos. You
can download great works of literature and docu-
ments such as the Declaration of Independence into
your classroom computer, and you can just as easi-
ly get instructions on how to build pipe bombs or
mix chemical explosives.
```

If you take a close look at this example, you can discern a combination of the text that appears in the normal viewing of a Web page and a series of tags (which appear in bold type in this example). These tags are just a set of commands that tell your system's browser

- where specific images should be placed:

```
<IMG WIDTH=220 BORDER=0 VSPACE=4
SRC="../OEFOLIO.GIF">
```

- where to display a link to another file:

```
<A HREF="MUSEUM.html">[Museums]</A>
```

- which text to display in a larger font:

  `<H1>`Caution and good sense keep Net safe`</H1>`

- which text to display in bold letters:

  `<STRONG>`January 1995`</STRONG>`

- where to place a hard return (which in Netscape appears as a line across the page):

  `<hr>`

Developing a Web page

Although the source code (as described in the above example) can make Web page development seem very confusing, it is not difficult to create a simple page for student work. Once you have grasped the basics, you can develop a Web page with instructions for an Internet research project and integrate links to the sites you want your students to visit. You can also develop a basic template for student reports that would allow you to display completed student assignments so your students can share their work online. Pages that you have developed can be accessed from a local hard drive. When you are ready to have the public view work that your students have done, transfer your files to a school or district Web server.

These days you will find many pages on the Web with complex features, such as interactive components and heavy-duty graphics. Fortunately, you don't need this to create a functional page. In fact, most teachers prefer simple pages that download quickly and are easy to navigate.

The process for creating an HTML page is to key in HTML tags to any plain text file. You can do this using your word processor. Most newer word processors have incorporated the ability to add HTML tags as a formatting option. It is, however, still important to learn about HTML codes in order to know how to use the range of tags available. Many people find it valuable to learn a few basic HTML tags before trying to develop Web pages using a word processor or other software.

Basic HTML tags

Most HTML tags appear in pairs, and the second tag in a pair includes a slash. (e.g., <H1> </H1>) The first of the two codes is placed at the start of the text you want to format and the second tag is inserted immediately after that text.

Tech Talk

Use the Save As ... option from the File menu to change a word-processed file into plain text. As you are prompted by the dialog box for a new file name, you will see a small window near the bottom of the screen identifying options for saving the file. Click on the arrow to see the list of options. Selecting Text Only or ASCII Text will delete all the special coding related to your word processor and save the file in text format. If you have added HTML tags to a plain text file, you can re-name the file with an .htm or .html extension that your browser will recognize.

Here are a few of the most important tags to know about:

Page formatting tags (These tags identify the different sections of a page and should be included in all HTML documents.)

\<HTML> \</HTML> These two tags signal the beginning and the end of a Web page.

\<HEAD> \</HEAD> These tags signal the beginning and end of the document header. The header provides information about a Web page, such as the title of a page and sometimes optional information that is not intended to be displayed.

\<TITLE> \</TITLE> These tags frame the title of the page. The title of the page displays in the title bar at the top of the browser, rather than on the page itself.

\<BODY> \</BODY> These tags frame the body of the document. The \<BODY> tag appears after the closing tag for the header and can incorporate some document detail, such as the background color information. The closing body tag \</BODY> should be included at the very end of the document, and just before the final \</HTML> closing tag.

Here is an example of what the above tags would look like in a document:

\<HTML>
\<HEAD>
\<TITLE>Assignment — Week 1**\</TITLE>**
\</HEAD>
\<BODY>
\<H1> Web Museum Reports **\</H1>**
This week you will visit a museum on the Web, blah, blah, blah!
\</BODY>
\</HTML>

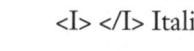

Geekspeak

Text formatting tags

1. Headings

\<H1> \</H1> This tag tells your browser to display text in the largest size available.
\<H2> \</H2> This tag will display text in the second largest size available.
\<H6> \</H6> Font size tags continue up to six; six represents the smallest size.

2. Emphasis

\<B> \</B> Bold text
\<I> \</I> Italics

3. Line Breaks

You will quickly discover that your browser pays no attention to line breaks unless you change the text size or use one of these tags.

<P> This tag adds a space. Use it to start a new paragraph.

 This tag inserts a line break, so that text is continued on the next line.
<HR> This tag adds a horizontal line as a break in the text.

4. Links

The examples below illustrate how to set up hyperlinks.
To link to another site:

<A HREF="http://www.gsn.org/"> Global SchoolNet </A>

The example above offers a link to the Global SchoolNet site. The URL is enclosed in quotation marks, exactly as illustrated. The URL can include directory and file names as well. Following the reference is any descriptive text you wish to display for the link (frequently the name of the site). *Additional tags can frame the text, such as a size tag (<H2> Global SchoolNet </H2>) or a tag for italics or bold.* The reference is closed with the **</A>** tag.

- To link to a document on your own server:

  <A HREF="assign1.htm">Assignment #1</A>

  In this example, the tags are exactly the same as those used in the previous example of a link to a Web site. In this case, the file is on your own server, so only the file name is required. Be sure to include any directory and subdirectory names if the file will not be in the same directory as the Web page you are linking from.

- To link to somewhere else on the Web page you are developing:

  <A HREF="#Evaluation">Evaluation </A>

  In this example, "#Evaluation" refers to a NAME anchor. A NAME anchor is a tag that you have set up as a reference. The NAME anchor tag looks like this:

  <A NAME="Evaluation"> Here are the points you will be marked on. **</A>**

  In this case, the text *Here are the points you will be marked on* is not a link, but simply a marked section in the text. Clicking on the *Evaluation* link described above will cause the browser to immediately bounce to this section of the document.

HINT Try EdWeb's HTML Crash Course for Educators: **http://ibiblio.org/edweb/htmlintro.html**.

- A link to an e-mail address:

  <A HREF="mailto:president@whitehouse.gov">
  Send a letter to the White House**</A>**

5. Lists

Lists are an efficient way to include a number of similar items on a Web page. As an example, you could use a list to identify the steps for a science investigation.

<OL> </OL> Use these tags to set up an ordered (numbered) list. The browser will automatically *number* the items designated <LI> within the list.

<UL></UL> This set of tags will give you a *bulleted* list.

<LI> Use this single tag to designate the start of each new item in a list.

Format example for a numbered list:
<OL>
<LI> beans
<LI> peas
<LI> cabbage
</OL>

Adding colors and images

1. Background Colors

You can add color to your Web pages by specifying a numeric code for each color you want to include. The numeric codes are hexadecimal values for RGB colors (Red/Green/Blue or #RRGGBB). If you do not specify colors on your Web page, the browser default colors will apply. The following example adds a background color (BGCOLOR):

<BODY BGCOLOR="#612f75"> The BGCOLOR tag is embedded into the body tag.

You can also specify colors for the text (TEXT) on a page, *links* (LINK), and *followed* links (VLINK):

<BODY BGCOLOR="#ffffff" TEXT="#000000" LINK= "#FF00FF" VLINK="##2F4F2F"> (In this case, the background is white and the text is black. Links are magenta and followed links are dark green.)

Although there is a method for calculating the RGB valuations for colors, it is easier to consult a color palette that provides these values. Many

Tech Talk

Found a Web page with a background color that you like? Check the BGCOLOR numeric code using the View Source option. You can use this option to learn how coding was done for other elements on a page as well. Another BGCOLOR tip is that for simple colors (e.g., white, black, yellow, red, purple, cyan, green) you can replace the numeric code with the word, as in *BGCOLOR = "WHITE"*.

Web site editors (discussed below) include hexadecimal codes for colors. A number of downloadable "HTML Color Pickers" are available for both Windows and Macintosh computers at TUCOWS (**http://www. tucows.com**). On the Web you can visit Dougie's Color Picker at **http://www.hypersolutions.org/pages/colorSel.html** or The ColorMaker Page at **http://www.bagism.com/colormaker**. At each of these sites you can look up the hexadecimal value for a broad range of colors and test how your color choices will look.

2. Images

To insert an image use the following tag:

<IMG SRC="sunflower.gif">

To position the image on the page add the ALIGN tag:

<IMG SRC="sunflower.gif" ALIGN=top>

The ALIGN attribute can be top, bottom, middle, left, or right. This attribute will affect how the text flows around the image.

ALT
<IMG SRC="applepicture.gif" ALT="[Apples]">

If you include the ALT= reference in the image tag, visitors to the page who have turned off the image loading feature on their browser will still be able to make sense of the page. Always use the ALT tag for documents that will be accessible outside of the school network.

3. Background images

You can add texture to your page by using a background image:

<BODY BACKGROUND="clouds.gif">

In this example, the browser will duplicate a graphic file called *clouds.gif*, filling the page and creating a tiled effect. Text and images on the page will appear against the tiled background. As with other image files, the image file referenced by the background tag needs to be in the same directory with the Web page, or directory and subdirectory names need to be included in the reference.

Use background textures carefully. Soft, subtle patterns work best. If background texture is too bold, the page will be hard to read. You will find lots of background textures at Hee Yun's Graphic Collection (**http://soback.kornet.net/~pixeline/heeyun/graphics.html**) and at AAA Free Backgrounds and Textures (**http://www.aaabackgrounds .com**). For a good collection of backgrounds, buttons and bars, visit Absolute Web Graphics Archive at **http://www.grsites.com/ webgraphics**.

HINT You can also add sounds to your Web page projects. Use Findsounds.com (**http://www.find sounds.com**) to locate sounds from rattlesnakes to sleigh bells.

HINT HTML no-brainer: try HomeMaker Online **http://www.kn.pacbell. com/wired/homemaker**. Type in information about yourself, select a color scheme, and click!

Tech Talk

An animated .gif is a graphic that moves. These can be added to a Web page as readily as a normal .gif. You can save the .gif by placing your cursor over the image and right clicking, then choosing the save graphic option. Then, just add the file name to a Web page as you normally would for a still image. Voila! It moves.

Web graphics

The simplest way to obtain graphics for your Web page is to download them from the Web. For links to many graphics sources, visit these sites:

Barry's Clip Art Server at **http://www.barrysclipart.com**

Freesite.com: Free Graphics and Clip Art **http://www.thefreesite.com/ Free_Graphics**

Clipart.com Clip Art Index **http://www.clipart.com**

Pics4Learning **http://www.pics4learning.com** (This site offers "copyright friendly" images for use by teachers and students in an education context.)

The ClipArt Connection **http://www.clipartconnection.com**

The Awesome Library Clip Art Page at **http://www.awesomelibrary.org** Click on the technology link to find the clip art resources.

Web Places Clip Art Review **http://www.webplaces.com/html/ clipart.htm**

You can also use a search engine to search for graphic images by name (teacher, Christmas tree, blue ribbon, etc.). AltaVista, Google and AlltheWeb all offer an image search. Searching is not exact, so that your search for a butterfly might also result in a picture of a butterfly pork chop, but this is nevertheless a good way to find images for such things as online portfolios or student reports. Sometimes searching for abstract concepts such as "success" or "friendship" or for phrases that capture an idea, such as "feeding the dog," may help you locate graphics for student stories.

When you want to download an image from a Web page, place your cursor over the image and click on the right-hand mouse button (PC), or just hold down the mouse button on a Mac. Then select **Save This Image As**. To ensure that copyright is respected, most search engines present you first with a thumbnail image, and then require you to go to the actual Web site where the image is posted to download the image.

Most of the images you will encounter on the Web end in *.gif* or *.jpeg*. Web browsers recognize both of these file formats. The .gif format is commonly used for line drawings and simple images (such as a cartoon image with big blocks of color), while .jpeg is generally used for photographs, paintings, and other images with considerable detail.

Sometimes you may have an image you want to include on a Web page that is in a format other than .gif or .jpeg. To convert other image formats (such as .pict, .pcx or .bmp), you will need a graphics editor. A graphics editor lets you open a graphics file in one format and save it to another format. You can generally also re-size a picture, cut out a section to create a new

HINT A very useful site for learning about how to develop Web pages is Pagetutor.com. This is an online tutorial that gives a step-by-step introduction to HTML. You will find the tutorial at **http://www.page tutor.com**. The lessons are listed at the bottom of the page.

image, and perform similar editing functions using a graphics editor. Here are some examples of graphics editors (viewers):

Windows:

20/20 (free) **http://www.hotfreeware.com/2020/2020wh.htm**

LView Pro **http://www.lview.com**

Graphic Workshop **http://www.mindworkshop.com/alchemy/ alchemy.html**

Macintosh:

Big Picture **http://www3.sk.sympatico.ca/tinyjohn**

You can find these and other graphics image viewers at TUCOWS: **http://www.tucows.com**. TUCOWS is a comprehensive site for Internet software.

If you are planning to create your own graphics, you will need a paint program. A number of good graphics programs are available for both Windows and Macintosh computers. One of the most popular and relatively inexpensive graphics programs for Windows is Paint Shop Pro at **http://www.jasc.com/products/psp**. NetStudio **(http://www.netstudio .com)** is a graphics program developed specifically for producing Web graphics, including buttons, banners and fancy text. The program makes it easy for beginners to to create professional-looking graphics.

Finally, if you want to try your hand at creating animated .gifs, try Cell Assembler at **http://www.gamani.com** or Pro Motion. Pro Motion is a drawing package that lets you create animations as well as still images. You can downlaod a trial version at **http://www.cosmigo.com/promotion**.

HTML editors

HINT You will find a list of additional Web editors for the Macintosh, as well as other Web publishing and Internet tools at Pur Mac **http://www. eskimo .com/~pristine/index. html**.

For many people, having to manually type HTML tags into a document is a form of slow torture. In addition, it's easy to make small typographical errors that can cause havoc on a Web page. The solution is to use a Web page editor.

A Web page editor will allow you to add HTML tags to your Web page using a graphical interface (drop-down menus, point and click, highlight and select). Editors include many useful features, such as the ability to select a background color from a color chart and simplified list creation.

Although most editors cost between US$100 and US$150, most are available as trial versions that can be downloaded from the Web. Some software browsers, such as Netscape Communicator, and the newest versions of Internet Explorer, include an HTML editor. If you have one of the latest browsers, you may find that the HTML editing feature is all you need to

develop basic Web pages. If you do not have a built-in HTML editor on your browser, try one of these:

Windows

Hot Dog (Sausage Software)

http://www.sausage.com
This is one of the most popular HTML editors. If you are developing a school site, you may want to choose the professional version, which includes a number of site management features.

HTML WebMaster

http://www.html-helper.com
This is a freeware program with lots of features.

Derekware HTML Author

http://www.geocities.com/SiliconValley/6763/html/dwhtml.html
This is another free program that is highly recommended. A built-in wizard helps with more complicated tasks, such as inserting images or tables.

CoffeeCup

http://coffeecup.com/editor
CoffeeCup is an inexpensive and very popular editor which includes a step-by-step design guide.

Netscape Composer

http://www.netscape.com
This editor provides image format conversion, a built-in spell checker and the ability to create an HTML-based discussion group. Netscape Composer is integrated with the Netscape Communicator browser.

FrontPage

http://www.microsoft.com/frontpage
This is a powerful, popular and easy-to-use editor, but it requires substantial hard-disk space.

Macintosh

PageSpinner

http://www.optima-system.com/pagespinner
This is an inexpensive very easy-to-use editor for Macintosh OS. PageSpinner lets you learn as you go.

Tech Talk

Using graphics is a great way to brighten up your pages. Unfortunately, graphic images can also slow down page loading.

Try to keep individual graphics below 50K (particularly on school Web pages that might be accessed outside of the local area network).

You can also "reuse" graphics. If you include several references to the same graphic on your pages, the image needs to be loaded only once. The browser's computer places the image in a computer storage area called a cache and will retrieve the image from there. To find out more about how to manage graphics for faster loading visit The Bandwidth Conservation Guide at **http://www. submitcorner.com/Guide/Bandwidth**.

BBEdit

http://www.barebones.com
This is a well-liked word-processing program with HTML add-ons.

AOL Press

http://www.mmsd.org/webpub/aolpress.htm
This is a free HTML editor from America Online. It is a good editor for beginners and it is available for Macintosh and Windows computers.

Where to learn more about HTML

There are many excellent resources that you can use to learn more about HTML. Try these :

Introduction to HTML and URLs by Ian Graham **http://www. utoronto.ca/webdocs/HTMLdocs/NewHTML/htmlindex.html**

The Barebones Guide to HTML **http://werbach.com/barebones**

The HTML Writer's Guild at **http://www.hwg.org/resources/ index.html**

You can find other HTML tutorials at The Web Masters Reference Library at **http://webreference.com/html/tutorials** and at the Web Developer's Virtual Library at **http://www.wdvl.com/Authoring/Tutorials.**

If you have students who are enthusiastic about going beyond HTML basics, you may want to introduce them to JavaScript. The JavaScript tutorial for the total non-programmer is the place to start. It's available at **http://www.webteacher.com/javascript**.

School Web pages

Once you have learned the basics for putting together a Web page, the challenge becomes figuring out how to use this technology in a meaningful way in a classroom setting.

Figure 6-2
A classroom Web page.

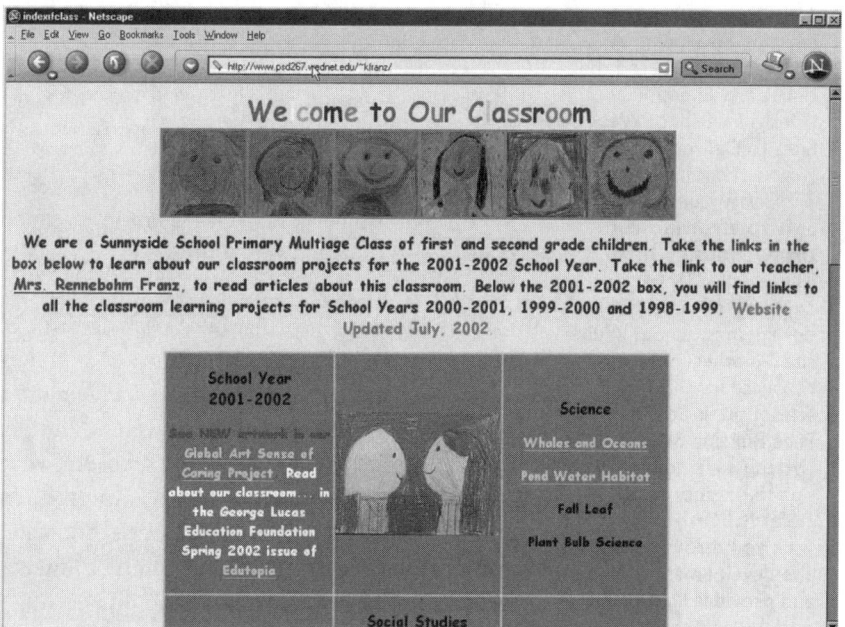

HINT To find out how classes can work together to develop Web pages, visit the Kinds of Web Pages link at West Loogootee Elementary School's Designing Web Pages site. This site also makes available tutorials and ideas for educational Web design. **http://www.siec.k12.in.us/~west/online/index.html**.

HINT Visit these great Web sites:

Cotton Fields pages (developed by seven-year-olds) **http://www.hipark.austin.isd.tenet.edu/arc/projects/first/cotton/cotton.html**

Bellingham Public Schools School Websites **http://www.bham.wednet.edu/schools/schools.htm**

Arbor Heights Elementary in Seattle, Washington **http://www.halcyon.com/arborhts/arborhts.html**.

The Yahoo directory

http://dir.yahoo.com/Education/K–12/schools

Provides links to hundreds of schools around the world, broken down by geographic location. This site offers an easy way to sample the range of school-produced Web pages. In addition to providing basic information about the school and sample class newspapers, many schools also include class projects, sample school publications, and links to useful curriculum sources that can be used by other teachers. Some provide information about the history of the school or information about the local community.

For a list of examples of the kinds of things that might be good to include on a school Web page, visit Exemplary School Web Sites at **http://www.wc4.org/expemplary_school_web_sites.htm**. You can sample school library sites on the Web through links available on Peter Milbury's School Librarian Web Page at **http://www.school-libraries.net**.

School Web pages have themselves become a way of contributing ideas to the rest of the world. One class collected Halloween stories from other schools (via e-mail) and developed a Web page based on them. Another class was given the task of identifying useful curriculum-based resources and establishing links that their classmates and teachers or anyone else accessing their site could use. Students can also use the Web to display their own research reports and creative writing or artwork, or they can profile local community services or events.

HINT For additional ideas on developing Web pages in schools, read the online article entitled "Designing School Web Sites to Deliver" from *From Now On Educational Technology Journal* available at **http://fromnowon. org/webdesign.html**. The article offers a good overview of reasons for developing a school Web site. Another useful resource for building a school site is School Home Page Building Blocks (**http://www.learning space.org/content/ default.html**) which will walk you through the Web site development process and provides links to many useful resources.

My students are excited and eager both to publish their own work and to see what other kids have done. They think of the Web as some kind of huge 'Just Grandma and Me,' except that they can make the click-places themselves. They love getting e-mail from people who mention seeing their work, and they love sending e-mail to others whose work they like.

— Clare Macdonald, Computer Teacher, Bernadotte School, Copenhagen, Denmark

But publishing Web pages is not just a way to broadcast the existence of your school to the world. Web publishing is also a significant classroom learning tool. Central to what students will need to master is how to gather, organize, and present information. Working through an activity that involves organizing a set of links or interrelated pieces of information is directly related to developing analytical thinking skills. Having to gather information from community groups or another class and develop a Web page offers the opportunity to build and refine verbal and written communication skills. Web pages can be the focus for a cultural exchange in which a school in one country teams up with one or more schools in another country to design a collaborative site on a topic of common interest, or as a way of highlighting each nation's history, culture, and diversity.

Class projects featured on School Web pages can be wide ranging. At Dublin Scioto High School in Ohio (**http://scioto.dublin.k12.oh.us**) many teachers have developed Web pages for their classes. There is an impressive gallery of student artwork and one mathematics teacher had her students develop PowerPoint presentations of math concepts and post these on the Web as tutorials for other students. The school site also features a homework center where individual teachers can post assignments and announcements of upcoming tests. Teachers provide directions for assignments as well as links to online resources that students can use in completing their work.

Ambleweb is the Web site for Ambleside C.E. Primary School in the United Kingdom (**http://ambleweb.digitalbrain.com/ambleweb/ ambleweb/ambleweb/index.htm**). It posts a rich variety of classwork, student research reports, personal Web pages done by students in the school computer club, an art gallery and updates for parents. This site also includes a "Book Reviews" database where students can read book reviews and submit their own and interactive quizzes and activities for students.

While this Web site may seem to be particularly sophisticated, Web publishing is not just for high schools. Atlantic View Elementary School has been using the Web to publicize student projects for several years. Topics from Grade 4 student Web pages have included

- student autobiographies
- student poems
- a cyberpals project

HINT Post your questions about creating Web pages to the edtech newsgroup or search the archive to get ideas. Subscription information available at **http://www. h-net.org/~edweb**.

- a sound clip from a student radio project
- report on an in-school performance by Razzmatazz for Kids
- their multicultural folk-dance program
- the participation of some of their students in the Nova Scotia International Tattoo
- information about an endangered species that nests in their community

For a view of school Web page development from a parent volunteer Webmaster and some some very good ideas about how schools can organize teams for developing Web pages and tips on how to keep them going, visit Terry Kearns Case Studies at **http://tk-jk.net/tk/Case_800_school_ websites.htm**.

Posting Web pages

Although student Web pages can always be accessed as individual files on a local computer, eventually you will want to post your pages for the world to see. If you are not running a server in your own school, it may be possible to post your Web pages on an existing Internet server for little or no cost. You may wish to contact a local university or Internet service provider about hosting your page. You could also use one of a number of Internet sites that offer posting for free or for minimal cost. While free sites are available, many are supported by advertising which can be intrusive in a learning context. Costs can be as low as US$30 per year for a basic hosting. Other sites offer features such as Web site development tools, collaborative work environments and online discussion. Web site hosting targeted to schools is available from

SchoolCenter (**http://www.schoolcenter.com**),
SchoolCity.com (**http://www.schoolcity.com**),
TeachNology (**http://signup.teach-nology.com**),
Homestead (**http://www.homestead.com**),
Lightspan (**http://lightspan.com**), and
Bigchalk (**http://schools.bigchalk.com**).

It is essential to have clear policies and guidelines for school Web pages. Guidelines address technical and design issues as well as questions such as who will contribute to the development of the Web site and how long student work will be kept on the site. For a good list of questions to be addressed in developing a school Web policy, visit The Missouri School Web Project Web Policy Guidelines at **http://schoolweb.missouri.edu/policy.html**. There are many good examples of school Web page policies available on the Web. Examples of permission forms for student Web publishing are available from the School Web Clubs site at **http:// support net.merit.edu/webclubs/permissionform.htm**.

Figure 6-3

The Cotton Fields project was developed by seven-year-olds at Highland Park Elementary School, Austin, Texas.

Newer versions of the Windows operating system include a Web publishing Wizard that will walk you through posting your Web pages on the Internet. The Wizard is located under **Programs |Accessories|Internet Tools**.

Figure 6-4

This project from Cotton Fields uses a scanned student drawing.

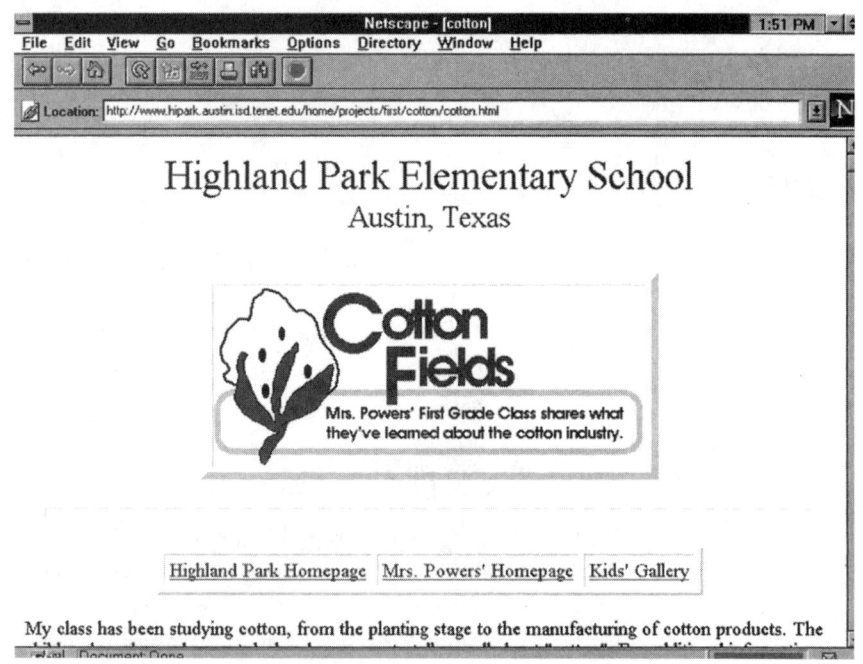

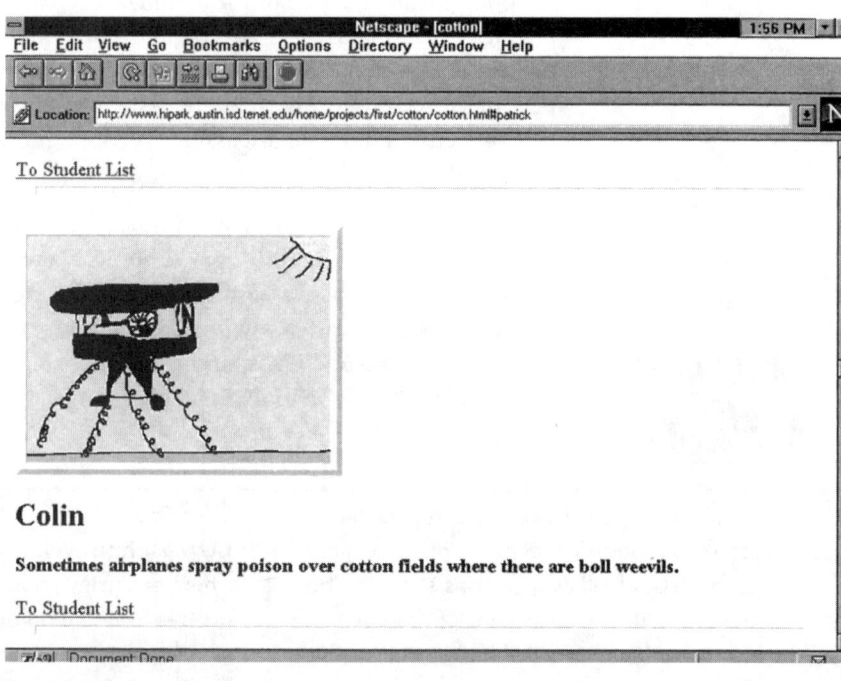

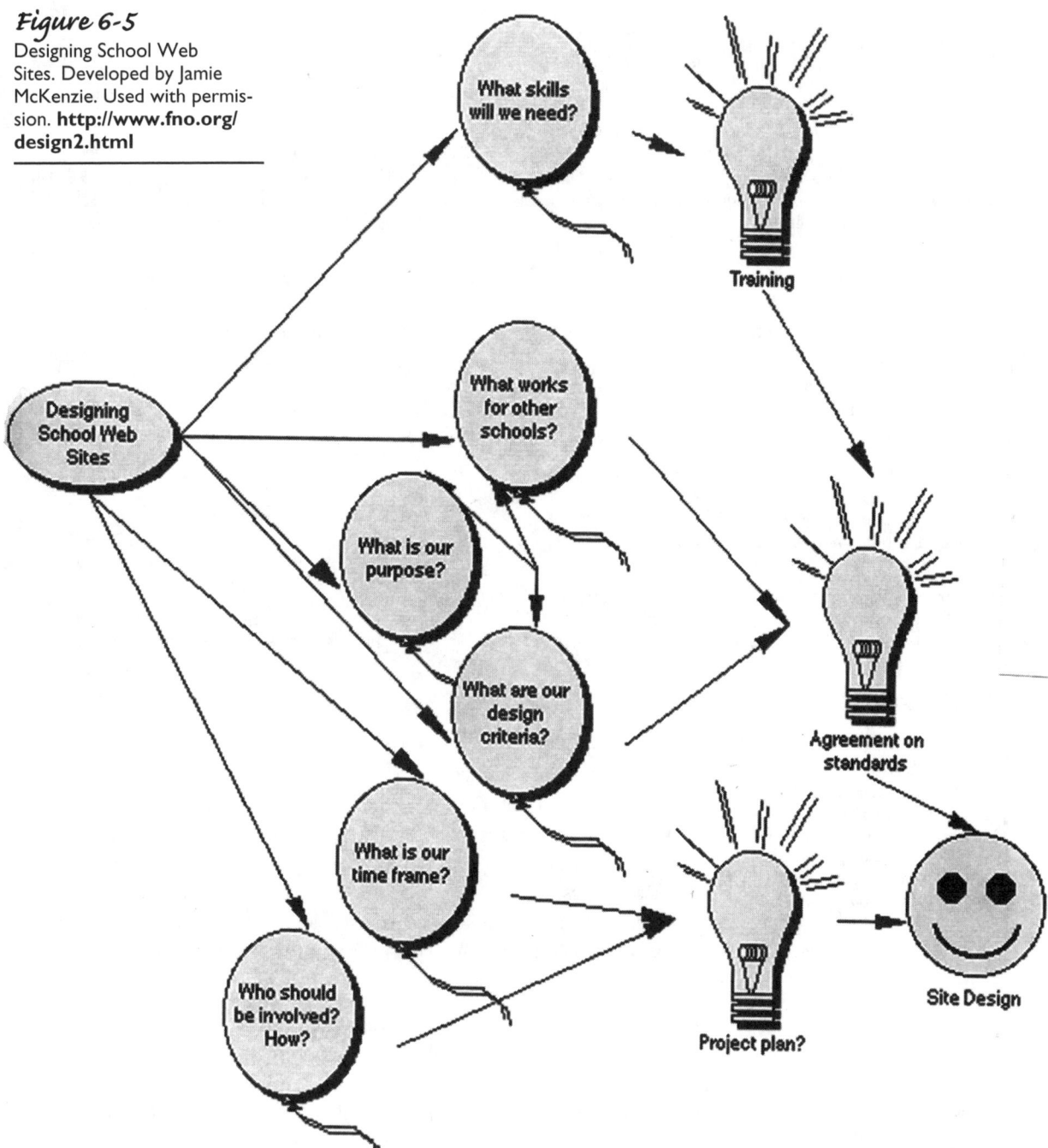

Figure 6-5
Designing School Web Sites. Developed by Jamie McKenzie. Used with permission. **http://www.fno.org/design2.html**

Tips for developing school Web pages

- Think of your Web page first as a communications and public relations tool, and as an information resource second.

- Start small. Develop a Web page of links for a unit of study, or a single page of teacher resources (distribute to teachers on a diskette!).

- Limit what's available at any one time. Use archives to store things as you focus on specific features.

- Don't have too many different things vying for attention: animated .gifs, busy background, many different font changes.

- Don't even think about putting your picture (or the principal's) at the start of your school Web page!

- Style should match content (check out the American Memory Collection: **http://rs6.loc.gov/amhome. html**).

- Think about design! Print Web pages and keep them in a notebook where you can jot down what you like in a Web site and what you don't like.

- Keep the site dynamic. Add new material, and try to develop resources around changing themes. At the same time, try to include something familiar — an established format, consistent banner, etc.

- Develop an archives for older material, in favor of keeping the latest up-front.

- As a general rule, include a brief description with each link you offer. This makes it easier for people to browse your site. It can also save time if access to a machine is an issue.

- When your Web page features something new, print a copy (ideally in color) and post it on a school bulletin board.

- Get others involved! (Kids, teachers, parents, community groups, librarians.) Try to make your site inclusive.

- Use templates for easy, consistent production. Find knowledgeable students to help with more complex tasks.

- Spend some time sampling school sites. What do you like? What don't you like?

- Use kids' artwork. Use great art, historical photographs, cave art. Be careful about copyright and seek permission from the student's parents before posting student work on the Web.

- Master the basics of a paint package (Paint Shop Pro or similar graphics package for creating simple graphics).

HINT At Think.com (**http://about.think.com**) teachers can create classes, projects, and a share material with students. School-based discussions are also possible. This is an excellent resource for class pages. Registration is necessary, but the resource is free.

HINT A good guide for planning and organizing a Web site is the Web Style Guide at (**http://webstyle guide.com**).

You can find more free and inexpensive hosting services reviewed at **http://www.1oobest-free-web-space.com**.

There are also a number of sites that allow teachers to create a Web page directly online. These sites offer templates and ready-made graphics so that even inexperienced Webmasters can easily post lessons, assignments and class activities. Frequently these sites are password protected, so that only students in the class and their parents can access the pages. If you want to post something on the Web without having to tackle HTML, try one of these sites:

TeacherWeb.com (**http://www.teacherweb.com**)
Teachers.Net (**http://www.teachers.net/tools**)
SchoolNotes.com (**http://www.schoolnotes.com**)
TeachNology (**http://teachers.teach-nology.com/web_tools/web_site**)
MySchoolOnline (**http://www.myschoolonline.com**) This site also offers an online quiz feature and an online gradebook.
E-board.com (**http://www.eboard.com**) Create an online corkboard for posting messages and files.
Schoolnotes.com (**http://www.schoolnotes.com**)

teaching tip

It's easy to jazz up your Web pages with an online quiz. Quia (**http://www.quia.com/web/index.html**) is a directory of online quizzes and activities which you can link to from your Web site. For a low subscription cost, Quia also makes available templates and tools that will let you create your own interactive learning activities, such as flashcards, matching challenges, memory tests and word searching exercises. You can also create quizzes for posting online using the software program, Hot Potatoes. Using this program you can create interactive multiple-choice, short-answer, crossword, and other types of exercises. Hot Potatoes is free of charge for non-profit educational users who make their pages available over the Web. You can obtain a copy of Hot Potatoes at **http://web.uvic.ca/hrd/ halfbaked**.

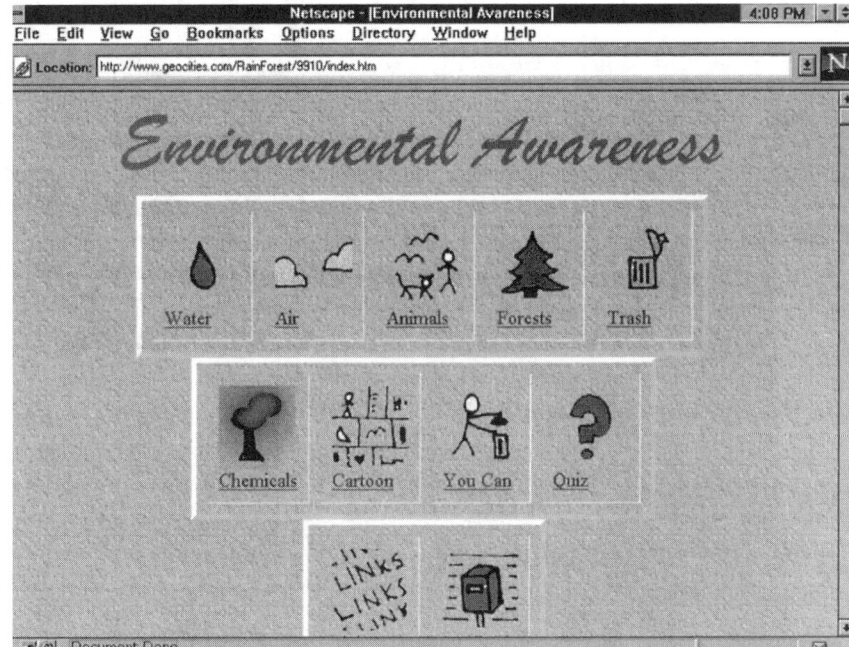

Figure 6-6
Environmental Awareness. This project was created by pupils in Vasaövningsskola in Finland.

Student Web projects

A number of resources on the Internet provide a context for students developing Web pages. One example is Global SchoolNet (GSN) (**http://www.gsn.org**), which was originally established in 1984 as FrEDMail. The purpose of this site is to foster the use of telecommunications to promote basic skills (reading, writing, and communications), along with cross-cultural understanding on a global level. Global SchoolNet sponsors a project registry to publicize online projects for schools, as well as several well-designed Internet projects that emphasize student learning.

HINT Evalute your school Web site using a rubric developed for the SchoolNet Grassroots project. The rubric can be used as a guideline for developing sites with good site design and content. You can also use the rubric in a workshop in which students or colleagues evaluate other school sites before developing sites of their own. The rubric is available at **http://www.schoolnet .ca/grassroots/e/ project.centre/shared/ SWSRubric.asp**.

For the International Cyberfair Contest (**http://www.gsn.org/cf/ index.html**), student teams are invited to develop and publish Web pages in one of eight categories. These categories include Local Leaders, Community Groups and Special Populations, Historical Landmarks, Environmental Awareness, Local Music and Art, making it easy to integrate student Web work into the curriculum. More than 30,000 students from 500 schools in 37 countries have participated in this event. Student projects vary widely. Past entries have ranged from a students in Australia exploring their town's history (**http://www.eps.vic.edu.au/history/histindex2.htm**) to a Grade 5–6 class in northern New Brunswick profiling people who have contributed to their First Nation community of Eel Ground (**http:// firstnationhelp.com/~eelground/leaders**) and to students in Minnesota discovering community stories from World War II (**http://www. isd77.k12.mn.us/schools/dakota/worldwarII/worldwarIIinterviews.htm**).

A similar initiative is ThinkQuest (**http://www.thinkquest.org**), which we discussed in Chapter 1. ThinkQuest projects tend to be very sophisticated, reflecting a level of teacher support that may not be available for most student projects. Having your students visit this site to see what has been produced, however, is a good way to motivate them. Your students may have some great ideas of their own about projects that can serve as learning resources for your school. Sample the library of online learning resources created by ThinkQuest student teams at **http://www.thinkquest.org/ library/index.html**.

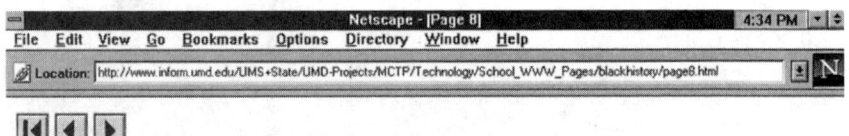

Jean Baptiste Dusable

by Michael

This stamp commemorates Jean Baptiste Dusable. He was the founder of Chicago. Jean was born in Haiti in 1818. He became a fur trader in St. Louis, Missouri. Then Jean moved to Peoria, Illinois, because the British took over St. Louis. The Native Americans help Dusable establish a trading business. During his trading business Jean passed by a place called Eschikagov. So in 1774 he built a cabin there, for his family. Then other people began to move there. The settlement grew and soon became Chicago. That is how Chicago became one of the greatest cities in the U.S.A.

Figure 6-7
Fifth-grade students at Fairland Elementary School develop Black history commemorative stamps.

At the Internet Science and Technology Fair (**http://istf.ucf.edu/**), students in middle school and junior high communicate with an online expert to investigate sophisticated technological topics such as AIDS vaccines, soil washing, and semiconductor lasers, and then develop project home pages to capture their research.

The sources listed above provide exciting opportunities for participation, but they can also be used to generate ideas for curriculum-based Web projects. Students and staff at Loogootee Elementary West in Indiana have developed a Web site that features some great student projects. A Grade 2 class at the school studied emus; their Web site offers an online quiz that was written by the class, and photographs of the emu eggs waiting to hatch. Third-grade through fifth-grade students developed and posted reports and pictures on endangered animal species. The Loogootee site (**http://www.loogootee.K12.in.us/west**) also includes steps for designing a curriculum-based Web project and links to other online projects. Fairland Elementary School (**http://www3.mcps.k12.md.us/schools/fairlandes**) also posts interesting examples of class projects, including projects done by students with special needs. The Fairland site makes available a number of ready-to-use handouts. Handouts and sample projects can be found in the KidsCorner. Putnam Valley Elementary Schools is also worth a visit. Putnam posts interesting examples of class projects as well as a list of technology learning benchmarks that have been incorporated into the curriculum.

I just finished a week-long HTML home page project with my eighth graders. We followed a simple recipe that allowed students who had some prior HTML knowledge to forge ahead and add fancier tags. The words were equally important to the coding. Students prewrote what would appear on their page. I noticed far fewer spelling and grammatical errors. The voice and style of their writing was clear. The students were very conscious of the fact that their page might be seen by others even though we do not at this time have Internet connectivity at our middle school. Their enthusiasim was enormous, in part because for them this is *new* information. Students came very early in the morning (7:30 A.M.), worked through their lunch and stayed until 5:30 in the evening to put in extra time. I was exhausted by the end of the week but delighted at the self-directed and collaborative learning that took place.

— *Inez Farrell ionez7@usit.net*

Summing up

The World Wide Web is central to the way in which the Internet is evolving as a tool for learning. Arguably, the Web derives its greatest value as a learning resource from the fact that students and teachers can actively participate in the development of the Web by contributing resources from their own communities and classrooms. For teachers, the ability to develop Web pages will become an increasingly valuable skill.

The chapters that follow describe some additional tools for using the Internet, but likely none of these will match the Web with respect to the impact they will have in the classrooms of today — and tomorrow.

ClassWebs (**http://classwebs.net**) and Teacherweb (**http://teacherweb. com**) are online bulletin board sites for teachers. A subscription lets you easily post Web pages, announcements and assignments.

Communicating over the Internet

"I think the Internet has the potential to help students realize that they are an integral part of a living, global community. Students in minority cultures can appreciate anew the value of their own culture by seeing it reflected in the interests and questions of others."

— Sandy McAuley, Secondary Programs Consultant, Baffin Divisional Board of Education, Northwest Territories, Canada

Although the World Wide Web is an exciting learning technology, some students (and teachers) are almost as enthusiastic about the learning that can happen through electronic mail projects. Electronic mail is a relatively simple technology for sending messages from one computer to another. In schools, students use electronic mail to gather data, connect with experts, communicate with students around the globe, and collaborate on projects. Teachers use electronic mail to keep up-to-date in areas of professional and personal interest, to exchange ideas and information with colleagues, and to work collaboratively with teachers at a distance. Despite the considerable attention given to the Web by the media, electronic mail is for many the mainstay of the Internet.

This is also an ideal technology for classrooms that have minimal connectivity, such as a single account on the library computer. Through the Internet, with just a simple (even somewhat slow) modem connection and a very basic computer, teachers and students can connect to the world. Electronic mail is the networking vehicle for many Internet inter-classroom projects. You can also use it to communicate with other teachers or subject specialists, to participate in educational discussion groups (listservers), and to subscribe to journals, request articles or take a course. More and more

Chapter goals

- ■ **To provide an overview of electronic mail on the Internet**
- ■ **To offer an example of how to use an electronic mail software package**
- ■ **To describe how mailing lists work and provide some examples of lists that would interest teachers**
- ■ **To explain how newsgroup discussion groups work**
- ■ **To explore how electronic mail can be used in a classroom and provide some ground rules for e-mail projects**
- ■ **To offer some examples of classroom-based electronic mail projects**

teachers now use e-mail as a convenient way to communicate with parents. Students and teachers both benefit when the link between home and school is strengthened. Despite the many sophisticated tools for accessing information over the Internet, electronic mail is not about information. Rather, it's about human communication, and as a result, it remains one of the most powerful aspects of the Internet. Sometimes messages sent to educational discussion groups are archived and can be retrieved using the Google Groups search engine. Figure 7-1 shows an example.

If you have not used electronic mail previously, begin by sending messages to yourself to learn the ins and outs of your particular mail software. Try all sorts of variations, including sending attachments. Experiment with setting up a mailing list by entering your own address a number of times. The advantage of using yourself as a recipient is that you have immediate

Figure 7-1

A sample e-mail message from the Google Groups archive.

```
From: net-happenings moderator <gsackmann@classroom.com>
Date: Fri, 22 Feb 2002
To: comp.internet.net-happenings
Subject: K12> Hit: Gifted websites and some ideas

Date:        Fri, 22 Feb 2002 08:52:30 +1100
From:        Trotter Christina
<trotterc@HAILEYBURY.VIC.EDU.AU>
Subject:     Hit: Gifted websites and some ideas
To:          LM_NET@LISTSERV.SYR.EDU
Thank you to everyone that sent me information on websites
for gifted and talented children.  It has taken me a
while to get find time to put it all together, but here
are the list of compiled websites that were sent through
and we found.
Also a few people recommended making sure that the kids
could evaluate what they were looking at and using the
wide range of web quests that are available on the net.

http://www.ehhs.cmich.edu/~tvantine/edgt.html
Teacher Tips Gifted & Talented Resources links

http://www.cec.sped.org/
CEC Council for Exceptional Children

http://seriweb.com/
SERI Special Education Resources on the Internet-extensive
index

http://www.nswagtc.org.au/index.html
Overview of giftedness, good booklists, looks at
related bullying etc

Thanks everyone.
Christina Trotter
```

feedback on whether your procedure worked. After mastering a few basics, you'll be able to communicate electronically with other teachers.

Later, this chapter will explore in detail some of the ways in which teachers can use electronic mail for classroom learning. But first, let's take a broad look at how electronic mail works.

Electronic mail: Overview

To send messages over the Internet, you will need (in addition to a computer that is connected to the Internet) your own Internet mail address and electronic mail software.

Internet mail addresses

If you have purchased an Internet access account from a local service provider, chances are you already have everything you need to send an electronic message. With an Internet account, you will receive, in addition to a place to log on to the Internet, an e-mail address on the Internet computer to which you are connecting. The messages you send out will be identified with this address, and this is the address that others can use to communicate with you. An Internet e-mail address looks something like this:

bscott@uoregon.edu

The format used for addresses on the Internet is essentially this:

username@hostname

The first part of this name is the user (you), commonly in some abbreviated form, and sometimes even a number. The second part of the name (after the @ sign) identifies the location of the computer that uses the electronic mail account. Here are some more examples.

anita-gibson@admin.ubc.ca

kwilliam@aol.com

bowenr@sheffield.ac.uk

library@ocicl.ou.utoronto.ca

nhenry@capaccess.org

12345.678@compuserve.com

meyer@educat.hu-berlin.de

If you look at an e-mail address carefully, you can often determine a bit about the location of the account. Following are some clues for reading an e-mail address.

- The final two or three letters in an address constitute the *top-level domain*. In the United States these are commonly descriptive domains that identify the type of institution where the address is located.

Domain	Type
.edu	Educational institution
.com	Commercial organization (used throughout the Internet)
.mil	Military site
.gov	Governmental office
.net	An Internet resource, such as an access provider
.org	Non-commercial organization
.biz	A new domain name for businesses
.name	A new domain for individuals

- In many instances, an Internet address will end with a two-letter designation for the country in which the account is located.

Domain	Country
.au	Australia
.ca	Canada
.de	Germany
.dk	Denmark
.es	Spain
.fr	France
.il	Israel
.jp	Japan
.ru	Russia
.uk	United Kingdom
.us	United States

- The .us (pronounced "dot U.S.") designation has traditionally not been used in favor of the basic descriptive domains for U.S. addresses, but is becoming more common as elementary and secondary schools connect to the Internet. When the .us appears, it is frequently used in conjunction with a two-letter state code. Here is an example of what an Internet e-mail address could look like for a teacher in Nebraska: **mnichol@esu3.k12.ne.us**

Free e-mail accounts

There are a number of places on the Internet where you can obtain free electronic mail accounts. With a free Web-based electronic mail account, you receive mail messages over the Web, so that you can access mail from a computer in the library and other locations away from your home account.

Teachers involved in telecommunications projects may find that free e-mail accounts provide a useful way to manage project mail. Students can obtain individual accounts or you can set up a single account for the project. Web-based mail can also be an advantage if you are currently sharing Internet access with other members of your family. Some services even let you check mail from other e-mail accounts that you may have. The downside is that free e-mail is supported by advertising. In addition, you must be connected to the Internet to manage mail messages. For some teachers the fact that it may be difficult to monitor student accounts is also a concern. Setting up accounts for teams or pairs of students can help to address this issue.

Free electronic mail accounts are available from

Eudora Mail **http://www.eudoramail.com**
ePALS **http://www.epals.com**
Yahoo E-mail: **http://mail.yahoo.com**
MSN Hotmail **http://www.hotmail.com**
Mail.com **http://www.mail.com**
Care2.com **http://www.care2.com**
Worldskip **http://www.worldskip.com**
Canoe Mail (Canadian Service) **http://www.canoe.ca/CanoeMail/home.html**
Gaggle **http://www.gaggle.net.** Gaggle is designed for classroom use.

Find out about other free e-mail options by visiting **http://www.emailaddresses.com/email_web.htm**.

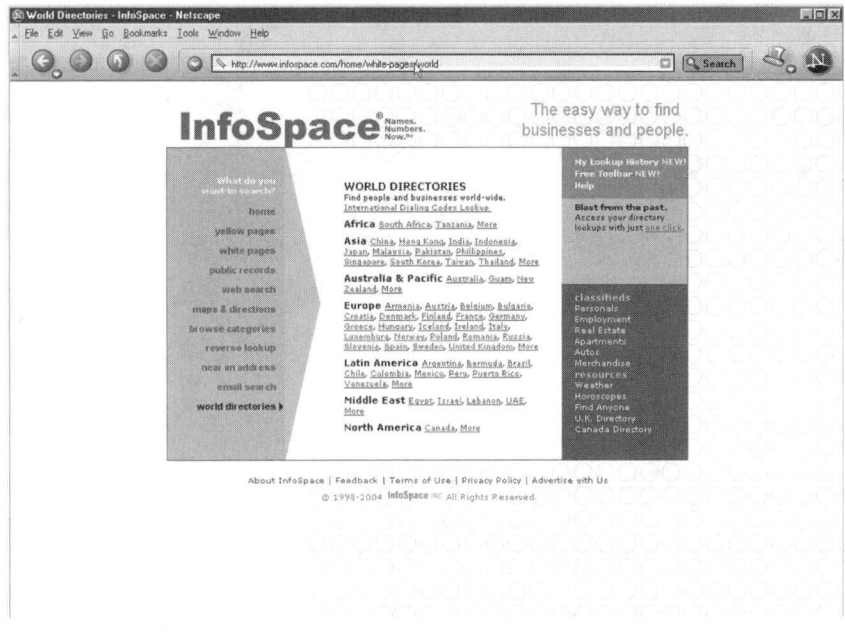

Figure 7-2

InfoSpace is one resource for finding mailing addresses on the Net.

Finding people on the Net: Use these sources to locate electronic mail addresses, phone numbers, and mailing addresses.

Four11:
http://canada411.sympatico.ca (Canada)

Infospace:
http://www.infospaceinc.com

Switchboard.com
http://www.switchboard.com

WhitePages.com (Includes many international directories)
http://www.whitepages.com

Yahoo People Search
http://people.yahoo.com

HINT Web2Mail is a service that lets you check your existing e-mail account over the Web. Web2mail is simple to use and it's free. Log on at **http://web2mail.com**.

Internet e-mail packages must be configured with information about your specific mail server. Many products have a wizard-type set-up that will simplify installation; however, you may still need to provide information about your account. You will also need to specify your name and e-mail address. If you are unsure of how to set up your electronic mail software, contact your Internet service provider.

Electronic mail software

Both Netscape (Navigator and Communicator) and Microsoft (Internet Explorer) include an electronic mail feature within their browsers. The latest version of each of these browsers offers well-designed, full-featured mail programs. Nevertheless, many people choose to use an electronic mail package that is separate from the browser.

In a Windows or Macintosh environment, you will have a choice of user-friendly mail packages. The latest versions of many electronic mail programs are designed to work with Web browsers, so that such things as clicking on a URL reference in an electronic mail message will immediately activate your browser. As with Web browsers, you don't have to stick with the product offered by your service provider. A range of options for electronic mail, including downloadable shareware programs, can be found at TUCOWS at **http://www.tucows.com**. Below are some examples of popular electronic mail programs.

Most e-mail programs will allow you to

- send electronic mail to a specified address,
- send one or more carbon copies,
- reply to electronic mail sent to you,
- forward electronic mail,
- set up an address book with "nick names" for addresses you use frequently,
- save messages to a file,
- send enclosures or attachments,
- automatically include a customized signature,
- delete electronic messages, and
- store messages in folders.

Use the Help function as well as vendor (e.g., Microsoft.com) and other online resources to explore the range of features available in your e-mail

Popular electronic mail programs

Eudora 5.1

Eudora is a very popular shareware package available in three versions: sponsored mode (includes ads), paid mode (no ads), light mode (no ads, but fewer features.) Eudora is available for Windows and Macintosh computers. It has a very robust system for filtering messages, and it is less vulnerable to e-mail viruses than Microsoft Outlook or Outlook Express.
Freeware or pro version
Available from: Qualcomm Inc. at **http://eudora.com**

Juno

This is a bare-bones e-mail client. Its primary recommendation is that it includes a free e-mail service available through dial-up across the U.S.
Available from: Juno Online Services, 1-800-654-5866 **www.juno.com**

Netscape Messenger

Basic mail functions along with newer features, such as HTML mail and the ability to search messages. Bundled with Netscape's latest browser, Netscape Communicator
http://www.netscape.com

Outlook Express

Outlook Express comes with Internet Explorer as well as Microsoft 98 and newer versions of the Microsoft operating system. Supports multiple accounts and will filter messages to a specific account. Also supports HTML tagged messages. Available for Windows and Macintosh.
Bundled with Internet Explorer.
http://www.microsoft.com/windows/oe

Pegasus Mail 4.0

Well-designed and solidly established electronic mail package. Nice "noticeboard" feature lets you post notices for viewing on a network. Includes the ability to annotate mail you have received. Freeware (printed manual available)
Available from: David Harris at **http://www.pmail.com**

Outlook

Outlook is a more complex version of Outlook Express. It comes with the Microsoft Office suite. Outlook includes a personal calendar, contact manager and other features. Outlook may be a suitable e-mail package for teachers, but Outlook Express is a less complex product and a better software choice for students.
http://www.microsoft.com

Poco Mail

This is an attractive, inexpensive mail client. It includes message templates and virus protection, multiple mailboxes and sophisticated filtering. 30-day trial available.
Available from: Poco Systems
http://www.pocomail.com

Webbox

Webbox is an online e-mail service. It works with your existing e-mail account and allows you to use a Web browser to manage your e-mail. Using this program, you can read your e-mail, reply, forward, delete and send new messages from any computer. This makes it particularly convenient for class projects.
http://www.webbox.com/new/default.htm

Tech Talk

MDaemon is a product that schools can use to route mail to an entire network through one connection and mailbox from an Internet Service Provider (ISP). An evaluation copy of this software is available from **http:// www. mdaemon. com**.

software program. If you have not used e-mail previously, practice send functions by sending messages to yourself. This is a quick and easy way to learn about messaging features and to see what happens on the receiving end. Practice using your e-mail software to become familiar with each of these functions:

- getting new mail
- deleting a message
- sending a new message
- responding to a message (sender only)
- responding to a message (sender and all recipients)
- forwarding a message

- setting up a new message folder
- moving messages to a new folder
- sorting messages (by recipient or by date)
- searching for messages (using your e-mail software's search function)

You may also want to try different formatting options for your messages. Most e-mail packages allow you to enhance the format of a message using different fonts and font sizes. If you want to include an e-mail link in your message, designate the complete address (including http://). Some e-mail packages include features that will allow you to use a pre-defined template and insert graphics into an e-mail message. You can also attach an HTML file to an e-mail message to send the message in a Web page format.

Use these sources to help you learn about the features of your e-mail software program.

Outlook Express:

Outlook Express Tutorials
http://www.tutorialfind.com/tutorials/microsoft/outlook/express
Links to tutorials for using Outlook on a PC or Macintosh.

Outlook Express Tutorial
http://www.millard.k12.ut.us/inservice/2000/outlook.htm
A slide-show tutorial from the Millard School District in Utah.

Outlook Express in the Classroom
http://www.actden.com/oe
Kid-friendly tutorial for Outlook Express.

Others:

Using Netscape Messenger for Email
http://wp.netscape.com/browsers/using/newusers/messenger
This site will walk you through the basics of using Netscape Messenger.

Web Safari
http://www.neisd.net/safari
Online tutorials for teachers developed for Texas teachers. The tutorials include an introduction to Netscape Mail.

Eudora Mail Tutorials
http://www.eudora.com/techsupport/tutorials

Electronic Mail
http://www.webteacher.org/winexp/email/email.html
Good introduction to e-mail featuring Yahoo mail.

HINT Find out how to set up an address book and filter mail using Outlook Express for Macintosh at the Mac Options site: **http://www. mac options.com/oe**.

Tech Talk

You will find that sometimes messages "bounce" (can't be delivered). When this happens, you'll receive a message from Mailer-Daemon or Postmaster. The subject line will start with "Returned mail." If you look carefully at the header information, you may be able to determine exactly why the message bounced. *Host Unknown* means that the computer address cannot be reached. Often that's just because of a typo you may then quickly spot. Another possibility is *User Unknown*. Again, this could be a typo, but it could also be that the person you are trying to reach is no longer at that location. Occasionally you might encounter network problems. For example, a server could be out of commission. Or you might run into a "traffic jam," which occurs when many systems are set up to resend messages automatically over several days before giving up.

Using advanced e-mail features

Signature files

Signature files are automatically appended to outgoing messages. They can lend a bit of distinctivenss to your messages. Many people choose to use humorous or thought-provoking quotes as part of their signatures. Some people also provide their phone number, address and fax number.

To set up a signature file, use a text editor or word processing. For example, using Windows "Word Pad," type in your text and then click on File and Save-As. Choose the folder where you want to save the file (My Documents is usually good). For "File Name," type in a file name that is easy to remember such as "sig." For "Save As Type" choose "Text Document." In a word processor, be sure to choose text only or ascii as the file type. Then click on "Save." If you get a message about losing all formatting, click "Yes." At this point your file is saved. Remember what you called the file and where it is located on your hard drive. (e.g., C:\My Documents\sig.txt.)

Your next step will be to locate in your e-mail software package the option for attaching a signature file. In Netscape, this is under **Preferences | Identity**. In Outlook Express, this is under **Tools | Options** or under **Tools | Stationary** and then the Signature tab. Your e-mail program will let you browse to select the file. You can test how your signature file looks by sending a message to yourself.

Figure 7-3
Signatures lend a distinctive touch to messages and tell something about the sender.

Using an Address Book

You will find it very helpful to use the Address Book feature of your e-mail program. By using an address book you can avoid having to type in a complete address each time you want to send a message, and you can establish mailing lists that will allow you to send a message automatically to many recipients without having to type in each address.

Locate the Address Book feature of your e-mail program. In Netsape Communicator, you can access the **Address Book** under the **Communicator** menu option. In Outlook Express, choose **Tools | Address Book**. Each of these programs will give you the option of creating a new individual entry, or a new list for a group of recipients. You can fill in appropriate contact information in each field and create "nicknames" if you like. Nicknames let you call up an address using a brief reference, rather than the complete name. Nicknames can also be used to designate a group of recipients. When you are ready to send a message, you can access your address book from within an e-mail message or simply type in a nickname.

Most e-mail programs will let you export and import your address book so that you can save a copy of your address book for use on other computers. Also, current versions of Outlook Express, Netscape and Eudora will all import address books from each other. There are software programs that will let you convert your existing e-mail address book to another format. If you are using an older program, you may be able to convert it using an online conversion service, such as Interguru at **http://www.interguru.com/mail conv.htm** or one of the software programs you will find listed at this site.

Attachments

This feature enables you to send files that have been prepared earlier in a word-processing application. With a single Internet connection, the **Attachments** feature may be the easiest way to have your students send messages. It's best to avoid attaching messages that include word-processing codes. You can prevent this by saving a file as a text-only (.txt or ASCII) file or rich text format (.rtf), which will preserve basic formatting, such as bold lettering. Usually this just involves investigating the various Save options in your word-processing package. With the text file format, you don't have to worry that the recipients will be unable to read your message because they don't use the same software as you. If you do want to preserve the word-processed format, try sending a test attachment to your recipient. Most newer word-processing packages will recognize files from other popular word processors.

The procedure for attaching files will depend on the type of e-mail program you use. Typically the following steps are involved:

- To attach a document, photo or picture file to an outgoing message, click on the Attachment (or Insert File) icon from with the message template.
- Browse your hard drive or diskette to locate the file you want to attach.
- Click on the file name and then select O.K. Repeat the process for additional files that you want to attach.
- When you send the message, the selected files will be attached.

If you are sending very large files as attachments, you may want to compress them before sending. This is particularly useful if you or the person you are sending an attachment to has a slower Internet connection. You can find out how to compress files in Chapter 8.

E-mail viruses
Teachers need to be aware that computer viruses can be sent as e-mail attachments. MyDoom is a recent example of a virus sent through e-mail that caused considerable upheaval. Never double-click on an attachment that contains an executable file that arrives as an e-mail attachment even if you know the sender. Executable files are those with an .exe .com .vbs or .pif file. Beware, .pif files sent via e-mail are almost always viruses. You can learn more about computer viruses in Chapter 8.

Binary files (such as word-processed files) must be coded before being sent as part of an electronic mail message.

Common formats for coding files for transmission include MIME, Uuencode, and Binhex. Netscape and Internet Explorer will code files automatically, but if you are using an older mail package, it may be necessary to select one of the above coding options. You can use MIME as a default, but try one of the others if your recipient is not able to successfully decode the message. Word-processed messages can also be converted to text before sending. If you are a Macintosh user and have trouble exchanging messages with the Windows world, check out an article on e-mail attachments from Tidbits at **http://www. tidbits.com/tb-issues/ TidBITS-515.html**.

E-mail filters

You can use e-mail filters to channel e-mail for a specific project into its own e-mail folder. You can also use filters to control spam. Eudora, Netscape Mail and Microsoft Outlook all include filtering capabilities. Some Web-based e-mail services also offer filtering. Basically, a filter allows you to pre-select some element of an e-mail message — such as subject, sender, date and have all messages meeting this characteristic filter into a specific folder — including the Trash folder.

For example, you could choose to set up a filter that would block all messages that contain the word FREE or $$$ in the message subject. You could also choose to filter out domain designations where you know you don't have any actual contacts, such as a .biz domain or country designation from a location where you know you do not have any personal contacts. A certain percentage of spammers use yahoo.com or hotmail.com addresses. You could choose to filter these addresses, but be cautious when using these addresses to filter on since these accounts are also used by legitimate senders. Many students, for example, have Hotmail accounts. You may want to set up a special "SPAM" folder where these messages will be deposited, and then quickly scan the file for legitimate messages before doing a batch (Select All) delete.

Finally, you should check with your Internet service provider to find out if they offer a filtering service. Some providers will filter out spam messages before they reach your mailbox.

Mailrings: Discussion groups via e-mail

Joining a mailring (also called listserv or listserver) is an immediate way to connect with other teachers who are using the Internet. To join a mailring, you need only basic knowledge of how to send an e-mail message and specific information on how to subscribe to any given list.

What is a mailring?

Mailrings are special-interest discussion groups available through the Internet. Members post messages, and listserv software redistributes them to all members of a given discussion group. To participate, simply send a subscription message ("subscribe <listserver name> <your name>") to the listserver address (e.g., listserv@msu.edu). Once you've subscribed, you will begin receiving messages from the list. You will be able to contribute your ideas and thoughts directly to the group, too, by using the group e-mail address (e.g., edtech@msu.edu).

The term *listserver* is often abbreviated *listserv*. Listserv is the original program developed to handle mailing lists. Today, a number of other

Figure 7-4

The Spaghetti Book Club posts student book reviews.

HINT Once you have subscribed to a listserv, you will receive important introductory information from the list owner. *Save this message!* It may be useful to print the message and keep it in a binder. Whenever you want to suspend your subscription, you will want exact information on how to *unsubscribe.*

programs, such as Listprocessor, Mailbase, Mailserv, and Majordomo, can also be used to manage mailing lists. Because there are variations on the Listserv software, the commands that you send to a mailing list can vary. For example, Majordomo requests your e-mail address, rather than firstname, lastname in the message area of a subscription request. To find out which commands pertain to a given list, contact the listserv address and send a one-word message: *help.*

You can also subscribe to many mailing lists by going to the Web site that hosts the list. When you subscribe to a mailing list, you may be asked to send in a confirmation message before you begin receiving messages. After subscribing, carefully follow any instructions provided in the confirmation request to complete your subscription. For a detailed explanation of listservers and mailing list software, go to the Mailing List links at Livinginternet.com: **http://www.livinginternet.com**.

Some discussion groups for educators

There are many resources on the Web that you can use to find interesting teacher discussions. Try sampling more than one group. It's easy to subscribe and unsubscribe to groups. Tammy Payton, a first-grade teacher and Web editor for Loogootee Community Schools, has posted some helpful links for learning about e-mail and listservers. Tammy's site at **http://www.siec.k12.in.us/~west/slides/penpal/index.html** posts a slide show

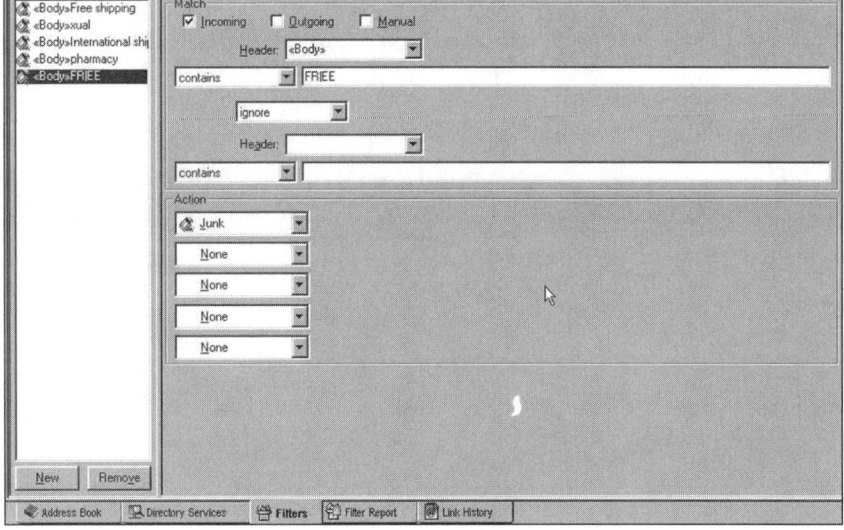

with tips for learning about e-mail exchanges, helps for finding penpals sample activities, as well as links to teacher resources for finding and using educational listservers.

Here is just a sampling of discussion groups for educators that are available on the Internet. For a more extensive list of education mailrings, check out Teacher Mailrings at the Teacher's Guide site at **http://www.theteachersguide.com/listservs.html**.

You can also visit Teacher.net. Teacher.net makes it easy to subscribe and unsubscribe to mailing lists at the "Teacher Mailring Center." If you are not quite ready to join an e-mail discussion group, you can sample the archived discussions from a number of education groups at the AskERIC Education Listserv Archive at **http://ericir.syr.edu/Virtual/Listserv_Archives**. You can find a list of discussion groups on scholarly topics at **http://www.kovacs.com/directory**.

ArtsEdNet Talk

Arts education discussion. Archives available from
> **http://www.getty.edu/artsednet/Talk/index.html**
Use the online form to subscribe.

Big6

An information literacy skills discussion group. Subscribe to
> **listserv@listserv.syr.edu**
Listserver archives are available at
> **http://ericir.syr.edu/Virtual/Listserv_Archives**
You can also subscribe to the Big6 e-newsletter at
> **http://www.big6.com**

Classroom Connect

An active list for K–12 educators who use the Internet in the classroom. This is a good place to post your questions. Subscribe to

crc@listserv.classroom.com

Archives can be viewed at

http://listserv.classroom.com/archives

Connected Teacher

A discussion list for K–12 teachers using the Internet for learning. A great place to share ideas and learn about new Web resources. Archives Available from

http://www.classroom.com/community/email/index.jhtml

Use the online form to subscribe to this list or one of the other discussion groups available at the site.

DEOS-L

This is a very busy mailing list about distance education. Subscription form and archives are available at

http://lists.psu.edu/archives/deos-l.html

If you are concerned about the number of messages generated by this list, consider subscribing to the "digest" version.

EDInfo

Subscribe to this list to receive U.S. Department of Education News. This is a good place to find out about funding opportunities, summer institutes and the latest research. Subscribe to

listproc@inet.ed.gov

Ednet

A discussion group for educational networking. Subscribe to

listproc@lists.umass.edu

Listserver archives are available at

http://ericir.syr.edu/Virtual/Listserv_Archives

Edtech

This is an active discussion group for using technology in education. You can post questions about hardware and software and learn about some of the best ways to use technology in the classroom. Subscribe to

listserv@h-net.msu.edu

Archives are available at

http://www2.h-net.msu.edu/~edweb

HINT Electronic periodicals that are published and distributed over the Internet are known as e-zines. Many of these newsletters and magazines are available through electronic mail. Consider introducing students to e-zines by allowing them to collaborate on publishing one of their own. You can find out more about electronic publications and how to get started publishing an e-zine at **http:// www.zinebook. com/directory/ zine-articles.html**. This site includes a four-page Teacher's Guide to e-zine publishing that can be duplicated and distributed to students.

Education Week

Education Week sponsors a number of e-mail newsletter publications that you can subscribe to. Teacher Magazine Update and Career Coach are examples. Subscription information is available at
> **http://www.edweek.org/emails**

Hilites

Project ideas, activities, and resources from Global SchoolNet. Archives are available at
> **http://www.gsn.org/lists/hilites.html**

Use the online form to subscribe.

IECC (International E-mail Classroom Connections)

A key resource for finding classroom keypals and e-mail projects. Lists are available for K–12, higher education and for intergenerational exchanges. Recent postings can be viewed at
> **http://www.iecc.org**

Use the online registration for Teacher.com to join the lists.

InClass

A Canadian source for educational discussion. Topics focus on subjects of interest to middle and high school teachers. Subscribe to
> **majordomo@schoolnet.ca**

K12admin

A discussion group for those interested in school administration. Subscribe to
> **listserv@listserv.syr.edu**

Listserver archives are available at
> **http://ericir.syr.edu/Virtual/Listserv_Archives**

K12small

A forum for education in small or rural schools. Archives are available at
> **http://listserv.uark.edu/archives/k12small.html**

Use the online form to subscribe.

Kidlink

The Kidlink listserv distributes official information about the Kidlink project. Subscribe to
> **listserv@listserv.nodak.edu**

You can also use an online form to subscribe and view the list archives at
> **http://listserv.nodak.edu/archives/kidlink.html**

Kidlit-L

A forum for the discussion of children's literature. Participants include teachers, librarians and others interested in children's literature. Subscribe to
listserv@bingvmb.cc.binghamton.edu

Kidsphere

Extremely popular list for elementary and secondary school teachers. Discussions range from queries about marking software, to great Internet project ideas, to instructions on how to make bubbles. The volume of mail on this list tends to be high, but it is a stimulating place to begin using the Internet as a professional tool. Subscribe to
kidsphere-request@vms.cis.pitt.edu

LM_Net

Busy list focusing on school library media interests. Subscribe to
listserv@listserv.syr.edu
Archives can be viewed at
http://ericir.syr.edu/Virtual/Listserv_Archives/LM_NET.shtml

Middle-L (Middle School)

A discussion group for teachers involved with the middle grades. Subscribe to
listserv@listserv.uiuc.edu
This group is also available online at
http://fc.burlington.mec.edu/Conferences

NCTE

The National Council of Teachers of English hosts mailing lists for elementary, middle and secondary school teachers as well as a number of special interest lists for teaching English. Archives and subscription information is available at
http://www.ncte.org/lists

Network_Nuggets-L

This is a newsletter about new Net resources. You can subscribe to the newsletter and check out the newsletter archives at
http://www.cln.org/nugget_index.html

Projects-L

This is a mailing list for project-based education in elementary and middle-school education. Subscribe to
listserv@postoffice.cso.uiuc.edu

More information is available at
http://www.project-approach.com/listserv.htm

TESLK-12

Teaching English as a second language in K–12. Subscribe to
listserv@cunyvm.cuny.edu

Teacher2Teacher

A high-traffic mailing list for teachers with options to subscribe to daily or "digest" versions. Subscription information is available from
http://www.teachnet.com/t2t/index.html

Teach Talk

General teacher discussion. Subscribe to this mailring at
http://teachers.net/mailrings
A number of special interest topics, such as special education and classroom management, are also available at this site.

Web Talk/Web Author

Teacher Web ring about Web development. Subscribe to this mailring at
http://teachers.net/mailrings

WWWedu

World Wide Web in education. This long-standing discussion group about the use of the Web in education is now an online forum. Join this discussion group and visit the archives at
http://groups.yahoo.com/group/wwwedu

> I joined the listserv Kidsphere, and that has opened many projects on various networks to me. Choosing listservs, group conferences, and newsgroups establishes relationships with others who have similar objectives and focus.
>
> — *Stephanie Stevens, Teacher, San Francisco, California, U.S.A.*

Finding other e-mail discussion lists

In addition to subscribing to some general education lists, such as Edtech or Kidsphere, you'll probably also want to locate some lists for specific subject areas, such as biology or geography. You can use these sources to find out about many more mailing lists

L-Soft at
http://www.lsoft.com/lists/listref.html
Here you can browse the extensive catalog of listserv mailing lists.

Join an Educational Mailing List at
http://www.siec.k12.in.us/~west/ edu/list.htm
This site includes lists for specific grade levels.

The Teacher's Guide: Mailing Lists for Teachers at
http://www.theteachersguide.com/listservs.html
Many specialized lists, such as lists for special education and for science teaching, are included here.

Teachers.Net Mailrings at
http://teachers.net/mailrings
E-mail discussion networks on many topics, as well as regional teacher discussion groups, including groups for teachers in Canada, Australia and the United Kingdom.

HINT Use this resource to find out more about e-mail, including how to start your own mailing list and how to deal with un-solicited e-mail: Everything E-mail at **http:// everythingemail.net**.

Newsgroups

For some people, one of the most exciting resources on the Internet are newsgroups. Through newsgroups (or Usenet), you can gain access to over 13,000 discussion groups on subjects ranging from fine arts to outer space. Messages from newsgroups are not sent directly to your mailbox. Instead, messages are posted centrally and you can access recent postings using a newsreader program.

Unfortunately, newsgroups are not an ideal classroom application. Some deal with adult, frivolous, or unsavory subjects, and most groups are unmoderated, so that no one screens messages before they are posted.

This is not to discourage teachers from allowing students to access Usenet newsgroups. However, you should be aware of potential problems and have a good idea in advance about how you want students to use these groups. Newsgroup science discussions or discourse around political issues can stimulate ideas and sharpen students' critical thinking skills.

You will undoubtedly want to access some of these groups in pursuing your own professional and personal interests. Newsgroups for teachers can be a valuable source of ideas. Also, they are less cumbersome than listservs, since messages are posted centrally rather than to your personal mailbox.

Some newsgroups are also available as listserv mailing lists, but many people prefer to access these discussions as newsgroups to avoid having to deal with excess e-mail. You might want to subscribe to listservs for one or two discussion groups that you are keenly interested in and opt for newsgroups for everything else. (Not all listservs are available as newsgroups. Also, there are many newsgroups that won't be available as listserv mailing lists.)

You can access newsgroups using your Web browser. Netscape, Internet Explorer (Outlook Express) and Opera all include a news reader. You will need to set your browser preferences to point to the news reader you are

Tech Talk

Newsreaders must be set up to access newsgroups from a particular news server. Most often your ISP will provide access to newsgroups and provide you with the correct settings. In Netscape, the Preferences menu offers an option for configuring Mail and News. The Internet server address for your news server should be inserted in the News (NNTP) Server window.

PERSONAL FAVORITES

Use this page to make notes on your own favorite listservs.

Listname: _____

Description: _____

Subscribe to: _____

Listname: _____

Description: _____

Subscribe to: _____

Listname: _____

Description: _____

Subscribe to: _____

Listname: _____

Description: _____

Subscribe to: _____

Listname: _____

Description: _____

Subscribe to: _____

Listname: _____

Description: _____

Subscribe to: _____

Listname: _____

Description: _____

Subscribe to: _____

Tech Talk

Google Groups is a 20-year archive of Usenet newsgroup postings. Use this resource to find out what groups are available. If you are searching for local groups, use the drop-down alphabetical menu to locate your city, state or province. There are, for example, 14 groups that start with Hawaii, including "Hawaii.education." The drop-down menu can be located under the "Browse complete list of groups."

HINT Some school-boards, universities, and ISPs offer access to local newsgroups. These news-groups can be of great interest because they are one way to stay aware of community events and be involved in discussing local issues. Also, some organi-zations offer semi-private news discussion groups for their members. Universities sometimes make private newsgroups available for course dis-cusssions. The organization sponsoring such discussion groups can inform you of how to access private or semi-private groups.

using. If you have not previously accessed newsgroups, your news reader will prompt you to view a list of newsgroups to which you may want to sub-scribe. This will involve having to download a lengthy list of newsgroups, but this needs to be done only once. After this, you can use your browser to search for groups of interest, subscribe and unsubscribe. Once you subscribe to a group, you can view messages by selecting the group name in your news reader and using the menu options to retrieve the latest items. Your news reader will also allow you to save and respond to messages, and to set up "filters" which can be used to block unwanted messages. This is a very useful feature as newsgroups are fertile territory for junk postings.

Here are some groups of interest to teachers.

alt.education.disabled
alt.education.distance
K12.ed.comp.literacy (computer literacy and applications in the classroom)
K12.ed.tag (for teachers of talented and gifted students)
K12.ed.math
K12ed.soc-studies
K12.ed.art
K12.ed.health-pe (for teachers of health and physical education)
K12 ed.music
K12 ed.business
K12.ed.life-skills
K12.ed.science
K12.ed.special (for teachers of students with special needs)
K12.chat.elementary (general bulletin board for youngsters, including keypal listings)
K12.chat.teacher

A easy way to sample newsgroups is to use the "Groups" option available from the Google search engine at **http://groups.google.com**. Google retains an archive of recent newsgroup postings. The Google archive is updated several times a day, so postings are kept current, and once integrat-ed into the archive, messages are kept indefinitely. You can browse the com-plete list of categories, or search for a specific category (such as K–12). When you select a group, the most current messages are displayed. The Google interface also allows you to respond to postings.

This service can also be used to search for keywords or for the name of a person posting a message.

FAQs

FAQs (Frequently Asked Questions) are a great way to get the "facts" about a wide range of topics, including how to use the Internet. You will find

Figure 7-6

Think.com can be a collaboration tool for your school.

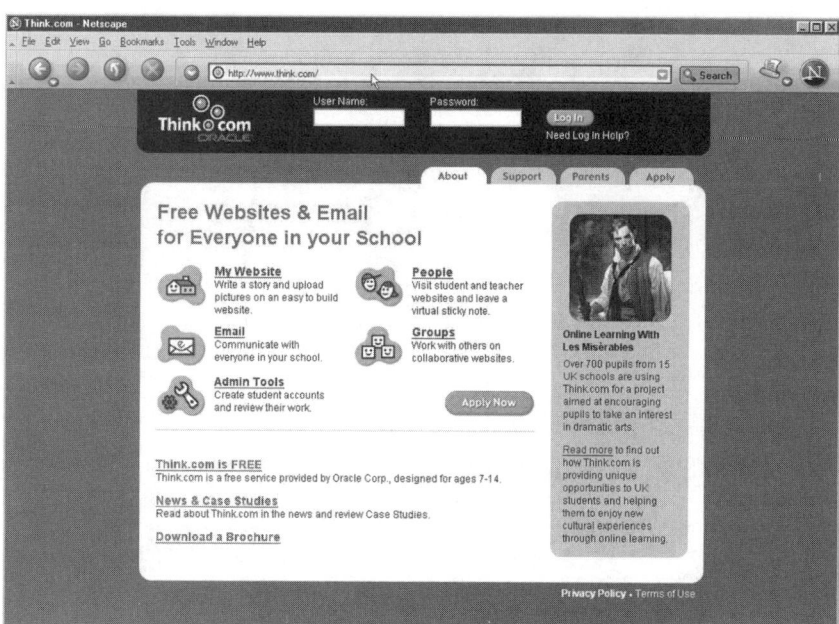

Newsgroup categories

Abbreviations at the start
of the name of a news-
group will tell you some-
thing of its focus or
content.

alt	Alternative
biz	Business
comp	Computers
K12	Primary and secondary educa-tion groups
news	General news and topical items
rec	Recreational (hobbies and arts)
sci	Scientific
soc	Social
talk	Debate on issues
misc	Miscellaneous

FAQs for many different newsgroups at **http://www.faqs.org**. Originally,
FAQs were associated specifically with newsgroup discussions, but these
days FAQ is used to refer to basic information about a topic. Try using one
of the heavy-duty search engines such as Google or AlltheWeb and use FAQ
as a keyword along with a topic of interest.

Online forums

In addition to listservers and newsgroups, a growing number of discussion
groups are published on the Web. These may be called online forums,
message boards, or online conferences. You can review current messages and
post replies directly on the Web. The downside to forums is that you need
to be online to view messages, and posted messages may be quite out of date
if a forum is not particularly active. Try these forums:

Teacher Talk
This is a busy forum with teachers, parents and students, from many
different countries.
  http://www.teaching.com/ttalk

Education World Message Boards
Early Childhood Education, Primary, Secondary, as well as subject boards
and special education discussion boards.
  http://forums.educationword.com

Netiquette: Internet etiquette for students using e-mail

DON'T type your e-mail message all in capital letters. This is considered the electronic equivalent of YELLING AT SOMEONE!

DO use meaningful subject lines on your messages. This helps the recipient to sort through messages quickly or delete those that might not be of interest.

DO try to keep your message to only one subject. This allows readers to decide quickly whether they need to read the message in full. Secondary subjects are easy to miss if the first topic being discussed is not of interest.

DO sign your message with your name, institution, and e-mail address. Not all mail systems allow the reader to see the address in the header of the message. Many e-mail packages will let you set up a signature file that can easily (or automatically) be attached to outgoing mail.

DON'T send short, unnecessary messages to groups (e.g., "I agree!). This increases traffic on the Internet and clutters mailboxes.

DON'T reply to a whole group when only an individual reply is warranted. Be sure to check to see where a message has been sent from before activating the "reply" function. Some embarrassing personal messages have inadvertently been posted to several hundred people.

DO respect the character of individual newsgroups. After joining a group, follow the messages for a week or two before jumping in with your own comments — particularly if you intend to take issue with the comments someone else has made.

DO use emoticons, or smileys :-). Smileys are used to convey the tone of voice that is absent in e-mail.

LD OnLine

This is an outstanding site dealing with learning disabilities. The site hosts a number of online forums (called bulletin boards), including forums for teaching reading, math and for teaching with technology.

> http://www.ldonline.org/bulletin_boards/index.html

Brain-compatible Learning Chatboard

This is a Teacher.net online forum focusing on brain-compatible approaches to learning in the classroom. You will find many other valuable forums (called chatboards) at Teacher.net.

> http://teachers.net/mentors/bcl

Teacher2Teacher

This is a math forum where teachers can ask questions and discuss math education. Join the forum by submitting your e-mail address at the site.

> http://mathforum.org/t2t

TeAch-nology Message Boards

Discussion groups for K–6, middle and high school levels and a technology Q&A.

> http://teach-nology.com

Yahoo Groups Yahoo Groups is an online forum hosting site. You can join an existing discussion group or set up one of your own and invite others to participate. It is necessary to register for this site the first time you use it, but once you set up an account, you can easily access all of the groups that you want to particpate in.

http://groups.yahoo.com

Many local boards and districts also host online forums. Watch for links to forum-type discussion groups and mailing lists at education portal sites and gateway sites for specific curriculum areas. You can also vist the Loogootee Elementary Teacher Chat page at

http://www.siec.k12.in.us/~west/edu/chat.htm.

Hosting your own online forum

Some online resources let you set up and host your own online discussion group. QuickTopic is an example. This resource is of particular interest because it is advertising-free, easy-to-use, and it will also allow you to host a document for group comments and review. Teachers can use this site to host a class discussion or have students work together on a research paper or creative writing exercise. If you post a table with each table cell representing a theme or topic where you want students to add their knowledge, you

---

Smileys* make the Internet a friendlier place :-)

Emoticons, or smileys, can give sparkle to electronic mail. They also help to communicate the writer's intention whenever a comment might otherwise be misinterpreted. Students enjoy smileys. As an interesting exercise, invite them to invent their own. Here are a few samples.

:-)	A smile: "I'm just kidding, joking, having fun." This is one you'll see used a lot — sometimes without the nose, as in :).		**A few less useful ones* but still fun:**	
			(-:	"I'm kidding, joking, or having fun — and left-handed."
:-(	"I'm sad." Often used to express displeasure with something that's just been written.		[ ]	Hugs
			: *	Kisses
\;-)	Wink (a variation on "just kidding")		*<:-)	Santa Claus
\;->	A winking, mischievous smile		%-)	I've been sitting at the computer too long.
:-o	Surprise		**Also watch for acronyms:**	
:-O	Shock		**BTW**	By the way
:-&	Tongue-tied		**FYI**	For your information
:'(	Crying		**IMHO**	In my humble opinion
			IMNSHO	In my not so humble opinion
			LOL	Laughing out loud
			TTFN	Ta Ta for now

Blogs (or Weblogs) appeal to students because they offer an immediate and interactive publishing venue. Try experimenting with a class diary, having students take turns writing entries. Students can also use Weblogs to record progress on a project. For more ideas about how blogs can be used for learning as well as a list of blogger tools, read Writing With Web Logs, published in the February 2003 issue of TechLearning: **http://www.techlearning.com/db_area/archives/TL/2003/02/blogs.html**.

can create a comprehensive study tool. Teachers can also use this site as a teacher-to-teacher collaboration tool. A "shared topics" feature lets you create a single place where related topics can be posted for access by a group. QuickTopic is at **http://www.takeitoffline.com**.

Another online forum hosting service is Community Zero (**http://www.communityzero.com**). Community Zero offers discussion group hosting and other features that support groups working together. Additional features include the ability to post announcements, Web links, files and a calendar. Community Zero can provide excellent support for class projects. Community Zero is used by many different types of interest groups, including families who post pictures and family news. If you are using this site for a class project, designate the site as a private space which means that only those people you allow in can participate.

Yahoo Groups (**http://groups.yahoo.com**) and Smart Groups (**http://www.smartgroups.com**) are two other sites that host group discussions. You can find out about other forum hosting services and conferencing software at Conferencing on the Web (**http://www.thinkofit.com**).

Blogs

The term Blog is short for Weblog. A Weblog is a chronological list of short notes, not unlike a diary entry. Blogs frequently incorporate professional notes with personal reflection. You can use a blog to record your own notes and ideas. Blogs are fun to create, fun to re-read and fun to share. Reading other people's blogs about education topics is a good way to gain knowledge about new technologies or special areas of exptertise. Frequently bloggers publish excerpts from other bloggers and in doing so create a kind of online community. Sometimes blogs are set-up as collaborative environments, so that visitors can post or comment on a site. In other instances blogs are kept private and that only invited guests can view postings.

Blogs can be used for student writing assignments. The online environment and shared nature of the writing space helps fire student's enthusiasm. Because blogs can be viewed chronologically, blogs can also be used for posting homework or keeping parents up-to-date.

HINT RSS files are used to exchange timely content, such as news headlines. They are also used to share blog content. For information about RSS files, visit Mike's News Feeds at **http://www.mikeshea.net/newsfeeds**.

Blogs are available through hosted online spaces. This means that you don't need to have an actual copy of the software on your system to use blogs, although the software may also be available for local or board-level server implementation. Easy-to-use templates are used for posting information, so blogs are a good tool for teachers who want to post information to the Web, but don't want to deal with the technical details of creating a Web page. A this stage, a number of Weblog sites offer free hosting. Others charge a small monthly or annual subscription cost. Be aware that many free

HINT The Moderators Home Page is a useful resource for teachers who want to start their own online discussion group for a class project, online learning activity or professional development. The Moderators Home Page is located at **http://www. emoderators.com/mod erators.shtml**. Also check out Electronic Collaboration: A Practical Guide for Teachers, available from **http://www. lab.brown.edu/public/ ocsc/collaboration. guide/index.shtml**.

services sooner or later turn to advertising revenues to support their service, or may offer basic services for free and enhanced services for a fee.

Popular bloging environments include:

Blogger.com (http://www.blogger.com). Free, hosted environment with advertising. Advertising-free upgrade available.

Weblogger.com (http://www.weblogger.com). Small monthly charge for hosting.

Movabletype (http://www.movabletype.org). Inexpensive environment for operation on a school server, or you can use the online version, TypePad for a small subscription fee. A 30-day free trial is available.

Manila (http://manila.userland.com). Intended for local implementation. Educational pricing available.

Schoolblogs (http://schoolblogs.com). is a hosted Manila site.

Many other software options for blogging are listed at the Weblogs Compendium at **http://www.lights.com/weblogs/index.html**.

Use these sources to discover more about how teachers are using blogs:

Using Weblogs in Education
http://www.weblogg-ed.com/
The creator of this space, Will Richardson, indicates that Weblogg-ed is "my place to collect ideas for Web logs in the classroom, to ask questions to the teacher Web logging community, and to reflect on my teaching." This site includes an FAQ explaining how Weblogs can be used in the classroom and a good list of links to articles about Weblogs.

Educational Bloggers' Network
http://www.ebn.weblogger.com/
A collaborative space for teachers and organizations using Weblogs.

Weblogs in Education
http://webtools.cityu.edu.hk/news/newslett/edublogs.htm
An overview of Weblogs for learning with links to examples and resources.

Finding E-mail projects

Links to e-mail projects and keypal sources are available from these sites:

ePALS Classroom Exchange (Includes access to e-mail accounts. Students can use this resource on their own to find keypals.)
http://www.epals.com
GSN Project Registry at
http://www.gsn.org/pr/index.html

E-mail projects can be built around electronic pen-pals or an electronic newsletter. Other ideas for e-mail projects include interviews with experts, impersonations, inter-cultural exchanges and surveys. Secure student e-mail accounts are available from Gaggle.net and ePALS.

Classroom Connect Teacher Contact Database at
http://www.classroom.net/classroom/teachcontact

Keypals at
http://www.teaching.com/keypals (International e-mail exchange)

Monster Exchange (Emphasis on descriptive writing skills with a great monster theme) at
http://www.monsterexchange.org

NickNacks Telecollaborate at
http://telecollaborate.net

Pitsco KeyPals at
http://www.keypals.com

E-mail Pen Pal at
http://www.tesol.net/teslpnpl.html

IECC (Intercultural e-mail classroom connections) at
http://www.iecc.org

E-Mail Classroom Exchange at
http://www.iglou.com/xchange/ece/ index.html

Getting Started
... with an E-mail Class Project

Guidelines for teachers

Classroom projects built around electronic mail are one of the principal ways that the Internet is being used in schools. These projects can range from a simple exchange of personal messages to sophisticated research and data collection.

The following guidelines can form the basis for many types of e-mail projects. (Be sure to also review the general guidelines for planning a project presented in Chapter 2.) Think of these steps as a framework around which to build your specific project.

Step 1: Establish the scope of the project.

Here are some key questions to consider:

• Will each student have a keypal, or will the class as a group compose messages for transmitting to another class?

A good resource for helping your students learn about effective online communication is "A Beginner's Guide to Effective E-mail," available from **http://www. webfoot.com/advice/ email.top.html**.

HINT The Teacher's Guide to International Collaboration was developed by the U.S. Department of Education to foster cross-cultural exchanges. It posts resources and describes some of the projects you and your students can participate in. It is also a good place to get ideas for classroom e-mail (and other) projects. You can access the online Guide at **http://www.ed.gov/ Technology/guide/ international/index.html**.

- If each student is to have a keypal, will the students all be in the same class, or from different locations? (Note: Collaborating with another class as a group is probably the easiest way to manage student communications.)
- Will your students' keypals be located in another state, province, or country?
- When will the project begin?
- Do you want to establish connectivity based on a particular project or theme (such as global ecology)?
- Do you want the correspondence between students to include specific learning objectives, such as research or data collection?

Step 2: Establish time frames.

Be specific about project phases and deadlines.

Step 3: Advertise your project.

To advertise your project, you can visit one of the e-mail project sites listed in the previous section, or you can post your project to a teacher mailing list or forum. You can also post on a more targeted list, such as Middle-L or a math teachers' discussion group for a project with a math component. Post at least eight weeks in advance. You may need to post more than once.

Step 4: Communicate formally with the other teachers involved.

Thank them for their participation and state exactly what you hope will be accomplished with the exchange of letters. Be sure to explain any specific instructions you would like followed. This is particularly important if the e-mail exchanges are to be integrated with a data collection project.

Step 5: Ensure that your own students are familiar with the procedures for sending electronic mail.

Posting specific instructions near the computer will help students learn the steps involved. Have them practice sending messages to one another, and walk them through any specific skills they will need, such as saving word-processed files as text or uploading files. Don't forget to cover netiquette, acceptable use, and safety on the Net.

Step 6: Discuss the project with your students.

Encourage them to contribute ideas on how to make it a success. Remind them in advance that they won't all receive responses at the same rate, and explain some of the reasons why messages can be delayed, such as limited access to a computer or occasional network problems.

Ten tips for success with e-mail projects

1. Post a list of safety and netiquette do's and don'ts.
2. Have students practice sending messages to one another.
3. Aim for short, frequent messages.
4. If your project focuses on individual Keypals, try to match learners with respect to language skills and word-processing skills.
5. Use a classroom map to track where messages are being sent from.
6. Seek out new keypals for any students who are not getting responses after sending two or three messages.
7. Establish time limits for composing student messages, especially if computer time is limited. Also, establish a policy for how long messages will be left on the system before being deleted (e.g., messages could be deleted once a reply has been received).
8. For more complex projects, consider having students work with partners or in small groups.
9. Use helpers, such as parent volunteers or older students.
10. Respond right away to those who offer to participate in your project, whether or not you are able to include them. Those who will be included may wish to seek other projects if participation in yours is limited.

Step 7: As participants are identified, prepare a reference sheet.

The reference sheet will list who is communicating with whom, along with relevant e-mail addresses. This will be a great help if messages are returned because of incorrect addressing or if a student loses a keypal's address. Post the list and have students check off when their messages have been sent and a response received.

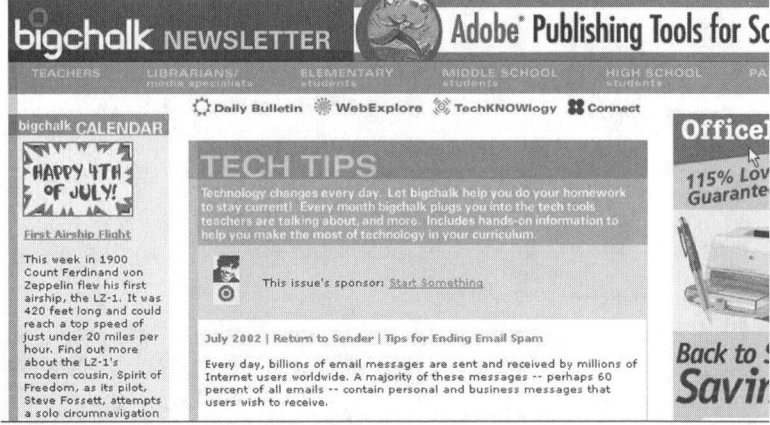

Figure 7-7
HTML pages can be sent as e-mail. Many newsletters are in HTML format.

Project Ideas

Student Keypals

Learning outcomes

- Students will exchange messages with other students around the globe.

Grade levels: 4–12

Getting started

- Visit ePALS (or other keypal resource or project). If you are using ePALS, use the "Find Classrooms" link and search for an existing class that matches your interests with respect to country and age level. You can also search for a keyword that appears in the participant's description. Once you find a suitable partner group, you can click on the contact link and send a message to the participant. In communicating with the other classroom teacher, include an indication of your expectations for learning outcomes.
- If you like you can also enter your own profile and identify the type of project you have in mind. Specify the focus, such as French-language exchange or messaging related to a particular project.

Developing

- Establish a process and timelines for the exchange. Use the Guidelines for Getting Started with an E-mail Class Project presented in the previous section to develop your project.
- Be sure that everyone is clear on project details — what is the purpose of the project; when will the project start and end.
- Ensure that everyone's expectations are clear: discuss when the project will start and finish, what its aims and outcomes are and how frequently messages will be exchanged.
- Confirm methods for accomplishing any peripheral activities related to the project, such as scanning images or adding in a video or online chat component to the project.

teaching tip

If your computer system allows you to create sound files, consider attaching a verbal message to an electronic mail message. This can be particularly enjoyable for younger students; however, do not let the vocal message replace the text message, since composing text messages helps develop writing skills.

Extending:

Using "snail-mail" can add texture and excitement to an electronic mail exchange, especially if you lack the equipment necessary to scan and upload photos and artwork.

Here are some ideas for a snail-mail exchange:

- Have students exchange class pictures, brochures, school newspapers, or travel brochures.

- Students can create drawings of their homes or neighborhoods and exchange them. Use the pictures as the basis for a classroom discussion about cultural differences.

- Have students create and exchange pictures around a theme, such as holidays, Earth Day, world peace, or helping the poor. Use these pictures as a starter for a class discussion of the chosen topic. The same topic can be used as the basis for the students' electronic messaging or reports.

- Students can select and exchange stories from their local newspapers. Deciding which stories best reflect the students' community can be an interesting class exercise.

Project Ideas

Introducing Friends

This is an easy and interesting project for those new to electronic mail. Students interview a friend and send their interviews via e-mail to students in another class. Then the students receiving the messages respond by introducing themselves. Invite other classes to participate using one of the listservers, or simply coordinate with another teacher in your school or another local school.

Learning outcomes

- Students will gain skill in interviewing, writing, and presenting information.
- Students will learn to send e-mail messages.

Grade levels: 4–12

Getting started

- Explain to the students that you will be meeting another group of students — but online, rather than in person.
- As a class, brainstorm a simple interview format that students might use with their interview partners. Typical questions might include likes and dislikes, unusual interests or talents, or humorous anecdotes.

Developing

- Allow class time for student pairs to take turns interviewing each other.
- Assist students to use their word processors to write their introductions. Here is one possible format for students to use in developing their messages.

   Paragraph 1: Describe what your friend looks like, and a bit about what he or she likes and dislikes.
   Paragraph 2: Tell about your friend's interests and opinions.
   Paragraph 3: Write an amusing story about your friend.
   Paragraph 4: Describe your friend's strengths and talents.

- If individual student accounts are available for both classes, have students send their introductions to individual students from the other class. Alternatively, students can send or submit their interviews to you for forwarding as a batch to the other class teacher.
- Complete the exchange by having the students in the class receiving the introductions send a reply in which they introduce themselves using a similar format.

Variations

- Devise a template with a list of interview questions. Send them to individual students using electronic mail. Have each student respond to the questions and send the replies back to you. Post or re-distribute the responses for the rest of the class to read.
- Use the format from the Introducing Friends project, but select a partner class from another country. Remind students that their interviews should include some information about the country in which they live. When the message exchange has been completed, have the class discuss some of the things they have learned about the other country from reading messages they receive.

I have been teaching LD kids for thirty years and have found the computer itself to be the best thing that ever happened for my students' writing. They are much more willing to sit and write, and make corrections because it is so easy. We are using the Internet for keypalling. The students jump at the chance to write someone from another country or state because it gives them a chance to open up and write freely about things they care about.

— *Cliff McCallum, Teacher, Seneca Junior High School, Holbrook, New York, U.S.A.*

Project Ideas

E-mail Surveys and Questionnaires

In this project, students develop a questionnaire based on the topic of personal "favorites."

Learning outcomes

- Students will develop and exchange electronic questionnaires.
- Students will incorporate an existing file into an e-mail message and/or forward a message.

Grade levels: 4–8

Getting started

- Have your students discuss and list possible "favorites" for discussion, for example:
  - favorite season
  - favorite color
  - favorite subject in school
  - favorite TV show
  - favorite book
  - favorite place to visit
  - favorite music group
  - favorite food
  - favorite movie
  - favorite sport

Developing

- Develop a questionnaire listing the selected questions. You can provide an electronic copy of the list to each of your own students; they, in turn, may send the file to each of their keypals. Students will enjoy comparing the responses they receive.

Variation

- Older students may wish to develop a questionnaire focusing on a research topic, such as a survey of students' leisure-time activities, their attitudes about violence on television, or their recycling habits. Suitable topics will flow from curriculum areas.

Extending

- Use the data collected in this project to build a database of responses. Plan in advance how to formulate the questions to simplify data input. Short-answer and multiple-choice responses will be easier to tally than open-ended responses.
- Using database software, collate and analyze the results of the surveys in a math or science lesson.

E-mail is and will always be the most powerful tool for educators. While it's nice for my students to access information from Web sites, the real power is their being able to contact others in their search. For example, my fourth grade students will soon be looking for information related to gold prospecting. I have found Web sites that have good information, but more importantly, from these sites I've been able to contact gold prospectors who have enthusiastically agreed to field any questions my students may have.

— *Gary Quiring (1995, December 21) "Benefits of Web/E-mail,"*
International E-Mail Classroom Connections.

Project Ideas

Exchanging Research Projects

Learning outcomes

- Using the library and the Internet, students will research a country.
- Students will conduct an online interview (using e-mail) with a student from the country they have chosen to research.
- Students will prepare written reports on their own country and submit them to their keypals for comments.

Grade levels: 4–12

Getting started

- Determine which country will be the focus for this project. Use the IECC listserv or Web site to advertise for participants.
- Have the class develop a list of topics to investigate as they learn about the country they intend to research. The list should include standard geographical information such as climate and location, but can also include topics of particular interest to students, such as favorite sports in a country or subjects that are studied in school.

Developing

- If students are able to use Internet tools such as the World Wide Web, they can explore the Internet for information on the country they have chosen.
- Alternatively (or in addition), they can use magazines and books from a local library to conduct their research.
- Once the students have completed their preliminary research, they should develop a list of questions to address to a keypal in the country they are researching. These questions will form the basis of an electronic mail interview.

Extending

- Once students have completed their interviews and written their reports, they should send what they have written to their keypal interviewees for feedback.

Variations

- Students enjoy exchanging their stories and reports with other classes. These can be a report they have completed for a unit of study or a creative writing endeavor.

- Have students put together a "travel guide" on their own country, state, province, or community and exchange them with other classes. This project is most exciting if more than one remote classroom is involved, so that each of the participating classes receives reports from more than one country, province, or state. If your students have access to Web resources, they can use them to research their reports.

- Have students research a current issue or event and create a "newswire" service. First, explain what a newswire service is, and clip some examples from a local newspaper. Then, have students research and prepare their reports. Students from another classroom can look at the reports and select their favorites for a simulated online news broadcast. Learning is enhanced when students have the opportunity to share their thoughts on world issues. Follow this project up with a discussion about the advantages and disadvantages of getting the news from a wire service.

- Join the International Newsday Project at **http://www.gsn.org/ project/newsday/index.html**. This is a student-developed news exchange. Students create a newspaper based on articles that are submitted by students around the world.

Project Ideas

Sharing Book Reviews

There are a number of places on the Internet where students can read and publish book reviews. Students are thrilled by the idea of having others read their work. Here's how your students can contribute.

Learning outcomes

- Students will access, over the Internet, book reviews written by other students.
- Students will create their own book reviews for posting on the Internet.

Grade levels: 4–8

Getting started

- Visit the World of Reading site at **http://www.worldreading.org**. Print a selection of book reviews and discuss them with students. Does the review make them want to read the book?
- As a group, decide what a good book review should contain.

The Spaghetti Book Club provides an environment where classes and after-school groups are provided with their own online space to publish student book reviews and drawings. There is also an online forum which allows parents and others to respond to the reviews that students have posted. A membership fee is involved; however, membership includes all the materials needed to implement the program, including lesson plans to help teachers guide their students through the process of writing and illustrating book reviews, publishing criteria, and consent forms. Visit **http://www. spaghetti bookclub.org** to learn more.

Developing

- Have each of the students write a review of a favorite book. Ideally, reports should be written using a word processor and sent to you using electronic mail.
- You can choose to submit all the reports to the World of Reading for posting or select a few class favorites from the group.
- To submit a report, cut and past the text into the online form provided. You will be asked to submit:

Student's First Name
Student's Age
Book Title
Author
Review
Teacher's Name (or other adult)
Teacher's e-mail (or other adult)
School or library name
School or library URL
City State/Province Country

You can also read and publish book reviews at

Kids Bookshelf
http://www.kidsbookshelf.com

Book Reviews for Middle Grades
http://www.kidsbookshelf.com

The Spaghetti Book Club
http://www.spaghettibookclub.org

Extending

- Have students share their reviews by reading them aloud or by sending them as an e-mail message to other members of the class.

Variations

- (Grades 4–8): Students can publish their own stories on the World Wide Web at KidsPub. For a small fee (about US$25 for class participation) classes can have a class page with unlimited posting of stories, pictures, and other creative work. Individual students can join as well. Visit the Building Rainbows Book Review and Discussion site at **http://www.buildingrainbows.com/home.php**.
- (Grades 4–12): Students can exchange e-mail book reviews with another class. Establish a format for the book reviews (similar to the format indicated above). Exchange reviews with a group of students from another

school. This activity can be particularly motivating if students exchange reviews with students from another country. Classes should be able to manage a common language at a similar level. Each group should read an author from their own country and write a review that will introduce the work to a class from another country.

- (Grades 7–12): A book rap is a book discussion conducted by e-mail. Identify the book to be discussed and set a start date for the discussion. Each week a coordinator posts one or more open-ended questions about the book and students respond. A range of different topics focusing on themes, characters, and other aspects of the book can be developed over several weeks.

Figure 7-8

```
Title: MacDonald Hall Goes Hollywood
Author: Gordon Korman
Published: 1991
Publisher: Scholastic
ISBN: 0-590-43941-3
Ages: 8 and up
Name: Darren Romijn
Age: 12 (grade 7)
Acadia Jr. High School
175 Killarney Ave.
Winnipeg, Manitoba
R3T 3B3


Review: This book is about a movie star that comes
to Macdonald Hall (a private school) to make a
film. Bruno tries to get into the movie but the
headmaster bans the students from the movie set.
Bruno won't stop until he gets to be in the movie.
This book was really funny! If you like funny
books you'll definitely like this one!
```

Summing up

While electronic mail is only one of the ways in which the Internet can be introduced into the classroom, it is potentially one of the most versatile. With a little creativity, teachers can use e-mail as an effective tool to achieve learning outcomes in basic skills such as computer literacy and communications, as well as in more specific subjects such as science, geography, or language studies. Through electronic mail projects, students can learn about teamwork and global cooperation.

Advanced users may want to experiment with using e-mail to transfer software, or to exchange graphics, sound, or even multimedia files. But for newcomers, electronic messaging can be wonderfully rewarding. A simple exchange of text messages can dissolve the walls of the traditional classroom and open a door to exploring the world.

The next chapter will look at some additional Internet technologies, including other methods for communicating online.

8
Chapter

Additional Internet Tools

"Physicists at MIT stood by and watched last week as scientists in California used the Internet to manipulate their fusion reactor from more than 3000 miles away.... Stephen Wolfe, the physics operations leader for the trial, said, 'We've shown that it doesn't much matter any more where the physicists and the machines are located, as long as you've got a fast link.' "

— Quoted in "The Incredible Shrinking Laboratory," *Science, 268* (5207; April 1995), 35.

While the World Wide Web and electronic mail represent the areas of greatest interest for teachers, there are a number of other applications that are good to know about. The Internet is a dynamic environment and as you gain skill, you will undoubtedly want to try some of the newer types of applications.

With faster Internet connections becoming available, audio and video applications are increasingly of interest. Streaming video projected into a classroom can be a rich new resource for learning. Using audio or video conferencing can enhance a global class project or provide an opportunity for a virtual field trip.

FTP (which stands for *File Transfer Protocol*) is an older technology that is still used for transferring files over the Internet. If you are setting up a Web page, FTP is important to know about. In addition, knowing how to set up your browser to accept plug-ins and helper applications, and being aware of Web utilities, such as offline browsers, will help you use the Web environment more effectively. While a Web browser on its own will go a long way toward meeting your needs, you can extend what you are able to do over the Internet by knowing about these additional applications and techniques.

As shiny new applications, such as streaming audio and streaming video, rapidly gain in popularity, we are reminded that the Internet is always evolving. There are more and more possibilities for communication and interactivity. As a teacher, you will want to be aware of how the Internet is changing and how it can be adapted for broader use in a learning context. In this chapter we will look at a number of technologies that will help you extend your use of the Internet.

Some of the tools included in this chapter are somewhat more complex than the World Wide Web. If you are a novice computer user, read each section carefully to determine how useful the feature is likely to be in your own classroom and how much technical detail there is to master. If the technique being described looks complicated, find a knowledgeable friend to walk you through it the first time you attempt to use it. Because these tools are less important than e-mail and the World Wide Web, you can take your time learning about them.

Video and audio Streaming

The Web is no longer an environment consisting of a lot of text and a few static graphics. Now, even with slower connections, it is possible to gain access to video and audio through a technology known as **streaming**. Streaming allows video or sound files to be played as they are being down-loaded. Many institutions, including colleges and universities, are exploring streaming video as a way to make lectures and conference presentations available over the Internet.

Webcasting is the term used when streaming is used to broadcast a live event. It is a way to attend conferences and lectures as they are being pre-sented. Teachers can use this technology for professional development. Streamed broadcasts can also be used in a class setting as a support for many different areas of the curriculum. For example, the Humane Society of the United States sponsors Animal Channel (**www.animalchannel.org**) which broadcasts documentaries about various animal species around the globe and their need for protection. Discovery Channel (**www.discovery.com**) broad-casts a weekly science show over the Web and has an archive of other inter-esting documentaries that can be accessed at any time.

Although some of the programming comes with a price tag, other programs are re-broadcasts of programs from television or radio and most of these are free. News broadcasts from other parts of the world can be a

Tech Talk

Less complex than video streaming is to stream PowerPoint slides. By stream-ing slides, you can make a slide-show, complete with audio, available over your Web site. To stream PowerPoint slides, you can use Microsoft's Media 7 Resource Kit. Step-by-step instructions, along with other streaming tutorials, are available from **http://ctl.clayton.edu/cid/tutorials.htm**.

HINT To find out more about streaming video, check out these tutorials from the University of Wisconsin–Madison: **http://streaming.wisconsin.edu**.

fascinating way to support a class in geography, politics or other issues. They can also be used to be used for a unit on media studies or for learning a foreign language. Travel videos can be used to study other countries.

Most streaming video comes in one of three formats: Microsoft Windows Media, RealNetwork's RealVideo and Apple QuickTime (available for both Windows and Macintosh computers).

Players for streaming video and audio formats are available free; however, the formats listed above are all distinct and students may need to have a copy of each of these on their computer, depending on the source of the video. Players will handle both video and audio formats. Many sites, such as news sites, provide files in more than one format, so you will have a choice of how to access the file. The sites also generally include a link to the necessary player, which will need to be downloaded and installed. You can download the latest version of the players at these sites:

Microsoft Windows Media
> **http://www.microsoft.com/windows/windowsmedia**

(Note this software may already be on your Windows computer. Check under **Accessories | Entertainment**.)

Real Media
> **http://www.real.com**

The basic player is available for free.

QuickTime
> **http://www.apple.com/quicktime/download/**

QuickTime is a popular format for educational video.

Sites from which players can be downloaded will provide specific information about the computer configuration required to access the video, but typically viewing video over the Internet will require a newer computer and high speed access.

A middle-school mathematics video showcase has been developed as a National Science Foundation project. You can view the video clips at **http://mmmproject.org/video_matrix.htm**.

Examples of streaming media

Use these resources to sample some streaming media applications:

CCNMTL Media Archive
> **http://www.ccnmtl.columbia.edu/projects/broadcast**

The Center for New Media Teaching and Learning routinely videotapes lectures, interviews and events at Columbia University. Selected events are made available online and can be accessed with the Real Media player.

University of Wisconsin Streaming Media Showcase
> **http://www.streaming.wisconsin.edu/showcase.html**

Learn about African Storytelling, the playwright August Strindberg, or Bloom's Taxonomy. The University of Wisconsin also makes available several streaming videos on how to create streaming presentations.

Yahoo Broadcast
http://broadcast.yahoo.com

This is and audio and video portal site. Good source for news, science and travel content.

iMovie Samples
http://homepage.mac.com/planclos/ade/iMovieexamples.html

Good selection of education videos from the Apple Distinguished Educator community.

Nova Online
http://www.pbs.org/wgbh/nova

Selected Nova science programs and special features are available in QuickTime and RealVideo.

Streaming Media Mania
http://www.kn.pacbell.com/wired/fil/pages/liststreaming.html

Streaming examples and resource list. Focus on streaming content for classrooms and streaming content produced by schools.

Tech Talk

You will find other kinds of audio files on the Web, in addition to streaming audio. If you encounter a *.wav* or *.au* file, you can play the file as long as you have installed the appropriate type of helper application.
Windows Media Player (included with the Windows operating system) will play both of these formats.

Figure 8-1
Quick Time technology is used for streaming media.

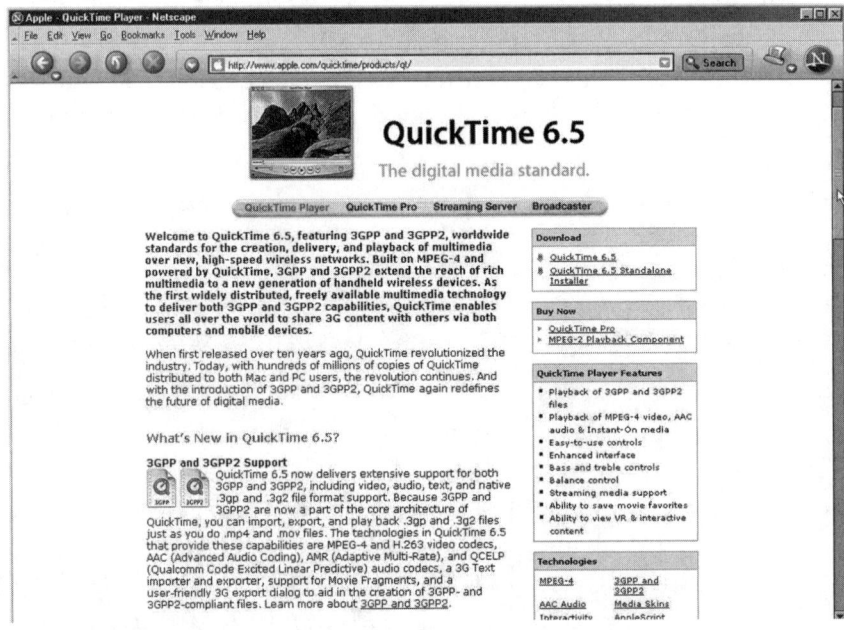

Teacher's Internet Companion

HINT Use the Fast Multimedia search to locate audio and video content on the Web: **http://multimedia. alltheWeb.com**. You can also use Pandia's Radio search to find radio and TV content from around the world.

HINT The Windows Media 9 Series in Education page at **http://www.microsoft .com/windows/windows media/Enterprise/ sectors/Education Sector/default.aspx** provides some case studies of streaming media use in education, including K–12. You will also find a tutorial here on how to use the Windows Media Encoder to produce streaming media.

If you are experimenting with using videoconferencing with a friend and need to find the IP address for your computer, click on **Start |Run** and type winipcfg in the **Run |Open** box. Click O.K. A window will pop up and display the IP address for your machine. When NetMeeting is installed, your IP address will be displayed in the NetMeeting Help Menu.

Producing streaming content

But streaming is not just about receiving video over the Web. In a classroom situation, with a few tools and some technical support, teachers can capture and broadcast events such as class debates or school sporting events.

Producing effective video for streaming requires a good quality video camera, ideally a digital video camera or recorder, a computer that is set up with special hardware and software to accept video and video editing software. A popular program for importing and editing digital video is iMovie. This program works on Apple's iMac DV computers and it has been designed as easy-to-use software for first-time movie makers. In the Windows world, you can use Microsoft's Movie Maker. It works with Windows XP, but remember that you will also need a video capture device and a computer with lots of space still available on the hard drive.

Once you have created a video, in order to stream videos you will need special encoding software. Again, Windows Media, RealNetworks and QuickTime all have different products available for encoding (or compressing) video. Visit one of these sites to obtain detailed information about products available and "how-tos" for streaming video:

QuickTime **http://www.apple.com/quicktime/products/qt**

RealNetworks **http://www.realnetworks.com/getstarted**

Windows Media **http://www.microsoft.com/windows/windowsmedia**

Videoconferencing over the Internet

Videoconferencing is another technology that is becoming more common as more people acquire faster Internet connections. In the best of all worlds videoconferencing involves dedicated videoconferencing equipment and a high-speed phone line; however, less costly videoconferencing can be done over the Internet, and that is where many teachers start. Experimenting with what can be done over the Internet with videoconferencing can help build a case for acquiring a more sophisticated videoconferencing system.

Internet-based videoconferencing requires:

- *A Webcam (est. US$100 — or even less if you shop around.)*
- *Speakers and a sound card*
- *Microphone (or a headset that combines speakers and a microphone)*
- *Conferencing Software (NetMeeting (free) and Cu-SeeMe are examples)*
- *Internet access @ 56 kbps +*

Conferencing software

Videoconferencing software allows users to talk to others in the conference
and see them on video at the same time. It is also possible with some software to display PowerPoint slides, to send a file across the network, to use
an online whiteboard for sharing ideas and to jointly surf the Web. Some
programs, such as NetMeeting, also allow participants to collaborate on the
same document.

The most popular software for desktop video conferencing is
NetMeeting which is available from Microsoft for free. Newer versions
of Windows come with NetMeeting included. PalTalk (**http://www.
paltalk.com**) and iVisit (**http://www.ivisit.info**) are similar programs that
include video conferencing, audio messaging and chat. The software for
these products is free, and can be used for point-to-point conferencing,
however, there is a subscription charge to access the conferencing reflector
sites — the server environment that allows multiple connections.

Many schools use CU-SeeMe software for videoconferencing. This is an
older software that is no longer being developed or supported, but it can
still be downloaded from **http://hoople_ny.tripod.com**. The advantage is
that CU-SeeMe still works on older computers with slower connections.

Figure 8-2
Classroom videoconferencing
using Cu-SeeMe, NetMeeting
or other software.

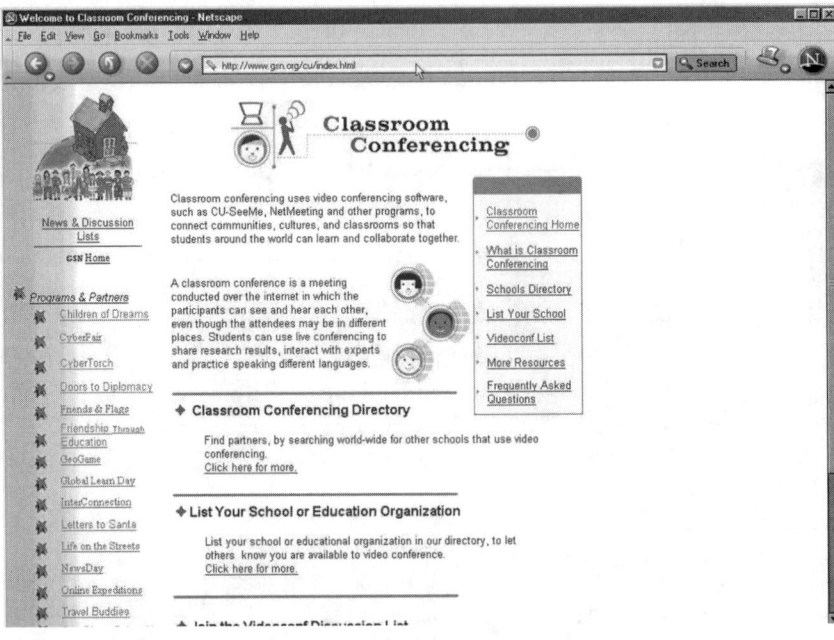

Teacher's Internet Companion

Webcams are cameras set up in strategic locations to capture still photos at closely spaced intervals for broadcasting directly to the Web. Webcams can also provide some interesting viewing. The BBC makes available links to Webcam shots (**http://www. bbc. co.uk/webcams**). There are travel cams and a number of animal cams, including selected shots taken in a bear's den. One school set up a Webcam to watch eggs hatching in a nearby birds' nest. If you want to learn how to set up a Webcam, you will find an excellent introduction to Webcams at Howstuffworks: **http:// www. howstuffworks. com/webcam1. html**. Myowncam.org provides free Webcam streaming software and free Webcam hosting.

HINT In a school situation you may also have to deal with a firewall or other issues related to the computer network before you can easily do video conferencing. Consult your local network technician if you encounter problems with videoconferencing.

Cathy Gunter has been using video-conferencing as a teaching tool at the Provincial School for the Deaf in British Columbia since the mid-1990s. Because deaf students are very visual and frequently have lower literacy skills than their hearing peers, videoconferencing is an invaluable tool to use to enrich their learning experience. As a teacher, Ms. Gunter finds that videoconferencing gives students a "fairly inexpensive method of connecting with the outside world and the ability to get information first hand." The school has held videoconferences for students in groups of as few as 8 students to as many as 150 deaf and hearing students. Conferences are interpreted using ASL (American Sign Language).

An early project using CU-SeeMe videoconferencing involved students at the school connecting to another school for the deaf in St. John's, Newfoundland. The project focused on having five student groups with members from both schools work together to plan an online trip between St. John's and Vancouver in British Columbia. Student teams researched the trip and created a Web page to present their findings. Videoconferencing was used to strengthen the connection between the two schools and to add to the excitement about working collaboratively.

The School for the Deaf has recently purchased a Polycom Viewstation MP. Although this is a more expensive videoconferencing product (than Cu-SeeMe), the cost is justified in that videoconferencing has now become fully integrated into the school as a teaching medium.

We have brought in deaf speakers to lecture to our students. We also had a videoconference with a famous Canadian futurist, Richard Worzel. He spoke to the students about the implications of technology on the jobs of the future and how it will impact the teenagers of today. We have visited the San Diego Zoo, the Elephant Sanctuary in Tennessee, learned about the Underground Railroad, had a lesson taught by a Quaker using the teaching style of the 1800s, and visited the Museum of Modern Art in New York. One very dramatic videoconference we were involved with was the Museum of Tolerance in Los Angeles. We talked with a holocaust survivor. He recounted the horrendous experiences he had while at Auschwitz. The students were moved to tears during the 90 minutes we spent with him. I think this was a life changing experience for us.

Pacific Bell has developed an excellent guide to videoconferencing in education. At their Videoconferencing for Learning site (**http://www. kn.pacbell.com/wired/ vidconf**) you can learn about the videoconferencing technology and instructional applications. They provide ideas and examples of how videoconferencing can be used for virtual field trips, multi-site projects and online tutoring. Internet-based videoconferencing is included. Global SchoolNet (**http://www.gsn.org/cu**) also provides information on classroom conferencing. Their site also includes a list of schools around the world that you can connect with using videoconferencing.

For some interesting examples of how video-conferencing can be used for learning, see the. Videoconferencing for Learning page at **http:// www.kn.pacbell.com/ wired/vidconf**.

Additional CU-SeeMe helps are available from yIKE's CU-SeeMe Links Page at **http://ilovereality.com/Yikes/links.html** and from the CU-SeeMe Cool Site at **http://www.rocketcharged.com/cu-seeme**. Newer choices regarding other desktop videoconferencing as well as audio and phone conferencing options, along with some product reviews can be found at **http://www.thinkofit.com/webconf/realtime.htm#video**.

If you have a high-speed Internet connection at home, try using NetMeeting with a colleague. NetMeeting can be a time saver if you need to work with a colleague located a distance away. NetMeeting is easy to use and has a rich set of features for collaboration; however, currently only two participants can use the video simultaneously. PalTalk, iVisit and CU-SeeMe work well for classroom collaboration because they accommodate more video participants.

In a classroom context videoconferencing can be used to connect classes working together on a project or to access an expert online. With a bit of advance setup, a single computer could be used to support the conference, and a computer projection unit used to involve a group of students in the experience. Students could select a moderator to relay questions from the group to the classroom or expert at the other end. Alternatively, if a phone line is available, a speaker phone can be used to support the audio portion of the conference in which case the interaction would not be dependent on a single computer microphone.

Internet videoconferencing works by connecting everyone in a conference to a conference server. In a multi-point conference, the server is responsible for mixing the incoming video from each conference participant and forwarding the video streams to other partipants. Most Internet-based videoconferencing software products provide access to publicly available conferencing servers. Alternatively, your board or district may have a conferencing server. Connecting to other participants is often simply a matter of knowing the IP address of the computer you want to connect to.

Because NetMeeting is free, it is a practical way to start experimenting with videoconferencing. If bandwidth is limited, you can still use an audio-only connection which should work acceptably at 28.8. Information on how to get started is available from **http://www.microsoft.com/windows/ netmeeting**.

Downloading software applications over the Internet

Downloading software from the Internet is very popular among teachers and students. There are a great many sites offering freeware and shareware. In addition many software producers provide trial or limited time versions of their products allowing you to sample the software before you actually purchase it. Software resources include programs for creating quizzes, graphics software for creating images and working with photographs and drawings, gradebooks, and software for learning, such as tutorials and drill and practice applications. E-books (books that you can read on a computer or PDA device) are also available over the Internet.

Once you have located a file or software program that you are interested in, you can download the file by placing your mouse over the name of the computer file and "right clicking," then selecting the "Save Link As" or "Save Target As" option, whichever is offered by your browser. You will be given the opportunity to select where on your computer you wish to save the file.

Sites for downloading software and educational resources

The following list describes sites where you can find software programs and other shareware or freeware that can be downloaded. Math tutors, typing programs, or lessons can all be downloaded for printing. Remember that shareware programs are offered as a way to let you try before you buy. If you plan to use a shareware program on a regular basis, be sure to pay the licensing fee. Licensed use of shareware programs is generally very reasonable.

Explorer

This site offers a collection of downloadable education resources for maths and sciences. The resources include instructional software programs. You can browse through the curriculum areas to find out what is available.

http://explorer.scrtec.org/explorer

WinSite

This is a major computer shareware site for Microsoft Windows software, with over 300 Mb of public domain software and shareware. You will find a good selection of programs for educators, including math tutors, marking programs, and more.

http://www.winsite.com

EASI (Equal Access to Software and Information)

If you are working with students with disabilities, visit this site for the latest information about adaptive technologies. The K–12 resource includes some pointers to math and science tutorial programs that may be of general interest.

http://www.rit.edu/~easi

File Transit

Software for many operating systems along with reviews and ratings.

http://www.filetransit.com

Figure 8-3
Find shareware at
http://www.download.com.

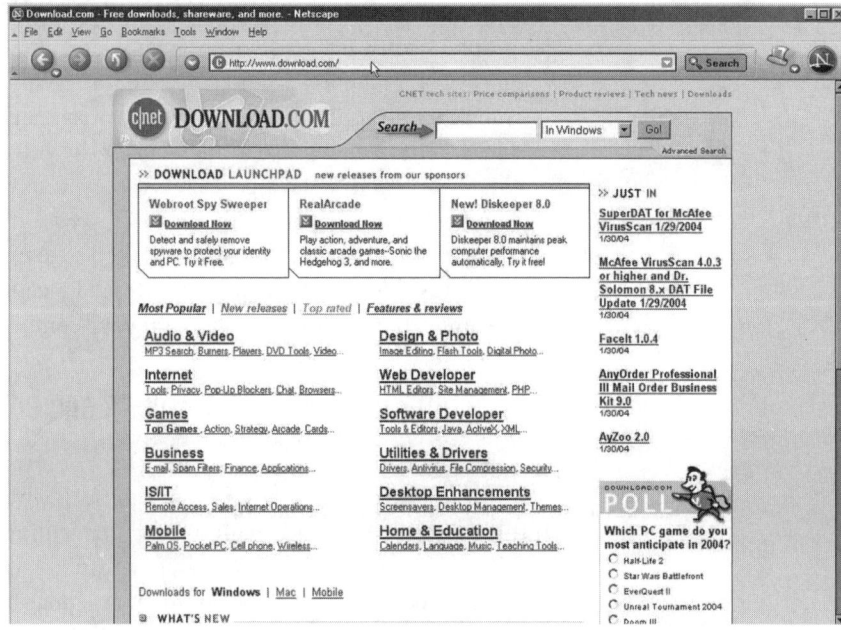

Download.com

This site includes an Education area and a Kids area, along with a number of other specific topics. If you browse in these areas, you will be able to pick out the "most popular," "newest titles," and the "topics" within each category.

http://www.download.com

HINT A list of links to freeware sites is available at **http://www.hotfree ware.com/freeware.htm**.

Shareware.com

The Shareware.com metasearch will let you simultaneously search a number of different shareware sites.

http://shareware.cnet.com

Educational Software Cooperative

A non-profit agency for educational software publishers and users.

http://www.edu-soft.org/index.shtml

Educational Software Institute

This is an important resource for finding out about educational software. From this resource, you can browse for software by curriculum area and by computer platform (Windows, Macintosh, etc.) Registered users can order many of the software programs online. Registration is free and there are frequent free software offers for members.

http://www.edsoft.com

Mathematics Archives

Searchable archives for teaching materials, software and Web links on mathematical topics. This site also includes a major set of links to other math software sites.

> **http://archives.math.utk.edu**

Online Books Page

Extensive collection of full-text book resources. These are books for which copyright has expired, or books for which the author has given permission to post the material. This site also makes available links to publishers of online books.

> **http://digital.library.upenn.edu/books**

Simtel

Popular Windows distribution source for freeware and shareware. You can download software directly or build your own CD-ROM with just the programs you have selected. The process is quite inexpensive and the vendor will ship to anywhere in the world. If you have a slower connection, this process can save you many hours in download time.

> **http://www.simtel.net**

TUCOWS

This is a major resource for Internet-related software. You will find other good software at TUCOWS as well for Windows and Macintosh. Check out the selection of tools for language learning.

> **http://www.tucows.com**

PERSONAL FAVORITES

Use this page to make notes on your own favorite download sites.

Site: _____

Description: _____

Note files: _____

Site: _____

Description: _____

Note files: _____

Site: _____

Description: _____

Note files: _____

Site: _____

Description: _____

Note files: _____

Site: _____

Description: _____

Note files: _____

Site: _____

Description: _____

Note files: _____

Site: _____

Description: _____

Note files: _____

Figure 8-4

A language learning site in the U.K. uses Hot Potatoes quiz software to help students learn to speak French. Hot Potatoes is at **http://web.uvic.ca/hrd/half baked**.

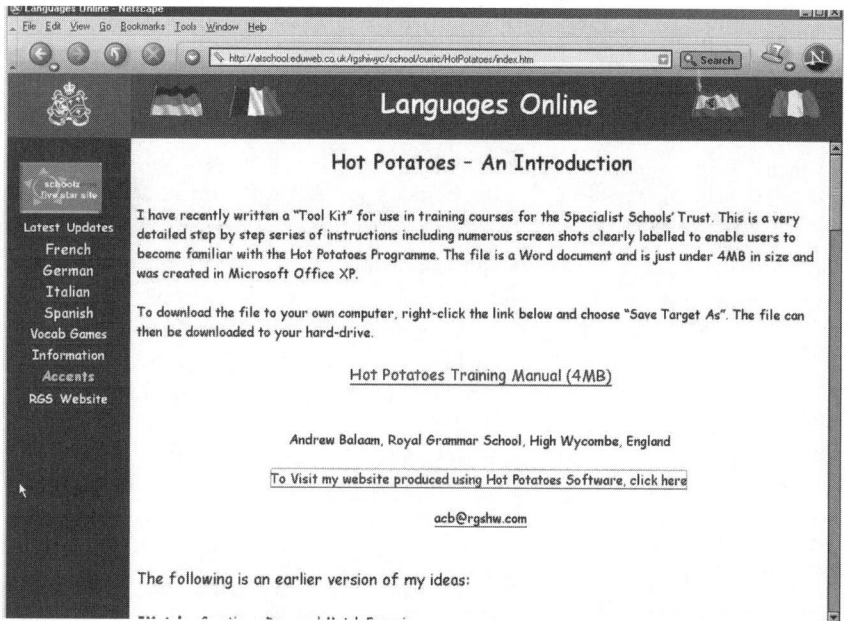

Bob Bowman's Guide to Free Educational Technology

Educational freeware, online tutorials, how-to guides, freeware graphics, downloadable Spanish course from the Embassy of Spain, etc. — free, free, free!

http://www.user.shentel.net/rbowman

Tech-Learning

This is an online site for Technology and Learning. There are many good articles to read about integrating technology into the classroom, and you can search for software reviews by subject and by grade.

http://www.techlearning.com

A word about computer viruses

If you are using the Internet it is essential that you and your students are aware of the potential damage that can be caused by computer viruses. Viruses are computer programs that damage other programs by modifying them in some way. They can cause your computer and its programs to behave erratically, and can damage your files.

Computer viruses can infect your computer in several different ways. They can travel from one computer to another through a shared floppy disk. On the Internet, viruses may be hidden in an e-mail message or in a program that you download. The notorious "Love Bug" virus which affected thousands of Microsoft Outlook users in 2000 was spread through e-mail and and replicated itself by manipulating files on a victim's hard drive.

The "Love Bug" was a type of computer virus known as a Trojan Horse. The malicious virus arrived disguised as a "love letter." Even a screen saver can harbor a computer virus, so teachers need to be aware and able to advise students about strategies for avoiding computer viruses.

To protect yourself from computer viruses from any source, you must have virus protection software installed on your computer. This software is designed to detect viruses before they can damage your computer. In a school context, your network administrator will have installed virus protection software on your school network, and you should be aware of policies and procedures that have been set up to protect school computers from viruses. You will also want to protect your own computer.

Here are some basic tips that will help you avoid computer viruses.

- If you do not already have an anti-virus program purchase one and install it on your own computer. Many new computers come with anti-virus software already installed. Make sure you know what program is on your computer and how to run it.
- Set your anti-virus software to run automatically each time your computer starts.
- Be sure to regularly update your anti-virus software. An older virus software program will not be able to detect new viruses. This does not mean that you need to buy a new anti-virus program. Virus software vendors stay up-to-date on new viruses and develop antidotes. Once you have

Tech Talk

Symantec Security Response provides a synopsis of the latest virus-related threats, including information on each virus, the damage it does and how to remove it. **http://securityresponse.symantec.com/avcenter/vinfodb.html**.

purchased the basic program you can reguarly download updates from the vendor's site.

- Do not open any type of computer file from an unknown source without checking it first for a virus.
- Be especially careful with e-mail attachments — even if you know the sender. Good anti-virus software will scan incoming e-mails for viruses.
- Explain to your students about the need to be careful and show them how to check floppy discs and files for a virus.

Two popular anti-virus software vendors are these:

McAfee VirusScan **www.mcafee.com**

Norton AntiVirus **www.symantec.com**

FTP

FTP is the process used to transfer files from one computer to another. As technology has advanced, FTP is not used as much as it once was for downloading files from the Internet; however, FTP is still the application most commonly used to upload files onto an Internet Web server. You may also sometimes use FTP to transfer files over a computer network, such as a wide area network for your school board. FTP can still be used to download software or other computer files from another computer; however, an Internet browser is more often used used for downloading individual files.

To transfer files to or from a remote computer you will need to log on to the remote site from within the FTP program, also called an FTP *client*. Typically you will need to specify the host name (machine.site.network), your user ID and password. If you are uploading files for a Web site, your service provider will provide you with information required for logging in. Some FTP sites allow "anonymous" logins. In this case it is a common practice to use the word *anonymous* for your user ID and use your e-mail address as the password. Once you have logged on to a remote system, the FTP software will display lists of files and allow you to move from one directory to another. Use the software to highlight a file name. Typically arrow buttons will allow you to move files from one computer to another with a simple click. FTP software is easy to use. The main things to be aware of are login information for the computer you need to connect to and finding your way around the remote system.

To find out more, check to see what instructions your Internet provider offers for uploading files. If this process requires you to use FTP, the vendor may have posted a set of instructions and even a link to FTP software that you can download. You can also check out the FTP New Users Guide located at **http://www.ftpplanet.com/ftpresources/basics.html**.

If your Internet service provider has not provided you with an FTP client, a selection of good FTP clients is available from TUCOWS (**www.tucows.com**).

Compressed files

While it is relatively easy to download uncompressed text files, sooner or later you will need to deal with a compressed file. These are files that have been "shrunk" using a software program in order to save disk space or to speed up the time required for transfer. There are many different programs that can be used to compress files. The key is to identify and obtain the particular type of software you need to decompress the type of file you have at hand.

One type of compressed file you will commonly see is *zipped* files. These have a .zip extension. To "unzip" these, you will need a shareware program called PKUnzip. This is available at **http://www.pkware.com**. Sometimes you will see the file automatically included with a group of zipped files that need to be unzipped. The latest version of PKUnzip includes a "wizard" that will walk you through the process for unzipping files.

Other programs for unzipping files include WinZip, available from **http://www.winzip.com**. In the Macintosh world, compressed (.sit) files can be unpackaged using Stuffit Expander or Stuffit Lite. Stuffit can be found at **http://www.aladdinsys.com**.

Real-time discussion on the Web

Online chat

There are a number of other ways to have real-time discussions online. Traditionally online discussions have involved text messaging in chat rooms which are online spaces that allow messages to be displayed (almost) instantaneously. Many students use desktop instant messaging software, such as ICQ or AOL instant messaging. Most of these technologies are not suitable for school use. Chat environments tend to be chaotic and the kinds of interactions that take place do not typically have a lot of value for learning. An exception is planned interactions at the start or end of a project. If groups of students at a distance from each other will be working together on projects, chat environments can provide a chance to get acquainted or form the basis for a fun finale to the work that has been done. If you are planning to use chat with your students, choose a chat service with an educational focus — such as ePALS (**http://www.epals.com/chat**), Tapped-in (**http:// www.tappedin.org**) or Teachers.Net (**http://teachers.net/chat**). Establish guidelines for appropriate messaging and set time limits for the session.

Tapped In is a real-time chat environment that operates over the Web. It has been developed for shared teacher professional development. Teachers can use this environment for sharing knowledge or collaboration with other teachers. You can visit Tapped In almost any time to get a sense of how to participate. Check the Tapped In events calendar to find out about scheduled discussion topics and online guests. Tapped In is at **www.tappedin.org**.

Students need to be skilled at keyboarding to participate, and it may help reduce the levels of chaos in the discussion to have smaller groups of students participating at any one time, rather than the whole class. Some online chat safety tips are available at ProtectKid.com at **http://www.protectkids.com/youthsafety/imchatipskids.com**.

Voice chat

Another opportunity for online communications is voice chat. With a microphone and speakers it is possible to set up an audioconference. Limited voice chat can been done with NetMeeting; however, if you want to do an audioconference with many different participants, you can use an audioconference service such as Talking Communities On-line at **http://www.talkingcommunities-online.com** or Orbitalk at **http://www.orbitalk.com/purchase/default.asp**. Both of these services use an audioconferencing software product called Chatterbox. If your school board runs a Web server and would prefer to purchase Chatterbox, it is available from Simple Software at **http://www.howudodat.com**. With your own copy of the software you can host unlimited audioconferences. It is possible to run the software off of almost any computer with a high-speed connection to the Internet. If you are not confident about your own technical skills you can ask a technical person in your school to help set up the server software. Once set up, the chat environment is easy to use, although individual users each must have a small program (downloadable at the Simple Software site) running on their computers.

Additional browser helper applications

Many browser applications require you to download a piece of software, viewer or "plug-in" application to use them. The streaming video and audio applications discussed above are examples.

One of the most useful plug-in applications is a viewer for .pdf files. PDF stands for Portable Document Format. Adobe Acrobat is the standard program used to create .pdf files. These files require the use of an Adobe viewer to access or print the document.

School boards, departments of education and government agencies commonly provide information such as newsletters or long reports in PDF format. Some education sites make activity sheets and lesson handouts available in PDF format. (You will find some examples at **Lessonplansearch.com**.) With PDF you can make a document available online in the same format that it was originally published in (preserving headlines, columns, graphics, etc.) PDF can help prevent illegal copying of material, and it ensures that a document will look the same regardless of which browser — or which computer platform — you are using.

Adobe's PDF viewer is available for free, and most sites that use PDF files provide a link to the PDF viewer for easy downloading. Usually, you need only click on the viewer link to download it to your own computer. The most recent versions of the PDF viewer will set themselves up to run with your browser once you run the install program.

Take time to explore the viewer's features, such as increasing the size of a display for easier reading. Editing features will vary. For example, although a PDF viewer will generally allow you to view and print a document, you may not be able to cut and paste from it.

You can find out more about Adobe Acrobat files at **http://www.adobe .com**. You can also create your own Adobe files online without having to purchase and install the software. A free trial is available at **https://create pdf.adobe.com**.

Software developers are always launching new applications requiring plug-ins and making them available via the Internet. You will find an extensive list of plug-ins. Generally, your browser will alert you when a plug-in is required. If you are downloading one of the newer versions of Netscape or Internet Explorer, you will have the option of downloading many different viewers at the same time. Be cautious about downloading too many viewers as they will gobble up space on your hard drive and take up computer memory.

You will probably need only a small selection of viewers. We have already discussed some of the most commonly used viewers — QuickTime for video, a player for RealAudio, and the Adobe Acrobat Reader for PDF files. Two other common presentation formats requiring plug-ins are Shockwave and Flash which are both used for multimedia applications. Shockwave is used for online entertainment and interactive games. Flash is frequently used for rich content presentation and animation. Shockwave and Flash are available from **http://www.macromedia.com**.

Your browser will alert you when a plug-in is required, and most plug-in applications will configure your browser when they are installed.

JavaScript and Java

JavaScript and Java are additional applications that work with your browser. They are both programming languages that can be used to run functions within a browser. JavaScript is used to create small applications such as page counters, clocks, banners and menus. JavaScript programming is incorporated right into an HTML document. If you are developing a Web page, you can access a JavaScript library such as **http://javascript.internet.com** and cut and paste JavaScript code into your own HTML document. Java is used particularly where there is a more sustained interaction required between your local computer and a remote server. An online tutorial, for example, might be created with Java. In both cases, it may be necessary to enable

HINT If you want to sample a .pdf document, visit the Explorer site at **http://explorer.scrtec .org/explorer**. This site offers a lot of useful curriculum material in .pdf format. You can also download back issues of *Speaking of Teaching*, a newsletter on teaching, at **http://ctl.stanford.edu/ teach/speakmenu.html**.

these features on your browser using the Internet Options Security menu or Advanced Preferences menu.

If you are on a school network, you should consult with your technical administrator prior to enabling Java on a network computer.

Offline browsers

It can sometimes be useful to download Web pages and associated graphics for viewing offline. You may want to do this if you are planning a demonstration or want students to have access to a site without having to worry about whether a connection is down. This is also a good approach for a one computer classroom and for schools with slow or limited Internet connectivity.

You can save individual Web pages using the "Save as" feature of your browser. Saving pages individually using your browser, however can be a time consuming process. If you are saving a selection of pages, a better approach is to use an offline browser. Remember that only links to pages that have been saved will work, so plan your lesson in advance to ensure that all the pages you need for viewing will work.

You can capture Web sites offline using any of the following products. Offline browsers commonly cost between US$40 and US$60. Most offline browsers are available as shareware so you can sample more than one to determine which one you like best before purchase.

Figure 8-5
An offline browser makes it easy to download Web sites for presentations.

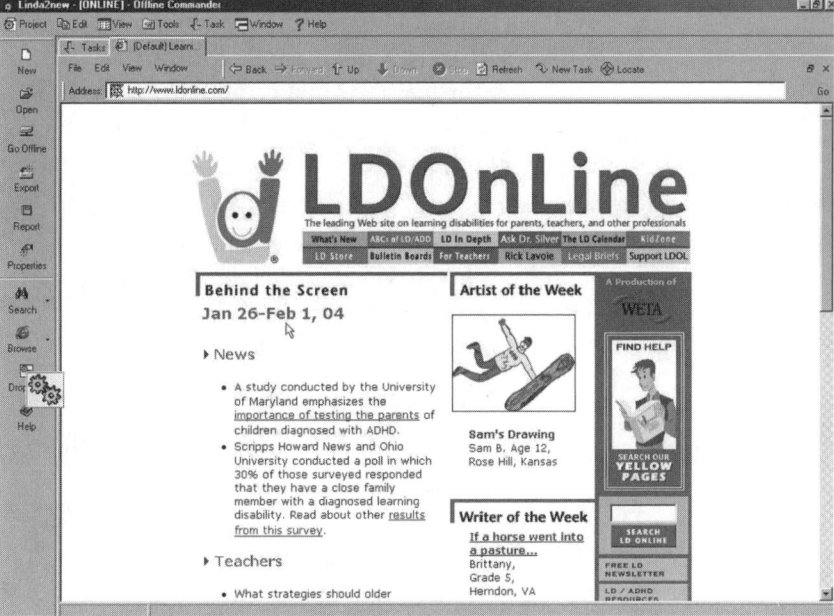

Grab-a-site

This is a good choice for downloading whole sites to a local network.

http://www.bluesquirrel.com/products/grabasite/grabasite.html

Web Whacker

This popular offline browser will let you organize saved pages into categories. Web Whacker can be scheduled to run in non-peak times. You can also use Web Whacker to create a CD to run automatically when inserted into Windows computers. BlueSquirrel recommends using Web Whacker with Edufy (**http://www.edufly.com**) for quick access to safe content by grade level.

http://www.bluesquirrel.com/products/whacker/index.html

Offline Commander

Use Offline Commander to automate many browsing tasks and download complete Web sites. A "drop box" feature lets you browse, and then just use your mouse to drag and drop a URL to the Offline Commander drop box icon for easy downloading.

http://www.zylox.com

Offline Explorer Pro

This offline browser has its own built-in browser, so that you can view downloaded pages even on a computer that does not have a browser installed. Offline Explorer will capture Web pages using newer technologies such as Java and Flash.

http://www.metaproducts.com

HTTrack

This is an easy-to-use "open source" offline browser. "Open source" means that the program is available for free.

http://www.httrack.com/index.php

Web Devil

An offline browser for Macintosh systems.

http://www.chaoticsoftware.com.

Summing up

Because the Internet is constantly developing, there will undoubtedly be other kinds of software available for audio- or video-conferencing on the Internet. If you feel that some of the applications discussed in this chapter are too challenging for a novice to tackle, be reassured that none of them are necessary to make good use of the Net. It's worth repeating that the real power of the Internet is as a tool for human communication, and although such applications as streaming video and NetMeeting are interesting technologies for classroom learning, much can still be accomplished with a simple e-mail connection. FTP will allow you to move files from computer to computer, but most users will probably find that the World Wide Web provides sufficient access to the resources that will be most useful to schools.

9 Chapter Bringing the Internet into Schools

" I think that the way to a teacher's heart is through the students. I doubt any teacher who sees the interest, the motivation, the skills, and the excitement in her or his students can long resist taking what, here in Quebec, we call 'le virage technologique' — 'the technology turn.' "

— Christiane Dufour, Teacher, Small Schools Network, Quebec, Canada

Because so much of a teacher's work is done after school hours, you are likely to find that you want to be connected to the Internet from both home and school. In order to access the many wonderful things the Internet has to offer, you need a computer, a modem, and a connection to the Internet. Once you have a connection, you will use the Internet for much more than schoolwork. You can find the latest news, take an online course, get up-to-date travel information, or communicate with colleagues, friends, and family.

If you are in the fortunate position of having Internet access through an already established school- or system-based infrastructure, getting connected may be as simple as turning on your computer and clicking on an icon or selecting from a menu. If not, you will need to deal more directly with the hardware and software required to get connected, whether at home or at school. Your school will be faced with such questions as, How many phone/data lines, computers, and modems do we need? Where should they be located? Who will monitor students as they use the Internet?

Change is rarely easy. School administrators, librarians, computer teachers, and classroom teachers all face the challenges of implementing this new technology. Problems are inevitable; in fact, we can't learn without them. When teachers discuss using the Internet in education, the hurdles of time, money, motivation, and technical training are mentioned time and again.

This chapter explores several different kinds of Internet connections and examines some of the ways in which schools are overcoming barriers that restrict Internet use. Although each school has different needs and resources, examining the various models described here will help you with technological and resource management decisions. This chapter will help plan for change in your school and will suggest some sources of funding to help make that change a reality.

What is a connection?

Remember that the Internet isn't a place or a thing; it is a network of computers linked together. You want to become a part of this global communications network in order to communicate with others and gain access to resources and information. Although approximately 20 million people use the Internet in some fashion, many have limited access, and many others use only e-mail. For educational purposes, you want to take advantage of the full range of resources available. The kind of connection you establish determines the type, format and download speed of the information that you and your students can access. This, in turn, affects learning outcomes for students. In order to plan for your integration of Internet resources into the curriculum, consider the kind of connection that will best suit your needs and the costs of the equipment and services that are required.

If your school is already connected, you can skip the next couple of pages. Still, it's useful to know how the connection works and why certain things may be possible while others aren't. Your students will certainly want to know! Or, you may wish to consider upgrading your existing connection.

Types of connections

There are many ways that individuals and schools connect to the Internet. The chart below describes some of the most popular.[1]

Connectivity method	Description
Dial-up connection	connecting to an Internet service provider/online service through a modem and telephone lines; 56Kbps modems can give reasonable speed
Dedicated connection	a direct connection between a school and an Internet service provider; 64Kbps (T1) to 45Mbps (T3)
ISDN line	a circuit-switched digital technology used to link to Internet service providers; two 64Kbps channels that can be bonded together to create one 128K connection

Connectivity method	Description
Cable-based modems	offered by Cable TV companies; about 30M, but shared bandwidth means that speed in the school is actually about 1Mbps
Wireless local multipoint communications systems	a broadband wireless service used to connect schools to an Internet service provider; speed varies
Multipoint communication systems	radio systems where a main hub radio station communicates with many locations in an area; speed varies
Satellite	Internet feeds to schools are via satellite, return via wireless; satellite broadcasts up to 400Kbps

An example of the outsourcing model is the Lemon Grove School District near San Diego, California, who worked with an ASP called Citrix® (**http:// www.citrix.com**). The Lemon Grove educators' goal was a "connected learning community" that could make use of inexpensive Windows-based terminals and the school's aging PCs. They created a network to connect the district's eight schools to homes, libraries, and community centers through cable hookups. Using a software suite called LemonLINK, teachers now deliver lesson plans digitally to students, families access news and information, and students complete homework online and submit it via e-mail. "This technology puts the power back into the hands of the child," says Barbara Allen, director of Project LemonLINK.[2]

Some of these are complex ways of connecting to the Internet, and explaining them in detail is beyond the scope of this book.

Schools and school districts may choose to leave high-end technical details to outside companies that specialize in hardware and software solutions. An application service provider (ASP) is a company that maintains groups of servers where software applications reside. Many school systems or districts act as their own application service provider by placing all of their applications on a central server; others choose to outsource this function by utilizing the resources of an independent ASP. The difference is that an outside ASP provides access to applications on a subscription basis and handles all technical maintenance and software upgrades from its own central location. Applications can be available over a computer network and/or over the Internet, which allows any device with a Web browser to have full use of applications from any location. This scenario also is called "thin-client computing." The International Society for Teaching in Education listed the thin-client computing model as one of the top ten models that had the greatest effect on school technology in 1999. One of the key reasons was the ease of administration promised by thin client vendors and application service providers. Consulting and technology services allow educators to focus on their core competency — educating students and though generally expensive, outsourcing may save the schools money in the end.

The following pages provide more details about the most common ways teachers presently connect to the Internet from home, and a glimpse into future possibilities.

Dialing into another computer

Many people get indirect access to the Internet by using a modem to dial in to a large computer (host) that is itself on the Internet. Your computer becomes a terminal that communicates with the host computer. Community freenets allow Internet access of this kind. When you log on to the central computer, you use its programs to navigate the Internet.

Joining an online service

Commercial services, such as the Microsoft Network, America Online, Sympatico, offer online banking, shopping, dating, entertainment, and connectivity to the Internet. Using these services in schools where students spend many hours online can be expensive, but they have been designed to be user friendly. Most of these services offer their own interface to the Internet, which can help reduce the learning curve for teachers and students. America Online offers a wide variety of educational resources, such as live classes, homework assignments, contests, awards, conferences for teachers, and complete graphical Internet access. The Microsoft Network is an online service built into Windows. You can join directly using a modem and your Windows software. The Microsoft Network offers full access to Internet facilities and e-mail, with different pricing plans from which to choose.

Commercial services vary in cost, and several cost options are available. For example, you might pay about US$23 per month for unlimited access or US$10 per month for five hours of online time with an hourly surcharge for additional time. Yearly subscriptions are generally less expensive. For specific details, contact the services directly. Be sure to ask which services are offered, as some offer only e-mail and may add personal message charges. Others may add surcharges for specific features. The best advice is to devote some time to exploring each service before joining. Look for current articles in computer magazines such as *PC World* or *MacUser* comparing the most recent offerings of the major commercial providers. Joining an online service is the easiest way to connect to the Internet, but it may not be the cheapest or the most inclusive. However, these companies are competing to make complete access for consumers easy, cheap, fast, and reliable.

Connecting through a LAN

Large organizations such as universities, school districts, and corporations purchase high-speed, high-volume direct connections to the Internet. They make use of these connections by developing ways in which hundreds of their users at a time can share that single high-speed central connection. Users may be physically dispersed throughout many buildings in laboratories, offices, and classrooms. Everyone is then connected by some technical means to a central server that controls the Internet connection.

Similarly, in many schools, all the computers in the school are connected on a local area network (LAN). By connecting a modem to the LAN, every computer on the network has Internet access.

Despite the complexity and expense of installing and maintaining an Internet connection through a LAN, most large schools have or will select this option because it provides such generous and complete access for students and teachers.

Establishing a SLIP/PPP connection

You can also get full Internet access by establishing a SLIP/PPP connection. You will see the acronyms SLIP (*Serial Line Interface Protocol*) and PPP (*Point-to-Point Protocol*) used interchangeably, although there are subtle differences between them. SLIP is the older of these two technologies and is now almost obsolete. The important thing is that a SLIP/PPP account gives you a temporary direct connection to the Internet from home or school. To get an account, you'll need to sign up with a company called an Internet service provider. For guidelines on selecting a service provider, see Appendix A. Service providers offer various levels of connectivity, as they provide connections to individuals, the business community and schools. Monthly fees for a standard dial-up phone line connection tend to be in the US$20 to US$30 per month or US$100 to US$150 per year range for unlimited online time. Your account may include a small amount of Web space for personal/professional but non-commercial use. This means that you'll be able to post your classroom Web site here if your school district doesn't provide space for you.

For faster connectivity, you might select a *Digital Subscriber Line* (DSL), which uses existing copper telephone wiring to deliver high-speed data services to businesses and homes. DSL, in its various forms, offers a choice of speeds ranging from 32 Kbps to more than 50 Mbps. These digital services may ultimately be used to deliver bandwidth-intensive applications like video on demand and distance learning. DSL takes existing voice cables that connect your home/business to the phone company's central office and turns them into a high-speed digital link. Over any given link, the distance between your home/business and the central office determines the maximum DSL speed. At your end, you use a DSL modem to connect the phone line to either a stand-alone computer or a local area network (LAN). Once installed, the DSL modem provides you with a continuous connection to the Internet. DSL line speeds are constant and provide the same speed in both directions. Unlike cable modems, DSL equipment is not accessing a shared infrastructure that slows down individual connection speeds when traffic gets heavy. You'll pay a flat monthly fee of up to about US$80 for a DSL line, plus the cost of the modem. Most providers also offer access via an ISDN line, but the cost of this service is usually prohibitive for home use. Once you have your SLIP/PPP connection, you can run Internet client software directly from the hard drive of your computer. This means you can use either the simplest or the most advanced Web browser available, according

The Virtual Classroom at Canada's Communications Research Centre is engaged in ongoing research to create broadband-enabled learning environments and applications that help develop collaborative learning skills. In a recent project, students participated in videoconferences with one another and with international landmine experts and then developed a Webzine addressing related issues. For more information about the Virtual Classroom, visit **http://www.virtual classroom.crc.ca/en/ html/virtualclassroom/ home/home**.

"As an educational leader and researcher, I am quite pleased to hear of this recent development and can wholeheartedly say that the education sector will require high speed Internet access to continue to meet the needs of students, staffs, parents, and the business community."[4]

– Mark Wylie, Principal, Alberta, Canada responding to the establishment of Canada's National Broadband Task Force

to your needs and the amount of memory in your computer. To open your Internet connection, whether at home or at school, you simply dial in to your service provider.

Cable-based connections

Many people who are already paying for cable TV find it convenient to add fast Internet access to their monthly cable bill. With assorted discounts and packages being offered to lure consumers away from the dial-up service providers, the cable companies' prices are becoming competitive. Cable lines can offer you broadband content and applications beyond the scope of dial-up Internet services. You are always connected; there's no need to dial up or log on and since you are connected on cable, you don't tie up your phone line while you are online. You must, however, purchase/rent a cable-modem and pay for installation.

High-speed connectivity

These days it seems as if the need for speed is everywhere, and school Internet connections are no exception. ISDN lines, dedicated connections, cable connections and satellite feeds are rapidly gaining prominence in schools because they allow faster and more flexible use of the powerful educational applications offered by the Internet. High-speed broadband, defined as "a high-capacity, two-way link between end users and access network suppliers capable of supporting full-motion interactive video application,"[3] is bringing new and exciting possibilities to expand the educational environment. For example, high-speed broadband was used in a 1999 Virtual Classroom project entitled "We Are the World." Participating student teams from across Canada assumed the role of international experts that were commissioned to make recommendations to the newly formed Global Council. Their task was to resolve the escalating crisis of preserving the earth's most precious resource, water. Teams shared information and collaborated in formulating their recommendations, which were presented at a culminating teleconference.

The U.S. Office of Educational Technology's e-Learning report (2001) states that "The quality of Internet access is critical. Broadband access will be the new standard. Slow, unreliable connections that cannot support interactivity or rich multimedia content will no longer be sufficient. To take advantage of access to technology for improved teaching and learning, it will become increasingly important to build and support network infrastructures-wired or wireless, desktop or handheld — that allow multiple devices to connect simultaneously to the Internet throughout every school building and community in the nation."[5]

In January 2001, the Canadian government established the National Broadband Task Force and committed to making high-speed broadband Internet access widely available in every Canadian community, no matter how remote, by 2004. The development of innovative content for education is supported through incentives and funding.

Models for schools

The Cadillac model: Wireless learning anyplace anytime

Economics may limit many teachers' dreams of a computer for every student in every class for a while yet, but it is becoming a reality in more and more schools each year through the use of laptop and hand-held computers. When all students have their own computers, a computer lab is no longer required. Participation in laptop programs has recently come to be associated with improved student attendance and engagement with learning. There are many advantages of laptops in classrooms:

- Students can share a laptop and take turns viewing, inputting, and analyzing data.
- Individuals or groups can transfer information using file sharing programs and/or wireless connectivity.
- Students at different locations can interact using e-mail or video-conferencing, using wireless connectivity or a modem.
- Students can check out laptops for use overnight or during vacations.
- Students have ready access to Internet resources from various locations.
- Students are able to process and graph data immediately, check estimates and make decisions about the next step of an activity in the field or laboratory.
- Students take responsibility for the computers and have more ownership in learning.
- Teachers can connect laptops to monitors or overhead projectors to review software, give multimedia presentations, teach from a Web site and clarify assignments.
- Teachers can easily record and organize notes on individual student progress and use the computers in conjunction with digital cameras and/or voice-to-text applications to record events for later student assessment.
- Teachers are provided with a tool to facilitate changes in their methodology.
- Teachers have more flexibility for homework assignments knowing that all students have a computer and Internet access available.

A study conducted from 1996 through 2000 by Rockman Et Al, an independent research organization, found that students using laptops in Microsoft's Anytime Anywhere Learning program spent more time out of class on schoolwork, scored higher in reading and writing assessments, demonstrated improved research and analysis skills, were more confident in their computer skills, and engaged in more collaborative work than non-laptop using students.[8] Laptops also proved to be a catalyst for teachers to use more constructivist teaching. Laptop teachers showed statistically significant change toward teaching practices that put students at the center of learning, use discussion rather than lecture, encourage student-led inquiry and emphasize thinking skills. Laptop teachers had a greater sense of control over their classroom instruction and management of student learning and used computers far more often in a wider variety of learning activities than non-laptop peers.[9]

- Laptops facilitate communication between students and teachers: using a laptop at home or in the field, students can submit assignments or questions via e-mail or wireless connectivity. [7]

Expense often comes to mind when the idea of a laptop computer for every student is considered. How are schools managing the cost of laptop programs? We are seeing a variety of options including the following:

- Students/parents purchase laptops according to school specifications.
- Students/parents lease laptops from the school district or an independent supplier.
- School and students/parents divide cost of either lease or purchase.
- School or district purchases laptops for students through re-allocation of funds.
- School or district applies for educational grants from the government or non-profit foundations.
- School district creates an educational foundation.

The "anyplace, anytime" theme also continues to be honed by hand-held devices of many kinds. The aim of the manufacturers of these devices is to compete with laptop programs for the most cost-effective and portable access to learning. Hand-held devices have come a long way since the first Palm Pilots of 1996. For schools, the key advantage of these computers is that they are small, powerful, inexpensive and easy to carry. The most common complaint at this time is that they cannot take the place of a laptop or desktop computer, but ongoing developments that expand the capabilities of hand-held computers promise to make them more viable very quickly. It is already possible to add peripherals such as digital cameras, scientific probes and extra memory. Hand-held computers are used in schools for

- sending and receiving of e-mail;
- reading of e-books;
- electronic calendars for teachers, students and administrators;
- science experiments in the field, with the addition of scientific probes;
- managing information such as grades and seating plans;
- math calculations using specialized calculators downloaded from the Web;
- vocabulary work using dictionaries downloaded from the Web;
- recording, storing and playing of MP3 music files;
- snapshots for Web pages by attaching a digital camera; and
- learning tasks with "pocket" versions of Microsoft Word, Excel, and PowerPoint.[10]

The impact of each student having a personal e-mail tool is profound. "Widespread and easy wireless access to the Internet using the palm-sized computers is at most one year away. This functionality is unprecedented in a classroom."[11] (Soloway et al./ 2001)

The standard sedan model: All computers in the school connected

Your students can access the Internet whenever they need to from any computer in the school. All the computers are connected to a LAN, which in turn is connected to the Internet. This kind of flexibility allows students virtually unlimited access to information and the ability to communicate worldwide. Information passes quickly in text or graphical form over a high-speed, dedicated data line. In every unit you plan, you can include a component that requires students to use the Internet. They can e-mail peers and experts in different fields, search for information, and telnet to remote sites to find particular documents. They can download pictures, video clips, and sound clips to include in their multimedia projects. Any project described in this book is easy to manage — the possibilities are endless.

The economy sedan model: Internet terminals in various locations in the school

Some schools have several phone lines, each with a modem-equipped computer, located around the school. In this case, school equipment dedicated primarily to Internet use might include

- two or more computers with modems
- two or more dedicated phone lines
- communications software (which often comes with your computer, and much can be obtained free of charge from the Internet itself)
- Internet access through a service provider, commercial online service, or even a community freenet (costs will vary, according to your choice)

HINT A good source for school networking information with practical advice on getting schools connected is the Schoolhouse Networking Operations Center at **http://sunsite.unc.edu/cisco/noc/index.html**.

Although students may have to leave the classroom, they can still have easy Internet access provided that the number of terminals is adequate for the student and teacher population of the school. Other schools have several modems but are limited to only one phone line. If your class is online and another unknowingly tries to connect, you'll be disconnected in the midst of your work. To avoid this inconvenience, you can obtain an inexpensive "line-in-use" indicator light from your local hardware store, although some modems don't draw enough power down the line to activate the light.

Typically, most terminals are located in the school library/resource center and the computer lab. This configuration allows each class structured Internet use for an hour or so per week but makes it difficult to integrate activities into the curriculum in a seamless, natural way. This model also works best with older students, where teacher supervision is not an issue. With younger students, the most useful location for a terminal is in the classroom. You'll need to plan for individuals or pairs of students to move freely to wherever the terminals are located at the times that they need them. The cooperation and teamwork of all staff members help to make this work. A schedule might be needed, especially in larger schools, so that all classes get a fair share of time. You'll also have to arrange for someone to be available to assist these students as they work, especially at first. Often, the librarian or computer teacher can be available. Parent volunteers and student experts are also invaluable.

If you are fortunate enough to have phone jacks in each classroom throughout the school, you might consider putting one or more modem-equipped computers on carts and creating a rotating schedule for their use. Modems on wheels allow access in the classroom, where you can use the technology most effectively to meet your educational goals. Depending on the type of connection you have, students may be able to access graphics or may be limited to text only. You can plan your Internet activities accordingly.

> The Internet becomes a valuable tool when it is accessible to the greatest number of students. It is difficult to find a location (when you have only one shared phone line) to allow all students supervised access. The computer room is supervised only when there is a class in attendance; the library is run by volunteers on a part-time basis. Each classroom needs its own access.
>
> — *Debra Killen, Teacher, Chelsea School, Chelsea, Quebec, Canada*

Checklist for connectivity

You're ready to surf the Internet when you have

- a modem of sufficient speed to sustain your work, unless you are connected through a LAN
- a personal computer and monitor of sufficient resolution for the text and graphics activities you wish to carry out
- a telephone line or high-speed data line
- a connection to the Internet in one of the ways described in this chapter
- instructions from your service provider on how to make and sustain a connection
- software to use once connected
- your service provider's customer service telephone number, should problems arise

Project Ideas

Cybernauts Only

Learning outcomes

- Students will participate in an Internet Club.
- Other outcomes will be determined by what projects the students become engaged in.

Grade level: Any

Getting started

- Invite students to join an Internet Club. (See sample invitation/ permission form.)
- Establish a time and place for weekly meetings.
- Select possible projects in which the students might get involved. (This book is full of them!)

Developing

- Begin with a student survey of Internet use. (See sample survey.)
- Propose some project ideas to the club members and get their ideas also.
- Come to agreement and start planning your first project!

Extending

- Many Computer/Internet Clubs are responsible for maintaining a portion of the school's Web site.
- Students should at least publish the projects of the Internet Club on the school's Web site.

Dear Parents of Future Internet Club Participants,

Internet Club for the _____ school year is open to all students in
Grade(s) _____ for the months _____ through _____.

Internet Club will begin on _____ at _____ in Room _____.

As a club member, your child will get opportunities to be involved in the
following learning experiences:

_____
_____
_____
_____

Club members will need the following supplies:

_____
_____
_____
_____

Students participating must have their Acceptable Use policies on file for this
school year. Please return the portion below to _____ by _____ .

Sincerely,

....

Date _____

My child would like to participate as an Internet Club member. I understand that
parents must provide transportation and have discussed with my child that participation is a privilege and appropriate school behavior is expected. My child's
Acceptable Use Policy for this school year is on file.

Student's Name   _____

Classroom Teacher's Name _____

Home Phone Number   _____

Work Phone Number   _____

Parent/Guardian Signature _____

Internet Use Survey

Name _____

Classroom Teacher's Name _____

Grade _____

Please circle your answer.

Do you have Internet access at home?	Yes	No
Do your parents/guardians have an e-mail address?	Yes	No
Do you have your own e-mail address?	Yes	No
Can you download files from the Internet?	Yes	No

What do you do **most often** on the Internet?
(pick one only)

- Send e-mail
- Visit chat rooms
- Play games
- Do homework

Please write your answer.

What Web sites do you like to visit?

_____
_____
_____

_____

What do you like about the Internet? What do you not like?

_____
_____
_____
_____

What would you like to learn about the Internet?

_____
_____
_____
_____

School implementation planning

The planning process gives school communities an opportunity to develop a vision of what they want their school to become and to plan the steps in getting there. A well-developed strategic school plan for implementing or expanding Internet use addresses current equipment and its present utilization, how and why these technological learning resources and their management need to be improved, who will be responsible for which aspects of the improvement, and how the school will evaluate its progress. Planning for curriculum and staff training are crucial elements too often ignored. Planning committees can include administrators, teachers, parents, and students. The committee will require help from individuals with curriculum, technological, and administrative expertise. Key issues should never be decided without consultation with others.

A good plan includes

- the names and contact information of committee members
- a brief philosophy and mission statement
- a list of anticipated beneficial student outcomes
- the planned integration of the technology across the curriculum
- proposed changes to current technology and its usage
- a hardware/software purchase plan, including proposed time of acquisition, cost, and sources of funding
- a detailed budget that includes costs of teacher training and support materials such as student learning guides, paper, duplication, and computer disks
- strategies to address upgrades, obsolescence, and maintenance
- the source and cost of ongoing technical and professional support
- the role of each person involved in the implementation, and timelines for their actions
- an explanation of how the project will sustain itself over time
- a description of how the project will be evaluated, including review dates

Everyone should understand that a good plan is not static: it is always being adjusted to take advantage of changes — in technology, in resources, and in teacher expertise. Since the plan will probably be used to solicit funding, it must be easy to understand. Thus, keep technical and educational jargon to a minimum. Prepare a brief summary as a handout. It's a good idea to have a catchy name and a student-designed logo for your package. If you have an opportunity to present your plan in a format other than print, try to use the very technology that you are advocating.

HINT Excellent resources for overall school and district technology planning can be found at the following sites:

Bellingham Public Schools Technology Plan
This Washington school district has long been a leader in technology planning and implementation. They provide a very comprehensive example here that makes a good starting point.
http://www.bham.wednet.edu/ technology/techplan.htm

ERIC Bibliography of Technology Planning Articles
A list of the ERIC documents related to this topic.
http://www.netc.org/tech_plans/ ericjournal.html

Mississippi State University: Guidebook for Developing an Effective Technology Plan
This manual, for preparing the written portion of a technology plan, was developed under the direction of Dr. Larry Anderson, professor of Instructional Technology, Department of Technology and Education.
http://www.nctp.com

National Center for Technology Planning
A clearinghouse for information related to technology planning such as school district technology plans available for downloading via a computer network, technology planning aids (checklists, brochures, sample planning forms, PR announcement forms), and/or electronic monographs on timely, selected topics.
http://www.nctp.com

North Central Regional Educational Laboratory
This is a document with excellent guidelines and links to school-based examples.
http://www.ncrel.org/tech/matrix/ plan.htm

http://www.ncrtec.org/capacity/ guidewww/gqhome.htm

WestEd Educational Technology Program
Resources available include examples for technology use, basic guidelines, and technology planning information on the WWW.
http://www.wested.org/cs/wew/ view/rs/619

Training

Motivation

As a teacher who has chosen to read this book, you must already be motivated to learn more about using the Internet in your classroom or school. You may now be wondering: How can you excite and motivate your colleagues to join you?

When asked what moved them to get involved in using the Internet in their classrooms, many teachers cited the availability of accounts at low (or no) cost, either through discounts from vendors, local or national grants, or pilot projects. Such advantages tended to trigger acquisition and implementation. Some teachers mentioned that their prior involvement with computers made using the Internet a natural evolution. Others found that a personal interest (such as planning a vacation, researching a hobby, or communicating with a family member) got them started on the Internet. In many cases, the enthusiasm of a friend, relative, fellow teacher, or student provided the motivation; a team approach eased the learning curve. The availability of a central resource, such as Canada's SchoolNet, Global SchoolNet, or EdWeb, was also helpful. Most importantly, all the teachers' comments reflected excitement and enthusiasm about the educational possibilities of the Internet.

> Our school district purchased thirty accounts and distributed them to personnel who were willing to volunteer twelve to fifteen hours of training time to the project. Its success has made some other teachers wish they had invested the time. The initial group will train others in Internet usage.
>
> — *Carol Willard, Teacher, Troy Junior High School, Troy, Missouri, U.S.A.*

Training yourself

A common response from teachers when they see the educational possibilities of the Internet is "This looks great, but there's so much to learn. Where do I begin?"

Start by examining the opportunities within your own school. Once you are committed to becoming Internet literate, look for learning partners and mentors among your colleagues. It's more fun, and more productive, to learn in collaboration than in isolation. Many schools hold inservice sessions, both during the day and after school. "Brown bag" meetings held during the lunch period offer an opportunity for users to share experiences, frustrations, and discoveries. You can save time by sharing lists of educational sites among colleagues who have visited them.

> We [twenty to thirty teachers] got together for Internet training using an LCD panel two separate times for four weeks, two hours a week. Our librarian did the training and each week provided us with practice activities that forced us to use our newly acquired skills. It was a great experience, and humbling, too. We felt "dumb" at times, just as our students sometimes do when we present them with new information.
>
> — *Carol Willard, Teacher, Troy Junior High School, Troy, Missouri, U.S.A.*

Your school and/or district probably has resource people who can assist you in a variety of ways. Ideally, resource people would be located in your own school so that they are available when needed. However, with the realities of today's shrinking budgets, this isn't always possible. Reach out for whatever services are available from these resource people, such as

- offering workshops for groups of teachers, parents, and/or students
- working cooperatively with you and your students on a project
- finding useful Internet sites to fit your curriculum
- putting you in touch with a focus group of interested teachers in other schools

- helping with technical problem solving
- recommending resource books, training manuals, and magazines
- providing lists of conferences and courses
- arranging a visit to another school or site

> We have given demonstrations to entire staffs as an introduction to the Internet. We have also given workshops for small groups of teachers who are interested in learning more about the Internet. This approach has worked well because it allows us to offer more one-to-one help. In addition, I have also been busy helping teachers who want to be connected at home. I go to their homes, set up their computers, and give them one-to-one tutoring.... Teachers who are comfortable enough to connect at school and at home will in turn help others in their own schools.
>
> — *Bonnie McMurren, Stony Mountain Elementary School, Stony Mountain, Manitoba, Canada*

Many school districts have established their own bulletin board system. Though these may not have Internet access, you can use such local bulletin boards to learn and practice the skills of sending and receiving e-mail, uploading and downloading files, general navigation, and netiquette. They also provide forums through which you can exchange resources and ideas with other teachers. And there are Internet-related discussion groups you can join. Other districts and states have established Web sites that assist teachers with curriculum matters as well as facilitating communication between peers and community organizations.

> Our school board features a mobile computer lab, the Micromobile. It travels from school to school, offering students and teachers opportunities to learn and use computer skills in a state-of-the-art facility.... Each school now has an Internet account and a Net manager — a teacher who is given a computer to take home for the summer to get comfortable with the Net. The Net manager then becomes an on-site trainer for other staff. We also have a school board BBS that provides access to, and help with, Internet and other computer-related topics.
>
> — *Peter K. McLeod (1995, June 22), "Training."* **Classuse@schoolnet.carleton.ca**

Some Canadian provinces and U.S. states offer training courses to assist their teachers in acquiring various computer competencies. These are often free of charge. For example, Utahlink, the state network, provides Internet training for all levels from beginners to advanced courses designed for technology specialists. You can look at their training calendar at **http://www. uen.org/utahlink**.

University courses in educational technology, including the Internet, are numerous today. Many of them focus on practical classroom applications. The advantage of taking a course during the school year is that you can try out new strategies immediately in your own classroom. Your local high school may offer evening or weekend courses focusing on a specific software package such as Netscape or a particular skill such as creating Web pages. These are very useful, as they tend to be brief, inexpensive, hands-on, and student centered.

> One teacher from each school that has Internet access was sponsored for an Internet course for new users, offered through the University of Calgary. Weekly assignments forced us to practice what we had learned. After five sessions we each had to present our project. This was excellent because each of us took on something entirely different. It gave us ideas for student projects and provided us with a list of resources that we could use in the classroom.
>
> — *Sharon Lewis, Teacher, Red Deer, Alberta, Canada*

Online learning offers convenience and flexibility. The choice of courses available is so vast you're sure to find something that suits your needs in terms of content, length and cost. Several accredited universities offer entire degree programs with no residency requirement; others use a combination of online and face-to-face arrangements. When you take advantage of online learning, you can work wherever you have an Internet connection and whenever you choose, within the parameters of the course. In addition, you get the opportunity to meet educators from other districts and other countries. Emerging technologies are making online courses and workshops more multimedia, interactive and easy to use. Highly motivated, self-directed, independent problem-solvers are most successful in online courses and you may find that you need to "shop around" a bit to find the type of course that suits your learning style. At the following sites, you can find surveys to help you decide if you are a good candidate for online professional development:

Minnesota Virtual University at **http://www.mnvu.org/mnvu/ 1503.jsp**

The Illinois Online Network at **http://www.ion.illinois.edu/ IONresources/onlineLearning/index.asp**.
In Chapter 10, you will find out more about distance education.

Conferences such as those offered by the International Society for Technology in Education (ISTE), the National Education Computing Conference (NECC), and the Educational Computing Organization of Ontario (ECOO) offer sessions for both beginners and advanced Internet users.

Several education-related agencies offer training for teachers, for a price. This may take the form of workshops, seminars, or courses, on or off line. Visit these Web sites for more details.

Apple Learning Interchange

Apple Learning's Professional Development Online Courses provide an array of self-paced courses designed to help educators integrate technology into teaching and learning. Each course consists of an interactive tutorial, and hands-on course projects.

http://ali.apple.com/nshelp/welcome.shtml

Classroom Connect's Connected University

Connected University offers educators more than 70 online guide-led courses, learning resources, just-in-time support, and peer interaction to help teachers integrate technology and improve student learning in their classrooms.

http://cu.classroom.com

Forefront Curriculum

Forefront Curriculum offers a great variety of seminars for K–12 educators and administrators throughout the United States. They will come to your school site and conduct seminars tailored to meet your specific curricular needs. Seminars include Internet Basics for K–12 Educators, Creating a Classroom Web Site, Intermediate Internet for Educators, Walking the Web with Special Ed, Internet Curriculum Club, Internet Basics for Administrators, One Computer in the Classroom, Internet Basics for Librarians, Technology in the K–12 Classroom, Child Safety on the Net, Improving Instruction with the 'Net, and Net Integration for Science Educators.

http://www.forefrontcurriculum.com/seminar.html

OnlineLearning

At OnlineLearning.net you can choose from nearly 50 courses designed just for educators, such as English Language Development, Inclusion, Reading, and Instructional Technology.

http://www.OnlineLearning.net

Some private agencies, such as Internet service providers and computer stores, also offer short workshops and longer training sessions. Though they may not deal specifically with educational applications of Internet resources, they can introduce you to general Internet tools and allow hands-on practice time.

Many teachers prefer to schedule their Internet training in a more flexible manner. You don't have to leave home to learn how to use the Internet; you can access distance education courses, tutorials, reference books, and Internet guides on the Internet itself.

Here are some of the many useful starting points on the World Wide Web. As you visit these sites, bookmark any you'd like to have your students or colleagues use.

Charm Net Learning Page

This provides links to books, tutorials, and hint sheets for Internet learning as part of the home page for the Charm Net service provider in Baltimore, Maryland.

http://www.charm.net/CN2000/Traverse/nu-learning.html

Electronic School Tour

Take a guided tour of the World Wide Web with the Electronic School. Developed specifically for educators, this site offers many educational resources, including the Library of Congress and the Louvre. This is also a good place to sample such sites as AskERIC and the Cisco Systems Meta-library of elementary and primary school Internet links.

http://www.electronic-school.com/surf.html

HTML Goodies

Joe Burns offers tutorials, HTML primers, free images, scanning service, video service, an archive file of frequently asked questions and much more.

http://www.htmlgoodies.com

Internet Island

An entertaining and informative Internet tour for beginners of all ages.

http://www.miamisci.org/ii/default.html

John December's Web Site

John December is a well-known author and speaker who has extensive experience in Web development, publishing, and research. His site is intended for both beginning and experienced Internet users. It has pointers to resources to help you learn about and use the Internet and the Web, master the art of Web development, and understand the significance of the online world.

http://www.december.com/works

Learn the Net

A comprehensive guide to the Internet, including help with digging for data; using search tools, mailing lists, and databases; exchanging files; and developing Web pages.

http://www.learnthenet.com/english/index.html

Figure 9-1

webTeacher provides free self-paced Internet training that includes both basic (Primers) and in-depth (Tutorials) information about the Web. Topics such as e-mail, videoconferencing, chat rooms, Web page design both beginning and advanced, Internet safety, and curriculum searches are included. The format is interactive so you get to put your new knowledge to work immediately through online exercises and activities. **http://www.webteacher.org/winexp/indextc.html**.

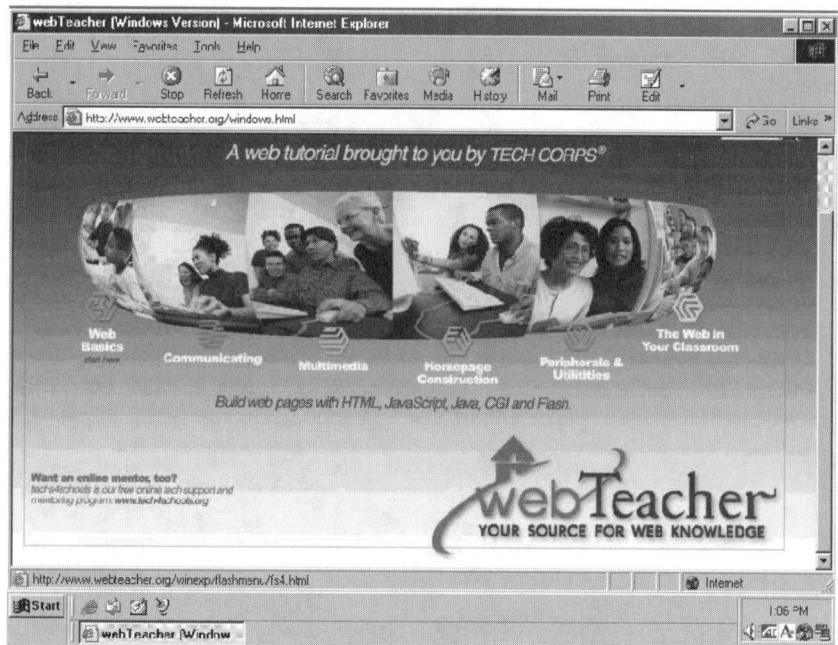

Oz-TeacherNet

This site is a starting point for Australian teachers who want to use the Internet for professional development and curriculum purposes. The project team will assist in developing online resources and tools for events and discussion.

http://rite.ed.qut.edu.au/oz-teachernet

SupportNet Online

SupportNet Online offers resources specifically geared to help teachers and technical support personnel in Michigan schools and libraries. SupportNet's free online training courses can also be used by anyone who wants to learn about communicating over the Internet, legal issues involving using technology in schools, security, networking, and different operating environments.

http://supportnet.merit.edu

TeacherLine

TeacherLine offers learning modules and resources for innovative professional development in mathematics and technology integration.

http://teacherline.pbs.org/teacherline/welcome.cfm

Figure 9-2
Internet Island: An Internet tutorial.

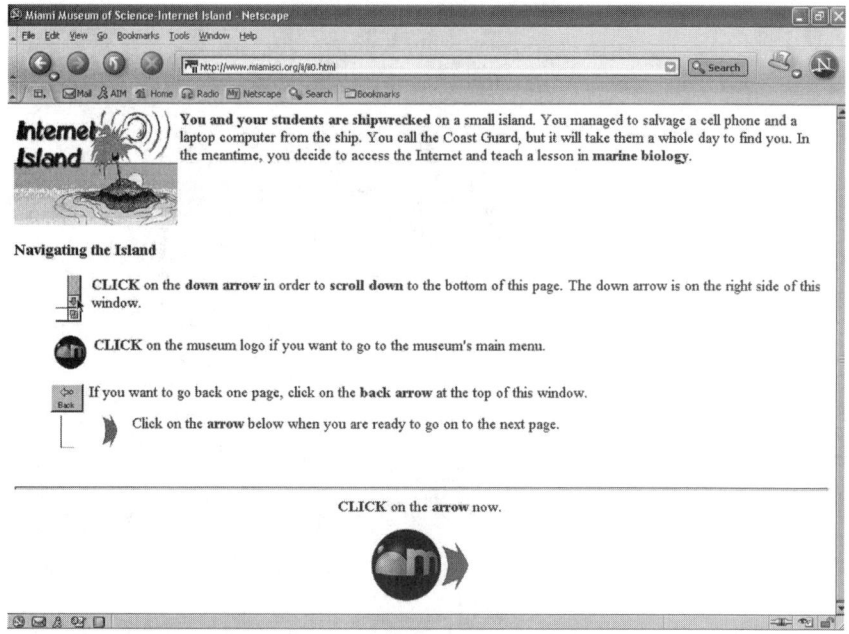

Yahoo's listing of Internet guides

Start here for links to all sorts of online learning materials.

http://www.yahoo.com/computers_and_Internet/Internet

> The Internet is like an elephant: you can eat it, but you have to take it one bite at a time!
>
> — *Christiane Dufour, Teacher, Small Schools Network, Quebec City, Quebec, Canada*

Training others

HINT The Internet Training site at **http:// december.com/ cmc/info** contains links aimed at instructors who provide Internet training, including lesson plans and resources.

Many different staff development strategies have been tried with mixed success. Staff development does not mean pouring information into teachers' heads or training them in a few technical skills, but rather providing meaningful contexts for learning, emphasizing collaborative problem solving and personal expression, and placing the learner at the center of the learning experience. Teachers, like their students, must see the relevance of what they are to learn or they are not interested. Thus, the Internet needs to be both understood and used in relation to its relevance to curriculum. Once its educational applications are apparent, teachers are motivated to take the time to learn how to use it.

Teachers teaching one another is one of the most successful professional development strategies. This might involve freeing one teacher to work as a teacher-trainer in another teacher's class for a given length of time. The teacher-trainer can assist by observing what goes on in the class, working with students and the teacher to learn a new skill, and suggesting ways in which that teacher could try to integrate the technology. This is valuable because it occurs within the "real" situation of the teacher, who can feel more comfortable knowing that help is at hand and thus may be more inclined to explore new ideas.

The "technology coach" model involves hiring itinerant teachers, who work at a number of schools within a district, to help teachers integrate various Internet applications into their existing curriculum. The coaches work in classrooms with students and assist teachers with the planning process.

If you are training other teachers, offer them a choice of opportunities to see the Internet in action, so that they can select the presentation that best fits their timetable.

You'll need to have a computer system available after school for teachers' use, with a co-trainer to attend when needed. Offer specific topic sessions, and build Internet awareness activities into scheduled meetings. After a brief introduction to the Net, encourage people to browse on their own. Stay close by to answer questions and give suggestions. Find out each teacher's interest, and then locate sites on the Internet that pertain to them. Show each teacher how he or she might use the Internet in the classroom — and remember what it was like for you when you were just beginning. Experienced users may accept such inconveniences as dropped lines or unavailable sites, but small irritations can be big roadblocks for people who are new to this technology.

> I believe in "just in time" training — that is, teaching people to use tools as they relate to projects they want to do now. Teaching Internet tools in the abstract is too overwhelming. But handing teachers a specific tool to do something they want to do makes learning easier.
>
> — *Christiane Dufour, Small Schools Network, Quebec City, Quebec, Canada*

Mentoring is a key element of a staff development initiative for technology literacy, and integration in Chicago's New Trier High School District 203. Teachers at New Trier develop Individual Technology Learning Plans. During the process of developing the plans, the teachers work with an assigned technology mentor who helps to assess their current technology skill level and to identify necessary steps to achieve their technology goals. New Trier's mentors are district-level technology staffers who can work in the classroom with their assigned teachers. As the teacher implements new software or strategies, the mentor may be there to assist or troubleshoot. Teachers meet regularly with their mentors for one to two years while they progress through the steps of the plan. As the teachers integrate the skills they learn into their teaching, they compile a portfolio to demonstrate proficiency with and integration of the technology as originally outlined in their plans. When the portfolio is accepted, teachers receive a stipend based on the scope of work undertaken.[12]

There's lots of help available on the Web for Internet trainers. For example, the webTeacher training modules (**http://www.webteacher.org/winexp/indextc.html**) are a series of individual scripts that are designed as lesson plans for those providing staff development training in areas of the World Wide Web, e-mail, and the Internet. Each script includes 70 to 90 minutes of class instruction, and is printable from the site.

Teachers who have had experience with Internet training courses recommend the following strategies.

- Ensure each pair of teachers has their own computer.
- Tie training to practical classroom needs.
- Be diverse in the activities you select, as not everyone responds with equal enthusiasm to the same activities.
- Reinforce learning by having teachers complete a project in conjunction with their training.
- Pair teachers with others in the school who are knowledgeable about the Internet.
- Create a few successful "pockets of good practice" within a school, even if this necessitates concentrating resources in a couple of early adopters rather than attempting to get everyone going simultaneously.
- Provide hands-on experience. The only way to learn something is to do it.
- Ensure a low instructor-to-student ratio to allow for individual assistance.
- Plan short instructional sessions followed by lots of practice time.
- Schedule ongoing training over a period of time rather than a one-shot inservice.
- Allow some release time from classes in order to pursue professional development whenever possible.
- Visit other schools to compare practices.
- Reward participants with certification or a recognized credit of some sort.

Staying current

With the pace of change today, it's a continuing challenge to keep up-to-date. The Internet is no exception; in fact, it's the fastest growing technology around. The Internet is always changing. We asked some teachers how they keep abreast of new developments. Here are their suggestions.

- Read magazines such as *Internet World, Web Week, Net Guide*, and *Leading and Learning with Technology*.
- Use the Internet as often as possible. Explore on your own, and do searches of topics that interest you.
- Subscribe to listservs that discuss issues relevant to technology in education, such as those listed in Chapter 7.

HINT One great way to stay current is to look at what other schools around your country and around the world are doing. An example of an individual school that always seems to have a lot to offer is Loogootee Elementary at **http://www.loogootee. K12.in.us/west**.

HINT The Visible Knowledge Project Web site at **http://cross roads.georgetown.edu/ vkp/resources/index. htm** provides links to online journals such as the *Journal of Technology Education, The Technology Source,* and *Computer-Mediated Communication Magazine.*

- Take a distance education course on the Internet.
- Have discussions with other teachers and individuals already involved in using the Internet.
- Search for tools or help to answer questions about practical needs that arise.
- Use the buddy system.
- Get involved in assisting other teachers to take advantage of the potential of the Net.
- Devote some time each day to surfing the Internet in order to discover new sites that might be useful at school. When a URL is recommended, view the site immediately, and if you like it, add it to your bookmarks. (Then, of course, share your bookmarks with others!)

Funding

In today's economy, money matters more than ever. But this is a good time to be seeking funds for Internet projects. With the emphasis on educational reform, global communications, and technology, you'll find there are a variety of sources of funding available. Designate several members of your planning team to pursue funding opportunities. Consider local community businesses, large corporations, private foundations, charitable organizations, provincial/state government agencies, and national projects that support technology in education.

The responsibility for finding sources of funding generally rests with your school administration and the school board or district. If you don't presently have Internet access, ask a local service provider or university to allow you to use their account for a demonstration to administrators. Once they see the World Wide Web in action as a learning tool, they will be more likely to pursue funding.

The best way to convince the decision makers of the educational benefits of the Internet is to have students demonstrate their learning and excitement. Invite trustees, parent councils, administrators, and community leaders to attend school technology fairs. Show them videos and slides of students at work using the Internet, and try to maintain a high profile for your technology projects. Collect a file of clippings about educational use of the Internet, and reserve a bulletin board for displaying current magazine and newspaper articles.

School fund raising

Many schools raise money for their projects through such efforts as fun fairs, technology fairs, school plays, bake sales, plant sales, math-a-thons, garage sales, and barbecues. You might not think of making a lot of money this

HINT You can find ideas for alternative sources of funding in the *Grassroots Funding Journal*, available from GFJ, P.O. Box 11607 Berkley, CA 94701 USA

The Grass Roots Fundraising Book: How to Raise Money in Your Community, by Joan Flanagan, is a book of practical advice and comprehensive information available from Contemporary Books, Inc.

way, but one school in San Francisco managed to raise nearly $100,000 in a year by preparing and selling hot lunches! An active, enthusiastic parent group can accomplish great things.

Corporate funding

Many large companies set aside funds specifically for community and educational projects. In the United States, these funds are often distributed through nonprofit foundations. In Canada, they are usually controlled by the Community or Public Affairs Branch of the national office of the corporation. In both cases, you'll find formal selection policies and application procedures.

Your first step is to list all the corporations in your area that might be interested in your project. Technology-related corporations are the most likely choice, particularly telecommunications companies; but don't limit yourself. Remember that the benefits to learners are the driving force, not the technology itself. Your community library may have a reference guide to corporate funding that includes contact information. The magazine *Technology and Learning* also includes a section on U.S. grants and funding sources and ideas.

Once you've identified possible sponsors, the next step is to find out what types of projects they support and what types of donations they provide. Ask them to send their application procedures and funding guidelines, then pare your list down to the top ten. Don't make the mistake of thinking that just because a project contributes to good public relations it will automatically be attractive to the company. Ideal prospects are those in which your project matches the stated objectives of the corporation's giving program and/or a senior executive has an interest in your project and will be an advocate within the corporation. Corporations generally prefer to donate to schools in their local area and may be more willing to contribute products or services than cash. You might approach them for donations such as telephone lines, equipment, or technical expertise. Corporate sponsors also tend to prefer to be the only ones of their kind involved in a specific project, so if you obtain significant funding from one source, don't solicit funds from competing companies in the same field.

Develop a succinct summary of your project, one or two pages long. Consider establishing levels of sponsorship, each with a set amount — for example, founding sponsors, $1000; major sponsors, $500; contributing sponsors, $100. Explain in your application how the sponsors will be given credit for their assistance. After clearing prospects with your school principal and board/district supervisors, communicate directly and personally with appropriate corporations. In large corporations, you'll want to talk with a specific person, often called the "giving officer." Use the name of any company executives who you know to support your project. After submitting your proposal, follow up and offer to provide further information or to do a more detailed presentation. If you are successful in securing a sponsor or receiving a grant, stay in close contact with your donor. Forward progress reports, news articles, and results. Invite company representatives to visit your school and see the project in action.

AT&T offers cash grants to educational institutions to fund projects that demonstrate effective and innovative uses of technology to support families, schools, and communities. There are no specific deadlines — grant proposals are considered as they are received and awarded as long as funds are available. The URL for the guidelines is **http://www.att.com/foundation/guidelines.html**. The grants are awarded regionally, so you will need to contact the AT&T regional contributions offices in your area. Their contact information is listed at **http://www.att.com/foundation/offices.html** You can also contact AT&T Foundation at

    32 Avenue of the Americas
    24th Floor; New York, NY 10013
    Phone (212) 387-4801

The program is open to all accredited public and private elementary and secondary schools as well as accredited public and private two- and four-year institutions of higher education and educational nonprofit organizations in the fifty United States, the District of Columbia, Puerto Rico, and all U.S. territories. The AT&T Learning Network Grants Program focuses on the use of technology, not on the equipment and infrastructure necessary to support that use. AT&T Learning Network grants will not fund requests that are exclusively for the purchase of computers, modems, wiring, or other infrastructure needs. Instead, the program provides resources to help families, schools, and communities understand how to use technology.

Some smaller hardware and software companies may give in-kind donations or offer reduced costs to schools. In-kind donations might include use of training facilities, printing and copying, surplus equipment, personnel for technical advice, or planning expertise. Don't hesitate to approach your school's parent community for assistance from local businesses, both large and small. Parents are often your best connections and are more than willing to assist when your planned initiative directly benefits their own children.

Business-education partnerships

Establishing a business partnership is different from asking a business for a grant or donation. True business-education partnerships are cooperative relationships in which partners share values; human, material, or financial resources; and roles and responsibilities, in order to achieve desired learning outcomes. For example, a local Internet service provider might give your school reduced access charges if teachers enroll in their training courses.

Employers and educators support business-education partnerships that:

- enhance the quality and relevance of education for learners;
- mutually benefit both partners;
- treat fairly and equitably all those served by the partnership;
- provide opportunities for all partners to meet their shared responsibilities toward education;
- acknowledge and celebrate each partner's contribution through appropriate forms of recognition;
- are consistent with the ethics and core values of all partners;
- are based on the clearly defined expectations of all partners;
- are based on shared or aligned objectives that support the goals of the partner organizations;
- allocate resources to complement and not replace public funding for education;
- measure and evaluate partnership performance to make informed decisions that ensure continuous improvement;
- are developed and structured in consultation with all partners;
- recognize and respect each partner's expertise;
- identify clearly defined roles and responsibilities of all partners; and
- involve individual participants on a voluntary basis.

— *The Education Forum, Conference Board of Canada (1995), "Ethical guidelines for business-education partnerships."*

HINT "Grant Proposal Development: An Educator's Guide" provides basic knowledge of grant writing at minimal cost from the Massachusetts Field Center for Teaching and Learning, University of Massachusetts at Boston, Harbor Campus, Boston, MA 02125. "Tips for Writing Grant Proposals" is free from the Association of Supervision & Curriculum Development, 1250 North Pitt Street, Alexandria, VA 22314; (703) 549-9110.

Handbooks and documents about business-education partnerships:

- *Bring Business & Community Resources into Your Classroom: A Handbook for Educators* — a partnership guidebook of practical advice, case studies, and sample surveys. #1851-6-00, US$19.95 from the NEA Professional Library, Box 509, West Haven, CT 06516; (800) 229-4200.
- The National Association of Partners in Education (NAPE) provides materials and training for partnership initiatives. Contact NAPE, 209 Madison Street, Suite 401, Alexandria, VA 22314; (703) 836-4880.
- *School Partnerships Handbook*, by Susan Otterbourg, published by Prentice-Hall, Inc.

ERIC Documents:
- "School-Business Partnerships: The Best of ERIC on Educational Management" — a five-page ERIC document, #ED291165, reviewing eleven documents and articles on the topic.
- "Business-Education Partnerships in California: An Overview and Guide" — a 156-page ERIC document, #ED348499.
- "Time to Teach a New World: Education and Technology in the 21st Century" — a twelve-page ERIC document, #ED332675, describing IBM's involvement with educational institutions.
- "Partnerships in Education: A Handbook" — a seventeen-page

ERIC document, #ED253620, with suggestions on developing partnerships between local schools and businesses.
- "Developing and Managing Technology Partnerships Between Industry and Higher Education" — a twenty-page ERIC document, #ED276861.
- "The Role of Private Business in Distance Learning: The Educational Partnership" — a twenty-eight-page ERIC document, #ED327144.
- "Establishing Partnerships Between the Business Community and Rural Schools" — a four-page ERIC document, #ED287650.

HINT The Apple Education/Business Partnership Program enables businesses that have established relationships with educational institutions to purchase hardware and software for their school partners at discount prices. Price lists and order forms are available in the Apple Education Resource Guide; call (800) 800-APPL to find out where to obtain a copy. For additional information about the program, call (800) 793-EDUC.

Partnerships can be formed with individual companies, colleges, and universities, or with groups of individuals representing several related businesses. For a school, the benefits of forming a business partnership might include leadership from experts in a particular technology, gifts or loans of equipment, opportunities for student internships, and/or the provision of support services. You'll find that many of the grants and award programs available today require evidence of one or more business partnerships. Here are some tips for finding a potential business partner.

- Identify companies in your local area and companies whose products you are already using.
- Explore personal contacts, such as parents within your school.
- Find out as much as possible about potential partners and their needs.
- Establish credibility by showing people from the business community some of the great things that are already happening in your school through the use of technology. Proposals in which the school raises a portion of the money and the business matches the amount raised are often successful.
- Generate as much publicity as you can for your venture. Try to establish your school as an innovative leader. Everyone likes a winner.
- Provide a detailed plan of your project and its benefits to all parties.

Government grants and awards

The US$1.5 billion federal funding for education technology comes from both targeted programs for technology as well as via core or "traditional" federal programs. In the former category of direct education technology programs are the Technology Literacy Challenge Fund funded at $425 million in 2000 and the Technology Innovation Challenge Grant program for stimulating technology-supported high performance learning environments, funded at $146 million in 2000.

Other specialized technology programs include these:

- Preparing Tomorrow's Teachers to Use Technology — US$75 million
- Community-based Technology Programs — US$32.5 million
- Stars School Program — US$50.5 million
- Learning Anytime, Anywhere Partnerships — US$23.3 million
- Technology and Media Services — US$36 million
- Assistive Technology for the Disabled Learner — US$34 million

An even greater portion of federal education technology funding support comes through core federal programs, which have made school hardware and software acquisition, as well as staff development for technology, a greater priority in recent years. These include Title I grants for basic and advanced skills, Title VI Innovative Education Strategies, Title II Eisenhower Professional Development, and the Goals 2000 Educate America Act. In addition to the federal investment in education technology, states and school districts contribute another $5.4 billion for instructional technology via a myriad of district-wide programs and competitive grants.[13]

Although education is not the direct responsibility of the federal government in Canada, schools can apply for government grants and awards sponsored by other federal departments. You can find out about these in the *Handbook of Grants and Subsidies of the Federal and Provincial Governments for Non-Profit Organizations.* The aim of this document is to keep citizens informed of all governmental assistance available. Funding opportunities

Enacted as a part of the Universal Service Program of the Telecommunications Act of 1996, the E-rate program provides discounts to public and private schools, libraries, and consortia on the costs of telecommunications services, internal access, and internal networking. In the program's first two years, tens of thousands of public and private elementary and secondary schools, and thousands more libraries received a total of $3.66 billion in discounts on connectivity and telecommunications services.[14] In the Spring of 2000, the Federal Communications Commission announced that the third year of the program would be funded at $2.25 billion, the maximum allowed, based on requests submitted by schools and libraries around the country.

include Education and Research, Cultural Affairs, Health and Social Services, and Employment and Development. The handbook and monthly updating service are available from

> Canadian Research and Publications Centre (CRPC)
> 33 Racine
> Farnham, PQ J2N 3A3
> (Phone: In Quebec, 1-800-363-8304. In all other provinces, 1-800-363-1400.)

Don't limit yourself to grants specifically designated for technology. Be creative in showing how the Internet will benefit students in at-risk, disabled, gifted, and workplace preparation programs. The time spent in writing a proposal is well worth it. Once you have prepared one funding application, you can easily modify it to meet the criteria of others. Apply well in advance of the anticipated launch of your initiative, and be patient as you wade through the red tape and bureaucracy.

Most state and provincial departments of education have recently created funds for technology initiatives. There are too many to list here, and they change yearly, so contact your local school district or school board to get the details of these programs for your area. You can also find extensive lists of links to sources of grants and funding at these sites:

* The Pitsco Technology Education Web at **http://www.pitsco.com**
* NASA's Grants and Other (People's) Money at **http://quest.arc. nasa.gov/top/grants.html**
* School Grants at **http://www.schoolgrants.org**
* TechLEARNING at **http://www.techlearning.com/grants.html**
* The Foundation Center at **http://fdncenter.org**
* WebTeacher Educational Technology Resources at **http://www. webteacher.org/cable/fundbk.html**

Many of these sites also include advice on writing grants, tips, samples and other related resources.

Private grants, awards and contests

Some computer companies and education-related businesses offer grants and awards of various kinds. At the following sites, you can enter a contest while contributing to a collection of exemplary classroom practices.

Canada's SchoolNet Grassroots Projects

The GrassRoots Program offers funding to schools for the creation of collaborative learning projects on the Internet. Projects must be initiated,

designed and implemented by teachers and students, be curriculum relevant and focus on learning activities carried out using the Internet. Students seek out online resources and carry out collaborative activities that result in a final report and Web site that are published on the Internet.
http://www.schoolnet.ca/grassroots/e/index.asp

CyberFair

CyberFair is one of the largest educational events of its kind on the Internet. This program has brought together more than 500,000 students from over 75 countries. For 2002, this international challenge encouraged K–12 students around the world to produce an educational Web site that tells a story about local community programs such as programs to help the sick or elderly, volunteer programs, community resource centers, meals on wheels, beach or park clean-up programs, or adopt-a-highway programs.
http://www.gsn.org/cf/index.html

The HP K–12 Technology for Teaching Grant

This initiative is designed to support innovative and effective uses of technology in the classroom setting. During 2004, HP will grant awards to K-12 public schools that are using a collaborative, team-based approach to implementing technology integration projects. The focus of the project must be on using technology to teach, rather than teaching students to use technology. HP will select teams of five teachers from at least 150 schools to receive the equipment, professional development and support they need to effectively integrate technology into their instruction. Preference will be given to low-income schools, relative to district or state free and reduced price lunch percentages and to projects that include integration of mathematics and/or science curriculum..
http://grants.hp.com/us/programs/tech_teaching/k12_main.html

International Society for Technology in Education (ISTE)

Each year since 1991, the Special Interest Group on Telecommunications (SIG/Tel) of ISTE has sponsored a contest for educators using telecommunications networks for innovative classroom practices. Winners are invited to share their work at two major conferences and the winning entries are published in ISTE's publication, the *Journal of Online Learning*. Winners also receive valuable prizes that facilitate telecommunications in their classroom, such as software, modems, robotics, and magazine subscriptions.
http://www.iste.org

Multimedia Mania

This awards program, hosted by HyperSIG, the multimedia special interest group of ISTE, is for students and teachers who use multimedia to teach and

The NetDay concept involves selecting a particular day on which volunteers from business, the parent community, and teaching and administrative staffs work together to get schools wired. Through volume discounts and corporate sponsorships, network kits are available at a reduced price to participating schools. NetDay has been very successful in many parts of the United States. At the NetDay site (http://www.netday.org) schools can register, volunteers can sign up, and you can find reports and helpful tips from past participants.

learn in a specific content area (e.g., math, science, social studies, language arts, art, music, physical education, ESL.) Students are invited to share their work with an international audience by creating dynamic multimedia projects related to any class or coursework. Participants are encouraged to incorporate 3-D design, video, animation, and any other multimedia techniques that may enhance the design of the project. The intent is to provide realistic models to share with other classroom teachers.

http://www.ncsu.edu/midlink/mmania.how.html

ThinkQuest

The ThinkQuest model involves students working in teams, coached by their teachers, to build Web-based educational materials that will help other students of the same age. For example, a team of students might create an entry that will introduce other students to the team's favorite books or that shows how the human digestive system deals with a peanut butter and jelly sandwich as it travels through the body. Those who create the entries learn as they collaborate within their team, focus on what will interest other students, and then plan and build their entries. More than $500,000 in cash, computer, and networking awards go to the winning teams of students, coaches, and their schools.

http://www.thinkquest.org

Time

One of the challenges to using the Internet most often articulated by teachers is finding time. They need time to

- learn Internet tools
- teach their use to the students
- find appropriate usable resources relating to the curriculum
- collaborate with other teachers on how to use the Internet in the classroom
- implement a project, given many user groups and limited access to computers
- re-think well-worn teaching strategies

I believe the biggest challenge is time and training. We must first learn how to use the technology. Then we must fit it to our curriculum in meaningful and appropriate ways. Next, we need to figure out how best to teach our students the power of the tool. We must also cut down the amount of "surfing" time, and devise ways to move right into classroom use.

— *Dave Lehnis*

"And just as I have stopped worrying about knowing everything, I've stopped worrying about the time it takes to oversee computer-related activities. You'd be surprised at how much time the kids themselves can save you. At the beginning of the year, I assign ongoing tasks, many of them computer-related, to students. We have an awards coordinator, a book-club coordinator, a name-tag coordinator, a paper coordinator, the Mac cleaner, the Kid Pix expert, and the Kid Works expert. The time invested in training kids to do these jobs more than pays off in the long term."

— Christine Arkwright Clemon, Teacher, online at **http://teacher.scholastic.com/professional/teachtech/technophobe.htm** 10/01/02

HINT NOVA Online now has over 500 resources for teachers on its site at **http://www. pbs.org/wgbh/nova/ teachers**. The site has a searchable database or viewers can browse the keyword list or the list of program titles. Some of the listed programs have accompanying activities, either printed (the print-able activities I saw were available both as PDF and HTML files) or online (some are HTML/Java Script quizzes, while some require Shockwave) and in some cases both. Many of the Shockwave-based activities are downloadable to be played as stand-alone applications. Searches can also be narrowed to pro-gram contents, printable activities, online activities, teachers' ideas or Web site overviews. Additional teaching resources include Teacher's Guide and Featured Teachers. Anybody who teaches kids (or who likes the NOVA series) will enjoy this site.

You don't have to master Internet tools before you start using the Net with your students. The overview provided in this book and some hands-on experience are all you need. Your ongoing training should focus on specific project needs. Rather than head out on your own, join an existing project such as those described in Chapter 2. Start small. If you run into a problem, you'll find that help is easy to get from the project leaders.

Nor do your students have to master many Internet tools before they begin. They'll learn to use the Internet within the context of their projects. This is authentic learning for a purpose. Arrange training for a few students, and then let them take the lead in training others so that you can move into the role of facilitator. Let parents, teachers-in-training, or older students work with small groups on the Internet while you manage the rest of the class.

> An ironic downside is that [the students] would rather be on the Net than in the book or attentive to the teacher. So we change the teaching style, relin-quish the direct power role, and become facilitators of their learning. I think "what's wrong with the schools today" boils down to too much teaching and not enough learning.
>
> — *Elizabeth S. Dunbar, Teacher, Baltimore City College High School,*
> *Baltimore, Maryland, U.S.A.*

The solutions to the challenge of finding time to locate useful resources on the Internet do not lie solely with the teacher. Such institutions as Canada's SchoolNet and its equivalents organize material in such a way as to make it easy for a teacher to find curriculum-related material and entry-level projects. When you begin, adopt a favorite general site, such as Canada's SchoolNet, EdNet, Global SchoolNet, Classroom Connect, or EdWeb, and stick with it rather than spending a lot of time sifting through the huge vol-umes of information on the Internet. You'll find that your horizons will broaden naturally as time passes and you become a more experienced user. One of the great benefits in collaborating with other teachers is the time saved by sharing specific useful sites among the group.

Rather than viewing Internet use as an add-on to your already heavy bur-den of curriculum, use it to replace more traditional methods. When you carefully document the learning outcomes you expect from your Internet project, you'll see how it accomplishes the goals of other activities you might have done in the past. As soon as you're confident that students will learn as well as or better than in the past, abandon the old in favor of the new. You can also use your Internet resources as an alternative to more traditional tools. For example, in a research project, have some students use books as information sources while others use Internet resources. In a project requir-ing communication, have some students use telephone or postal services while others use e-mail.

A common pitfall for be-
ginners is to not allocate
enough time to provide
for unforeseen difficulties.
What happens when a
member of a student team
is ill? What happens if a
particular task proves to
be more difficult than
anticipated? What happens
if a needed piece of equipment is out for repair?
A carefully prepared plan
must build in an extra
allocation of time and
other resources.

Summing up

With effort, creativity, and commitment, you can find the time, money, resources, and equipment you need to get connected and travel the information highway with your students. You will find yourself less isolated, better informed, better equipped with skills for today and the future, and empowered to be a knowledge builder. Because the educational reform movement advocates change and encourages schools to use new technologies such as the Internet, there are literally thousands of funding sources available for technology-related projects. The energy and inspiration you need will come from the collaboration and support of colleagues, students, parents, and the community.

Notes – Chapter 9

1. Adapted from *Connecting Canadians* (2001), Canada's SchoolNet, Industry Canada.

2. Online at **http://www.citrix.com/site/NE/news/news.asp?newsID=9957** 17/02/02

3. *The New National Dream: Networking the Nation for Broadband Access* (2001), Industry Canada, p 4.

4. Voisin, J. (Fall 2001) *The Wired Future: Keeping Canada on the Leading Edge*. SchoolNet Magazine, p 5.

5. *e-Learning Report*, U.S. Office of Educational Technology online at **http://www.ed.gov/Technology/elearning/index.html** 06/02/02

6. *Bringing the Internet to Students Faster* online at **http://www.telesat.ca/satcache** 01/02/02.

7. Tolbert, T. L. (Sept. 1984) "Industry Access to University Technology: Prospects and Problems," in *The Private Sector/University Technology Alliance: Making It Work*. Proceeding of a conference of the National Council of University Research Administrators, Dallas, TX. ed E. J. Friese pp 24–28.

8. Murray, C. Eight Great Steps to Getting Corporate Sponsors, online at **gopher://cwis.usc.edu:70/00/Librar…chers/Corporate_Funding/ 8steps.txt** 05/94.

9. Johnson, M. (1999) *New Roles for Educators*. Electronic School online at **http://www.electronic-school.com/2000/01/0100f1part1.html**

10. O'Donovan, E. (October 2000) *Small Wonders* Technology and Learning, pp 15–19.

11. Soloway, E., Norris, C., Curtis, M., Jansen, R., Krajcik, J., Marx, R., Fishman, B., Blumenfeld, P. (April 2001) *Making Palm-Sized Computers the PC of Choice for K–12*, Learning and Leading with Technology pp 33–34.

12. Oates, R. (2001) excerpted from *Technology Professional Development for K–12 Educators*, National School Boards Association online at Electronic-School 05/02/02

13. *The Power of the Internet for Learning: Moving from Promise to Practice*. Report of the Web-based Education Committee online at **http:// interact.hpcnet.org/webcommission/index.htm** 05/02/02

14. *E-rate: Keeping the Promise to Connect Kids and Communities to the Future*. Education and Libraries Network Coalition, 2000.

10
Chapter

Beyond the Classroom Walls

"Professionally, I see the chance to help my students experience the world outside rural Kansas. I see the chance to share ideas in forums I never thought possible; to gather information that's not in any local library; and to help others who might never have found the answers to their questions without such a wide base to draw from. Teachers often feel isolated. The Internet makes us a community that doesn't have to meet at any set time in a world that seems over scheduled already."

— Heddi Thompson, Teacher, Chase County Elementary School, Cottonwood Falls, Kansas, U.S.A.

The world of telecommunications is truly expanding learning beyond the confines of the traditional classroom. The Web is a fantastic resource for students that lets them search and research from home and find more information than we would have ever dreamed possible a few years ago. Of course, finding information is only one small piece of the research process; knowing what to look for and what to do with it once it's found are important skills usually taught within the school. Homework help on the Web tends to focus around research, but there are also places for drill and practice of basics, to sharpen problem-solving skills, and to get answers to specific questions. For parents who teach their children at home, the Web is a valuable link to resources, curriculum, and other parents who have chosen this route. The Internet has contributed immensely to the growing field of distance education, as it allows for interactive, multimedia, online courses. The formerly limited learning opportunities and isolation of those who are institutionalized, homebound, or living in remote locations are now overcome by new technologies.

Chapter goals

■ **To illustrate some resources available on the Internet that can help students with day-to-day homework and projects**
■ **To describe ways that the Internet assists with homeschooling**
■ **To examine the development of distance learning on the Internet**

Homework helpers

Web sites specific to homework are popular these days. A simple search will reveal thousands of homework helper sites, posted by individuals, schools,

Figure 10-1

Along with providing general help in math, science and literacy, Eureka! connects students with teachers live online through their special ask-a-teacher chat feature. The teachers answer homework questions and provide online tutorial support during designated hours. Their purpose is to guide students in thinking through a problem and to suggest other ways of finding solutions to their homework problems. A shared whiteboard is available with enough basic tools to visually describe problems.

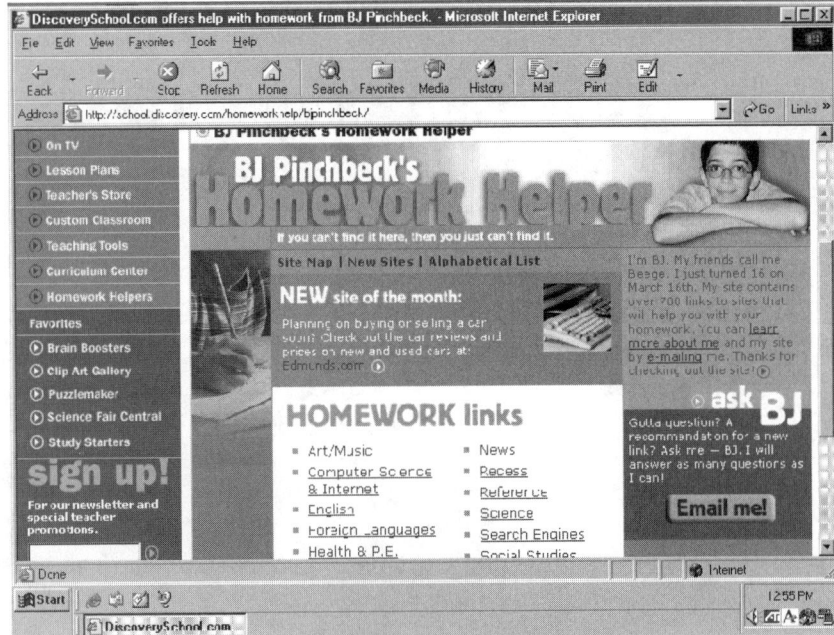

libraries, and some private companies. One of the most well-known is B.J. Pinchbeck's Homework Helper (**http://school.discovery.com/ homeworkhelp/bjpinchbeck**). Beege is a 15 year-old who has compiled, with help from his dad, more than 700 sites that can help you find any information that you need. B.J.'s page at Discovery School gets more than 10,000 visitors every day and between 20 and 40 e-mail messages. The reference section is particularly useful.

Here are just a few of the many other homework helpers available:

Ask Earl

Submit your own questions or browse through others' questions by category.

> http://www.yahooligans.com/content/ask_earl

Chatterbee's Homework Help Center

Chatterbee's Homework Help Center exists to help middle school, high school, and "early years" college students with their homework. Their stated goal is to guide students to only the best freely available Internet educational resources. Sites included in their database are reviewed for content, design and navigation.

> http://chatterbeeshomework.homestead.com

Discovery School

Discovery School features an encyclopedia, links organized by subject and opportunities to connect to a tutor for a free 15-minute session.

http://school.discovery.com/students/index.html

Fact Monster

This reference site for elementary students combines a user-friendly format with flashy graphics. It features an almanac, atlas, dictionary and encyclopedia made especially for kids. In addition, you'll find a daily famous birthday, event in history, a quiz, interesting topics in the spotlight, plus games, and a homework help center where you can also ask questions.

http://www.factmonster.com/homework

Gary's Homework Help Page

Developed by a busy parent of two children, this Web site was designed to be an efficient and effective use of your time. Gary's Homework Help Page contains hundreds of links to thousands of Web pages to help you with math, science, history, geography, language, art and literature. The links are relevant and updated regularly.

http://www.homeworkhelppage.com

HomeWork Elephant

Resources are available by subject at this British site. There is also a reference section and a hints and tips service.

http://www.homeworkelephant.co.uk/index.shtml

Homework Planet

Homework Planet makes it easy for students to find homework and research resources, tutoring services, reference tools, learning games, content experts, college information and more.

http://www.homeworkplanet.com

Homework Spot

This site has links to themes, online encyclopedia, field trips, study tips and a variety of questions in a "You Asked for It" section.

http://www.homeworkspot.com

Jiskha Homework Help

Jiskha Homework Help publishes educational content to help students with homework and provides instant-answer services for teens who need urgent help. Over 200 contributing writers have been involved since this service began in 1996. Visitors are invited to work as news reporters, newsletter writers, and content submitters getting their own works of writing published online.

http://www.jiskha.com

Math Goodies

Math Goodies is a free educational site featuring interactive math lessons, homework help, worksheets, puzzles, forums, and more. It is designed primarily for Grades 5 through 8.

http://www.mathgoodies.com

My Homework Helper

Here you'll find an extensive set of useful links organized by grade level and subject as well as links to lots of general reference tools.

http://www.refdesk.com/homework.html

The Shakespearean Homework Helper

The Shakespearean Homework Helper is a site to assist high school students and teachers in learning more about Shakespeare.

http://hometown.aol.com/liadona2/shakespeare.html

Not all homework helpers are free. Commercial companies have entered the homework domain also. If you believe that you'll get better quality when you pay for it, try one of these services.

Homeworkhelp.com

A yearly paid subscription to Homeworkhelp.com entitles you to access over 1,800 lessons in math, science, social studies, and English along with animations and interactive quiz questions on these subjects.

http://service.homeworkhelp.com

StudyWeb

StudyWeb is a long-standing site that was established to assist anyone doing research to find information easily. It has officially become part of The Lightspan Network and is now available only by school subscription. You can try it out in a free 30-day trial.

http://info.studyweb.com/brochure.htm

Electric libraries

Subscription-based electric libraries on the Web are also useful schoolwork resources for students. Teachers using these electric libraries find that they don't need to take as much extra time with their students emphasizing the authenticity and authority of the information as they do when students search for Internet resources. Also, students may function at a greater level of competency and confidence when they have fewer sources, but the sources are pre-selected and reviewed. Infonautic's Electric Library is an online reference tool for students of all ages. Though designed for the novice user, it is powerful enough for an experienced researcher. Its reference library incorporates more than 100 newspapers, 400 magazines, 2,000 books, 18,000 television and radio transcripts, thousands of color photographs and maps, and several encyclopedias and almanacs. Students retrieve information by asking questions in plain English, and documents are returned to the questioner in order of relevance. For example, a search for "Who said, 'Et tu Brute?'" will yield citations to an encyclopedia article about Julius Caesar, the full text of Shakespeare's play, and common references and allusions from newspapers, magazines, and other sources. Students can also narrow the search to particular dates, authors, subjects or publications, as well as confine it to materials appropriate to a certain reading level.

eLibrary Canada (**http://elibrary.bigchalk.com/libweb/canada/ do/login**) provides Canadian schools with a range of online reference services that help students, teachers, and administrators find quality information online. Like Infonautic's Electric Library, eLibrary Canada features natural language and Boolean search capabilities. Publications in its database include *Maclean's*, *National Post*, *World Book Encyclopedia*, *Fortune*, *60 Minutes* (CBS), *Time*, *Earth Explorer*, MapQuest.com, *Canadian Encyclopedia*, and hundreds more.

Not only are there resources available that can help students with day-to-day homework, the Web is also a great source of information for projects and essays on any imaginable topic. At the simplest level, students can find information in online encyclopedias such as Microsoft Encarta, which is a free abridged version of the multimedia CD-ROM product. Most of the other CD-ROM encyclopedia publishers — e.g., Grolier, Compton's and Britannica — have more complete versions available — for a price, which ranges from about US$30 to US$85 per year. These online subscription encyclopedias provide traditional content plus Web links. Britannica's content is the most adult oriented, thus not really appropriate for elementary school students.

Sites such as Canada's SchoolNet (**http://www.schoolnet.ca**) provide links to selected resources by subject geared to school-age children. The

HINT You can do a word search on any of Shakespeare's plays at the Complete Works of Shakespeare at **http:// the-tech.mit.edu/ Shakespeare**. You can find an entire "clickable" table of periodic elements at **http:// www-tech.mit. edu/Chemicool**.

National Atlas on SchoolNet lets students create customized theme maps that can be printed and included in a project. The Discovery Channel (**http://www.discovery.com**) and Sympatico (**http://www1.sympatico.ca**) are also worth looking at for student project information on various topics, though you may have to search a bit to find what you are looking for. Another useful homework and project resource site is Yahooligans! (**http://www.yahooligans.com**), the children's version of the popular Yahoo index. It filters out clearly adult material, and students can search using the tree-structure subject index or with a keyword search. The Homework Answers subheading takes you to a variety of sites that may assist with school assignments; it also includes five dictionaries and an Ask-an-Expert section. iTools (**http://www.iTools.com**) includes dictionaries, thesauruses, and translators. Here a student can look up quotations, find maps on the Web, and search factbooks. Flashcards for Kids (**http://www.edu4kids.com/math**) is a place for students who need extra help with addition, subtraction, multiplication, and division facts. They can select the level of difficulty and whether they want to keep score. The problem of the week sites described in Chapter 2, when used with parent assistance, are also helpful to students who require extra practice.

The Info Zone, produced by the Assiniboine South School Division (**http://www.assd.winnipeg.mb.ca/infozone**), focuses on links to help students with the research process. It's organized in the categories of wondering about something, seeking information, choosing information, connecting useful information you have found, producing information of your own in a new form and judging the entire process and your product. This site is also an excellent resource for teachers.

Plagiarism

Although the Internet is a great research tool, teachers need to be alert to the possibilities of students taking material directly from the Internet and submitting it as their own. "Recent studies indicate that approximately 30% of all students may be plagiarizing on every written assignment they complete."[1] In some ways, powerful search engines make it easier than ever to track instances of plagiarism. Copying a key phrase from a student submission into a meta search engine is likely to turn up the source if it has been

Figure 10-2

Turnitin's plagiarism prevention system provides instructors with a customized report for each paper they submit. "The report is an exact copy of the submitted manuscript, supplemented with color-coded passages corresponding to sources on the Internet. Each report includes an Overall Similarity Index, along with links to the Internet sources in question. Clicking on the bar called "direct source comparison" under each link opens a new browser to the source in question and color-codes suspect passages for easy comparison to the submitted paper. Reports are generally available 24 hours after submission. You can get five free trial reports at **www. Turnitin.com**." [3]

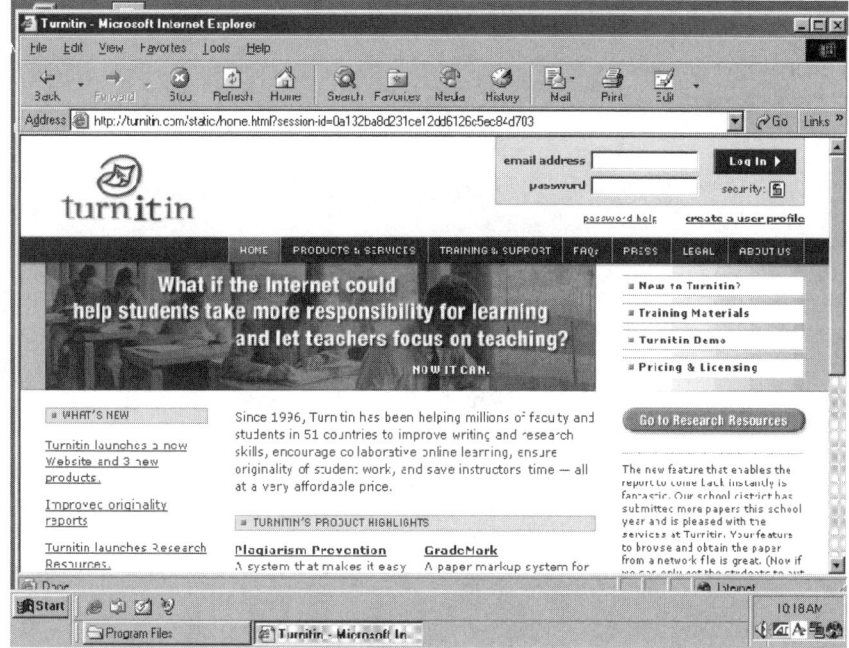

taken directly from a Web page, but teachers don't have time to be detectives. Students know this, according to a *US News and World Report* poll indicating that 90% of students believe that cheaters are either never caught or have never been appropriately disciplined. [2]

There are over 200 sites on the Internet that sell essays and other types of writing commonly assigned in schools. This type of cheating is not new. Indeed, one agency claims to have been operating for over 25 years! Teachers should be aware of some of these services that sell term papers:

An Evil House of Cheat

This is one of the pioneers in the industry, with a large user population and a database of more than 9,500 essays. It also provides other services such as "Tips and tricks on how to cheat an exam."

http://www.cheathouse.com

Other People's Papers

This site boasts that the number of visitors keeps rising along with the number of papers, which now totals 10,000. You can search for a paper by topic or click on the categories provided.

http://www.oppapers.com

Plagiarism.org (**http://www. plagiarism.org**) is an online resource for educators concerned with the growing problem of Internet plagiarism. This site is designed to provide the latest information on online plagiarism including facts about Internet plagiarism and a report on the growth of "cheatsites" online.

SchoolSucks.com

Here, "your homework worries will disappear" as you "download your workload" by choosing from a large collection of free, inexpensive and expensive papers. School Sucks claims they have already had well over one million visitors.

http://www.schoolsucks.com

Term Paper Sites.com

Term Paper Sites.com advertises thousands of free and searchable high quality term papers. A list of links to member sites is provided, including one at which you can have a paper custom-written for you.

http://www.termpapersites.com

One good way to avoid having students tempted to use these services is to incorporate unique elements into an assignment that are hard to duplicate generally, such as insisting that a literary analysis be done from the point of view of a character in the story. Teachers can also demonstrate their Internet-savvy to students by providing a list of "cheatsites" and allowing students the option of going to one of these, downloading five existing book reports on the chosen book and grading them. Require students to justify their grading by making references to the work being reviewed and backing up their comments with their personal observations about the book. This task may be harder than writing an original review and, since the students know that you are aware of the online paper sites, they are less likely to try to pass someone else's work off as their own.

Another way is to pay for a service that detects plagiarism. A handful of companies, like Plagiarism.org and the Essay Verification Engine (**http://www.canexus.com**), offer Internet-based anti-plagiarism technology that teachers can use for a fee. Fees start at about US$20 a year for a class of 30, with cheaper rates for larger contracts. The most complex of these services compare student term papers with millions of Web pages and the archives of online sites that offer free term papers. While the anti-plagiarism services do not have access to the databases of operations that sell term papers, they are able to spot many commercial term papers in teachers' online databases of papers from past semesters. If the service finds similarities, it notifies the teacher, who must then decide whether the similarities are justified by proper footnotes or are incidents of deliberate plagiarism.

Homeschooling

For some students, learning at home involves a lot more than homework. These are students whose families have, for one reason or another, decided to join the homeschooling movement. For an increasing number of students, home is where the classroom is. In the United States, the number of students being taught at home has increased from roughly 18,000 in the late 1970s to an estimated 800,000 today (some claim the figure is closer to one million). In Canada, there are approximately 50,000 students learning from home today — up from a meager 2000 in the 1970s.

There are many different reasons why parents choose to home-school. Some seek this option for religious reasons, while others feel that their children will benefit from a high level of individualized instruction that is simply not possible in schools. A child may have a chronic illness that prevents her or him from attending school. An Ottawa family has gone the home school route to allow them to embark on a two-year sailing venture around the world. They are able to send and receive e-mail from anywhere in the world using an Innarsat satellite dish.

In many ways the Internet is radically changing the nature of learning at home. On the Internet, home schoolers can connect to courses, online tutors, and learning services. Once isolated in their own communities, such students can now participate in live online discussion groups, projects, and activities with other children being schooled at home. Eagle Academy is an example of the learning services now available to home schoolers. Eagle Academy is like a private prepartory academy that is accessible via the family computer. The Academy provides curriculum, mentoring, and evaluation services and helps children develop their academic portfolios. Students can also meet other students online via a virtual classroom. (**http://forethought.net/index.html**)

Parents choose to home-school for many different reasons.

School boards have also recognized that they too have a role to play in the burgeoning homeschooling arena. The New Directions in Distance Learning is a British Columbia virtual school offering Kindergarten to Grade 12 programming to residents of the province. In Ontario, the EDEN project is a consortium of school boards offering courses online. The Virtual School for the Gifted is an Australian school offering courses on challenging topics, such as Existentialism. Home schoolers are also supported by many private agencies and community schools. The Puget Sound Community School facilitates online conferencing and student exchanges through their online education program. Their target student population is high school students who are not formally enrolled in schools. The Keystone National High School is specifically designed for home schoolers.

> Puget Sound Community School is unique. We don't have a school site; instead, we hold classes in libraries, community centers, and other public places. All our students have dial-up Internet accounts from their home (we help families without computers to get them). We do a lot online; besides our MOO, students also create their own home pages, and a team of students creates home pages for local organizations in exchange for free meeting space.
>
> — *Andrew Smallman, Director, Puget Sound Community School, Seattle, Washington, U.S.A.*

Home schoolers, whether or not they subcribe to formal online courses, are among the most active educational users of the Internet. Many of the Web sites set up by home school families are interesting places to visit, both to get a closer look at the homeschooling movement, and to locate many carefully selected learning activities. Here are some homeschooling sites worth visiting:

Canadian Home Based Learning Resource Page

This site features links to all Canadian provincial and territorial sites, a chat room, access to the Canadian Homeschool Mail List and the Association of Canadian Home-Based Education as well as links to all sorts of other homeschooling sites and pages published by home schooled students.

http://www.flora.org/homeschool-ca

Jon's Homeschool Resource Page

This site is a good one to start with. It is the work of Jon Shemitz, who has created a site so extensive that it's hard to imagine a resource he's missing. He has pointers to various FAQs, research on homeschooling, newsgroups, legal resources, mailing lists, local support groups, organizations, resource lists for several states, and much, much more.

http://www.midnightbeach.com/hs

The Caron Family's Homeschool Homepage

During their four years of homeschooling, this family has discovered many great resources available on the Internet. Their home page includes answers to some common questions about homeschooling, 800+ links to home-education resources on the Internet, help with finding curricular materials, books, magazines, and software on the Web, homeschooling and television links to networks and programs suitable for home school use, resources for the home schooled high schooler looking ahead to college, and links to their own family's pages plus local Maine resources. You can also join the The Homeschool Webring from this site.

> http://www.megalink.net/~caronfam

About Homeschooling

Homeschooling information from About.com. This site provides weekly feature articles and links to many of the best homeschooling and educational sites. A section on "unit studies" provides curriculum and project ideas for cross-curricular thematic units, many of which would work just as well in a classroom. There are also links to state information about homeschooling, curriculum sources and distance learning.

> http://homeschooling.about.com

A – Z Home's Cool Homeschooling Web Site

This is an excellent site with information about teaching methods and styles, lesson plans and reading lists. Internet links include a link to online French lessons, links to arts and crafts sources, and "kids links" where students can find out about bugs and body parts. There are even recipes for gak, oobleck, flubber and silly putty!

> http://www.gomilpitas.com/homeschooling

Texas Homeschoolers (Not just for Texans!)

A very good set of links to homeschooling resources, including associations, publications, distance learning services and many articles about the homeschooling movement. This site also offers a page of links to Free Educational Stuff on the Web.

> http://www.texashomeschoolers.com/txhs.htm.

Learn in Freedom

This is an award-winning site. Teachers who are interested in alternative education will find this site interesting. The focus is on homeschooling and education reform. The ideas presented are challenging and thought provoking. This site contains many informative articles, as well as a list of recommended books and capsule reviews of other homeschooling sites, including homeschooling sites around the world.

http://learninfreedom.org

Homeschool World

Homeschool World publishes Practical Homeschooling and Homeschool PC and makes many articles available online. This is also a good place to participate in online forums with others interested in or involved in home-schooling.

http://www.home-school.com/

E-learning – Learning at a Distance

An area that has seen even more growth in recent years than homeschool-ing is e-learning, or distance education. While the Internet is a relatively new medium for delivering distance education courses, distance learning is not a new phenomenon. Indeed, correspondence courses were first devel-oped by universities in the middle 1800s. In the 1930s, radio broadcast became a prevalent medium for delivering distance education, and many of us are familiar with educational television. But interest in distance education has increased considerably since the introduction of Internet technologies. The Internet offers a new medium for instructional delivery that has the potential to go much beyond the earlier one-way instructional delivery systems.

In addition to providing an easy and inexpensive vehicle for providing lessons, the Internet makes it possible to create dynamic learning communi-ties in which participants can ask questions and exchange ideas. Learning environments available through telecommunications technologies now come close to matching the level of interactivity previously available only in face-to-face learning situations.

Teachers are interested in distance learning for several reasons. In some small or remote schools, distance learning is a way to provide students with access to courses that cannot be offered locally, often because the low enroll-ment would not justify the cost. With distance education, advanced students can be given the opportunity to reach ahead by taking a university course while still in high school. Arrangements such as these allow schools to continue to offer challenging opportunities to their students, even as bud-gets for special programs are shrinking.

Some teachers are already involved in developing and delivering distance education courses. They may be dealing with students in a non-traditional school setting (such as the homeschoolers described above), developing online training materials for a commercial agency, or they may be using the

Internet or other telecommunications technology to present a course to students located at another school. Many more teachers are taking advantage of the range of opportunities that distance learning offers for professional development or pursuing personal interests.

A significant number of colleges and universities now offer some form of distance education. In one example, CU-SeeMe videoconferencing has been used to allow supervisors of technology teacher education to observe student teachers. A course on electronic networking for educators from the University of New Brunswick included asynchronous communications using Web-based conferencing and synchronous chat rooms for weekly discussions of assignments. A physiology course from Mount Royal College in Alberta featured Shockwave (multimedia) presentations with explanations provided using clips. In an Educational Science and Technology course at the University of Twente in the Netherlands, students learn to design and develop multimedia products for learning-related use and work in groups to carry out collaborative projects. There are more than 50,000 courses available over the Internet, many offered by accredited institutions. University and college course online offerings range from Baroque art to calculus, from criminology to bee keeping.

Although distance education has grown more quickly at the post-secondary level, a growing number of agencies are now offering high school courses online. Even a few elementary school level subjects have appeared on the Internet, most of them intended for homeschoolers.

HINT You can search for distance education courses available online at these sites: Telecampus Online Course Directory at **http://courses.tele campus.edu/subjects/ index.cfm**, the Globewide Network Academy at **http://www.gnacademy. org**, ICDL (International Centre for Distance Learning) at **http:// icdl.open.ac.uk**, and World Wide Learn at **http://www.worldwide learn.com**.

Figure 10-3
COOLSchool is an electronic alternative school for K-12 students.

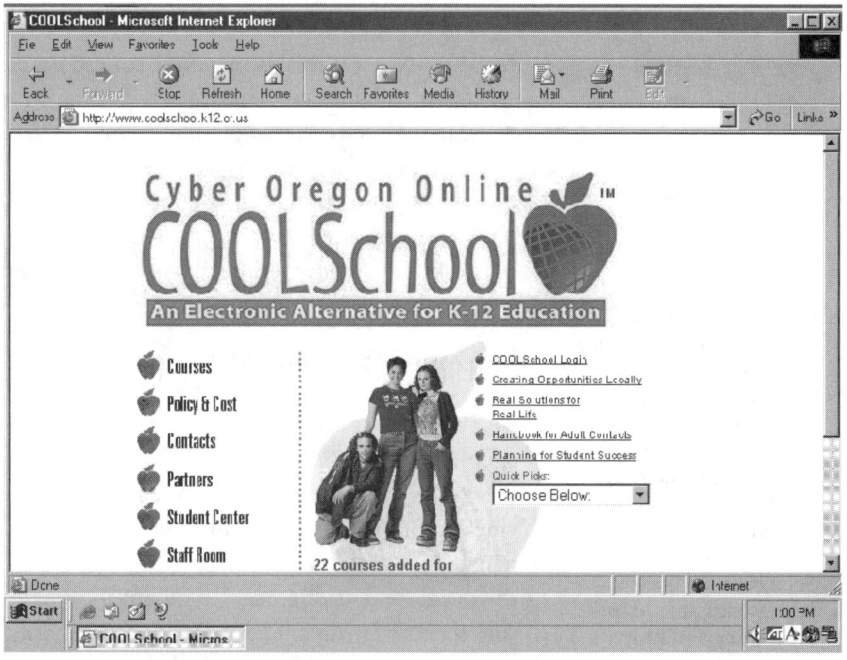

HINT Examples of agencies offering high school courses online:

Compuhigh
http://www.clonlara.org/ compuhigh

e-Schoolhouse
http://www.e-schoolhouse.org

Mindquest
http://www.mindquest.org

COOLSchool
http://www.COOLSchool.k12.or.us

Michigan Virtual High School
http://www.mivhs.org

Mesa Distance Learning Program
http://www.mdlp.org
St. Paul's Academy
http://www.redeemer.ab.ca/spa

Virtual High School
http://www.govhs.org/website.nsf

Virtual Learning Centre
http://vlc.virtuallearning.ca

It is not difficult to understand why interest in distance education is growing. Increasingly, the Web is allowing us to overcome the barriers of time and space in teaching and learning. Agencies offering courses at a distance have the potential to reach non-traditional students (such as students in the workplace), and students from around the globe. With the Internet, once the infrastructure for course delivery is in place, learning modules can be created relatively inexpensively and updated easily. Even textbooks are appearing in electronic format.

The technologies used for course delivery and interactivity can include

- basic electronic mail
- electronic mail for text-based lessons, online tutoring, and submitting assignments
- listserver or other group conferencing environment for class discussion and learning circles
- Web-based tutorials in print or multimedia format
- downloadable tutorials as text, .pdf, or multimedia files
- real-time, interactive discussion or simulations using voice transmission technology or chat
- streaming technologies — audio or video for delivering lectures and demonstrations
- desktop videoconferencing — for collaboration and interactivity

HINT You can find reviews for many learning management systems at Bruce Landon's site at **http://www.edutools .info/course/index.jsp**. Also, you can find many excellent resources for planning and developing an online course at the TeleEducation New Brunswick site at **http:// teleeducation.nb.ca**.

Learning management systems

Many schools are choosing to purchase or acquire access to a learning management system (LMS or LCMS for learning content management system) for delivering online courses. A learning management system typically provides an online environment that is already set up with many of the tools needed by teachers to develop and deliver courses. Features are available for the development of content, student interaction and administrative tasks, such as registering students and posting marks.

Figure 10-3a

Some publishers are providing Web-ready content using the WebCT learning management system.

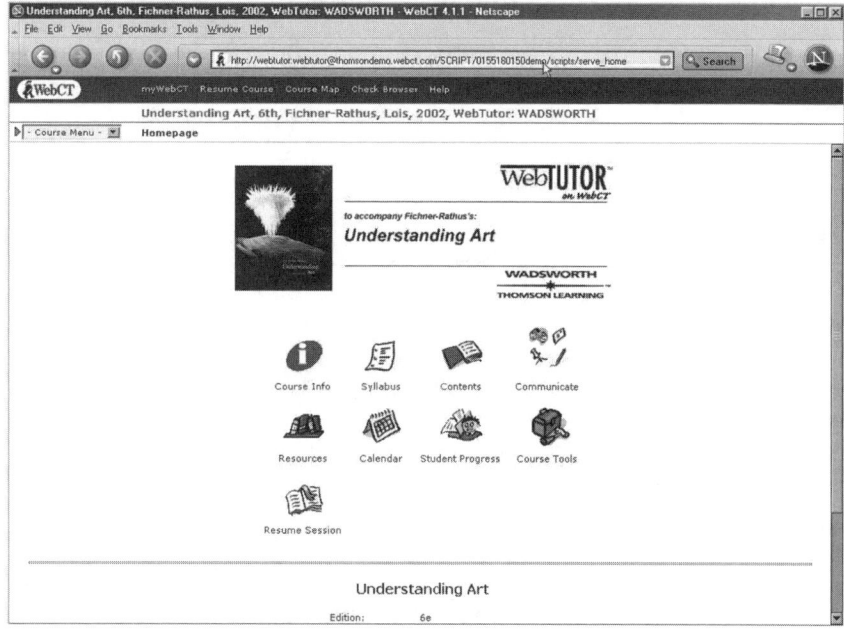

Most learning management systems provide an easy tool for creating course content in HTML format. Many will also make it easy to upload word-processed documents, PowerPoint slides and other generic content. Teachers use these tools to post learning content, assignments and links to study helps and resources. Some systems also include instructional templates and tools for creating interactive quizzes.

Online communications is another major feature of a learning management system. An LMS will include an online conferencing feature for Web-based discussions and some also provide a whiteboard for presenting slides and a "chat" space for real-time text discussions. Some also offer a built-in e-mail feature making it easy for students to submit assignments and for teachers to send comments to individual students. Still others offer a "group work" feature. Student groups are set up by the teacher and teams are assigned their own Web page and discussion space allowing students to work together on projects. Finally, a learning management system includes the ability to register students. The more sophisticated systems can use data from an existing student database and monitor student performance. Popular learning management systems include these:

ATutor

A free Web content and delivery system. Non commercial cources can be developed and delivered for free using the LDRC course server.

http://www.ldrc.ca/projects

Blackboard.com

Blackboard is an extremely popular LMS, used by many colleges and universities as well as high schools. Without knowing any HTML, teachers can quickly create their own course site. Course sites are available for a 60 day trial period.

http://www.blackboard.com

WebCT

This is another leading LMS. WebCT offers templates that can be extensively customized and good support for teacher to student and student to student communications and collaboration.

http://www.webct.com

LearnerWeb

LearnerWeb supports online enrollment and course delivery. DazzlerMax is an award-winning authoring tool from the same company that can be used to develop multimedia presentations and interactive tutorials.

http://www.maxit.com

First Class

First Class is an online communications and collaboration system that has been used by schools for online learning. First Class can support curriculum-driven online conferences, discussions and projects or to share curriculum and instructional materials.

http://www.firstclass.com

Manhattan

Manhattan is a less complex product than many other systems available; however, it is simple to use and it provides basic features at an affordable cost. You can download Manhattan for free. Manhattan requires a Unix operating system.

http://manhattan.sourceforge.net

Synchronous learning refers to situations in which the instructor and students are online at the same time. Asynchronous learning refers to online learning situations where learning content, assignments and discussions are posted so that individual students can access them at any time.

MetaCollege.com

MetaCollege provides inexpensive access to course building tools. MetaCollege offers an easy way for individual teachers to deliver an online course or set up an online space to enhance classroom communication.

http://MetaCollege.com/

There are many other learning management systems available. You can find out about other systems at **http://www.edutools.info/course/index.jsp**.

Virtual classrooms

The term *virtual classroom* is frequently used to refer to synchronous learning environments. In a synchronous learning environment everyone is online at the same time. Teachers present content using PowerPoint slides or HTML pages along with voice communications. Voice can be one way or two way. Some virtual classrooms support interactive voice, while others use a conference call for audio. HorizonLive is an example of a virtual classroom. HorizonLive allows instructors to present using slides, desktop sharing, a whiteboard, streaming audio or video. Users can submit questions or send messages using text chat and teachers can do on-the-spot surveys using a variety of question formats. HorizonLive sessions can also be archived. This is very valuable as a way for students to review or access a class they may have missed. You can sample online instruction based on HorizonLive at **http://www.horizonlive.com**. You can also experience a demonstration of this product at LearningWeek Live which is a weekly Webcast about technology and learning. Other virtual classroom products include Centra (**http://www.centra.com**), WebEx (**http://www.webex.com**), and Raindance (**http://www.raindance.com**).

Synchronous environments can be expensive, but may be worth the investment in situations where boards need to share a teacher between two or more schools or for teacher professional development. A virtual classroom environment can save travel costs and time.

New roles for teachers

E-learning represents a new opportunity for teachers. Not only is it increasingly valuable in small rural schools, and as a way for school boards to reach students who are not able to attend school on a regular basis, but it also rep-

HINT Take a class! You will find many free or inexpensive classes available at these sites:
Virtual University
http://www.vu.org
SkyLight
http://www.skylightedu.com/courses
Connected University
http://cu.classroom.com
Learn2Store
http://www.tutorials.com
Concept to Classroom (A series of online workshops on education topics)
http://www.thirteen.org/edonline/concept2class
Barnes and Noble University
http://barnesandnobleuniversity.com

Find out about more free courses at Distance Learning from About.com:
http://distancelearn.about.com.

Courseware authoring tools

Although many LMSs have built-in authoring tools, these tools can also be used to create course content.

Dazzler Max
http://www.dazzler.net

PowerPoint
http://www.microsoft.com/office/powerpoint

ReadyGo Web Course Builder
http://readygo.com

Toolbook Assistant
http://home.click2learn.com/products/assistant.html

Authorware
http://www.macromedia.com/software/authorware

Some of these are more complex to use than others. You can sample the demo versions before you buy.

resents a major opportunity for schools to develop more services for adults and for teachers to reach out to areas of the world where educational opportunities have traditionally been limited.

Sometimes, online learning is used to supplement a classroom experience. Some schools are purchasing online curriculum activities to be used in conjunction with classroom teaching. In universities, many professors now use learning management systems to complement classroom lectures. Learning management systems provide a place to post readings, assignments and links to resources as well as a place where students can ask questions and continue to discuss ideas that are introduced in class. Sometimes, when a group of learners are not able to be physically together, the online space necessarily becomes the classroom.

Some teachers have been critical of distance learning. Online learning is still relatively new, and there are certainly many examples of ineffective distance learning courses — courses where there has been little thought given to the principles of good instructional design, where the technology is unreliable and where there is little or no individual support for students. But to dismiss distance learning because of some poor examples is akin to the Wright brothers giving up when their first attempts to launch a flying machine failed.

As technology improves and developers gain experience, we are now seeing some excellent applications of distance learning. Most significantly, distance learning is becoming more effective as dedicated and motivated teachers become involved. Although developing distance learning courses is frequently a team effort, teachers are needed to establish learning goals, outline and develop instructional content, identify appropriate learning activities, recommend evaluation strategies, facilitate course delivery and motivate students.

More and more teachers are becoming knowledgeable about the methods and potential of learning online. They are seeing it as a complement to their work in the classroom.

These sources will help you to learn more about distance education on the Internet:

Connected University

A place for teachers to take online courses. A trial subscription is available. You can choose self-paced, guided study, or Recipes4Success, an excellent collection of software tutorials. Connected University is a division of Classroom Connect which focuses on helping teachers integrate technology in their classrooms.

http://cu.classroom.com

Distance Education at a Glance ...

This is another good introduction to distance education from the University of Idaho. There are 14 guides in all; they discuss topics such as instructional television and strategies for learning at a distance. This resource includes as Guide #12, *Distance Education and the WWW.*

> http://www.uidaho.edu/evo/distglan.html

Distance Education Resources from TeleEducation New Brunswick

This is a valuable distance education directory of resources. The site provides links to papers and reports, conference proceedings, information on integrated distance learning environments, resources for developing Web-based distance education courses, as well as pointers to other important sources for distance learning information.

> http://teleeducation.nb.ca

Distance Educator.com

This site provides good background and links related to distance learning. There is also a list of online journals, daily news and an e-zine for keeping up-to-date.

> **http://www.distance-educator.com**

e-Learning Centre

This is a major European portal for e-learning. The resources listed are extensive and relevant to anyone involved in distance learning. Topics include how to select a learning management system, online tutors, and using streaming media for e-learning. In its vendor area, e-Learning also features top ten lists, including the top ten free tools.

> **http://www.e-learningcentre.co.uk/eclipse/default.htm**

One particularly interesting and often cited study is entitled the "No Significant Difference" Phenomenon (**http://teleeducation.nb.ca/nosignificantdifference**). In his paper, Thomas L. Russell, director of the office of Instructional Telecommunications at North Carolina State University, reports on the results of 248 research reports, summaries, and papers that compared a range of different teaching methodologies. The studies date back to a 1928 study that compared the levels of achievement attained by college level correspondence students with those of classroom students. Their conclusion — and the conclusion of all of the other studies in the report — is that there is no significant difference between these groups. Some of the studies compare two different technologies. Again, in each case no significant difference was found in the performance levels of the groups under study.

Experts argue about what conclusions should be drawn from Russell's study, but many educators feel that this research paper confirms that the method for delivering educational content matters less than the thought that goes into instructional design and the ability of the learning environment to respond to individual learner needs.

Heritage Institute Online

A distance education resource specifically for K–12 educators. Contains links to courses, along with opportunities for global travel and study.

http://www.hol.edu

Learnativity

Learnativity is a site devoted to the exchange of ideas about new ways of learning. It's not just about distance learning, but it includes links to many distance learning resources. There are many informative articles at Learnativity that will help provide context for online learning.

http://www.learnativity.com

Learning Circuits

Answer Geek, e-learning 1.0 — the basics of digital learning, and regular articles on timely topics about e-learning. At the site, you can subscribe to Learning Circuits Express, a free companion newsletter for the site. This site is sponsored by ASTD, the American Society for Training & Development.

http://www.learningcircuits.org

OnlineLearning.net

Good selection of online courses from California universities. Here you can enroll in a program to learn about teaching online.

http://www.onlinelearning.net

Steven's Web: Knowledge, Learning, Community

Steven Downes has been involved with distance learning for many years. His site is a good place to find out about new directions for technology and learning. There are many thoughtful articles posted here.

http://www.downes.ca

TEAMS Distance Learning

This site offers resources for distance learning as well as a range of teacher helps. TEAMS makes available TV in the classroom as well as Internet distance learning activities for K–12 and for teacher professional development.

http://teams.lacoe.edu

The Commonwealth of Learning

The Commonwealth of Learning is very involved in distance education. They have published some excellent guides for getting started and training guides. The guides are available in PDF format, and some can be ordered as print publications for teacher workshops.

http://www.col.org/resources

University of Wisconsin Distance Education Clearinghouse

This site provides information on distance education programs, courses, and technologies. Although this resource focuses on distance education in Wisconsin, the clearinghouse includes a useful selection on definitions and introductory materials. If you are new to distance learning, this is a good place to browse.

http://www.uwex.edu/disted/home.html

Web Based Learning Resource Library

This page is an educator's resource for delivery and management of learning over the Internet. The resource includes an overview of issues in distance learning, as well as links to tools, course catalogs, newsletters and e-zines.

http://www.knowledgeability.biz/weblearning

World Lecture Hall

Only some of the courses here are totally online. Other listings are for classroom-based courses that make use of the Internet to deliver course materials, such as course syllabi, assignments, lecture notes, exams, class calendars, multimedia textbooks. For many teachers, offering one unit of study or some component of a course online is a good way to explore online technologies.

http://www.utexas.edu/world/lecture

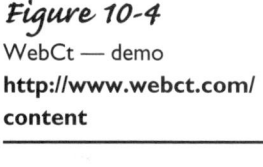

Figure 10-4
WebCt — demo
**http://www.webct.com/
content**

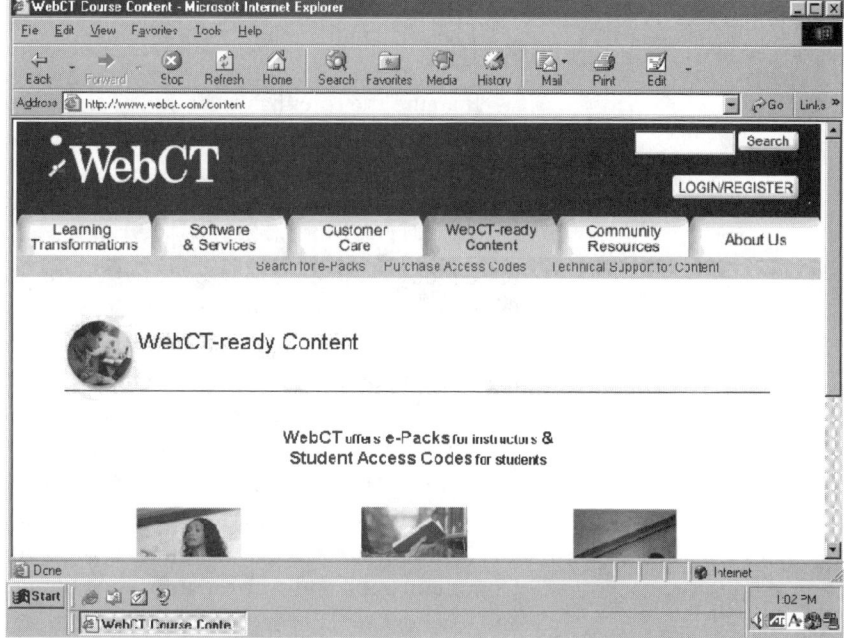

New directions

There is no doubt that the world of education is changing in ways that few of us would have envisioned just a few years ago. The trend toward home-schooling and distance education will probably continue to grow, but these alternative approaches to learning will not replace classroom-based education, which for most students still affords the richest environment for learning. Yet many things about how learning happens in the classroom undoubtedly will change.

What will schools look like further into the twenty-first century? We cannot predict this exactly, but as we plan for the future, it helps to consider current trends. Some of the most pervasive trends in educational reform include

- inclusion of all learners
- students taking responsibility for their own learning
- a shift from all students learning the same things to students learning different things individually
- learning outcomes and performance assessment
- education for global stewardship facilitated by communications technologies
- collaboration, communication, and the integration of visual and verbal thinking
- the changing role of teacher from expert to facilitator, mentor, and partner in learning

These changing parameters give us some vision of schools in the years ahead.

Imagine the role that technology, and specifically the Internet, can play in helping to integrate these trends into daily learning. It's not technology that will *create* change in education, but rather the power of technology that will *allow* teachers and students to make necessary changes.

Through the power of telecommunication, traditional hierarchies are broken down and education becomes the responsibility of *communities* of learners — students, teachers, and parents. Students now have access to a wide variety of information resources. They can be more involved in designing learning outcomes as part of functioning teams in which people change roles all the time, just as they do in the real world. This kind of teamwork sees students assuming leadership roles as well as being part of the team.

As we approach the excitement and challenge of exploring the educational potential of the Internet, we have the opportunity to be lifelong learners, and by doing so we set an example for the students with whom we work. Communication and collaboration skills are enhanced when both students and teachers are engaged in authentic learning.

Much experimentation is required to figure out the practical aspects of transforming teaching and learning, and it is sometimes difficult not to be overwhelmed by the technology itself. Improvements happen not suddenly, but over time. Continuous reflection and evaluation are critical to the process of change. At some point, teachers will undoubtedly view the Internet as an integral tool for professional growth and learning. Today, our challenge is not to master it, but rather to discover what is most important and most useful for learning, and how to reorganize classroom practices to take advantage of these aspects.

The Internet is a dynamic environment that can sweep students into a world of constant change. In the midst of this dynamic activity, integrative techniques such as metacognition and reflection will help teachers to establish the islands where students can pause, think about, and share their learning experiences.

> It all seems amazing: to be able to send messages halfway across the world with the press of a single button; to get national news before most of the world does; and to meet some of the people who made that possible. Just to be able to sit in this room and type on these computers is a privilege, but to understand what's happening, and how we're doing this, is magnificent. I think that the Internet has influenced me.... When I watch the news on TV, I get all the information I want, but do I really understand it all? On the Internet, when friends tell me the news in words that I can understand, it doesn't just sound like pieces of a puzzle that don't seem to fit together; all the pieces join as one ....
>
> When my computer teacher asked what I will demand in the future, I started thinking.... I will expect more in middle school and in high school. I will expect to be able to communicate with anybody in the world. I will demand to continue to challenge and encourage us, and I will want the future to be even better than the present.
>
> — *Meredith Geremia, Student, Grade 6, West Windsor Plainsboro*
> *Upper Elementary School, Plainsboro, New Jersey, U.S.A.*

Notes – Chapter 10

1. Online at **http://www.plagiarism.org/problem.html** 17/12/01

2. *US News and World Report* poll quoted online at
    http://www.plagiarism.org/problem4.html 17/12/01

3. Online at **http://www.plagiarism.org/sample.html#** 17/12/01

PERSONAL FAVORITES

Use this page to make notes on your own favorite distance education sites.

Site: _____

Description: _____

Note files: _____

Site: _____

Description: _____

Note files: _____

Site: _____

Description: _____

Note files: _____

Site: _____

Description: _____

Note files: _____

Site: _____

Description: _____

Note files: _____

Site: _____

Description: _____

Note files: _____

Site: _____

Description: _____

Note files: _____

Glossary

Agent An intelligent program or "agent" that you can instruct to search the Internet for information about a particular subject. These agents are the focus of intense software research and development.

Anonymous FTP One of the Internet's main attractions is its openness and freedom. FTP (*File Transfer Protocol*) Internet sites let you access their data without registering or paying a fee.

Applet A small Java application used to run programs through a Web browser. Java applets are often used to create interactivity. An example of a Java applet might be a calculator that can be accessed over the Internet.

Archie A search tool that helps you locate information stored at hundreds of anonymous FTP sites around the Internet.

ASCII (Ask-ee) *American Standard Code for Information Interchange*, plain text without formatting that's easily transferred over networks. (Got a question? Just ASCII.)

AUP Acceptable use policy. Rules and policies related to the use of a particular computer system.

Backbone The main communication line that ties computers at one location with those at another. Analogous to the human nervous system, many smaller connections, called *nodes* or *remote sites*, branch off from the backbone network. (Don't slip a disk!)

Bandwidth An indication of how fast information flows through a computer network in a set time. Bandwidth is usually stated in thousands or millions of bits per second. See Ethernet.

Baud Unit of speed in data transmission; maximum channel speed for data transmission.

Bit The basic unit of data. It takes eight bits (a byte) to represent one character (e.g., a letter or number) of text.

Blog   Short for Web log. A blog is a Web page that serves as a publicly-accessible personal journal. Blogs are often updated daily and frequently reflect the personality of the author. The term blog can also be a verb.

Bounce   Return of e-mail that contained a delivery error.

Bozo filter   A program that screens out unwanted and irritating incoming messages. (Both messages and filter can be breaches of netiquette.)

Burner   A CD-R (Compact Disk-Recordable) drive used to write data to a CD.

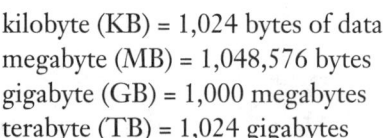

Byte   The memory space required for storage of one character — eight bits.

> kilobyte (KB) = 1,024 bytes of data
> megabyte (MB) = 1,048,576 bytes
> gigabyte (GB) = 1,000 megabytes
> terabyte (TB) = 1,024 gigabytes

CD-ROM   *C*ompact *D*isk *R*ead-*O*nly *M*emory. CD-ROM can hold the equivalent of 1,500 floppy disks. It is the most popular carrier of interactive multimedia programs that feature audio, video, graphics, and text.

Chat and Talk   A chat program lets you electronically "converse" online with many people simultaneously. A talk program is like a personal telephone call to a specific cybernaut — only in text. See IRC (Internet Relay Chat). Chat usually refers to text messaging

Client   A desktop personal computer that communicates with other PCs and larger computers, called *servers* or *hosts*.

Client/server computing   Combining large and small computers in a network so data are readily available when and where they are needed. For example, in a retail store, information is collected from customers at point-of-sale terminals. Then it is directed to a server in the store and forwarded to a larger enterprise server for inventory management and other functions.

CNRI   *C*orporation for *N*ational *R*esearch *I*nitiatives, an organization that is exploring different ways to use a national information highway.

Computerphobe   Someone who is afraid of using computers. (Now, who could that be?)

Copyright   The legal right granted to a copyright owner to exclude others from copying, preparing derivative works, distributing, performing, or displaying original works of authorship of the owner. Copyrighted works on the Internet are protected under national and international laws. Examples

of copyrighted works include literature, music, drama, pictures, graphics, sculpture, and audiovisual presentations.

Cybernaut   Someone who explores the vast world of cyberspace where only the brave dare venture.

Cybernetics   In 1948, Norbert Wiener coined this term to describe the "entire field of control and communication theory, whether in the machine or in the animal." *Cyber-* has become a popular prefix for many Internet terms: *cyberlingo, cyberwonk, cybercast.* (What hath Norbert wrought!)

Cyberspace   Word coined by William Gibson in his 1984 sci-fi novel, *Neuromancer.* Refers to all the sites that you can access electronically. If your computer is connected to the Internet or a similar network, then it exists in cyberspace. Gibson's style of fiction is now called *cyberpunk.*

Daemon   Web software on a UNIX server; a program running all the time in background, providing special services when required.

Dedicated line   A telephone line that is leased from the telephone company and used for one purpose. In cyberspace, dedicated lines connect desktop systems to servers.

DES   The *Data Encryption Standard* represents a set of criteria for providing security for transmitted messages. Standards like this lay the groundwork for electronic commerce over the Internet.

Dial-in connection   A way to access a computer on the Internet using a PC, telephone line, and modem. Slower than connecting directly to the Internet backbone, but provides accessibility from many sites and does not require specialized equipment.

Domain   The system of organizing the Internet according to country or type of organization, such as educational or commercial. For instance, an educational institution such as The Franklin Institute Science Museum in Philadelphia, Pennsylvania, would have ".edu" as a suffix to its domain name (sln.fi.edu). Other typical suffixes include ".com" for commercial organizations and ".org" for non-profit groups.

Domain Name System (DNS)   The scheme used to define individual Internet hosts.

Download   When you transfer software or other information from the Internet to your PC. *Upload* refers to transferring content to a server from a smaller computer or a PC.

DSL   DSL (Digital Subscriber Line) is one type of high-speed Internet access. DSL is typically available from telephone service providers.

E-mail   Electronic mail. The term has several meanings: the network for sending messages; the act of sending a message electronically; and the message itself. It all comes down to using a computer network to send electronic messages from one computer user to another. Fortunately, all the electronic junk mail you receive is environmentally friendly since it generates no paper — unless you print it.

Electronic commerce   Buying and selling products and services over the Internet.

Ethernet   (Not an illegal fishing device.) A common type of network used in corporations. Originally limited to 10 million bits of information per second, technical improvements have raised Ethernet bandwidth (how fast information flows through a computer network in a set time) to 100 million bits of information per second — in concept, enough speed to transfer the entire contents of the *Encyclopaedia Britannica* in one second.

E-zine   A Web-based electronic publication.

FAQ   List of *F*requently *A*sked *Q*uestions (and answers) about a particular topic. FAQs can usually be found within Internet discussion groups that focus on specific topics. Read FAQs before asking a question of your own — the answer may already be waiting.

Finger   A program that provides information about someone connected to a host computer, such as that person's e-mail address.

Firewall   A mechanism to keep unauthorized users from accessing parts of a network or host computer. For example, anonymous users would be able to read documents a company makes public but could not read proprietary information without special clearance.

Flame   Rude or ludicrous e-mail. Advice: Don't reply to flames, just extinguish them by deleting.

Flash   A graphics/animation technology used to develop bandwidth friendly Web animations. Flash is a commercial technology owned by Macromedia.

Freenet A community computer network, often based on a local library, that provides Internet access to citizens from the library or sometimes from their home computers.

FTP *File Transfer Protocol* is a program that lets you transfer data from an Internet server to your computer.

Gateway A system that connects two incompatible networks. Gateways permit different e-mail systems to pass messages between them.

Geek A person who is so involved with computers and the so-called "virtual world" as to have only a tenuous hold on the real world. (But then again, what is reality?) Similar terms: *nerd*, *propeller head*, and *techie*.

Gigabyte A unit of data storage that equals about 1,000 megabytes. A CD-ROM holds about two-thirds of a gigabyte (650 million bytes). That's enough space to hold a full-length motion picture. (Don't forget the popcorn.)

Groupware Software that allows groups to share documents, databases, text conferencing, schedules, etc. Some groupware applications are available as services over the Internet.

GUI *Graphical User Interface*, software that simplifies the use of computers by letting you interact with the system through graphical symbols or icons on the screen rather than coded commands typed on the keyboard. Microsoft Windows and the Apple Macintosh operating systems are the two most popular GUIs.

Hacker The best reason of all to put up a firewall. Originally some of these pranksters breached computer security systems for fun. Computer criminals have created chaos on computer networks, stealing valuable data and bringing networks down for hours or days. See DES (Data Encryption Standard).

Home page Document displayed when first accessing a Web site.

Host A server computer linked directly to the Internet that individual users can access.

Hotlists Frequently accessed URLs (*Uniform Resource Locators*) that point to Web sites. Usually organized around a topic or for a purpose, e.g., a hotlist of museums on the Web.

HTML *HyperText Markup Language*; the codes and formatting instructions for interactive online Internet documents. These documents can contain hypertext, graphics, and multimedia elements, including sound and video.

Hypermedia   Multimedia and hypertext combined in a document.

Hypertext   An electronic document that contains links to other documents offering additional information about a topic. You can activate the link by clicking on the highlighted area with a mouse or other pointing device.

Information Highway   Also referred to as I-Way, Internet, Infobahn, Autostrada, National Information Infrastructure (NII), Global Information Infrastructure (GII). The network is evolving to make existing computer systems more efficient at communicating and to add new services, such as electronic commerce, health information, education, polling — just use your imagination.

Infrastructure   The base on which an organization is built. It includes the required facilities, equipment, communications networks, and software for the operation of the organization or system. But most important, it includes the people and the relationships that result.

Instant messaging   A type of Internet chat technology that allows two or more people to communicate, primarily using text. Some messaging programs also allow file exchange. When your instant messaging program, your contacts will detect that you are online and can send you a message at any time. Microsoft's MSN Messenger is an example of a popular instant messaging program.

Internet   An interconnection of thousands of separate networks worldwide, originally developed by the U.S. federal government to link government agencies with colleges and universities. Now thousands of companies and millions of individuals use graphical browsers to access information and exchange messages. See Mosaic.

InterNIC   The *Inter*net *N*etwork *I*nformation *C*enter. This NIC is run by the U.S. National Science Foundation and provides various administrative services for the Internet.

IP   *I*nternet *P*rotocol is the communications language used by computers connected to the Internet.

IRC   *I*nternet *R*elay *C*hat, a software tool that lets you hold keyboard conversations. See Chat and Talk.

ISDN   The *I*ntegrated *S*ervices *D*igital *N*etwork defines a new technology that delivers both voice and digital network services over one "wire." More important, ISDN's high speed enables multimedia and high-end interactive functions over the Internet, such as videoconferencing.

Java   A programming language developed by Sun Microsystems. Java is sometimes used for developing Web applications. Java applets are small-scale Java applications that can be downloaded from a Web server and run using a Java-savvy Web browser.

JavaScript   A programming language developed by Netscape to allow the creating of interactive sites. JavaScript can be incorporated into HTML coding. It is a simple way for Web authors can create dynamic content. Prc-programmed JavaScript functions can be downloaded from the Internet.

LAN   *Local Area Network*, a collection of computers in proximity, such as an office building, that are connected via cable. These computers can share data and peripherals such as printers. LANs are necessary to implement client/server computing since the LAN allows communication to the server.

Listserv; Listserver   An electronic mailing list used to deliver messages directly to the e-mail addresses of people interested in a particular topic, such as education.

Luddite   Person who believes that the use of technology will diminish employment.

Lurking   The practice of reading about a newsgroup in order to understand its topics and tone before offering your own input.

Mbone   *Multicast backbone* is an experimental system that sends video over the Internet.

Mosaic   This sophisticated, graphical browser application lets you access the Internet World Wide Web. After the introduction of Mosaic in 1993, the use of the Internet began to expand rapidly.

MP3   A coding scheme for compressing audio data. MP3 is one of a number of MPEG standards. It is a format commonly used for music downloads.

MPEG   (pronounced m-peg.) Moving Picture Experts Group is a working group of the International Standards Organization responsible for developing compression standards for digital video and related formats. Standards developed by the group are named using the acronym MPEG (as in MPEG-4) or MP (as in MP3).

Multimedia   Multiple forms of communication including sound, video, videoconferencing, graphics, and text delivered via a multimedia-ready PC.

Net surfing   The practice of accessing various Internet sites to see what's happening. (A whole new world for the Beach Boys!)

Netiquette   Standards of behavior and manners to be used while working on the Internet. For example, a message in ALL CAPS can mean the sender is shouting.

Network   People connected via computers to share information.

Newbies   Newcomers to the Internet.

Newsgroup   The Internet version of an electronic discussion group where people can leave messages or post questions.

Newsreader   A program that helps you find your way through a newsgroup's messages.

Newsserver   A computer that collects newsgroup data and makes it available to newsreaders.

NFS   The *Network File System* lets you work with files on a remote host as if you were working on your own host.

NNTP   *Network News Transport Protocol*, an extension of TCP/IP protocol; describes how newsgroup messages are transported between compatible servers.

NSFNet   Large network run by the U.S. National Science Foundation. It is the backbone of the Internet.

Packet   A collection of data. Packet switching is a system that breaks data into small packets and transmits each packet independently. The packets are combined by the receiving computer. (Danger! We may have crossed over into geekspace.)

PDF   Portable Document Format. A file format for online viewing of documents that retain the look of the printed document. PDF, rather than HTML, is sometimes used to post such things as forms, brochures, newsletters, or longer documents on the Web. Adobe PDF is the most common technology used to create PDF documents. Viewing Adobe PDF files requires the Adobe Acrobat reader.

Peer-to-peer (P2P)   A type of network in which each workstation has equivalent capabilities and responsibilities. Compare to client-server. Napster and some other music exchange environments are based on peer-to-peer networking.

Plug-in   A piece of software for viewing a specific type of file format, such as audio or video files. A plug-in works in conjunction with a Web browser. For example, Apple QuickTime audio and video files require the QuickTime plug-in for accessing from within Netscape or Internet Explorer.

Point Of Presence (POP)   A method of connecting to an Internet service locally. If a service company has a POP in your area, then you can connect to the service provider by making a local call. POP is also used for *Post Office Protocol*.

Portal   A Web site or service that offers a wide range of resources and services, such as e-mail, discussion groups, directories, search engines, and on-line shopping. The term portal can also be used to describe a Web starting point for specific topic (e.g. health information portal).

Postmaster   The person at a host who is responsible for managing the mail system.

PPP   *Point-to-Point Protocol* connects computers to the Internet using telephone lines; similar to SLIP, but not as widely used.

Protocol   Rules or standards that describe ways to operate to achieve compatibility.

Public domain software   Computer programs you may use and distribute without paying a fee. *Shareware* is distributed at no cost, but you are expected to pay the author a fee if you decide to keep and use it.

Resource hog   A program that eats up a large amount of network bandwidth.

Robot   A program designed to automatically perform a particular computer task. A spider is a robot that has been programmed to follow Web links and gather Web page content for search engines.

Router   A device that acts as a traffic signal to direct data among different networks. Routers often have enhanced processing capabilities that enable them to send data on an alternative path if one part of the network is busy.

RSS   RSS stands for Rich Site Summary or Real Simple Syndication. A method of distributing content. RSS files are created and registered with a RSS document publisher for re-distribution by those who choose to "subscribe" to RSS files in a particular content area. News headlines, events and excerpts from discussion forums are typical RSS content.

Server   Equivalent to a host, a machine that works with client systems. Servers can be anything from PCs to mainframes that share information with many users.

Service provider   A company that provides a connection to the Internet.

SIG   *Special Interest Group.* (Also nickname of Wagnerian opera hero.)

Skins   Skins are used to give a piece of software a different graphical look. Some software comes with various skins that can be altered to suit your personality or your mood. The functionality of the software is not affected.

SLIP   *Single Line Internet Protocol* is a technique for connecting a computer to the Internet using a telephone line and modem. Also called Serial Line Internet Protocol. See PPP.

Smiley   Manipulating the limited potential of keyboard characters to show goodwill, irony, or other emotions with a "smiley face." There are a number of text-based effects, for example, (–: and ;–).

SMTP   *S*imple *M*ail *T*ransport *P*rotocol, the Internet standard for transmitting electronic mail messages.

Sneakernet   The 1980s way of moving data among computers that are not networked, by storing data on floppy diskette and running the disks from one computer to another. (Very good for the cardiovascular but not the information system.)

SNMP   *S*imple *N*etwork *M*anagement *P*rotocol is a standard of communication of information between reporting devices and data collection programs. It can be used to gather information about hosts on the Internet.

Spamming   Indiscriminately sending a message to hundreds or thousands of people on the Internet, e.g., unsolicited junk mail. Not good netiquette.

Streaming   Audio, video, and text available for viewing on your computer even as it is in the process of downloading to your system from a Web site.

T1   Telecommunications lingo for digital carrier facility used to transmit information at high speed. (T1 is to the Web what passing gear was to the '64 Cadillac.) If you want to turbocharge your network backbone, many companies are expanding to the even faster T3 service.

TCP/IP   *T*ransmission *C*ontrol *P*rotocol/*I*nternet *P*rotocol; communication rules that specify how data are transferred among computers on the Internet.

Telnet   Software that lets users log on to computers connected to the Internet.

Token ring   Featured on LANs (Local Area Networks) to keep control messages (tokens) moving quickly among the users.

Trojan horse   A destructive virus-type program that is disguised as something benign such as a game or screen saver.

UNIX   Software operating system that provides the underlying intelligence to Internet servers. Mosaic and other browser programs have helped increase Internet usage by hiding the complexities of UNIX from the average cybernaut.

URL   Abbreviation for *U*niform *R*esource *L*ocator, the Internet addressing system. (What's your URL?)

Usenet   *Use*r *Net*work, an array of computer discussion groups, or forums, that can be visited by anyone with Internet access.

Video conferencing   Face-to-face communications using a video hook-up and telecommunications connection. Internet video conferencing involves two or more people using a webcam, conferencing software (such as NetMeeting) and an Internet connection to interact..

Virus   Destructive computer program that invades by means of a normal program and damages the system.

War driving   A technique for cracking wireless computer networks by driving through a neighborhood with a wireless-enabled notebook computer and mapping locations that have wireless access points. In the vicinity of an unsecured wireless network, hackers can anonymously gain access to free high-speed Internet connections.

Webcam   A video camera that is designed for using with a computer to capture and transmit live images and send them over the Internet using a Web browser

Web site   A sequence of related Web pages normally created by a single company or organization.

White Pages   Because they remind people of the old telephone book, services that list user e-mail addresses, telephone numbers, and postal addresses.

Winsock   *Win*dows *Sock*et, an extension program designed to let Windows applications run on a TCP/IP network.

Worm   A computer program designed to replicate itself. A worm-type virus is an application that destroys information on a hard drive. Worms proliferate when the virus is programmed to send a copy of itself to everyone in the computer's e-mail address book.

WWW   The *World Wide Web* is a hypertext-based collection of computers on the Internet that lets you travel from one linked document to another, even if those documents reside on many different servers.

XML   The Extensible Markup Language (XML) is a type of document mark-up language designed to work over the Web as does HTML. Where HTML tags Web pages on the basis of how the text should appear, XML attempts to code documents based on their actual content. For example, XML content tagging might look like this: <greeting>Hello, world!</greeting>. Similar content in HTML would typically just designate font size and style. XML has been derived from SGML, a mark-up language used in the print world.

A
Appendix

Selecting a Service Provider

A service provider is a company that charges a fee to provide Internet access through a direct SLIP/PPP connection, a cable connection or an indirect commercial online service. Look for lists of service providers in computer magazines, business magazines, Internet books, phone books, and newspapers. There are a large number of providers available, and they offer a wide variety of subscription plans. Get recommendations from friends and colleagues.

Once you register with a provider, you are assigned an Internet e-mail address, like a phone number, which others use to communicate with you. If you've ever had to change your phone number, you know how inconvenient that is. The same is true of your Internet e-mail address, so selecting a reliable, stable provider from the huge number available is important. Consider the following factors.

Services offered

What do you want to do on the Internet? What do you want your students to be able to do? Make sure the service provider offers the time and connectivity speed you need.

Cost

For many users, this is the first consideration. Ask for detailed fee schedules, and spend some time examining and comparing different packages. Usually, the charge depends upon what services you use and the amount of time you spend online. Many services have a flat-fee monthly rate for a given number of hours (from US$15 to US$35 for thirty hours per month or more) and surcharges if you exceed the designated limit per month. Others charge a basic fee plus an hourly rate based on the exact amount of time you spend online. Cable connections generally have no time limits, as the cable is always active. Thus, one provider's rate might be better for people who spend a lot of time online, but not as good as another's for those who spend less time. Reasonable cost is nice, of course, but as with many other things in life, you are likely to get what you pay for from an Internet service provider.

Access

Access relates to cost if there is no local number for the service you want to use. Find out how you would connect — via a local call, a long distance call, or a 1-800 number. Long distance charges can add up quickly. Don't assume that a 1-800 number is free, either; you'll pay for it through a surcharge. For home or school use, a local number is best. If you travel frequently, find out if the provider has local numbers in other major cities or if you can access your e-mail through a Web site. Access also relates to the number of lines and modems the service has. How often will you get a busy signal when you dial in? You can ask the provider for their user-to-line ratio, and you can ask others who use the service if they ever have trouble getting connected. Customer assistance/technical support

This might be the most important factor for beginners and even experienced users. Find out the answers to these questions.

- Does the service provider supply some help documentation?
- Do they staff a help desk?
- During what hours is assistance available? (evenings? weekends?)
- Is there an extra monthly charge for help?
- When you call, do you get a machine or a person?
- How quickly do they respond to requests for help?

The best way to get an honest, unbiased answer to these questions is to talk to someone who uses the service.

Track record

New service providers used to pop up frequently and some were short lived for a variety of reasons. Others suffered from technical problems that caused their system to shut down more frequently than users liked. A history of reliable service can be a sign that a provider is here to stay; these days the large companies tend to take a lion's share of the market.

Software

What software will you need to do what you want to do? Access providers should give you a package of software (on a diskette or CD-ROM with clear instructions for loading) or access to a Web site from which you download the required software. Some providers will tell you that everything you need is available on the Net — but unless they tell you exactly how to get it, choose another service. When you connect to a commercial online service, you may need a special software package. Sometimes this is an added cost, and you might prefer to use your own communications software. Check with the provider to find out if your software will work.

B
Appendix

Curriculum Links: Online Resources

Introduction

The following list is a selection of some of our favorite links to curriculum resources on the Internet. Although the list is not comprehensive, it provides a sampling of curriculum resources available in a range of specific subject areas. You will find these and hundreds of other wonderful resources on the Web site that accompanies this book.

While the thought of exploring hundreds of Internet resources is not a task for busy teachers, the brief listing included here can serve as a quick reference to the kinds of sites available, and it will help you pinpoint the topic areas that will be of most interest to you, such as Mathematics or Science — Hands-On Activities. Once you have an idea of the kinds of sites you would like to explore, use the Web site to easily access these and many more. Be sure also to check the many curriculum and general resources included in the text. Some of the very best resources are identified in the text as favorite sites, or along with project ideas. In addition to the specific links to curriculum subject areas, this list and the Web site include listings of special needs resources on the World Wide Web, additional sites for kids, and additional sites of professional interest to teachers.

Take your time exploring and think about how the individual sites might be useful for your students. If you bookmark your favorites, you can easily return to them. You can also print a Web page from a site as a visual reference, and make notes on how you could use the site in your teaching.

How to use this Appendix

Following is a list of the curriculum area resources included in this Appendix.

1. Aboriginal Native Education
2. Art
3. Astronomy/Space
4. Biology/Life Sciences
5. Careers
6. Chemistry

1. Aboriginal native education

Aboriginal links to Internet resources about Aboriginal peoples of Canada. This huge collection includes organizations, treaty information, government, art, and human rights issues.

   http://www.aboriginal-canada.com/native1.html

Appendix B: Curriculum Links

Assembly of First Nations. The official Web site of the Assembly of First Nations has links to other sites so that every aspect of Aboriginal life is covered.

　　http://www.afn.ca

Native American Curriculum Resource. Visit this site for its list of guides and other resources appropriate for several different levels.

　　http://ali.apple.com/features/natamerican.shtml

Native Web. The Indian Resources site, maintained by Will Karkavelas, offers over 700 well organized international referencelinks to sites concerned with Native America.

　　http://www.nativeweb.org/listing.phtml

First Peoples on School Net. Here you will find links to projects, programs and celebrations relevant to Canadian Aboriginal peoples.

　　http://www.schoolnet.ca/aboriginal

2. Art

Arts Sites for Educators. This is the place for art educators. Regularly updated, it covers all of the arts on the Web and will e-mail updates to sites to help the busy teacher.

　　http://www.ceismc.gatech.edu/busyt/art.html

ArtsEdge. This major site for art education materials was established and continues its development under a cooperative agreement between the John F. Kennedy Center for the Performing Arts and the National Endowment for the Arts (with additional support from the U.S. Department of Education).

　　http://artsedge.kennedy-center.org

ArtsEdNet. You'll find teaching and learning materials, including art images. The resources are organized so that ArtsEdNet visitors can easily find the sort of information they want.

　　http://www.getty.edu/artsednet

The Incredible Art Department. The site has links to elementary and secondary school art departments, lessons, museums, and art magazines. It's an excellent resource for art teachers that includes lessons, art site of the week, pet peeves, and much more.

　　http://www.artswire.org/kenroar

Inside Art. This online game explores a painting from the inside out. During an art museum tour, you're sucked into a vortex and find yourself inside a mystery painting. Your only hope of escape is to answer the questions "Who? What? Where? How?"

> http://www.eduweb.com/insideart/d4.html

KinderART. The creators of this handy teacher resource have combined their backgrounds in education and the visual arts to develop a site to meet the needs of busy teachers. An absolutely wonderful find!

> http://www.kinderart.com/lessons.htm

Michael's Kid's Club Online! From the well-known craft store, this Michael's Web site is devoted to kids and features lots of neat projects and arts and crafts ideas! This is a resource to share with your fellow teachers, especially the art teacher!

> http://www.michaels.com

SmARTkids. This site from the university of Chicago helps students aged 7 to 11 learn to analyze and interpret visual art. Extensive use of Flash makes it engaging, entertaining and interactive.

> http://smartmuseum.uchicago.edu/smartkids/

Princeton HS Virtual Museum. An interactive set of lessons for high school students makes art fascinating and fun! Students explore paintings, art objects, and architecture to learn more about world and American history, literature, and the creative arts.

> http://www.prs.k12.nj.us/Schools/PHS/History/World_History

3. Astronomy/Space

Astronomy Cafe. "The Web site for the astronomically disadvantaged" was developed by a professional astronomer. It provides unusual information about the research scene, data collection, and anatomy of a published research paper, Ask-an-Astronomer, and software suitable for science fair or classroom projects.

> http://www.theastronomycafe.net

NASA Today@NASA.gov. This is NASA's outlet for daily updates to its activities. It includes press releases, many student-related activities, Internet happenings, and information on upcoming missions.

> http://www.hq.nasa.gov/office/pao/NewsRoom/today.html

Nine Planets. Here's an excellent site to find information on astronomy: planets and moons, spacecraft, astronomical names, a glossary of technical terms and proper names, and a chronology of space discovery.

> http://www.seds.lpl.arizona.edu/nineplanets/nineplanets/
> nineplanets.html

Quest: NASA's K12 Internet Initiative. NASA's educational outreach program includes Passport to Knowledge, a series of interactive projects designed to stimulate student learning about space.

http://quest.arc.nasa.gov

Sea and Sky: The Sky. This site has lovely gallery photos, an informative tour of the solar system, links, a Challenger memorial, and Java games. Very well put together, it's an all around beautiful site.

http://www.seasky.org/sky.html

The Space Educators' Handbook. This interesting site uses science fiction to help teach about space technology and scientific laws. You can download the software version (Mac and Windows) of the Space Educators' Handbook. The site also includes a collection of QuickTime movies and other surprises.

http://vesuvius.jsc.nasa.gov/er/seh

4. Biology/Life sciences

Access Excellence. Access Excellence is a national education program that puts high school biology teachers in touch with other teachers and scientists. This excellent resource for biology teachers and students contains online mysteries and other interactive resources.

http://www.accessexcellence.org

Cells Alive. This is a great site to see cells in action. The topics (Anatomy of a Splinter, When a Cell Commits Suicide, This Strain Kills White Blood Cells, and others) have descriptions of each step of their process, and animated gifs and QuickTime movies to see actual cells!

http://www.cellsalive.com

The Natural History of Genes. Learn how enzymes digest food, or how an arm is genetically different from a leg. This thorough site explores DNA and genetics in the real world, with excellent sections on hands-on experiments and teacher activities.

http://raven.umnh.utah.edu

Sea and Sky: The Sea. This is a great site with a gallery of wonderful photos, information on all kinds of reef animals, links, and Java games such as a word search, a crossword, and a slider.

http://www.seasky.org/sea.html

Seeds of Change Garden. The site is the result of the Smithsonian Institution's Natural Partners Initiative and was created by the New Mexico State University College of Agriculture and Home Economics. There are

garden activities for all seasons, recipes, and lots of wonderful information about the origins of food crops.
http://horizon.nmsu.edu/garden

5. Careers

Quintessential Career and Job Hunting Resources Guide. This comprehensive, well-organized job search site offers cover letter and resume advice, job and career sites (with great reviews), a step-by-step guide to job-hunting on the Internet, a marketability test, interviewing help, and more.
http://www.stetson.edu/~rhansen/careers.html

Showing the Children of Today, the Possibilities of Tomorrow! The site contains a description of educational career awareness video programming from Takeoff Multimedia. With a career library of over 125 career fields, the Takeoff collection offers something to satisfy every student's interest.
http://www.iwc.com/careertv

6. Chemistry

Chemicool Periodic Table. The clickable periodic table gives in-depth information on each element and is the most complete periodic table seen on the Web to date.
http://www.chemicool.com

The Chemistry Place. You've found an excellent chemistry Web site to supplement your course. An outstanding team of educators collaborate to provide you with interactive Web activities for your students, art and animations to enhance your lectures, links to a collection of appropriate Web sites, research news, and much more.
http://www.chemplace.com

The Molecular Expressions Photo Gallery. Thousands of full color photomicrographs (photographs taken through a microscope) and digital images selected from their many collections.
http://micro.magnet.fsu.edu/micro/gallery.html

WebElements from the College of Chemisty UC Berkeley. On the clickable periodic table, find the atomic weight for beryllium or gallium or any element. It's an excellent chemistry resource.
http://www.cchem.berkeley.edu/Table/index.html

7. Computers

7.1. E-mail Help Links

An Educator's Guide to Email Lists. The Prince Edward Island Department of Education presents an easy-to-read "How to" for educators.
http://www.edu.pe.ca/resources/listserv/default.asp

Lizst. If you're wondering if an e-mail discussion group exists about a particular topic, try this useful directory of mailing lists. Enter any word or phrase to search over 32,000 listserv, listproc, majordomo mailing lists and independently managed lists from nearly 900 sites.
http://www.liszt.com

7.2. Tutorials

Adobe Online Training. Online courses in Adobe Acrobat, Photoshop, and InDesign are available here for only USD$59. You can try out a free sample courses in Adobe Photoshop 7.0 and Adobe InDesign 2.0 to give you an idea of how the courses work. Adobe product support also provides product specific tutorials.
http://adobe.elementk.com/

Atomic Learning. With a subscription costing USD$49.99 per year, you can learn your favorite software programs such as AppleWorks, Dreamweaver, Hyperstudio, KidPix, Powerpoint and many others by viewing tutorial movies with narration. Free tutorials presently offered include iMovie2, iPhoto, Mac OS X, and Kidspiration.
http://www.atomiclearning.com/

Beginners Guide to Dreamweaver and Fireworks. These two tutorials teach the basics of Dreamweaver and Fireworks. The 6 Dreamweaver tutorials cover planning your first web site, creating a site structure, working with text, design templates, simple swap images, and pop-up menus. Fireworks tutorials address creating new documents, bitmaps, animations, transperancy maps and rollovers.
http://www.dw-fw-beginners.com/

Computer Skills for Integrated Learning Teacher Resources. This site contains a description of resources that provide technology-integrated units for single-subject and cross-curricular work.
http://www.linkidea.com

Desktop Video. Links to everything you'd ever want to know about equipment, planning, shooting, capturing, editing and sharing desktop video.
http://desktopvideo.about.com/

FrontPage in the Classroom. Cathy Chamberlain's Electric Teacher site provides step-by-step instructions for tasks such as working with text, graphics, hyperlinks, tables and special components of FrontPage. Though aimed specifically at teachers, this tutorial could also be useful to students.

http://www.electricteacher.com/tutorial2.htm

Get Connected to Learning Using the Internet. What is ICONnect? Developed especially for school library media specialists, teachers, and students, ICONnect offers anyone the opportunity to learn the skills necessary to navigate the Information Superhighway.

http://www.ala.org/ICONN/index.html

iMovie. In this excellent illustrated tutorial you will learn how to preview, move, arrange and edit clips, work with audio and export to tape or QuickTime movies.

http://etc.sccoe.org/i2000/oomod/l_mm/imov.html

Internet Island. If you want to learn how to use the Internet in a classroom, start here. Internet Island is designed to be a safe environment where novice Internet users learn and practice navigation skills.

http://www.miamisci.org/ii

Microsoft Education: In and Out of the Classroom. These practical tutorial guides are designed to help students, teachers, and administrators learn how to use Microsoft software in the classroom. They include Office XP, Office 2001 and v. X for the Mac, Office 2000, FrontPage 2000, Publisher 2000, PowerPoint 97 and Word 97.

http://www.microsoft.com/education/?ID=IOCTutorials

Short Courses. This is a great site to learn about digital cameras and digital photography, everything from the basics to to more advanced skills such as editing, image sizes, filters and accessories.

http://www.shortcourses.com/

7.3. The Internet and World Wide Web

Armadillo's K12 WWW Resources. You'll find one of the most comprehensive collections of board policies and acceptable use policies along with many articles on issues such as censorship and filtering. Armadillo also contains resources covering networking projects; educational databases and lesson plans; learning and instruction; and grant resources. The site also lists great Internet resources for each of the major curriculum areas.

http://chico.rice.edu/armadillo/Rice/Resources/reshome.html

Best Information on the Net. This is a nicely organized and comprehensive list of selected sites. You'll find pages for hot topics such as affirmative action, drug issues, and human rights, as well as many Internet guides and resources.

http://library.sau.edu/bestinfo

Classroom Connect. The site presents a rich assortment of good information to support the Internet-ready teacher and school. One excellent list of resources listed by school subjects and topics is GRADES+. Classroom Connect also offers a resource station; searching; a classroom Web — a listing of school Web sites; and a teacher contact database.

http://www.classroom.net

Finding Information on the Internet ... A Tutorial. Getting started? This is a good introduction to the Internet and has great strategies for searching.

http://www.lib.berkeley.edu/TeachingLib/Guides/Internet/ FindInfo.html

ICONN. Online Internet Courses and Information for School Librarians. Developed especially for school library media specialists, teachers, and students, ICONnect offers anyone the opportunity to learn the skills necessary to navigate the Information Superhighway.

http://www.ala.org/ICONN

Internet Information Gateway for Educators. From Planet K–12. This vast site of wonderful resources is a onestop information shop for teachers of all subjects.

http://www.planetk12.com

LETSNet. Learning Exchange for Teachers and Students through the Internet (LETSNet), designed for the K–12 classroom, contains a collection of teaching units with online student activities that incorporate reading, writing, and research skills.

http://commtechlab.msu.edu/sites/letsnet/noframes/Subjects/la

NetAdventure. You'll find challenging activities for middle and high school students at this site. Each weekday they post a new topic such as Fibonacci numbers or Monarch Migrations. Every NetAdventure has three interesting challenges, starting with one most 12-year-olds could master in an hour to one that would challenge even the most advanced student.

http://www.concord.org/netadventure

The Online Internet Institute. This results-driven organization offers professional development workshops to help students and teachers improve classroom achievement.

http://www.oii.org

Pitsco Educational Technology Web Site. At this first-rate resource for teachers, you can access an excellent set of links to curriculum resources, grant information, acceptable use policy information, and much more.
http://www.pitsco.com

Premier Tracks. You'll find a collection of K–12 Web-based lessons for a variety of subject areas created by SCR*TEC's TrackStar. To use this tool, teachers enter a list of Web site addresses, annotations, and questions for TrackStar to organize them into an interactive, online, ready-to-use lesson.
http://www.4teachers.org/premier

The Spider's Apprentice. Search the Web more efficiently. Check out this site to learn the principles of smart searching. Find ratings and analyses of popular search engines, too.
http://www.monash.com/spidap.html

ThinkQuest USA. In this exciting contest, student teams, coached by their teachers, build Web-based educational materials for their age group and submit them for evaluation.
http://www.thinkquest.org/tqusa/index.html

Web 66: A K12 WWW PROJECT. A project of the University of Minnesota's School of Education, this server sets out to: help K-12 educators learn how to set up their own World Wide Web Internet servers; link K–12 WWW servers and the educators and students at those schools, and help K–12 educators find and use appropriate resources on the WWW.
http://web66.coled.umn.edu

7.4. Integrating Computers

An Inch Deep and a Mile Wide: Electronic Tools for Savvy Administrators. This article presents and explains web-based resources for 1) standards development for administrator, teacher and student technology skills and knowledge; 2) standards development for accessibility, connectivity, and software; and 3) national and state resources such as diagnostic tools, school data/statistics, and other technology-related information.
http://ifets.ieee.org/periodical/vol_3_99/awalt.html

Consortium for School Networking. "CoSN is a nonprofit organization formed to further the development and use of telecommunications in K–12 education." Visit the site to locate articles on the use of technology in schools and the latest information on the E-Rate.
http://cosn.org

EdWeb. An educational resource guide specifically written for K–12 use, the guide focuses on the interconnection of education reform and information

technology and provides numerous examples of how networking and computers have affected and will affect the classrooms of today and tomorrow.
http://www.edwebproject.org

Global Campus. The creators describe the site as "a collaborative multimedia database containing a variety of educational materials such as images, sounds, text, etc. to be used for nonprofit, educational purposes."
www.csulb.edu/gc

Harnessing the Power of the Web: A Tutorial. This material from Global SchoolNet Foundation focuses on student preparation and lesson planning.
http://www.gsn.org/web/index.html

Internet Classroom Projects. This huge site with links to all subjects includes classroom project ideas for teachers, broken down by subject area. A must stop on the highway.
http://www.ket.org/Education/IN/projects.html

Mid Continent Regional Educational Laboratory. Take advantage of Technology Connections, which "provide some of the best online resources available to help educators, administrators, and parents answer common questions and solve problems related to the implementation and use of technology in education."
http://www.mcrel.org/connect/tech/index.html

NickNacks Telecollaborations. This site is updated monthly and features projects for class participation and subject-specific Web links for students and teachers. A great site — bookmark it!
http://telecollaborate.net/education/edprojects.html

Organization for the Advancement of Educational Technology in the Classroom. OAETC.org is dedicated to advancing the use of sound, proven educational technologies in public and private classrooms. One of their goals is to identify good educational websites for the classroom.
http://www.oaetc.org/

United Nation's Cyber School Bus
Designed for students and teachers everywhere, the site carries projects and resources about the United Nations and the world we all share. An outstanding site that can be used by all learners.
http://www.un.org/pubs/cyberschoolbus

7.5. Technical Information

Multimedia Mania. Here's a contest for students and teachers who use multimedia in the classroom. HyperSIG (Multimedia Special Interest Group of the International Society for Technology in Education) invites you and your students to dazzle your global peers by creating dynamic multimedia projects that relate to any class or coursework.

http://www2.ncsu.edu/unity/lockers/project/midlinknc/mmania.how.html

7.6. Searching Tools

The Spider's Apprentice. Search the Web more efficiently. Check out this site to learn the principles of smart searching. Find ratings and analyses of popular search engines, too.

http://www.monash.com/spidap.html

7.7. Videoconferencing

Videoconference Resource Center. This promising site is hoping to become an open forum for videoconferencing professionals and interested parties.

http://www.videoconference.com

Videoconferencing for Learning. Pac Bell's info on using videoconferencing for distance learning includes links to related directories.

http://www.kn.pacbell.com/wired/vidconf/index.html

8. Dictionaries, glossaries, and more

Dictionary.com. More languages, more dictionaries and more of what you've asked for.

http://www.dictionary.com

Encyclopedia.com. This free encyclopedia includes over 17,000 articles from the *Concise Columbia Electronic Encyclopedia*, Third Edition. The articles are generally short but most include links to related topics.

http://www.encyclopedia.com

Human Languages Page. Searchable dictionaries, grammar guide, and tutorials for over 20 languages.

http://www.june29.com//HLP

The Internet Sleuth. Track down all kinds of information. The site offers access to over 1,500 searchable databases. Visit the Reference area for a selection of dictionaries and encyclopedias.

http://www.isleuth.com

MetaSearch Engines — Teaching Library Internet Workshops, University of California, Berkeley. In a metasearch engine, you submit keywords in its search box, and it transmits your search simultaneously to most of the popular search engines and their databases of Web pages. Within a few seconds, you get back a compilation of results containing matching sites from all of the search engines queried.

http://www.lib.berkeley.edu/TeachingLib/Guides/Internet

My Virtual Reference Desk. This online reference source has a Fast Facts section with sources for finding out about population, weights and measures, plus a search engine for a multitude of online dictionaries and glossaries.

http://www.refdesk.com

OneLook Dictionaries. Use this site to search over 200 dictionaries on the Internet.

http://www.onelook.com

Researchit. You'll find Roget's Thesaurus, a translator, map resources, Merriam Webster and rhyming dictionaries, CMU pronouncing dictionary and language identifier, a biographical dictionary, area codes and phone directories, a currency converter, UPS and FedEx package tracking, and more!

http://www.iTools.com/researchit/researchit.html

The Wordsmyth English Dictionary-Thesaurus. This claims to be the only integrated English dictionary and thesaurus in electronic form! It has 50,000 headwords with definitions, pronunciations and examples, providing exact synonyms and similars (near synonyms).

www.lightlink.com/bobp/wedt

9. English

9.1. Language

11 Rules of Writing. This site is a concise guide to some of the most commonly violated rules of writing, grammar, and punctuation. It is intended for all writers as an aid in the learning and refining of writing skills. Explore each of the rules to see examples of its application, and use the references to find additional explanations and examples on the Web or in print.

http://www.junketstudies.com/rulesofw

A+ Research and Writing. This step-by-step guide for high school and college students will take them through the process of writing a research paper from getting the assignment to gathering the information and writing the paper.

http://www.ipl.org/teen/aplus/stepfirst.htm

AdmitOne. Created by the Artists Right Foundation, this site offers a practical guide to film making that includes general interest topics such as "what a director does," hands-on exercises and links to specific topics such as sound editing and costume design.

http://www.admitone.org

I Know That. Activities such as MadLibs, Word Builder, Word Match and Grammar Galaxy are featured at this online subscription site. The cost is USD$199 for a yearly subscription for a class of 30 students. The activites ar engaging and well though out. Open-ended and creative opportunities are provided. The site also includes math activities, a painting lab and a science lab.

http://www.iknowthat.com

Inkspot. This award-winning site is a writer's best friend on the Internet. Inkspot offers a well-organized and comprehensive index that addresses every writing issue.

http://www.creators-child.com

KidPub. More than 40,000 stories written by kids from all over the planet! If you would like your students to write a story and publish it on the Web, then this is the place for you. A template has been set up for kids to write a story, fill in some information about themselves and send in for publishing.

http://www.kidpub.org/kidpub

LinguaCenterGrammar Safari. This site is designed for bold students of English who would like to broaden their horizons by leaving the safe confines of the grammar book and venturing out into the unruly jungle of real-world English usage.

http://www.iei.uiuc.edu/web.pages/grammarsafari.html

Reading A to Z. At this unique site, you can print an unlimited supply of levelled books for K to Gr 5 students at a cost of USD$29.95 for a 6-month subscription. A wide variety of books in English, French and Spanish are available including fiction, non-fiction and poetry. Each book is downloadable in PDF format for easy printing. Other resources such as flashcards, worksheets and teaching ideas are also available.

http://www.readinga-z.com

The Favorite Poem Project. Robert Pinsky, the 39th Poet Laureate of the United States, founded the Favorite Poem Project shortly after he was appointed in 1997. The Favorite Poem Project is dedicated to celebrating, documenting and promoting poetry's role in Americans' lives. The collection includes 50 short video documentaries of individual Americans reading and speaking personally about poems they love, 200 poems along with readers' letters about their attachments to the poems, and an extensive database of favorite poems.

http://www.favoritepoem.org

The Mind's Eye Monster Exchange. The curriculum projects are WinStar For Education's solution for integrating Internet technology into the current core classroom curriculum. Each project has been mapped to the New York State Standards for Learning and has proven to meet many areas in a way that is fun and exciting for the kids.

http://www.win4edu.com/mindseye

Vocabulary.com. Here at Vocabulary University, you are able to participate in free vocabulary puzzles to enhance vocabulary mastery. Register, complete 12 sessions (learning 144 words), and you earn your diploma!

www.vocabulary.com.

What Makes a Good Short Story? This site presents the elements of a good short story. A sample short story is presented as a model.

http://www.learner.org/exhibits/literature

9.2. English Literature

Alex. Alex is a comprehensive catalog of books and other works that enables users to find and retrieve the full text of documents on the Internet. It currently indexes almost 1,800 books and shorter texts by author, title, subject, language, and year of publication.

http://www.infomotions.com/alex

Carol Hurst's Children's Literature Site. This is a collection of reviews of children's books and ways to use them in the classroom. You can look them up by title, author, type, or age, and browse them in categories such as curriculum area, subject, and theme.

http://www.carolhurst.com

Children's Literature — Resources for Teachers. This is a good starting point for any language arts teacher. You will find book awards, publishers, and authors, illustrators, and a multitude of other links. This is an outstanding site with links to resources and lesson plans with a focus on reading and literature.

http://www.ucalgary.ca/~dkbrown/rteacher.html

CyberGuides. These are supplementary units of instruction based on core works of literature, requiring students to use the World Wide Web, and are meant to be used as collections of Web-searching activities that lead to a student product. They may be used in a classroom with one computer, connected to the Internet.

http://www.sdcoe.k12.ca.us/score/cyberguide.html

Pizzaz! ... People Interested in Zippy and Zany Zcribbling. Created by Leslie Opp-Beckman, the site provides creative writing lessons and activities with royalty-free student handouts. The site features explanations of various kinds of poetry from limericks to haiku to quatrains.

http://www.uoregon.edu/~leslieob/pizzaz.html

Researchpaper.com. Here's a great resource for those needing inspiration. The site has tips and ideas to help with your writing. The site even includes a chat room so you can talk to other students. The topics index is searchable and there's also a writing center, research center, and chat.

http://www.researchpaper.com

Weblit. The Internet is still waiting for a perfect literary index. Until one is developed, you should check out Weblit. Its simple design and four-star site rating system put most of the best author and poet sites at your fingertips.

http://www.weblit.info/offsite/research.html

Writers In Electronic Residence (WIER). This site links Canada's writers to Canada's schools. The writers join classrooms electronically to read and consider students' work, offer ideas, and guide discussions between students.

http://www.wier.ca

10. The environment

An Amazon Adventure. A wonderful site! Students from elementary, junior high, and high schools created the majority of this site and the results were checked for accuracy.

http://jajhs.kana.k12.wv.us/amazon

Arctica. The site, an Access Excellence Science Mystery sponsored by Genentech, Inc., can be completely downloaded for use off the Internet. A breathtaking Web site.

http://www.accessexcellence.org/arc

Blue Ice: The Food Web. You can visit Antarctica to learn of the fascinating interrelationship between the animals of the Antarctic and their environment. This is a program packed with information and daily activities.

http://www.onlineclass.com/bi/blueice.html

Boreal Forest Watch (BFW). BFW is an educational outreach program for the Boreal Ecosystem Atmosphere Study (BOREAS). It involves high school students in conducting real research as part of their educational experience. BFW takes place in the boreal ecosystem region of northern Saskatchewan, Canada.

http://www.teachearth.com/programs/Boreal_Forest_Watch.html

Carolina Coastal Science. This innovative, inquiry-based, science resource utilizes the interactive technologies of the World Wide Web to explore science in coastal Carolina. It has been created based on the goals stated in the National Science Education Standards.

http://www.ncsu.edu/coast

Journey North. One of the best and most successful online science learning communities for K–12 students, this site engages students in a global study of wildlife migration and seasonal change.

http://www.learner.org/jnorth/jnorth.html

MayaQuest '98: Mysteries of the Rainforest. This outstanding long-term project provides meaningful interactions between students around the world and the MayaQuest team. Subscribe to get biweekly updates and reports that include glorious images and stories about real people met along the way.

http://www.classroom.com/mayaquest/default.html

Sierra Club. The club is a nonprofit member-supported, public-interest organization that promotes conservation of the natural environment by influencing public-policy decisions. Test your scientific sleuthing in "River of Venom," the new science mystery from Access Excellence.

http://www.sierraclub.org

WeatherNet. This is the Internet's premier source of weather information, providing access to thousands of forecasts and images, and the largest collection of weather links.

http://cirrus.sprl.umich.edu/wxnet

World Wildlife Fund. This organization works to fight environmental pollution and support endangered species. Get the latest environmental news and read special features on protecting species and habitats.

http://www.panda.org

11. ESL and non-English languages

C.B. Putnam's Home Page. The site has been created for Foreign Language Teaching on the Internet. Resources with teaching activities.

http://www.ea.pvt.k12.pa.us/htm/Units/Upper/modlang/putnam/putnam.htm

Dave's ESL Cafe. Visit this site for ESL/EFL students and teachers from around the world.

http://www.eslcafe.com

English as a Second Language. The site is sponsored by Online Bilingualism and Language Network (BLN) and provides links to relevant ESL resources for students and teachers.

http://www.talkeasy.co.uk/link/esl/esl.html

12. Geography

Amazon Adventure. Follow a New Zealand traveler as he reports back on a nine-week trip to the Amazon and other destinations in South America. Schools are encouraged to participate.

http://jajhs.kana.k12.wv.us/amazon

Atlapedia Online. A virtual world almanac of planetary proportions, Atlapedia Online provides facts and vital stats for every country on the globe, and it's free. The simple, alphabetized index lets you click a letter, choose a country and get its geography, climate, people, religion, language, history and economy.

http://www.atlapedia.com

Earthrise. This database of Earth images was taken by astronauts from inside the space shuttle. Users can search the image database by keyword or by clickable topographical and political maps.

http://www.space.com

GeoGame. This unique, e-mail project helps students learn geographic terms and how to read and interpret maps, and increases awareness of geographical and cultural diversity.

http://www.gsn.org/project/gg

Geography. This is The Mining Company's Geography section. If you'd like someone who loves geography to precede you on the Net, picking out the best sites and describing them, you've hit the jackpot.

http://geography.miningco.com

Geography — GeoMystery Project. Students can brainstorm what is unique about where they live. They create drawings or take photos of the place, then add captions. Through a successive series of clues, participants will attempt to locate each school.

http://kalama.doe.hawaii.edu/hern96/pto53/GOMYstery/ geomys.html

GeoNet Game. "A fun new geography game based on the national geography standards," GeoNet offers low and high band width versions as well as easy and hard questions in many categories. Part of Houghton Mifflin's Education Place.

http://www.hmco.com/hmco/school/geo/index.html

The Great American Landmarks Adventure. The National Park Service, The History Channel, and The American Architectural Foundation offer 3,000 years of U.S. history through word and picture.

http://www.cr.nps.gov/pad/adventure/landmark.htm#olds

Himalayas — Where Earth Meets Sky. A culmination of collaboration among three high school students and their coaches from separate continents, the project forms an entry in ThinkQuest (1997), an annual contest that challenges students to use the Internet as a collaborative teaching and learning tool.

http://library.advanced.org/10131

Internet Resources for Geography and Geology. This is a great geography resource. Choose from a dozen topics including world geography, government resources, and teaching helps.

http://www.uwsp.edu/geo/internet/geog_geol_resources.html

Map Machine. Here you and your students can search for all types of maps and get printer-friendly versions. You'll also find some good lessons in the Xpeditions database.

http://www.nationalgeographic.com/maps

Mapmaker, Mapmaker, Make Me a Map. This is an entertaining page, geared for kids, that explains maps. The author explains how Will Fontanez, a cartographer, goes about making maps when he gets a request.

http://pr.tennessee.edu/utkids/maps/map.html

National Geographic Online. In addition to its famous features on individual cultures, National Geographic offers a wide range of options including talk, answers to your geography questions, and scenic drive information with lodging, maps, and even car games. A great site.

http://www.nationalgeographic.com

Seven World Wonders. The list of the Seven Wonders of the Ancient World was originally compiled around the second century B.C. Each wonder has been beautifully reconstructed, including attractive graphics, detailed description, historical background, and location, all woven together with helpful hypertext references.

http://ee.eng.usf.edu/pharos/wonders

World Surfari. Each month World Surfari takes you to a different country. This site has colorful images and lots of information on the country they are focusing on.

http://www.supersurf.com

Worldtime. Spin an interactive globe to see where the sun is shining, or zoom in on particular countries.

http://www.worldtime.org

13. Geology/Earth science

AskaGeologist. Do you have a question about volcanoes, earthquakes, mountains, rocks, maps, ground water, lakes, or rivers? Each message goes to a different USGS earth scientist.

http://walrus.wr.usgs.gov/docs/askage.html

Interactive Multimedia Educational Resources. The Penn State College of Earth and Mineral Sciences has established this site to provide access to a series of interactive multimedia educational resources for teaching introductory earth science. Highly recommended!

http://www.ems.psu.edu/Courses/earth002/Resources.html

NJNIE Curriculum Page. New Jersey Networking Infrastructure in Education (NJNIE) Curriculum Page contains several curriculum modules, related to earth science, plus many excellent links.

http://njnie.dl.stevens-tech.edu/curriculum.html

Volcano. This Web site delves into the study of volcanoes both on Earth and on other planets. It contains information about currently erupting volcanoes; photos and video clips; classroom activities; and a searchable database of volcanoes.

http://volcano.und.nodak.edu/vw.html

14. History and current events

American Immigration Home Page. The page was started as a part of a school project for a 10th-grade American History class. It has evolved into a treasure trove of information about the immigrant experience.

http://www.bergen.org/AAST/Projects/Immigration

American Memory. Loads of primary source material from broadsides to early documents, photographs, audio, and film can be found at American Memory. Multimedia material relating to American culture and history.

http://lcweb2.loc.gov

Ancient World Web. Bookmark this site for excellence. The Ancient World Web, created by Julia Hayden, is a master index to Internet sites "discussing, spotlighting, or otherwise considering the Ancient World."
http://www.julen.net/aw

Biography. You can search over 20,000 short biographies from the Cambridge Dictionary of Biography.
http://www.biography.com

Flints and Stones: Real Life in Prehistory. The British Museum of Antiquities takes kids on a virtual trip to the Stone Age in this appealing site, which also relates ancient history to today's world, making it more real.
http://www.ncl.ac.uk/~nantiq/menu.html

Frontier Girl—Laura Elizabeth Ingalls. The site contains a brief menu to subject pages, a full A–Z index, "The Story of Laura's Life" with lots of links, and for younger readers, "The Log Cabin in the Big Woods."
http://webpages.marshall.edu/~irby1/laura.htmlx

History Channel.com. Upper elementary and secondary students along with their teachers will find this site useful. In addition to a searchable database of articles, it includes This Day in History, quiz questions and a discussion question for the day.
http://www.historychannel.com

History Link 101. History Link 101 is a resource site appropriate for upper-elementary and middle school students. It is divided into six categories for each culture or time period: art, biographies, daily life, maps, pictures and research. Currently the cultures/time periods of Prehistory, Africa, China, Egypt, Greece, Aztec, Mayan, Olmec, Native Americans, Mesopotamia, Middle Ages and World War II are completed with the aim to cover the entire scope of World History.
http://www.historylink101.com

HyperHistory Online. HyperHistory is an expanding scientific project presenting 3,000 years of world history with an interactive combination of synchronoptic lifelines, timelines, and maps. Over 2,000 files are presently interconnected throughout the site, with over 50 MB of images and text files. HyperHistory also provides several hundred links to the world wide web. This is a great research site for middle and secondary school students.
http://www.hyperhistory.com/online_n2/History_n2/a.html

The Encyclopedia of World History. This is a comprehensive chronology of more than 20,000 entries that span the millennia from prehistoric times to the year 2000. Middle school and secondary students will find this site useful for research.

http://www.hyperhistory.com/online_n2/History_n2/a.html

The Heritage Post Interactive. This wonderful site offers stories from Canada's historical past. The story of Canadian aviation is available here as well as information on *The Bluenose* and the Water Pump, a Canadian-designed hand pump used in poorer countries for drawing water. Well worth the time to check it out.

http://heritage.excite.sfu.ca/hpost.html

Horus. This is the first Egyptian Web site for kids. It is bilingual (Arabic and English) and contains more than 300 pages of information and illustrations covering Egypt's 7,000 years of civilization (Ancient, Coptic, Greco-Roman, Islamic and Modern).

http://www.horus.ics.org.eg

Mr. Donn's Ancient History Page. Mr. Donn teaches ancient history to sixth graders in Maryland. This impressive site offers his own units on Ancient Greece and Mesopotamia (detailed daily lessons, activities, a unit test) plus wonderful teaching resources he's gathered on a dozen ancient cultures including Egypt, Rome, China, Africa, and Aztec.

http://members.aol.com/donnandlee/index.html

The Mythos: Zeus Speaks! This interactive 12-week project explores Greek mythology. It's a great place to do Ancient History via writing and drama.

http://www.onlineclass.com/Mythos/mythos.html

The North American Quilt. Be part of a great virtual exploration of this wonderful continent, researching your local communities to learn more about the land, the earth systems, and the people.

http://www.onlineclass.com/NAQ/NAQhome.html

OLD NEWS. What a unique way for kids to learn about history! This site is in a newspaper format and has stories about old news — the *Titanic*, a 1900 hurricane, Sitting Bull, Harriet Tubman, and more.

http://www.oldnewspublishing.com

This Day in History. Although mainly American in its content, this site provides a list of important happenings for each day, as well as a list of birthdays, music, and so on. Choose the month and day to learn about events that happened throughout history.

http://www.historychannel.com/today

You Be the Historian. Here's a fun way to explore American history by looking at artifacts. The site asks visitors to "figure out what life was like 200 years ago for Thomas and Elizabeth Springer's family in New Castle, Delaware."

http://www.si.edu/organiza/museums/nmah/notkid/ubh/oointro.htm

15. Kids' links

15.1. Kids with Computers

Bonus.com. What a great site! It uses Java to open up a separate window that kids can use to navigate the site easily, and there's a Parents and Teachers path as well. Bonus.com offers 900 activities, some linked and some original.

http://www.bonus.com

Kids Food Cyber Club. The site is rated "Among the Best" with 23 out of 25 points by Nutrition Navigator, a rating guide for nutrition Web sites!

http://www.kidsfood.org

KidsWeb: A World Wide Web Digital Library for School Kids. The site, which links to the arts, the sciences, social studies, and more, is very simple to navigate, and contains information targeted at the K–12 level. Each subject section contains a list of links to information that is understandable and interesting to schoolkids.

http://www.npac.syr.edu/textbook/kidsweb

Moose. In this virtual community for kids online, kids can "build" things in their community. It helps them help others get started. What they're really learning to do is object-oriented programming. Wow!

http://www.cc.gatech.edu/elc/moose-crossing

15.2. Kids with Others on the Internet

Children's Express. The site is created "by children for everybody." With a wealth of news from six news bureaus, it's packed with content. You can also participate in an electronic round table, submit your own story ideas, answer polls, and respond to articles.

http://www.ce.org

Digital Education Network (DEN). Six DENs let students obtain up-to-date information, learn, and practice their skills in such areas as math, news, writing, and the Internet.

http://www.actden.com

International Kids' Space. This interactive, educational site helps kids learn about science, transportation, animals, the Internet, and more. Kids perform musical pieces and present their artwork, poems, and stories in Kids' Space.

http://www.kids-space.org

16. Mathematics

The Annenberg/CPB Math and Science Project. This organization has funded more than 40 projects to improve K–12 math and science education. These projects educate and support the key groups of adults that have a hand in changing the way math and science are taught.

http://www.learner.org/content/k12

The Center of Excellence for Science and Mathematics Education (CESME). This site offers a variety of math resources including classroom-related and professional development information. You can find a sample lesson on the history of mathematics and computer spreadsheet applications developed by teachers.

http://cesme.utm.edu

Eisenhower National Clearinghouse. ENC is a one-stop gateway for math and science resources. Search the catalog or check out the Digital Dozen, a monthly list spotlighting great Web sites to visit.

http://www.enc.org

Fractory. An Interactive Tool for Creating and Exploring Fractals is an educational site designed by students that lets you design your own fractal and learn about their uses and the mathematics used to generate them.

http://library.advanced.org/3288

The Largest Known Primes. If you or your students are fascinated with prime numbers, you'll love this site. It gives information about prime numbers and the largest primes that have been generated.

http://www.utm.edu/research/primes/largest.html

The Math Forum. The information and projects offered at this site are devoted to geometry and to math education. For teachers, The Math Forum offers electronic newsgroups, articles on math education, learning, and research, math workshops, resources, and more.

http://forum.swarthmore.edu

Mathworld Interactive. Join an online community of students working on math challenges! Since 1991, this successful community has offered its participants a new math challenge every nine weeks.

http://www.mathworldinteractive.com

Mighty M&M Math. This will help you teach fractions and percentages in a motivating and mouthwatering way. Using bags of M&M's, it answers these questions: What is the percentage of each color? Are the percentages similar worldwide?

http://www.iphysique.com/school

Pi Mathematics. A multidisciplinary project designed around the concept of pi, involving math, history, English, and problem-solving skills, this site is designed for Grades 5–8 and guides students in discovering the approximate value of pi, using measurement data, formulas, and various problems and activities. Pi Mathematics also offers a downloadable movie and software as inclass resources.

http://www.ncsa.uiuc.edu/edu/RSE/RSEorange.html

Suzanne's Math Lessons — Math Forum Web Units. Cover many different aspects of math using this wonderful site of creative units ready for application in your classroom.

http://forum.swarthmore.edu/alejandre

This Is MegaMathematics! Under the auspices of the Los Alamos National Laboratory, MegaMath attempts "to bring unusual and important mathematical ideas to elementary school classrooms so that young people and their teachers can think about them." Some of these very interesting projects would be fun for older students as well!

http://www.c3.lanl.gov/mega-math

17. Music

Internet Resources for Music Teachers. Cynthia Shirk, a music teacher, has compiled a list of links that are useful to teachers. A special feature on the page is the Music Box of Sound and Software with complete downloadable music compositions in QuickTime format.

http://www.isd77.k12.mn.us/resources/staffpages/shirk/music.html

K12 Resources for Music Educators. This site has many resources and links for music educators and students at all levels of education.

**http://www.isd77.k12.mn.us/resources/staffpages/shirk/
cindys.page.k12.link.html**

18. News and media

18.1. News

ABC Hourly News Report. You'll get real audio updates every hour. The site does require you to register, but it's free. Follow the link to "News Alerts."
http://abcnews.go.com

CBC: Canadian Broadcasting Corporation — Canadian Arts, Information, and News. Information, downloadable radio programming, including selected archived material dating back to 1965.
http://www.cbc.ca

18.2. Media

Cyberspace Film School and Movie Web. This is an online resource center and educational facility. Learn how to produce a film, find an agent, direct your first feature, or sell your script.
http://www.hollywoodu.com

Discovery Channel Online. An amazing Web site, it's packed with information about what's on the Discovery cable television channel as well as other unique content. Very well designed.
http://www.discovery.com

Electronic Elementary. ELink magazine is a nonprofit, educational project that highlights interactive projects and creations of elementary grade students around the world (for ages 5–12).
http://www.inform.umd.edu/UMS+State/MDK12_Stuff/
homepers/emag

Media Literacy OnLine Project. This is probably the best place on the Web for resources related to the influence of media in the lives of children, youth, and adults.
http://interact.uoregon.edu/MediaLit/HomePage

MediaFinder. They say, "If it's in print, it's here." They offer search tools in a number of print media categories such as catalogs, newspapers, and magazines. Thousands of periodicals list their subject, subscription, and circulation information in summary for your perusal.
http://www.mediafinder.com

19. Physics

Computer as Learning Partner (CLP) Project. The site provides a one-semester integrated energy curriculum unit teaching the physical science topics of heat, light, and sound to eighth-graders.
http://www.clp.berkeley.edu/CLP.html

Physics Lecture Demonstrations. If you are interested in physics, this site is a must! From astronomy to magnetism to waves, the site covers it all.
http://www.mip.berkeley.edu/physics/physics.html

Science at Home (Los Alamos National Laboratory). This is a collection of physical science activities developed to demystify science for adults and children while fostering scientific inquiry and analysis.
http://www.lanl.gov/temp/Education/Contents.html

20. Special needs

disABILITY Information and Resources. This great list of Internet resources on disabilities was developed by Jim Lubin, who is a C2 quadriplegic, completely paralyzed from the neck down and dependent on a ventilator to breathe. The pages are meant to serve as a resource to provide useful information; therefore, they do not contain a lot of useless, pretty graphics, which take a long time to load.
http://www.makoa.org

LD Online. This site offers a wealth of information regarding learning disabilities and Attention Deficit Disorder. You can be kept up-to-date on current events, locate help nationally and by state, participate in discussion groups, and more. What a find!
http://www.ldonline.org/index.html

SNOW (Special Needs Opportunity Window). This is *the* site for special education resources. A central goal of the project is to foster an online community of educators, organizations and special needs students, who share common interests.
http://snow.utoronto.ca

Special Needs Network. Resources for parents, teachers, schools, and other professionals dealing with special needs education. The network supports a number of valuable discussion groups focusing on special needs issues.
http://www.schoolnet.ca/sne

21. Science

21.1. Hands-On Activities

Canadian Young Inventors' Fair Page. *It's Cool to Be Creative!* says the page of the Canadian Young Inventors' Fair Society, a not-for-profit registered B.C. society dedicated to forming invention fairs across Canada and helping teachers learn to teach innovation to our young adults.
http://www.rimart.com/cyif.html

Design and Discovery from Intel. Design and Discovery is a free curriculum and supporting resources for implementing a program to interest youth ages 11-14 in design and engineering. The curriculum provides a hands-on, inquiry-based experience with identifying and designing creative solutions to everyday problems in the designed and engineered world. Students are introduced to fundamental design and engineering concepts and follow a design process that leads to building prototypes of their ideas.
http://www.intel.com/education/Design/index.htm

Hands on Science Centers Worldwide. They have the greatest Web sites and here they all are, all at once. Take it slow, there is so much to see and do. Don't get overloaded!
http://www.cs.cmu.edu/~mwm/sci.html

The K–8 Aeronautics Internet Textbook. This site is an electronic multimedia text, teachers' supplement and student workbook to be used over the Internet with the World Wide Web. For a study of the science of aeronautics at a level elementary and middle school students and their instructors can easily understand.
http://wings.avkids.com

Kit and Kaboodle. Students in Grades 3, 4, and 5 can learn science concepts as they tackle real-world problems through this highly interactive, online curriculum.
http://www.kitkaboodle.org

NYE Labs Online. Bill Nye, the Science Guy, brings science to life by describing fun experiments kids can do with things around the house, helping them understand complex scientific theories.
http://www.billnye.com

OLogy. OLogy means "the study of." On the American Museum of Natural History's OLogy Web site, you can study and explore many cool OLogies such as biology, paleontology and astronomy.
http://www.ology.amnh.org

Professor Bubbles — Official Bubble Homepage. Don't be fooled by those "unofficial" bubble homepages. This is the "official" one and with a name like "Professor Bubbles" you'd better believe him.

    http://bubbles.org

Science Is Fun. Learn through home science activities, presentations, videos and home experiments. Among the home experiments on offer is the rather interesting sounding "bending water." A superb site that delivers what its title suggests.

    http://scifun.chem.wisc.edu/scifun.html

Space Games. Students can play games related to space science. Simple graphics and clearly explained tasks make the games engaging learning activities.

    http://www.cbc.ca/kids/main.html

The Tech Museum of Science. This online scientific playground for kids and adults is a great way to learn about how technology affects our lives. The interactive exhibits are a delight.

    http://www.thetech.org

Thinking Fountain. In addition to the wonderful mould activities, this site developed by the Science Museum of Minnesota has a variety of projects for children as well as a gallery of student work, book reviews, and slide shows.

    http://www.smm.org/sln/tf/nav/thinkingfountain.html

21.2. Resources

Ask Dr. Science. This is a great site! You can ask scientific questions and participate in e-mail discussion with Dr. Science. People Magazine OnLine and InFinet nominated it as "Cool Site of the Year!"

    http://www.drscience.com

Center for Excellence for Science and Mathematics Education (UTM). The mission of the CESME is to encourage and support the improvement of science and mathematics education at all levels. To further that goal they have uploaded 40 physical science activities in Word (Mac) and WordPerfect (Windows) format, spreadsheet templates, and activities written to make use of existing freeware and shareware.

    http://cesme.utm.edu

Mad Scientist Network. The site contains questions and answers on a huge range of scientific topics. If you don't find the answer you're looking for already here, be sure to ask a question of the mad scientist.

    http://www.madsci.org

New Scientist Planet Science. This is a vast and wonderful site by Britain's *New Scientist* magazine. It presents a guide to science sites on the Net, including personal recommendations.
http://www.keysites.com/keysites/hotspots/hotspots.html

Ontario Science Centre. You'll need Shockwave to get the most out of this site, which offers a number of hands-on science experiments online. An excellent application of the best in Web technology to further learning.
http://www.osc.on.ca

ScienceNet. This site includes a monthly feature and a link to an episodic science mystery for kids; a searchable bank of reviews of science sites, categorized by topic; standards-based classroom activities; an Internet help section; and a discussion board.
http://www.sciencenet.org.uk

Whelmers. You'll find five new science activities, each month, which have been aligned with the National Science Education Standards.
http://www.mcrel.org/whelmers

The Why Files. The site covers "science behind the news." The Why Files, a product of the National Institute for Science Education, is an effort to illuminate the science, math and technology that lurk behind the headline news.
http://whyfiles.news.wisc.edu

22. Especially for teachers

22.1. Curriculum, Assessment, Evaluation

The Big Six Information Management Skills by Michael B. Eisenberg and Robert E. Berkowitz. Big Six is a systematic approach to information problem solving applicable to any classroom in which students conduct research.
http://ericir.syr.edu/big6/bigsix.html

Content Knowledge. The site contains standards in math, science, history, geography, and other fields, and information on how to interpret and implement them.
http://mcrel.org/standards-benchmarks

Creating Your Own Rubrics. Steps to follow, recommendations, tips and questions to ask yourself as you develop your own rubrics.
http://www.2learn.ca/projects/together/START/rubricc.html

Critical Thinking, Collaboration. Ruth Sunda's Assessment Rubrics for Elementary Schools.

    http://www.kyrene.org/schools/brisas/sunda/litpack/ critical_thinking_rubric.htm

CyberLibrary. Links to several assessment and subject-based evaluation rubric sites.

    http://www.rainbowtech.org/CyberLib/assess.htm

Kathy Schrock's Guide for Educators. This extensive collection of links to a wide variety of assessment rubrics will be helpful to you as you design your own. Links include Student Web Page Rubrics, Subject-Specific and General Rubrics, Educator Technology Skills Rubrics, Electronic Portfolios, Report Card Comments and Progress Reports and Related Articles.

    http://school.discovery.com/schrockguide/assess.html

MidContinental Regional Educational Lab. The MidContinental Regional Educational Laboratory consists of three affiliated entities but they share a common mission: to make a difference in the quality of education and learning for all through excellence in applied research, product development, and service.

    http://www.mcrel.org

Project-Based Learning Checklists. This site helps you to make a project checklist for your students. You select the grade level for the type of project you want your students to do (writing, presentation, multimedia, or science projects), choose from a list of project guidelines, and make a checklist with the touch of a button. You can also add your own criteria to personalize your checklist.

    http://4teachers.org/projectbased/checklist.shtml

RubiStar. Customizable rubrics for student projects, reports, oral presentations, multimedia projects and more. A special tool allows you to enter data at the end of the project and find out which skills students found difficult.

    http://rubistar.4teachers.org/index.php

Student Web Page/Multimedia Project Rubric, An assessment template adapted from the Multimedia Mania contest to help you evaluate student created Web pages and multimedia projects. Critria include storyboard development, organization, originality, copyright and documentation, subject knowledge, graphic design and teamwork.

    http://www.ncsu.edu/midlink/rub.mm.st.htm

TERC — The Regional Alliance Hub. TERC houses articles, curriculum, and project reports organized by key topics in education reform: Assessment Equity | Professional Development | School Reform | Science | Standards and Curriculum | Technology.

http://ra.terc.edu/alliance/HubHome.html

The Partnership for Lifelong Learning Web Olympics Scoring Rubric. Use this rubric for evaluating the effectiveness of your class or school Web site.

http://www.remc11.k12.mi.us/rubric.html

22.2. Lesson Plans

Curriculum Units by Fellows of the Yale–New Haven Teachers Institute. The site consists of hundreds of teaching units prepared by dozens of teachers on scores of themes.

http://www.cis.yale.edu/ynhti/curriculum/units

ENC — Eisenhower National Clearinghouse for Math and Science. This site provides teachers with ways to increase their effectiveness with lessons, activities, articles, and the highlighting of 13 outstanding sites every month.

http://www.enc.org

Lesson Plans for Technology. Technology 'Nformation for Teachers (T'NT) is a database of over 225 technology-related lesson plans developed by Florida teachers for Grades 4–12.

http://fcit.coedu.usf.edu/tnt

Library in the Sky. Provided by Northwest Regional Educational Laboratory (NWREL), the site contains hundreds of K–12 lesson plans for a variety of curricular subjects.

http://www.nwrel.org/sky

Outta Ray's Head. The site has lesson plans with handouts for writing and literature for Grades 7–12.

http://home.cogeco.ca/~rayser3/

The Teacher's Internet Use Guide. The intent of this site is to walk teachers through a four-step process of creating their own Internet-based lessons that are aligned with state standards (in this case, Texas) and that have an assessment piece.

http://www.rmcdenver.com/useguide/index.html

22.3. General Sites for Teachers

Amazing Picture Machine. This searchable index of Internet graphics will help you find images for your lessons. Supporting a wide variety of topics from historical photos to science diagrams, the site also includes lesson ideas and search tips.

> http://www.ncrel.org/ncrtec/picture.htm

AskERIC's Collections (Educational Resources Information Centre). The site includes AskERIC, an Internet-based question-answering service for teachers and others involved in education, and AskERIC Virtual Library (resources for education).

> http://ericir.syr.edu

Firn (Florida Information Resource Network). The Web site offers instructional resources that seem to provide access to almost everything related to curriculum and teaching.

> http://www.firn.edu/instruct.html

Going to a Museum? A Teacher's Guide. The guide was written and compiled by teachers and students in the "Museums and Education" course at the University of Virginia Curry School of Education, and offers a collection of lesson plans and resources for field trips to specific museums.

> http://curry.edschool.virginia.edu/curry/class/Museums/
> Teacher_Guide

Just for Teachers. This is a collection of premier sites for teachers. It's from Knowledge Source, which also offers "Just for Librarians" and "Just for Kids."

> http://www.sirs.com/tree/teach.htm

Kathy Schrock's Guide for Educators. This highly rated resource is a guide that provides annotated hotlists for teachers in a variety of subject areas. The information is presented clearly and the lists are comprehensive.

> http://www.capecod.net/Wixon/wixon.htm

The Kindergarten Connection. Be sure to show this site to the kindergarten teacher! Ideas, lessons, projects and many links concentrating on the kindergarten curriculum.

> http://www.kconnect.com

ShURLy. Although designed as a Web directory for students, this is an excellent place to locate topical resources by grade level.

> http://learningedge.sympatico.ca/shURLy/boom.htm

Pathways to School Improvement. Visit this well-designed site, which looks at critical issues in education and provides extensive research-based materials in a user-friendly format.

http://www.ncrel.org/sdrs/pathways.htm

Sympatico Learning. Sympatico offers a number of well-designed sites aimed at students, teachers, and parents. These can be accessed through Sympatico's regional home pages.

http://www.sympatico.ca

Teacher Pathfinder: An Educational Internet Village. The Schoolhouse at this site provides a well-organized list of resources for assessment, arts, language arts, mathematics, and physical education.

http://teacherpathfinder.org

WWW4teachers. The site provides a space where educators can encounter new ideas about technology's role in education, express their opinions and share experiences, get and give moral support, and be inspired and educated by other teachers' narratives about using technology in educational settings.

http://www.4teachers.org

Bibliography

Chapter 1:

Grau, Isidro, IV and Judy Bartasis. Utilizing the World Wide Web to Advance Student Education into the 21st Century. **http://129.7.160.115/INST5931/ paper.html#SLC eval,** November 20, 1997.

Learning Theory, **http://www.etc.bc.ca/tdebhome/inservice/itpd/pedagog.html**, November 20, 1997.

Matte, Armand. Marsville: An Educational Odyssey Through Science and Technology. *The Reporter*, Fall 1997, pp. 31–34.

Rogers, Al. Living the Global Village. *Electronic Learning Magazine*, May/June 1994, pp. 28–29.

Rowe, G.R. Educating in the Emerging Media Democracy. *Educational Technology*. September, 1994, pp. 55–58.

Strommen, Erik F., and Bruce Lincoln. Constructivism, Technology, and the Future of Classroom Learning. **http://www.ilt.columbia.edu/k12/livetext-nf/docs/con- struct.html**, November 20, 1997.

Tapscott, Don. *Growing Up Digital: The Rising of the Net Generation*. McGraw-Hill, 1997.

Chapter 3:

Drawbacks of Filtering Software. *From Now On*, Vol. 5 No. 5 March/April 1996 **http://www.pacificrim.net/~mckenzie**

Planning Your Own Project. *Educational Network of Ontario*, **http://www. enoreo.on.ca/students/success.htm**. June 12, 1997.

Protecting Our Children from the Internet and the World. *From Now On*, Vol. 4 No. 10 June 1995 **http://www.pacificrim.net/~mckenzie**

Rogers, Al, Yvonne Andres, Mary Jacks, and Tom Clauset. Telecommunications in the Classroom: Keys to Successful Telecomputing. *The Computing Teacher*, 1990, Vol. 17 No. 8, pp. 25–28.

Chapter 9:

Forefront Curriculum: Internet Training and Curriculum Development for K–12 Educators **http://www.4forefront.com/home.html** June 3, 1998.

Murray, Chris. Eight Great Steps to Getting Corporate Support, **gopher://cwis. usc.edu:70/00/Librar...chers/Corporate_Funding/8steps.txt** May 1994.

Panepinto, J. The Year of the Web. *Family PC*, March 1997.

Teachers, Educational Computing and Professional Development, Education. Au, Limited, **http://www.educationau.edu.au/archives/crt/index.htm** June 3 1998.

Teacher's Internet Companion

Index